STRAIGHT NEWS

▼

BETWEEN MEN ~ BETWEEN WOMEN
LESBIAN AND GAY STUDIES

LILLIAN FADERMAN AND LARRY GROSS, EDITORS

BETWEEN MEN ~ BETWEEN WOMEN

LESBIAN AND GAY STUDIES

LILLIAN FADERMAN AND LARRY GROSS, EDITORS

Corinne E. Blackmer and Patricia Juliana Smith, editors, *En Travesti:*
  Women, Gender Subversion, Opera

Alan Bray, *Homosexuality in Renaissance England*

Joseph Bristow, *Effeminate England: Homoerotic Writing After 1885*

Claudia Card, *Lesbian Choices*

Joseph Carrier, *De Los Otros: Intimacy and Homosexuality Among Mexican Men*

John Clum, *Acting Gay: Male Homosexuality in Modern Drama*

Gary David Comstock, *Violence Against Lesbians and Gay Men*

Laura Doan, editor, *The Lesbian Postmodern*

Allen Ellenzweig, *The Homoerotic Photograph: Male Images from Durieu / Delacroix*
  to Mapplethorpe

Lillian Faderman, *Odd Girls and Twilight Lovers: A History of Lesbian Life in*
  Twentieth-Century America

Linda D. Garnets and Douglas C. Kimmel, editors, *Psychological Perspectives on Lesbian*
  and Gay Male Experiences

Richard D. Mohr, *Gays / Justice: A Study of Ethics, Society, and Law*

Sally Munt, editor, *New Lesbian Criticism: Literary and Cultural Readings*

Timothy F. Murphy and Suzanne Poirier, editors, *Writing AIDS: Gay Literature,*
  Language, and Analysis

Noreen O'Connor and Joanna Ryan, *Wild Desires and Mistaken Identities: Lesbianism*
  and Psychoanalysis

Don Paulson with Roger Simpson, *An Evening in the Garden of Allah: A Gay Cabaret*
  in Seattle

Judith Roof, *A Lure of Knowledge: Lesbian Sexuality and Theory*

Claudia Schoppmann, *Days of Masquerade: Life Stories of Lesbians During the Third Reich*

Alan Sinfield, *The Wilde Century: Effeminacy, Oscar Wilde, and the Queer Moment*

Thomas Waugh, *Hard to Imagine: Gay Male Eroticism in Photography and Film from Their*
  Beginnings to Stonewall

Kath Weston, *Families We Choose: Lesbians, Gays, Kinship*

Carter Wilson, *Hidden in the Blood: A Personal Investigation of AIDS in the Yucatán*

STRAIGHT NEWS

▼

GAYS, LESBIANS, AND THE NEWS MEDIA

Edward Alwood

Columbia University Press   New York

Columbia University Press

New York   Chichester, West Sussex

Copyright © 1996 Edward Alwood

Library of Congress Cataloging-in-Publication Data
Alwood, Edward.
    Straight news : gays, lesbians, and the news media / Edward
Alwood.
       p.   cm.— (Between men–between women)
    Includes index.
    ISBN 0-231-08436-6 (cloth : acid-free paper)
    1. Mass media and sex.   2. Gays.   I. Title   II. Series.
P56.S45A44   1996
305.9'0664—dc20
                                                                        96–526
                                                                          CIP

⊗

Casebound editions of Columbia University Press books are printed on permanent
and durable acid-free paper.
Printed in the United States of America
c 10 9 8 7 6 5 4 3 2 1

BETWEEN MEN ~ BETWEEN WOMEN
LESBIAN AND GAY STUDIES

LILLIAN FADERMAN AND LARRY GROSS, EDITORS

Advisory Board of Editors
Claudia Card
Terry Castle
John D'Emilio
Esther Newton
Anne Peplau
Eugene Rice
Kendall Thomas
Jeffrey Weeks

Between Men ~ Between Women is a forum for current lesbian and gay scholarship in the humanities and social sciences. The series includes both books that rest within specific traditional disciplines and are substantially about gay men, bisexuals, or lesbians and books that are interdisciplinary in ways that reveal new insights into gay, bisexual, or lesbian experience, transform traditional disciplinary methods in consequence of the perspectives that experience provides, or begin to establish lesbian and gay studies as a freestanding inquiry. Established to contribute to an increased understanding of lesbians, bisexuals, and gay men, the series also aims to provide through that understanding a wider comprehension of culture in general.

To the memory of my parents,
William and Mary Alwood

The ability to present news objectively and to interpret it
realistically is not a native instinct in the human species; it is a product
of culture which comes only with the knowledge of the past and acute
awareness of how deceptive is our normal observation and
how wishful our thinking.

WALTER LIPPMANN, 1922

CONTENTS

PREFACE

My interest in the relationship of gay men, lesbians, and the news media began in the late 1970s when I worked as a reporter for a Washington, D.C., television station. I was among those thousands of men and women who marched down Pennsylvania Avenue from the Capitol to the Washington Monument in October 1979 in the first National Gay and Lesbian March on Washington. At that time it was the largest gathering of its kind ever held.

Afterward, I followed coverage of the event in newspapers and on television as closely as anyone, but from the perspective of participant and journalist, and I was struck by the imbalance of what I saw and read in the news. Although march organizers estimated a crowd of 250,000, newspapers nationwide relied on smaller estimates ranging from 25,000 to 75,000 provided by the police. *Newsweek* and *Time* ignored the march, although by any measure it was a historic event.

For many years crowd estimates have been one of the most contentious issues for minorities and the news media. Because the media routinely rely on police figures, they have reported official estimates that have tended to be significantly lower than those made by the organizers. One of the most recent examples was the 1995 Million Man March on Washington. Whereas the Nation of Islam claimed more than one million participants, the initial estimate from federal park police was less than half that number. In his book *Inventing Reality*, political scientist Michael Parenti says the press "makes a regular practice of undercounting the size of demonstrations." Sociologist Todd Gitlin in his book *The Whole World Is Watching* terms the phenomenon "disparagement by numbers" and suggests the downplaying by police officials is intentional.

Although ambiguity is often a part of life for gays and lesbians, the discrepancies between what I saw on Pennsylvania Avenue in 1979 and what was portrayed in the news were startling for someone who had made journalism his career. It was this experience that led me to a much wider inquiry. This book represents my attempt to document the role the news media have played in constructing a public image of homosexuality and to understand the factors that have shaped that image. My primary goal is to describe patterns of news coverage about gays and lesbians since World War II, but I also suggest important reasons for the inadequacy of that coverage. My new understanding of the failings of the media has been greatly aided by the work of a number of media scholars, particularly Walter Lippmann, Warren Breed, William Rivers, Herbert Gans, Edward J. Epstein, Gaye Tuchman, Leon Sigal, and Todd Gitlin, who provide a framework for understanding how the news media operate.

I began this book in the spring of 1990 by interviewing gay and lesbian journalists. The first was a gay man in Florida with whom I had worked at an Orlando television station. Although he wanted to describe his experience of working in the media spotlight, he clearly found the interview unsettling. Making matters worse, his lover was in the final stage of AIDS and died a few months later. Although I tried to contact him again several times, he did not respond to my calls before his own death in 1993. It was as though he had told his story for the first time and did not care to return to his memories of a painful chapter of his life.

As I continued to interview gay and lesbian journalists, I began to grasp certain complexities. With only a few exceptions, people I had known and worked with were eager to help me. Those who did not know me or my work were more reticent. Several at the *Los Angeles Times* refused to meet with me, claiming that a book about gays and lesbians in the news media was unnecessary. But in other cases, such as at the *New York Times*, many reporters were surprisingly willing to relate their personal stories to a stranger.

Within the first year I began to understand that the experiences of gay and lesbian journalists were only part of the story. Clearly, the stories they told would have to be put in a context that readers could understand. This required a search for historical detail in archives and libraries on both coasts and in the deep South. Veteran gay activist W. Dorr Legg, who died in the middle of my research in July 1994 at the age of eighty-nine, was kind enough to allow me to spend a few days crawling around the basement of the *One* Institute, where I worked with his rich treasure of records from the original Mattachine Society in the early 1950s. I spent hours at the Library of Congress paging through copies of the *Miami Herald*, *Atlanta Constitution*, *San Francisco Chronicle*, *San Francisco Examiner*, *Chicago Tribune*, *Chicago Sun-Times*, *Minneapolis Star*, and other newspapers for articles that predated databases. Gay and lesbian archives in San Francisco, Los Angeles, Chicago, and New York helped me track down copies of newsletters of the early gay and lesbian organizations. All this was essential to gain an understanding of what the media covered, how they had covered it, what they ignored, and how activists of the day responded.

As I soon realized, records of much of our gay and lesbian history do not exist, precisely because mainstream newspapers and magazines were either silent or presented a distorted picture. The *Advocate*, established in Los Angeles in 1967, became the newspaper of record for the gay community; it provides the broadest—and virtually the only—continuous historical record of the emergence of the nation's gay and lesbian liberation movement.

When I began this project in 1990, author-journalist Randy Shilts at the *San Francisco Chronicle* was the only widely known, openly gay journalist working in the mainstream news media. Six years later the National Lesbian and Gay Journalists Association has more than twelve hundred members. Some have written about their sexuality in their own publications. However, broadcast journalists continue to be the most reluctant to step forward, perhaps because of the inherently tenuous nature of broadcast employment. It was extremely difficult to find broadcast journalists who were willing to speak openly—no lesbian broadcast reporter consented to be interviewed.

In the past half century much has changed about how the news media portray gays and lesbians. Fifty years ago we were nearly invisible. Today news articles about life in the gay and lesbian subculture and its interaction with the larger society are almost commonplace. How gays and lesbians are viewed by the public has also changed. A 1993 Gallup poll found that more Americans support equal job opportunities for gays than ever before, 80 percent compared with only 56 percent in 1977. Is there a connection? I think so.

ACKNOWLEDGMENTS

This book would not have been possible without the interest and support of Professor Larry Gross, of the Annenberg School for Communication at the University of Pennsylvania, and Ann Miller, associate executive editor at Columbia University Press. I am grateful for their expert guidance, unending patience, and keen insights as it evolved into a manuscript.

A book of this nature could not be written without the generous help of many people and institutions. Among those to whom I am indebted are Jim Kepner and Pat Allen at the International Gay and Lesbian Archives (Los Angeles); W. Dorr Legg at the Blanch M. Baker Memorial Library at the *One* Institute (Los Angeles); Richard Wandel at the New York Gay and Lesbian Archives (New York); Karen Sendziak at the Gerber Hart Gay and

Lesbian Library and Archives (Chicago); Melanie Yolles and Chris Alksnis at the International Gay Information Center of the New York Public Library (New York); Bill Walker at the San Francisco Bay Area Gay and Lesbian Historical Society (San Francisco); Mattie Sink at University of Mississippi Mitchell Memorial Library; Robert Bray at the National Gay and Lesbian Task Force; and the University of Michigan Information Transfer Source.

I am indebted to several individuals who helped me craft the manuscript. Chris Bull was an enthusiastic supporter of this project from its inception and helped me distill my thoughts as the book evolved. He was a constant source of encouragement, guidance, and friendship throughout. Likewise, Jeffrey Escoffier lent his considerable editorial skills to help me define the themes of this book and find a structure in which they could be understood. Veteran gay activist Ronald Gold generously reviewed drafts of the manuscript and helped me understand how the gay and lesbian community continues to influence what we see and read in the media today. Bill Kelly, Don Slater, and Dale Jennings painstakingly reviewed chapters and sections of the manuscript for historical accuracy. Jack Nichols, a pioneer of the gay rights movement and the gay press, enthusiastically reviewed drafts and was always available as a sounding board as I learned to understand the complexities of the earliest days of gay and lesbian activism. Hans Johnson and Maggie Lyons spent countless hours proofreading the manuscript to find glitches and rough spots when I could no longer see mistakes.

At Columbia University Press I wish to thank managing editor Anne McCoy, designer Maria Guiliani, and assistant editor Sara Cahill for their expertise in guiding the book through the production phase. I have been fortunate to have as my copy editor Polly Kummel, whose sharp editorial skills and passionate interest in the news business helped enormously to make this a better book.

For their unbending support and encouragement I wish to thank Doug Abbey, Jim Anderson, John Andriotte, Danny Beyer, Don Brown, Tom Donegan, Bill Hadelstadt, David K. Johnson, Bob Jordan, Michael Kaminski, Steve Lee, Tim Mason, Tom Morgan, John Plank, Larry Reynolds, Mark Weinress, Dennis Wholey. I am indebted to friends who encouraged me in the earliest stages of this project and whom I lost to the AIDS epidemic: Albert "Buzz" Bryan, Alan Grooms, and Naulty Kileen. I also wish to thank the friends of Bill W. who sustained me by sharing their experience, strength, and hope.

STRAIGHT NEWS

▼

INTRODUCTION

In the fall of 1953 news accounts in the *Miami Herald* described how authorities had become agitated over a strip of beach at Twenty-second Street that
was "a hangout for males with a feminine bent." The story and later accounts
revealed much about the hysteria that surrounded gay issues in that era, but
they also showed how journalists routinely responded to one of society's
most incendiary topics.

Prominently displayed on the front page of the local news section, the
Herald story of November 21, 1953, explained that the police chief had
inspected the beach area personally and called for a police wagon to take
twenty-one men to police headquarters for questioning. The *Herald* told its
readers, "The chief said that he has been 'getting lots of complaints' that men

21 Rounded Up for Quiz

Turn-About Not Fair Play, Say Beach Police

By STEPHEN J. FLYNN
Herald Staff Writer

Angered by complaints that the beach at 22nd st. was becoming a "hangout for males with a feminine bent," Miami Beach Police Chief Romeo J. Shepard made a personal inspection Friday—and then called for the wagon.

As a result, 21 persons were taken to Beach police headquarters and questioned before being released.

But Chief Shepard said the raid served notice on "this questionable type of individual" that they're not wanted on Miami Beach.

The chief said that he has been "getting lots of complaints" that men with girlish-looking hair-dos and flimsy, Bikini-type . tights . "have been prancing around the 22nd .st. public beach in droves."

The area, he explained, has been acquiring a reputation as a congregating place for males who try hard to look and act like women.

Some police officers had muttered about the situation, but, there had been no concerted drive until Shepard's action Friday.

"It's gotten so, I'm told, that respectable people don't want to go to that particular public beach," Chief Shepard said.

The chief said the 21 persons taken to headquarters —all males—were questioned about their employment and identification.

"We had no charges we could book them on," Shepard said.

"But it's just a question of cleaning up a bad situation and letting undesirables know they're not wanted here."

Miami Herald, August 13, 1954 (© Miami Herald, used with permission)

with girlish-looking hairdos and flimsy, Bikini-type tights 'have been prancing around the 22nd Street public beach in droves.' The area, he explained, has been acquiring a reputation as a congregating place for males who try hard to look and act like women."[1]

Miami readers were entitled to an objective, unbiased account of the incident, told in a manner that would help them understand; this is the traditional role of the news media in a democracy. But rather than serve as a conduit of factual information, Miami newspapers became a pipeline for propaganda from the local police. The journalists never asked why police felt compelled to herd law-abiding citizens off a public beach to let them know they were unwelcome. "We had no charges we could book them on," the chief told the *Herald*. "It's just a question of cleaning up a bad situation and letting undesirables know they're not wanted here."[2]

The following year, when Miami police were investigating several attacks on young children, the *Herald* again echoed the attitudes of local police toward homosexuals. In one case, an intruder broke into a local couple's home, sexually assaulted their young granddaughter, and brutally killed her. As newspapers explained, police launched a massive hunt that focused on a cluster of gay bars the police had dubbed "Powder Puff Lane." "The rapists and molesters are mental incompetents; they are killers per se, with uncontrollable passions," the *Herald* said in an editorial on July 28, 1954.[3] The editorial failed to explain why gay men would be prime suspects for molesting a young girl. None of the articles quoted homosexuals or reflected their point of view in any way.

In the late summer of 1954 news coverage became hysterical after police found the body of William Simpson, a twenty-seven-year old flight attendant with Eastern Air Lines, on a remote strip of highway known as Lover's Lane. Detectives later learned that he had been killed by two men who lured him into a trap by promising sex. PERVERT COLONY UNCOVERED IN SIMPSON SLAYING PROBE, read the headline in the *Miami Daily News*. Apparently unaware that homosexual men used the word *queen* to jokingly refer to one another, the writer began the article, "A colony of some 500 male homosexuals, congregated mostly in the near-downtown northeast section and ruled by a 'queen,' was uncovered in the investigation of the murder of an Eastern Air Lines steward."[4]

The *Herald* fueled the hysteria with a front-page article written by Lieutenant Chester Eldridge, a veteran Miami police detective; its headline read, OFFICIAL URGES SOCIETY TO FACE PERVERT PROBLEM. Eldridge explained the scope of the problem and provided readers with an image of homosexuality no one was likely to forget: "We are extremely fortunate that there have been no more violent crimes in Miami involving them. The sex pervert or deviate is an individual who has reached the age of reason, yet knowingly disregards the idea of reproduction. They comprise a group that ranges from relatively harmless homosexuals to the fierce sadist who horribly mutilates and tortures his victim."

Estimating the number of homosexuals in the Miami area at five thousand to eight thousand, Eldridge suggested the state address the problem by building psychiatric hospitals for homosexuals "so they can be removed as a social blight and become useful citizens."[5]

The climate for gays and lesbians worsened after police charged two men with the flight attendant's death. The *Herald*, for one, blamed the crime on homosexuals who "threatened the wholesome growth of Greater Miami." CLEAN THIS PLACE UP! urged the headline on a *Herald* editorial that quoted the eighteen-year-old bride of one suspect. "Miami did this to us," she told reporters, lashing out at the city for allowing homosexuals to tempt "normal" people into committing such a crime. The editorial observed, "For police to say they can't rid the city of this concentration of perverts is ridiculous."[6]

The next day a large contingent of Miami Beach police launched a crackdown on the Twenty-second Street beach area shortly after noon. BEACH POLICE ROUND UP 35 IN PERVERT CRACKDOWN, the *Herald* reported on the front page of its local news section. The article explained that the police had raided the beach after receiving "numerous complaints" that the area had become a congregating spot for "males who act mighty like girls." According to the *Herald*, most of the thirty-five who were taken to police headquarters were

Beach Police Round Up
35 In Pervert Crackdown

Public Area
At 22nd St.
Raid Target

Miami Herald, August 13, 1954 (© Miami Herald, used with permission)

released after questioning. But six were booked on disorderly conduct charges. "We made the raid to serve notice that Miami Beach doesn't want this type of individual," the police chief told the paper. "Maybe after a few more raids of this kind, they'll take the hint and congregate somewhere else."[7]

The *Herald*'s Letters to the Editor columns made clear the influence its coverage was having on readers. "It seems to me that there would be far less child molestation problems if when these wretches were caught, given a quick and fair trial and found guilty, they be quickly exterminated like the dangerous rodents they are," a reader wrote the *Herald* on July 18, 1954. "So the police round up 75 or 100 known child molesters and perverts," wrote another. "If known, what are they doing walking the streets? Are the police waiting for them to strike again?"[8]

Miami soon enacted ordinances that made it illegal for bar owners to allow "two or more persons who are homosexuals, lesbians or perverts" to patronize their bars. Theater owners set up antimolester patrols during Saturday matinees for children. Acting Governor Charlie Johns threatened to oust Dade County Sheriff Dan McCarty for "coddling perverts." Johns also created a secret legislative committee to investigate and expose homosexuals and communists that lasted from 1956 until it was dissolved in 1964.[9]

At about the same time Miami newspapers began their crusade against gays, the *Atlanta Constitution* reported on October 11, 1954, 1,500 SEX DEVIATES ROAM STREETS HERE. "Bulging files of secret police information tell a shocking story of child molesters in the Atlanta area," warned reporter Jack Nelson. "A great majority of the deviates are homosexual, usually not violently dangerous, but—as the investigator pointed out—potentially dangerous if in fear of being caught."[10]

The following year and hundreds of miles from Atlanta and Miami, a front

2 ● **THE ATLANTA CONSTITUTION, Monday, Oct. 11, 1954**

1,500 Sex Deviates
Roam Streets Here

Alverson and Hoover Warn
Parents on Child Molesters

By JACK NELSON
Copyright 1954, The Atlanta Constitution

Bulging files of secret police information tell a

Miami Herald, August 13, 1954 (© Miami Herald, used with permission)

page article in the *Idaho Daily Statesman* set off a similar witch-hunt in Boise, Idaho. Readers were stunned to learn on November 2, 1955, of a sex scandal involving men and teenage boys. Although the article lacked specifics, it said authorities suspected "several" other adults were involved with "about 100 boys." Parents were thrown into an instant panic and began assembling a list of "known perverts."[11]

CRUSH THE MONSTER was the incendiary headline on the *Statesman*'s editorial the next day. It said that one of the accused men had "confessed to violations involving 10 teenage boys" and called for "immediate and systematic cauterization," yet it never explained the scope of the problem so readers could assess it for themselves. Instead, the editorial irresponsibly fueled the mounting public hysteria. "It's a challenge of greater danger than any of us could have thought possible here," it said.

Tensions escalated further when the *Statesman* quoted a pledge by the district attorney to "eliminate" all homosexuals. Reading the article over breakfast, a local schoolteacher went to his bedroom, packed a suitcase, and drove off to San Francisco. When worried school officials sent someone to check on his absence two days later, they found his cold eggs, toast, and coffee still sitting on the breakfast table.[12]

The press has a long history of cooperating with police officials to control homosexual acts in public places. One of the most blatant examples occurred in February 1978 when the New Jersey State Police asked the media to print the names of men who were being charged with soliciting at a rest stop on the

Garden State Parkway. According to a brief article in the *New York Times:* "In making the request, the police said a crackdown begun last October had had little effect despite the arrest of 84 men by police undercover agents. . . . Though the names of persons arrested are generally considered public record and are available to newsmen on request, the spokesman said that until now the state police had not volunteered information on homosexuals' solicitation arrests to reporters making general inquiries."[13]

THE NEWS MEDIA AND PREJUDICE

There are no conclusive measures of the degree to which the mass media influence public opinion. But a large body of social science research going back to the 1940s strongly suggests that the news plays a critical role in shaping people's image of the world around them. The stories chosen, sources interviewed, placement selected, language and descriptions used, and many factors that are a part of everyday journalism influence what people consider important or unimportant. When society faces a problem, the media suggest a proper response.[14]

The gay rights movement and the AIDS epidemic have resulted in significant changes since the mid-1980s in how the media portray gays and lesbians. The *New York Times* ran its first front-page story about gays and lesbians in 1963; the nation's newspaper of record described them as "deviates" who were "condemned to a life of promiscuity." There was no significant network television coverage of homosexuality until 1967, when a CBS documentary characterized it as "a mental illness which has reached epidemiological proportions." In one of the first major articles on the subject in a mass-circulation magazine, *Look* produced a 1967 feature, THE SAD 'GAY' LIFE, and described homosexuality as a "distorted mirror image of heterosexual life." Even as late as 1974, a front-page article in the *Los Angeles Times* described the gay patrons of an all-night grocery as "fags."[15]

The capacity of the news media to create and perpetuate prejudice is one of the most unsettling and frightening aspects of American journalism. The news media have long been one of the public's few sources of information about homosexuals, given the closeted existence that most have been forced to live to escape social stigma. For much of American society, what people see and hear in the news is what they accept as reality. But in the case of homosexuals, for far too long what the media delivered was a dose of propaganda that was handed to readers, viewers, and listeners as news.

This book is an attempt to understand how and why the news media perpetuated antigay stereotypes through much of this century, even as journalists claimed to adhere to long-standing professional standards of accuracy and unbiased, well-balanced coverage. Some media critics would blame the prejudice and bigotry on individual journalists or on slipshod reporting techniques. But in taking an in-depth look at the relationships of gay men, lesbians, and the news media over five decades, I found far more complex explanations. The history I recount here repeatedly shows that the widespread antigay attitude in news coverage has been rooted in a structural bias of the media, one that causes journalists to favor the established power base and defend the status quo while shunning the perspectives of those who are politically powerless—as were gays and lesbians for so long in this country.

In promising readers, viewers, and listeners that the press has the ability to establish and convey the truth, the news media have created a set of myths about journalism that they cannot always live up to. Journalists, in their quest for truth, rely on professional standards of "fairness," "balance," and "objectivity" and on procedures that are intended to assure a high level of accuracy. As this book demonstrates, routine practices in newsrooms cannot assure that the news will be accurate, fair, or objective. Although the patterns of coverage of gays and lesbians have begun to shift in recent years, there is a long history of so distorting "news" about this segment of our society—even when it was based on substantiated facts—that the truth was smothered.

MYTHS OF AMERICAN JOURNALISM

The self-deceptions, or myths, under which the media operate are so germane to this history of coverage gone awry that they are worth describing here at some length.

The Myth of the Neutral Observer
Journalists have long held themselves to be neutral observers, claiming to be able to put aside their personal prejudices in order to deliver the news fully and fairly to the public. "We don't make the news; we report it," contended CBS News president Richard Salant in the 1970s. "Our reporters do not

cover stories from their point of view. They are presenting them from nobody's point of view."[16]

But in practice, journalism is a far more complex process. More than most people realize, much of what we see and hear in the news results from a sophisticated and complex filtering process that determines what becomes news and what is ignored. To a large degree what we see and hear in the news is there because some editor or producer thought it was interesting, important, or both. In the absence of any clearly defined standards that distinguish news from non-news, journalists have little choice but to rely on their subjective experience—as limited and distorted as it may be.[17]

The way in which events become news has held especially important consequences for the nation's gays and lesbians. Although journalists try hard to prevent their personal biases from influencing the news, they cannot completely detach themselves from their assumptions about the world around them. "The values in the news are rarely explicit and must be found between the lines—in what actors and activities are reported or ignored," wrote media sociologist Herbert Gans in his groundbreaking 1979 book *Deciding What's News*.[18]

It is at this point in the process that "the heterosexual assumption" becomes the underlying perspective of the news. For many years, newsrooms have been almost exclusively controlled by white, middle-class, heterosexual men who have relied on a common set of assumptions to guide them in how they reflect the world through their work. Although bias is traditionally regarded as an intentional distortion of the facts, another form of bias results from unwitting ignorance.

A good example of how this affects a minority community came in the summer of 1965 when urban riots erupted in the Watts area of Los Angeles. More than thirty people were killed, nearly four thousand arrested, and a five-hundred-square-block area was burned and looted. The news media came under sharp criticism for fostering racial tensions by having concentrated on the white middle-class to the exclusion of the inner-city poor. "The one aspect of the Negro world that most whites are able to experience vicariously through the mass media is riotous and torn from its context," William Rivers wrote in a 1971 assessment of the coverage. "Few whites see Negroes except when the Negro community is inflamed."[19] Because no minority reporters were working in the *Los Angeles Times* newsroom, the paper resorted to sending messengers from the advertising department to cover the riots.

Following the assassination of Martin Luther King Jr. in 1968, riots broke out in Detroit, Newark, and Washington, D.C., and news coverage of the tumultuous upheaval reignited criticism. "If the media are to report with understanding, wisdom and sympathy on the problems of the cities and the problems of the black man—for the two are increasingly intertwined—they must employ, promote and listen to Negro journalists," concluded the Presidential Commission on Civil Disorders.

This blind bias may have been even more pronounced in news coverage of gays and lesbians, given their closeted existence. In the late 1890s when *New York Tribune* police reporter Jacob Riis learned that the police had raided a group of homosexuals, he reportedly cried, "Fairies! What are fairies?" When his assistant tried to explain the term, Riis shouted, "Not so! There are no such creatures in the world."[20]

"This is the whole history of newspapering," observed Nan Robertson, a Pulitzer Prize–winning *New York Times* reporter who championed the rights of women journalists. "Journalism was overwhelmingly male, overwhelmingly macho, overwhelmingly drinkers, smokers, fuckers, all of these things. Women lost by it, blacks lost by it, gays lost by it, everybody lost by it, because it did not reflect the diversity of this country."[21]

The Myth of Objectivity

Closely allied with the notion that journalists are neutral observers is the concept of objectivity, a pillar of modern American journalism. Many writers have pointed out its flaws, but it is such an overarching factor that it also must be considered here.

"Objective" news reporting initially grew out of the desire of turn-of-the-century newspaper publishers to boost circulation to a mass audience. If they could maintain a "middle-of-the-road" editorial policy and avoid partisanship, they reasoned, they could attract the greatest number of readers and, as a result, charge premium prices for advertising. Since that time "objective" news reporting has evolved into a professional standard that encompasses both an attitude and a practice. Although neutrality involves the journalist's supposed frame of mind, objectivity dictates how neutrality is reflected in the news.

The goal in following the prescribed procedures for gathering and reporting news is to separate journalists' opinions and attitudes from news—to achieve objectivity. Even today young reporters are often admonished by their editors to "tell the news, and tell it straight." By "straight" news they mean stories that are based on verifiable statements from recognized experts, public documents, and official sources—police, elected officials, public office holders—almost anyone's opinion but their own.[22] But the unacknowledged drawback in this quest for objectivity is that the media are far more accessible to the defenders of the status quo than to advocates of change. In the case of gays and lesbians the standard of objectivity encouraged reporters to rely on information from politicians, police, clergy, psychiatrists—historically society's most forceful antigay detractors.

Closely allied with this reliance on experts is the concept of "balance." Journalists are taught to satisfy the standard of objectivity by including "the other side" (as if there were always only two sides to a story). But the determination of when a story needs "balance" and how it should be balanced is quite subjective, and that determination has had strong repercussions for gays and lesbians. For years, when stories about gays and lesbians were positive, they were deemed controversial and in need of an opposing viewpoint. When the stories were antigay, however, editors saw no need to quote other points of view. This pattern was particularly evident when gay men and lesbians appeared on talk shows. Radio and television producers felt compelled to include antigay perspectives to offset criticism from viewers who might accuse them of condoning homosexuality.

The Myth of Autonomy

The final widely held misconception that strongly influences journalists' coverage of gays and lesbians is the claim that their decisions about news content are not influenced by pressures from outside newsrooms or from their superiors. But journalists are not free agents. Newspaper reporters, for example, are the lowest level of a hierarchal structure that consists of layers of editors who report to an editor-in-chief hired by the publisher. Publishers set overall policy, and the editors enforce it. Therefore, the sense of autonomy among journalists is more often an illusion than reality.[23] More than many journalists realize, they must conform to a set of suggestions that is really a set of thinly veiled orders.

Reporters learn the unwritten rules of the newsroom by reading or watching the news at their newspaper or broadcast station, seeing how their successful colleagues cover stories, including who they interview and what words they choose or avoid. They learn from seeing who is hired, fired, and promoted. The more that journalists fit the mold, the more opportunities they have to climb the ranks. This pressure to conform may be so subtle that many journalists are unaware of the extent to which the culture of the newsroom influences what becomes news and how it is reported.[24]

The situation has only grown worse in the past twenty-five years as large newspaper chains have snapped up newspapers with close ties to their local communities and have hired "tame" reporters and editors who can be counted upon not to rock the boat. The same trend can be seen among magazines and the broadcast media.[25]

Los Angeles Times media writer David Shaw has described how his newspaper altered a key fact in a story about a sixty-nine car pileup on the Pomona Freeway. Concerned that the figure might offend readers, the *Times* reported the number of cars in the accident as seventy. "The editor who made that change said he had done so to avoid 'titillating or offending readers' by reminding them of the sex act of the same number," wrote Shaw.[26]

Often journalists learn the limit of editorial policy by unwittingly crossing it. This was the case in August 1980 when David Harris, a writer for the *New York Times Magazine*, wrote a revealing profile of Allard Lowenstein, the late New York congressman slain in a Rockefeller Center law office five months earlier. In it Harris cited sexual advances Lowenstein had made toward young men, including one directed at a mentally disturbed man who years later became his assassin. But after Lowenstein's supporters learned what the article was to say, a national columnist based in New York, a member of the New York City Council, and a former member of the U.S. delegation to the United Nations telephoned the magazine to say the information was "unfounded" and tantamount to character assassination.

BLOODY END OF '60S DREAM appeared on August 17, 1980, with no reference to Lowenstein's homosexuality, although Harris had explained to his editors that he had firsthand knowledge of Lowenstein's advances. "I myself had had such an experience, and numerous other sources said they had heard stories of similar incidents," he wrote in his 1982 book, *Dreams Die Hard*.[27]

An even more common practice among the media has been the failure to acknowledge the homosexuality of deceased individuals in their obituaries, even of those who had publicly acknowledged being gay. In numerous cases newspapers have gone so far as to say "there were no survivors" when the individual had maintained a long-term gay relationship. Such practices and procedures are so ingrained that journalists go about their jobs without realizing the conflict with their overall mission to report the truth.

INSIDE THE NEWSROOM CLOSET

Many journalistic practices that have influenced the portrayal of gays and lesbians in the news will be familiar to students of mass communication; some practices have over the years distorted coverage of blacks, women, farm workers, the student movement of the 1960s, and other political and social minorities. The same phenomena also guided and shaped news coverage of gays but with a difference—the newsroom closet. Often going to great lengths to conceal their sexual orientation, gays working in newsrooms knew instinctively that no one was likely to subject them to discrimination so long as they kept their sexual orientation secret. This set off a continuous cycle in which gay journalists felt intense pressure to keep their knowledge of gay life to themselves, lest they be stigmatized, leaving the media—and therefore their audiences—unenlightened about the many complexities of homosexuality. In this self-perpetuating information vacuum gays continued to appear abnormal and threatening to the public as they continued to hide in their closets.[28]

Leroy Aarons was a reporter at the *Washington Post* on April 17, 1965, when he heard a voice on a police radio describe ten picketers outside the White House. Compared to protests in that era that drew as many as 200,000, the ten men and women representing the Mattachine Society of Washington seemed insignificant. But they braved public ridicule and even arrest to stage a demonstration of historical dimensions. It was the nation's first gay-organized picketing against discrimination.[29]

As Aarons listened to the police describe the scene, he felt his dual identities come dangerously close to colliding, and the personal risks were enormous. What made him so uncomfortable was the recognition that he and the protesters has something in common. But, unlike the protesters, he desperately wanted to keep his homosexuality secret: "I thought they must be totally reckless or weird—using their names and talking to reporters for quote. My second thought was: What's that got to do with me? I had my job, I had my gay life, and I had my straight life. I had totally compartmentalized my life and I didn't like those elements of my life getting confused."[30]

Long before he had become a highly regarded reporter on the metropolitan desk at the *Post*, Aarons knew his career would depend on his ability to hide his homosexuality. If anyone learned his secret, he would be branded a mental case, a pervert, or a criminal—regardless of his achievements and his exemplary career.

Members of the Mattachine Society, however, had decided to throw caution to the wind and follow the lead of the civil rights movement by using public protests to confront prejudice. The members who were bold enough to participate had sent press releases to the *Post* and other media outlets in hopes of publicizing their fledgling cause. Except for Aarons and other gays who secretly worked in the media, most reporters focused on some ten thousand students from across the nation who were in Washington that day to stage the largest protest ever held against the war in Vietnam. Amid the chaos the gays garnered one small story that appeared a few days later in the *Washington Afro-American* headlined 10 OPPOSE GOV'T ON HOMOSEXUALS.[31] The *Post* and the *Washington Star*, the city's two daily newspapers, as well as local broadcast media, ignored the gay picketing.

Far away from Washington, Perry Deane Young also understood the danger of revealing one's homosexuality. When he arrived in Saigon on January 30, 1968, the North Vietnamese were launching a huge campaign against the South, an onslaught known as the Tet Offensive that proved to be the deadliest of the war.

Young had done everything possible to avoid the war while serving in the Army Reserve, but as a reporter he knew he had to be there to cover the war for the giant worldwide wire service United Press International. At the same time he knew that a heteromasculine pretense was a prerequisite of war reporting: "Very little was ever written about gays in Vietnam but Saigon had a very active social life; there were all those troops and no women. Because the war was so overwhelming, almost any type of behavior was tolerated. You had to be careful, but you had to be careful about everything. Friends knew what was going on, but as far as what went on in private, people didn't care. Those Marines were awfully good to me."[32]

News reporting had been a lifelong ambition for Young, so much so that he recognized his attraction to it long before he realized he was attracted to other men. In high school he wrote for the student newspaper, and at the University of North Carolina at Chapel Hill he majored in news writing and impressed his journalism professors by selling freelance articles to the *New York Times*. Between classes he hustled to cover news for the local paper, the *Chapel Hill Weekly*.

Young recalled clearly the afternoon his editor asked him to look into a rumor about the sudden firing of a university professor who had been named Most Valuable Instructor a year earlier. Young contacted the university chancellor to find out why. "Because the guy's a queer," the chancellor told him. The comment only confirmed the everyday reality of life as a gay man. "Looking back, it's hard to remember all of the games we played," he said. "Hiding was just part of the way all of us lived."[33]

The closet also divided work life and leisure. Rockford, Illinois, had no exclusively lesbian bars in the early 1970s when Sharon Shaw Johnson was an editor at the *Rockford Morning Star* (which later became the *Register Star*). She had grown accustomed to driving to either Milwaukee or Chicago to live another life in another city so that her private life as a lesbian would remain secret: "I was the city editor, the first woman city editor the newspaper had ever had, and I knew I was living in a spotlight. At that point in my career I was thinking that I probably wanted to stay in journalism, and I suspected that being a lesbian and being a journalist weren't compatible. Of course I wouldn't come out and neither did anyone else. There was absolutely no question."[34]

For women like Johnson it was difficult to know which facet of their lives stirred the greatest hostility. Being a feminist was more socially acceptable than being a lesbian, although they often went hand in hand in the public's eye. Feminists may have been considered trouble makers, but lesbians were downright evil.

GAY NEWS IN A MODERN ERA

Gay and lesbian journalists did not begin to emerge from newsroom closets in significant numbers among the mainstream media until 1990. Their willingness to play a role in shaping how gays and lesbians were portrayed by the media was one of several unrelated but simultaneous developments that changed the long-standing antigay tone of the news media. Not only were gay and lesbian journalists writing about gays and lesbians, many were openly writing from their own experience and expertise. In an earlier era this would have been tantamount to professional suicide. At the least it would have been judged a conflict of interest and unethical.

As gay journalists were beginning to speak out, the upper ranks of the media were undergoing a transition from the old guard to a more open-minded generation of editors and publishers. Even if they were not younger in age, they were younger in attitude about the world around them. In some cases women and blacks were beginning to move into ranks from which they had been excluded. The new breed questioned many time-honored assumptions, including those that had guided the coverage of gays and lesbians for decades.

AIDS was another important factor that changed how gays were seen in the news. By any measure mainstream media virtually ignored the epidemic until Rock Hudson's death in 1985, when the story's newsworthiness finally began to override the prejudice of outdated editors and publishers. Combined with unresponsive government policies, the media's lack of concern helped to mobilize gay and lesbian activists. The message became even clearer when closeted journalists began to contract the disease, making it virtually impossible to continue hiding behind a heterosexual facade. These factors helped to wake up the media and change how gays and lesbians were portrayed in the news.

By the mid-1990s coverage of gays and lesbians in major newspapers, magazines, and television networks had become frequent and practically routine. To many readers, viewers, and listeners this change may have seemed sudden. But as this book demonstrates, what we see in the news today is the result of a long struggle against the "business-as-usual" newsroom attitude that was entrenched behind the media's First Amendment right to be wrong. For millions of readers, viewers, and listeners gays and lesbians who had been silent and separate became vocal and visible.

PART I

▼

THE NEWS MEDIA DISCOVER HOMOSEXUALITY:
WORLD WAR II TO STONEWALL, 1943–1969

I

A COMMUNITY DISCOVERS ITSELF

Until World War II homosexuals were unmentionable in American newspapers and magazines. The few sporadic print references were typically in small neighborhood or tabloid newspapers. The African American press in some major cities was among the first to acknowledge the existence of homosexuals in its communities, with articles about annual drag balls during the 1930s. Most of these articles were written in a gossipy condescending tone that characterized homosexuals as a menace to society. 1931 DEBUTANTES BOW AT LOCAL 'PANSY' BALL, reported the *Baltimore Afro-American* on March 21, 1931. FAG BALLS EXPOSED, cried the New York neighborhood newspaper *Broadway Brevities* on March 14, 1932.[1]

While the sensational press mocked homosexuals, the more established press was virtually silent on the subject until military psychiatrists began a campaign to weed gays out of the armed forces. The Washington *Sunday Star* reported in 1943 HOW THE NAVY'S 'MIND DETECTIVES' SEEK MEN OF SOUND NERVE FOR WARFARE. Complete with Navy Department photos of young men at induction centers, the page-long feature explained the role of psychiatrists in the national war effort: "They want to weed out the epileptics, homosexuals, alcoholics, mentally deficient, those who have traces of a conflict in their personality, those who are psychopathic and those borderline cases where the strain of war may be just enough to tip the youth over the border of mental health."[2]

Military publicists made certain that similar articles appeared in newspapers and magazines across the nation, including a January 1944 feature in the *Saturday Evening Post* entitled HOW WE SCREEN OUT PSYCHOLOGICAL 4-F's. It explained the importance of the tests administered by military psychiatrists, particularly questions that determined whether draftees were homosexuals. "A selectee's sexual practices may seem to be of little concern to the Army, but his attitude toward sexual matters gives an indication of his emotional maturity," the magazine explained.[3]

Almost every description of homosexuals during the war years was in the context of how they were unfit for military service. Although homosexuality had been defined as criminal behavior for many years, military psychiatrists during World War II established it as a mental condition and, as military staffing needs eased, implemented screening procedures designed to identify homosexuals before they joined the ranks.

The press may have been receptive to publicizing the military's antigay campaign because of the government's strict wartime constraints on what the press could report. Newspaper editors often were hard-pressed to satisfy the public's insatiable appetite for information and were eager to report almost anything related to the military. At the same time the relatively new "science" of clinical psychiatry was beginning to establish itself in the public consciousness as a profession. With heightened coverage psychiatrists became increasingly recognized as experts on homosexuality.

Newsweek provided the first public acknowledgment that the military had intensified its antihomosexual campaign when it reported in its June 9, 1947, issue,

Although Army regulations strictly forbade the drafting of homosexuals scores of these inverts managed to slip through induction centers during the second world war. Between 3,000 and 4,000 were discharged for this abnormality; others were released as neuropsychiatric cases. Last week, with most of the records on homo-sexuals tabulated, Army medical officers, for the first time, summed up their strange story. To screen out this undesirable soldier-material, psychiatrists in induction-station interviews tried to detect them (1) by their effeminate looks or behavior and (2) by repeating certain words from the homosexual vocabulary and watching for signs of recognition.[4]

The negative tone of the wartime press continued until 1948, when Alfred Kinsey published his eight-hundred-page book *Sexual Behavior in the Human Male* and made human sexuality a legitimate topic for public discus-sion. Among his many startling findings, readers were especially shocked that homosexuality was far more prevalent than anyone had previously imagined. Previously, most people considered same-sex intercourse to be anomalous, especially because most states outlawed it and some judges gave defendants the choice of a harsh prison term or castration.[5] But Kinsey determined that although few Americans were exclusively homosexual, half the men inter-viewed acknowledged erotic responses to other men, 37 percent had expe-rienced orgasm during at least one postadolescent homosexual encounter, and 4 percent were exclusively homosexual throughout adulthood. His 1953 study of women's sexual behavior reached similar conclusions, although the percentages were lower.[6]

Kinsey's work did not claim gays and lesbians to be a distinct minority. He viewed everyone as equally capable of engaging in homosexual acts. This alone was deeply disturbing to the average American, but Kinsey went on to suggest a deep contradiction between the behavior many Americans preached and their actual practice. His study suggested that age-old laws that were supposed to regulate such behavior were out of step with everyday American culture.

As the public became more willing to discuss sexuality openly, editors at newspapers and magazines were left in a quandary. Kinsey had created the first real opportunity to write about the topic realistically, but many editors were afraid sales would plummet if parents suddenly found their children reading about sex in a family publication. Some went to great lengths to pro-tect readers' delicate sensibilities. The *Raleigh Times*, for instance, refused to print the story about the Kinsey report when it appeared on the wire ser-vices but informed readers that they could order the story by mail. More than nine hundred requests arrived in the first week alone. The Great Bend

Tribune in Kansas began a series about the book but abandoned it when, after the first article, the paper was deluged with angry telephone calls. The *New York Times* refused to accept an advertisement for the book. In a 1953 article on Kinsey's study of women's sexual habits, the conservative *Chicago Tribune* described Kinsey as a "real menace to society."[7]

Some magazine editors, on the other hand, were more willing to take risks, treating the story as good practical journalism. Articles appeared in some of the nation's leading family-oriented publications, including *Life*, *Time*, *McCall's*, and *Ladies' Home Journal*. The publicity pushed the book's sales to new heights, even though it was written in clinical terms that were far from erotic. Kinsey's publisher boosted the initial run of 10,000 copies to 25,000 and ran the printing presses around the clock to meet the huge demand. The book roared onto best-seller lists, and a sixth printing boosted the number of copies to 185,000. One newspaper editor remarked that it was "the least read best-seller ever produced." It appeared on the *New York Times* list for twenty-seven consecutive weeks. A public opinion poll in 1950 found that people were more familiar with Kinsey than with the postwar Marshall plan to revitalize Europe. Within five years sales had climbed to more than 300,000, and the book was translated into six languages. When Kinsey published his volume on women in 1953, *Time* put him on its cover.

Although the books and the headlines they generated told people more about homosexuals than they had ever known before, the information provided little real insight into who homosexuals were and what they were about. For millions of Americans—including large numbers of isolated gay men and lesbians—homosexuality remained an enigma. In this information vacuum the medical profession assumed a major role in defining homosexuals and shaping how they were portrayed to the public through the nation's newspapers, magazines, radio stations, and later television.

In New York radio station WMCA carried one of the first broadcasts on the subject on November 1, 1948, after a listener complained of the growing number of homosexuals who were being singled out for arrest by police. "I was in a subway toilet one day when a man came in," the listener explained in a letter. "He made advances to me which meant only one thing. Since I am in this pathetic mental condition, I reciprocated his advances. Whereupon, this 'gentleman' pulled out a badge and told me that I was under arrest."[8]

The letter prompted the radio station to invite New York City's chief magistrate, Edgar Bromberger, and the eminent psychiatrist Frederic Wertham to appear on a program entitled, "Something Ought to Be Done." Their atti-

tudes were typical of how the general public viewed homosexuals after
World War II:

DR. WERTHAM: I see behind these troubles one thing and that is an
enormous lot of human suffering. And I think that
psychiatry is well enough advanced to alleviate this
suffering a great deal.

JUDGE I don't think that he has the right to criticize the
BROMBERGER: manner in which he was arrested because, after all,
to detect crime, we must have people who will
detect crime and the fact that he may have been
invited into the offense merely emphasizes his
problems and is no cause for criticism of the
detecting authorities.[9]

Increasingly, individuals who engaged in homosexual behavior were
labeled "perverts" by psychiatrists and police who considered them closely
linked with child molesters, rapists, murderers, and others believed to be
mentally unstable. As the public became more aware of homosexuals, many
people thought their numbers were rising. News reporters turned to psychiatrists and police officials to explain the phenomenon, further fueling
negative stereotypes and irrational public fears. *Newsweek* carried one such
article in its October 10, 1949, issue. The story, QUEER PEOPLE, explained:
"The sex pervert, whether a homosexual, an exhibitionist, or even a dangerous sadist, is too often regarded merely as a 'queer' person who never hurts
anyone but himself. Then the mangled form of some victim focuses public
attention on the degenerate's work. And newspaper headlines flare for days
over accounts and feature articles packed with sensational details of the most
dastardly and horrifying of crimes."

It was within this atmosphere that questions about homosexuality suddenly arose during a routine congressional hearing in Washington in
February 1950. Republican senator Styles Bridges of New Hampshire asked
a witness whether he knew how many State Department employees had been
dismissed for security reasons. Only days earlier Wisconsin's Republican senator, Joseph McCarthy, had leveled shocking allegations that communists had
infiltrated the State Department and claimed to have some of their names. In
response to Bridges, Assistant Secretary of State John Peurifoy blurted out,
"Ninety-one persons in the shady category, most of them homosexuals."[10]

New York Times, April 19, 1950
(© New York Times, used with permission)

His stunning revelation was the first indication the purge of homosexuals, begun in the military, had been extended to include all federal employees.

The Senate launched an investigation into the "Employment of Homosexuals and Other Sex Perverts in Government," and homosexuality became synonymous with communism in the nation's best-read newspapers and magazines.[11] PERVERTS CALLED GOVERNMENT PERIL, reported the *New York Times* on April 19, 1950. OBJECT LESSON: PROBLEM OF HOMOSEXUALS IN THE GOVERNMENT, said *Time* in its December 25, 1950, issue. On July 2, 1953, the *Los Angeles Herald-Express* reported STATE DEPARTMENT FIRES 531 PERVERTS, SECURITY RISKS. Between 1947 and 1953 the government ousted 425 employees with "homosexual proclivities" from the State Department alone. Although dismissals at government agencies had averaged only five per month from 1947 through March 1950, the number surged to a monthly average of sixty through the rest of 1950. Accusations of homosexuality accounted for more firings than being a communist did.[12]

One of the few reporters to question the justification for such witch-hunts was Max Lerner, a popular writer and columnist at the liberal *New York Post*. In the summer of 1950 his twelve-part series, PANIC ON THE POTOMAC, promised to "help take the problem out of the darkness of rumor, into the open; out of wild procession of hunters and hunted, into the area of fact and science." Among the questions he posed was why society felt so troubled by homosexuals and why the government felt an obligation "to hunt them down and destroy them."[13]

As a columnist Lerner had wide latitude to express his opinions. He used it to ridicule claims by politicians that homosexuals were a risk to national security because they could be blackmailed. "I have tried to show, from the evidence of the psychiatrists, that to make a loose category like 'homosexuals' the basis of government policy is worse than useless—it is senseless," he wrote. "When the security officers of government agencies start firing people because their sexual habits seem strange, it is a case of the sick being pursued by the sicker."[14]

Lerner's admonitions had little effect. News coverage of homosexuality turned still darker after 1950 when newly elected President Dwight Eisenhower signed Executive Order 10450, which declared "sexual perversion" to be grounds for barring suspected homosexuals from federal employment. The order was described as a step to ensure that government employees were "reliable, trustworthy, of good conduct and character, and of complete and unswerving loyalty to the United States." NEW SECURITY PLAN ISSUED; THOUSANDS FACE RE-INQUIRY, announced the front page headline in the *New York Times*.[15]

Dependent for survival on government licenses, the major broadcast networks soon adopted similar exclusions. For instance, DuMont Television, a pioneer TV network that later failed, posted large signs in its studios that read: "Attention, producers directors and talent: Your audience is the average American family—Mom and Dad—Junior and Sis—Grandma. You are a guest in their living-rooms. Any violation of this privilege through the use of material in bad taste, immoral business, situations, dialogue, lyrics, routines or costuming will not be tolerated by the DuMont Television Network."[16]

All those who appeared or spoke on television broadcasts were required to sign an employment contract that contained the same warnings. People who appeared on television were not to engage in any activity that would embarrass the network or a major advertiser. Among the television and movie studios in Hollywood, suspected communists were scorned and blacklisted, which made employment virtually impossible.

Attention turned to the print media in 1955 when the Senate Internal Security Subcommittee called hearings on the influence communists might have on American newspapers. Of the thirty-eight reporters and editors who were called to testify, six acknowledged that they had had communist ties at some point in their past. The six included writers and editors at the *New York Times*, *Time*, and *Life*, all of whom either lost their jobs or were demoted.[17] This produced a chilling atmosphere for almost any journalist, but particularly for closeted gays and lesbians working in newsrooms. A lesbian editor at a national newsmagazine who still wishes to remain anonymous put it this way:

> The reason we got ahead was World War II. All of the men had gone to the war, and somebody had to write the magazine and get it out. This was our great opportunity to leap forward. But we knew the FBI checked into every damn thing we did, so it never occurred to me to go out looking for another woman. Nor would I join a fringe group—although I knew actors, singers, and musicians who did and unfortunately let their name be used. I didn't think that was safe and I warned them. The FBI was watching every damn thing we did.

Although Kinsey never estimated the number of gays and lesbians in the United States, police in several cities used the percentages in his books to draw their own conclusions. Fearing their communities were on the verge of becoming havens for homosexuals, police set up special units to crack down on parks, movie houses, and subways where men had been seen engaging in sex. Using one-way mirrors and ventilation ducts, they stepped up efforts to lure men into committing a crime in order to arrest them. As a result of these entrapments, arrest figures exploded, feeding the notion that homosexuals were out of control.

In 1959 alone New York rounded up more than five hundred men in the subway system as suspected homosexuals, many of them married with families. In Washington, D.C., where the largest number of federal employees were concentrated, police netted more than one thousand "perverts" each year during the early 1950s. Similar crackdowns took place in Baltimore, Wichita, Dallas, Memphis, Seattle, Ann Arbor, New Orleans, and Salt Lake City.[18] News media fed the antigay hysteria by publishing the names of the men arrested, along with their addresses and the names of their employers, which in some cases amounted to journalistic lynching. The publicity cost many of them their jobs and in some cases their homes.

With the military purge of homosexuals, the hunt for gay and lesbian federal employees, and increased police crackdowns, the oppressive atmosphere became self-perpetuating, combining to generate an endless stream of negative headlines and news articles. All these factors further defined homosexuals as degenerates and justified their portrayal as a menace.

FORGING A GAY COMMUNITY

Before homosexuals could attempt to influence their portrayal in the news media, they would have to develop a self-concept. The first attempt at self-discovery was the formation of the Mattachine Society in 1950 to push for homosexual rights. The United States had had only one other such organization, a short-lived group in Chicago in 1924 that collapsed after the wife of one of the men called the police and had them arrested.

The Mattachine Society was founded in 1950 by five Los Angeles men. The chief organizer was Harry Hay, a Hollywood actor whose interest was sparked by the Kinsey report two years earlier and the realization that vast numbers of homosexuals across the nation could form a political bloc, much as the National Association for the Advancement of Colored People (NAACP) had for blacks. The name was borrowed from medieval jesters who wore masks and were allowed to speak freely without retribution. Hay was an early advocate of the idea that homosexuals were an oppressed minority, a concept put forward by Donald Webster Cory (the pseudonym of Edward Sagarin, a closeted homosexual who later became a sociology professor at City College of New York) in his landmark 1951 book *The Homosexual in America*.

It made perfect sense for this particular group of men to create such an organization. With backgrounds in Marxist organizing, they were already social renegades. Hay had joined the Communist party in the 1930s. In 1951 he was thrown out of the party after members accused him of trying to protect suspected homosexuals.[19]

The Mattachine Society eventually provided a refuge where homosexual men and women could talk freely about their sexuality. But the group also worked hard to protect the identities of its members, many of whom held security clearances at Southern California aircraft factories and would have been ruined had their homosexuality been revealed. They were careful to make sure membership records did not fall into the wrong hands.

Because California considered such gatherings illegal, members would draw the shades and post a lookout for police before each meeting held in a private home. Although raids never materialized, some members were convinced that an informant had infiltrated the organization but that the police found the group's activities too innocuous to bother with. "We didn't have time for sex," remembered Dale Jennings, one of the original members.

"There were meetings, meetings, meetings every night of the week. When the police realized we were a bunch of commies debating legal questions, they must have realized there wasn't any reason to arrest us."[20] By the end of the first year, a second group had formed.

The organization quickly learned how to take advantage of the news media's concerns that homosexuality and crime were connected. In the spring of 1952, an undercover cop followed Jennings home from a public park and arrested him on charges of vagrancy and lewdness. Hay immediately saw an opportunity to persuade the news media to expose entrapment. Although the Mattachine Society maintained strict anonymity for individuals, it needed publicity to attract new members. The Jennings case seemed like a perfect opportunity. "I'll never forget the next morning when Harry came to bail me out," Jennings recalled. "He said we could make a big thing out of it if I told the court I was homosexual but not guilty. He said we could probably get in the papers for the first time. But we didn't. The papers ignored us."[21]

A Colorado native, Jennings had served in the Philippines during World War II and then settled in Los Angeles, where he took a job with an advertising agency. Like many closeted gay men in the 1940s and 1950s, Jennings was married but also "fooled around" with men from time to time. He had joined the Communist party after the war, believing its promises of a perfect society. But one night a woman member baited him to find out whether he was gay and then testified against him when party officials demanded his membership card. When he learned of Harry Hay's plans to create an organization for homosexuals, he became one of the first to join.

Jennings's decision to plead not guilty was quite unusual. Most gays pleaded guilty in order to avoid the expense of trial and the embarrassment of additional publicity. But publicity was exactly what Jennings and Harry Hay wanted. Their problem would be finding a lawyer, because the respectable ones considered cases against gay men a losing proposition. In Southern California only two lawyers were known to take perversion cases. Most charged exorbitant fees and advised gays to plead guilty to a lesser charge and pay a fine, eventually costing the client everything he had.

Under the name Citizens' Committee to Outlaw Entrapment, the Mattachine Society raised money for a defense fund and convinced George Shibley, a heterosexual Long Beach attorney, to take the case. Hay sent letters to the local news media explaining the problem of entrapment and the case against Jennings. "Now Is the Time to Reveal . . . the Full Threat to the

Entire Community of the Special Police Brutality Against the Homosexual Minority," the two-page, single-spaced letter began. But none of the newspapers, radio stations, or television outlets contacted responded.[22]

In the meantime Jennings's trial had begun with an aggressive defense from Shibley, who told the jury that "homosexuality and lasciviousness are not identical." He argued that his client's acknowledgment that he was homosexual did not mean that he was soliciting. Shibley went on to condemn the tactics used by police to lure innocent men into committing a crime. "The only pervert in this courtroom," he told the jury members, "is the arresting officer."[23]

After deliberating for forty hours the jury announced that it was hopelessly deadlocked, 11 to 1. The lone dissenter vowed to hold out for a guilty verdict "until Hell froze over." After the judge declared a mistrial and the district attorney unexpectedly dropped the charges, Jennings became the first gay person in California history to successfully challenge police entrapment. Not only was it a tremendous personal victory for Jennings but Harry Hay and the others were ecstatic for political reasons. They had stood up against an oppressive judicial system and won. The Los Angeles press, however, remained silent. Jennings recalled,

> We could have burned down a nursery at high noon on Sunday, and they wouldn't print it because we were all queers. At that time several judges were giving homosexuals a choice between a sentence as long as fifty years or castration for sodomy convictions, and the papers printed nothing about it. Or, if they did, they wouldn't mention this dreadful choice. Straights thought we were exaggerating. We knew we were going to have to do something ourselves to get through to the public to let them know the horrors that were going on.[24]

Unable to crack the media barrier, Jennings and some of the others grew increasingly frustrated with the long tedious Mattachine Society meetings. Don Slater had attended several meetings but never joined. "I was not interested in self-serving self-pity," he later recalled.[25] Although most Mattachine members were skeptical that a magazine would survive, Slater, Jennings, Martin Block, Tony Reyes, and Guy Rousseau founded a pamphlet-size magazine they named *One.* The editors boldly put their names on the masthead, knowing that if trouble came, they would be the first to be arrested.

In addition, W. Dorr Legg, who had joined the Mattachine Society shortly after Jennings's arrest in 1952, set aside his career as an urban planner and became *One*'s business manager. For several years he enthusiastically pro-moted sales of the magazine at Mattachine Society meetings, making him the first full-time gay activist.[26]

They used a printing press in the basement of the home of Jennings's sis-ter and brother-in-law, producing the first issue of *One* in January 1953, the first time American gays had written about their concerns in a publication intended for mass distribution. "The magazine stood for the assimilation of homosexually active persons into the larger community," Slater recounted. Like Alfred Kinsey, the founders of *One* considered homosexuality a behav-ior that any person was capable of experiencing. "We certainly didn't want to institutionalize homosexuality, á la heterosexuality, or make ourselves into a special class or culture group," Slater said.[27]

Jennings wrote a feature article for the first issue, TO BE ACCUSED IS TO BE GUILTY, in which he described his arrest and his landmark victory. The article quickly proved a boon to *One*'s circulation and produced a surge in member-ship and morale for the Mattachine Society. Attendance at meetings grew rapidly, and new groups began to spring up from San Diego to San Francisco. Jennings quickly became a cause célèbre, except among the mainstream media, which continued to ignore his crusade.

In the spring of 1953 the Mattachine Society made another attempt to attract publicity, this time by conducting an opinion poll on gay issues. The society solicited opinions from candidates for city council and the Los Angeles school board on such topics as police harassment, sex education in the schools, and civil rights for homosexuals. Copies of the questionnaires were also mailed to news reporters, including Paul Coates at the *Los Angeles Daily Mirror*. Coates was fascinated by it. After making several telephone calls and finding little information about the organization, Coates wrote about it in his daily column on March 12, 1953. "The already harassed and wary can-didates for public office were whacked with a broadside from a strange new pressure group," he wrote. "An organization that claims to represent the homosexual voters of Los Angeles is vigorously shopping for campaign promises." The columnist went on to explain that he had learned that the Mattachine Society's legal adviser had been an unfriendly witness before the House Un-American Activities Committee. "If I were a member of that club," he wrote, "I'd worry."[28]

Harry Hay was so thrilled with the organization's first publicity that he arranged to have thousands of copies reproduced to distribute to the mem-bership and the general public. But he faced a major problem. Most members of the Mattachine Society were not aware that some leaders had once been members of the Communist party. They were particularly paranoid because the House Un-American Activities Committee had scheduled hearings in Los Angeles on the Communist party's influence on the motion picture industry. The city's daily newspapers were saturated with reports that McCarthy's anticommunist crusade had spread to Hollywood.

Frightened members of the Mattachine Society called for a general meeting to discuss the issue. Hay quickly realized he would have to resign if the organization were to survive. The new organization—which kept the Mattachine name—abandoned Hay's idealistic vision of a homosexual minority and reconstituted itself as a service organization that would help homosexuals learn how to survive in an oppressive society. "Our guiding principle was evolution," wrote board chairman Ken Burns, "not revolution." Where the earlier organization had stressed homosexuals' differences, the new one considered gay men and lesbians as "exactly the same as everyone else—except in bed."[29]

To succeed Hay the membership chose Harold Call, the former publisher of several small midwestern newspapers who had worked as an advertising salesman for the *Kansas City Star*. His association with the *Star* has lasted until the newspaper learned he had been arrested in Chicago in 1952 because police suspected he and another man had engaged in sexual activity in a parked car. Although a judge later dismissed the charges, the *Star* asked him to resign. Soon after that he moved to San Francisco and joined the Mattachine Society.

By the spring of 1954, *Daily Mirror* columnist Coates also had a weekly television program called *Confidential File* on a local Los Angeles television station (KTTV). Like his newspaper column, the TV show thrived on gossip and sensationalism. That spring a producer for the program contacted officials of the Mattachine Society and asked whether they could supply a homosexual for an on-air interview. The producer also asked permission for a film crew to attend a discussion group in order to show the public what the organization was about. Conservative members feared any contact with television. "It was like handling nitroglycerine," Legg remembered.[30] But the more liberal members prevailed and agreed to both requests. The group's twenty-two-year-old secretary volunteered to appear on camera for an interview.

On April 25, 1954, television viewers tuned in to see twenty ordinary-looking men and women standing around a table in a homey living room, drinking coffee, and eating cookies. This was not riveting television. Viewers who might have hoped to glimpse a bunch of mental cases were disappointed. The show featured interviews with a psychiatrist, a police officer, and the Mattachine Society's secretary, who used the pseudonym Curtis White and whose identity was disguised by a black rectangle superimposed on his face. Careful that he not offend his viewers, Coates had asked a PTA group to review and bless a transcript before the program aired; the PTA approved.[31]

During the interview White said that he rejected the common psychiatric description of homosexuals as neurotic and considered himself a happy well-adjusted person. Coates asked whether his family knew about his sexuality. "Well," White responded, "they didn't up until tonight. . . . I think it's almost certain that they will. . . . I think I may very possibly lose my job too." Surprised by the response, Coates wanted to know why he would agree to go on TV under those circumstances. "Well," White responded, "I think that this way I can be a little useful to someone besides myself."[32]

The next day accolades poured in from several quarters. "Without sensationalism, Coates and his cohorts managed to present this delicate subject in an adult and informative way," the *Daily Mirror* said. "Coates handled the difficult subject with taste and dignity, pinpointing the social problems raised by the presence in this area of some 200,000 sex variants," wrote *Daily Variety*, the entertainment industry newspaper.[33]

The positive response stood in stark contrast to White's reception at his job. Despite the efforts to hide his identity, his boss recognized his voice and fired him. *One* carried a full-page tribute in its next issue:

> May his courage serve as the example for more and more of us to stand up and be counted. The day will come when thousands and thousands of our people will rise proudly to demand social equality and civil rights. When that day comes—when enough of us have the kind of courage Curtis has—legislators, jurors, educators and clergy will no longer be able to ignore our needs and problems. And our first great victory—lifting the curtain of silence—will have been achieved.[34]

Two months later White wrote to *One* to report on his fate since: "While I lost my job the next day, I am again employed and in a position somewhat better than what I had, and at a salary nearly half again as much as I was making."[35]

With each issue the importance of *One* became clearer. Although much of its content was *Saturday Evening Post*–style fiction and poetry, it also provided

its readers with valuable information, including scientific and scholarly articles. It provided a forum within which homosexuals could safely develop a
concept of their culture through diverse—and often conflicting—views.
Letters from readers in many parts of the nation documented intolerance
and harassment by local police. Articles told of witch-hunts conducted by
police, the government, the military, and private industry. These were the
only sources of information about homosexuals that had not been filtered
through heterosexual editors in the mainstream media.

"We used a million different pseudonyms as bylines on the articles so people would think we had a tremendous number of writers," Slater recalled.
"But there really were only a handful of us."[36]

A few newsstands sold it openly, but many refused to carry it. "We finally
got a newsstand on Cahuenga and Hollywood to keep a couple of copies
under the counter because people would ask for it," Jennings recalled.
"Pretty soon it was on the counter. Then the owner asked, 'Can you bring
fifty next time?'"[37]

In 1954 monthly sales of *One* peaked at 16,000, most of them mailed to
subscribers. But in October 1954 the magazine came dangerously close to
being silenced. The Los Angeles postmaster suddenly refused to accept that
month's issue, claiming it was obscene. His concerns centered on a fictional-
ized story about a twenty-year-old woman who left her fiancé so she could
live with her female college roommate, described in the story as a lesbian.
Although the magazine contained no pictures and the story offered no
explicit descriptions of sexual encounters, the word *lesbian*—and even the
word *homosexual*—was considered obscene.

Slater, a feisty gay man whose slight build belied his belligerence, proposed that they "sue the bastard." *One* slapped the postmaster with a lawsuit
citing the First Amendment right to free speech (*One, Incorporated vs Otto K.
Olesen*). The suit set off a legal tug-of-war that lasted for years. In the meantime *One*'s success served as an incentive for the Mattachine Society to launch
a newsletter in January 1955 called *Mattachine Review*. The newsletter quickly
became the primary link for members and a growing number of chapters,
which now (at least intermittently) included Los Angeles, Long Beach,
Chicago, and San Francisco. In addition, several chapters published their own
newsletters.

The editors of *One* lost their initial case in 1955 and went on to lose their
appeal in 1957 when a panel of judges ruled that the magazine was "filthy and
obscene," containing "nothing more than cheap pornography calculated to

promote lesbianism." But then on Monday, January 13, 1958, the U.S. Supreme Court handed down one of the most important victories of the homophile movement by unanimously reversing the decision. In essence, the Court determined that homosexuality per se was not obscene. The victory eliminated the final barrier to the emergence of a gay press.[38] But once again the significance was either overlooked or downplayed by mainstream newspapers, including the *Los Angeles Times*, for which *One*'s lawsuit was a local story.[39] The *New York Times* and the *Washington Post* missed the significance of the story and relegated it to their back pages.

Even with the emergence of *One* and the Mattachine newsletter, Del Martin and Phyllis Lyon had never heard of the Mattachine Society. The two women met in 1950 while working on a trade journal in Seattle. Lyon had been the first woman editor of the *Daily Californian* at the University of California at Berkeley, where she had studied journalism. She later became a crime reporter at a small newspaper in Chino before moving to Seattle. Aware that their opportunities in the male-dominated news business were severely limited, they abandoned journalism and headed for San Francisco, where they set up house together.

Borrowing an obscure name from an erotic prose poem by Pierre Louÿs, they launched the Daughters of Bilitis, the nation's first lesbian organization, in September 1955. It quickly became a safe place for women to meet one another—lesbian bars were struggling to survive because the threat of police raids was unrelenting. In their second year Martin and Lyon realized that the organization needed some way to reach out to more women; they created the *The Ladder*.[40] "We tried to cover a huge range of subjects," said Barbara Gittings, an early member who became editor in 1963. "We wanted people to know they had lots of company, they weren't alone, they were all right, they were good people, they shouldn't listen to the propaganda, and they should begin to stand up for themselves and try to do something about their situation. We told them we needed their help and cooperation."[41]

Meanwhile the mainstream media continued to ignore both the Daughters of Bilitis and the Mattachine Society. In January 1956 the New York chapter's founders had sent letters to newspaper editors throughout the city but received no response until 1958, when a producer for a lunchtime talk show contacted chapter president Tony Segura and asked whether the organization would provide someone to be interviewed about homosexuality.

A chemist by profession, the Cuban-born Segura was one of the more courageous and outspoken members of the New York group. But as a homosexual he was well aware that he was living in dangerous times. Homosexual behavior was a felony in New York State, and a conviction carried a maximum sentence of twenty years in jail. Individuals had been arrested for merely talking suggestively about gay sex.

Segura agreed to appear on the program, provided he would not be identified. On March 10, wearing a hood that covered his face, he became the first homosexual to appear on an East Coast television station, WABD. He was joined by psychologist Albert Ellis and Gerald Sykes, the author of an article on Freud and Jung for *Harper's*. As one of the more enlightened members of his profession, Ellis urged homosexuals to adjust themselves to a "heterosexual mode of living." Segura, through his heavy Cuban accent, talked in positive terms about the Mattachine Society, explaining that the organization was attempting to help homosexuals achieve acceptance through its educational programs. When asked why homosexuals had become more visible since World War II, Segura speculated that the public's increased awareness accounted for the difference. But in fact gay activists were struggling to raise the public consciousness.

For a second segment on the subject to be aired the following day the producers had scheduled a second panel to discuss lesbians, inviting a Daughters of Bilitis representative to discuss the subject with well-known author Fannie Hurst. But the segment was killed fifteen minutes before air time. Hurst appeared on screen to explain that the program had "undergone severe censorship." Instead of discussing lesbianism, she said her guests would talk about handwriting analysis.[42]

Although the new-found visibility was limited to only a handful of media outlets, it was sufficient to generate a backlash from an increasingly vocal group of psychiatrists. One of the most outspoken was Edmund Bergler, a psychiatrist who had studied under Freud in Vienna before moving to New York in 1927. Although Freud never offered a complete explanation of the causes of homosexuality, his attitude was clearly tolerant. This was reflected in his letter to a homosexual's mother in 1935 in which he wrote that it was "nothing to be ashamed of, no vice, no degradation, it cannot be classified as an illness; we consider it to be a variant of the sexual function."[43]

But Bergler, in his 1956 book *Homosexuality: Disease or Way of Life?* characterized homosexuality as "neither a biologically determined destiny, nor incomprehensible ill luck" but a curable perversion that posed tragic consequences for the nation's impressionable youth. He went on to level harsh criticism at the press for failing to describe the misery homosexuality causes, especially to spouses and parents. "Serious-minded people are alarmed, but unfortunately this alarm has not yet communicated itself to the editorial offices of newspapers and magazines," he wrote.[44]

The admonition struck a nerve with the news media. *Time* carried news of the book to a national audience with a supportive review on December 10, 1956. The book also prompted a response from Max Lerner, the *New York Post* columnist whose 1950 series was one of the earliest in-depth features on the subject. Among his comments, Lerner wrote: "I agree with Bergler that their 'way of life' has been given an undeserved glamour by some of their writers. Where I disagree sharply with him is in his belief that by scolding, condemning and attacking them we shall get very far with the problem."[45]

Despite the setbacks, familiarity with the Mattachine Society and Daughters of Bilitis was spreading across the nation. Just as *One* had spurred membership in the Mattachine Society, *The Ladder* boosted membership in the Daughters of Bilitis. By the late 1950s the Mattachine Society had added even more chapters—in New York, Boston, Denver, Philadelphia, and St. Louis. The Daughters of Bilitis had added chapters in New York, Los Angeles, Chicago, and for a time Rhode Island. However, they were but a fraction of the nation's gay and lesbian population. By the end of the 1950s the Mattachine Society had about 230 members, whereas the Daughters of Bilitis had only about 110. Despite the attention the organizations had managed to garner from the media in Los Angeles and New York, most Americans understood little, if anything, about homosexuals and what they wanted.[46]

2

OUT OF THE SHADOWS

In September 1958 the Mattachine Society held its fifth annual convention in New York City. Because it was the first time the gathering had been held outside California, energetic members thought they might attract some publicity from the New York press. Not only did they want to make their existence known to closeted, isolated gays and lesbians, they wanted to educate the general public about homosexuality. But the big city dailies, citing their family orientation, proved to be formidable obstacles. Although editors routinely ran articles about rapes, murders, and drug dealings, stories that portrayed homosexuals in a positive light were another matter.

"One managing editor refused to print an interview written by one of his reporters on the grounds that this material was 'not fit to print in a family newspaper,'" Del Martin, president of the Daughters of Bilitis (DOB), wrote in *The Ladder*. "Our attempts to bring homosexuality into the open and clarify a much misunderstood subject were relegated to a 'conspiracy of silence.'"[1]

The following year Mattachine members held their convention in Denver, where the media response was dramatically different. Both metro dailies, the *Denver Post* and the *Rocky Mountain News*, carried stories before and during the convention. The *Post* called the gathering "a serious, intelligent and open discussion of a basic human problem." But the coverage did not sit well with some readers. "This is simply revolting," one wrote in a letter to the editor. Another said, "I've heard that the late Senator McCarthy called your newspaper the 'Rocky Mountain Daily Worker' (a Communist organ) and it seems as though you are furthering this belief when you print articles on the furtherance of homosexuality in America."[2] Even so, the coverage was the best the Mattachine Society had received in the mainstream media. But Denver members of the organization paid a steep price. Within a month, Denver police raided the homes of several, arresting one on morals charges.

Backlash was also brewing in San Francisco. At its Denver convention, the Mattachine Society adopted a resolution praising Mayor George Christopher of San Francisco and Thomas Cahill, the police chief, for their "enlightened attitudes" toward homosexuals. Mounting a challenge to the mayor, city assessor Russell Wolden used a radio interview to accuse the two officials of allowing the city to become "the national headquarters of organized sex deviates." WOLDEN IN SMEAR CAMPAIGN, reported the *San Francisco Examiner*. The uproar set off a weeklong flurry of news articles, the most recognition the city's newspapers had ever given the surging number of gays and lesbians. "A million dollars worth of publicity," is how *The Ladder* described it. And Wolden's grandstanding backfired. Both dailies rallied to Christopher's defense. In a front page editorial two days after Wolden leveled his charges, the *Chronicle* called on Wolden to drop out of the race: "The notoriety he has acquired has left its embarrassing mark. He has degraded the good name of San Francisco. A man who would recklessly and spuriously do this shows himself unfit for office. Wolden should apologize to the people of San Francisco and withdraw as a candidate for Mayor."[3]

It later became apparent that the Mattachine Society's resolution was part of a publicity stunt the Wolden forces had cooked up to embarrass the mayor. The instigator was Wolden supporter Patrick Brandhove, who had managed to convince the Mattachine Society that such a resolution would be seen as a goodwill gesture toward the mayor. Brandhove sent a copy to Wolden, who attacked it on the radio program. Even so, Christopher won reelection by a healthy margin. In the meantime Wolden accused the newspapers of "racing at full throttle to destroy a man."[4]

Soon after the election nonprofit radio station KPFA-FM in Berkeley broadcast a two-hour special titled "The Homosexual in Society." The program consisted of two separate panels, one called "The Role of the Homosexual as an Individual and as a Member of Society" and the other titled "The Role Society Should Play in Solving the Homophile Problem."

Guests on the radio show included Harold Call, president of the Mattachine Society, and Blanche Baker, a San Francisco psychiatrist who was one of the most compassionate and enlightened of her profession. "There are those who feel it is a neurotic problem and others who call it glandular, or even a hereditary problem," she explained to the radio audience. "For myself, from many years of work, I consider the homosexual first of all a human being."[5] The program was among the first in a series of landmark broadcasts that ran on the Pacifica radio stations, the broadcast equivalent to the underground press. Pacifica stations in Berkeley, Los Angeles, and New York built a reputation on their willingness to tackle homosexuality and other controversial topics in a no-nonsense straightforward manner.[6]

But the heightened attention sparked a ferocious media backlash. The San Francisco *Examiner* ran a series of articles the next summer about gay men who were using Buena Vista Park to find sexual partners. In June and again in October 1960 editorials in the *Examiner* and the *Chronicle* set off police crackdowns in city parks, public squares, and bus depots.[7] Tensions escalated even more in August 1961 after police arrested eighty-nine men and fourteen women at the Tay-Bush Inn, a popular dance club. It was the largest bar raid in the city's history. There might have been even more arrests except that about one hundred people fled before police were able to load them into police wagons. The *Chronicle* said the scene looked "vaguely reminiscent of leading sheep from a packed corral" as three wagons shuttled seven loads of prisoners from the club to the city jail. The newspaper explained that police launched the raid after a neighbor complained that men could be seen through the windows dancing with one another and kissing. "That many, in a place that small," one police officer told the *Chronicle*. "How could they be dancing?"[8]

Police intensified their raids, and the San Francisco newspapers egged them on, focusing even more public attention on efforts to clean up the city.

In October 1961 the *Examiner* reported that state liquor agents were training young attractive police officers to patrol gay bars, teaching them what to look for and how to act and dress so they would appeal to gay men. Some reported being solicited for "unnatural acts" and witnessing "fondling or kissing among male patrons, and [that] patrons were permitted to engage in lewd conversations," grounds for revoking liquor licenses. In a year's time the number of gay bars in the city was cut by nearly half, from thirty in 1960 to eighteen in 1961.[9] Frightened gays and lesbians flocked to the Mattachine Society and Daughters of Bilitis for safety. A third organization, the Tavern Guild, sprang up to help victims pay court costs. That group later expanded and served as the nucleus for the Society for Individual Rights (SIR), which by the late 1960s was the largest homophile organization in the nation.[10]

The San Francisco newspapers remained hostile until 1964, when more than five hundred gay men and lesbians attended a New Year's Eve ball sponsored by the Council on Religion and the Homosexual, a new coalition gays had established with Protestant ministers from several denominations. Although the vice squad was included in the planning and permitted the event to take place, police tried to convince the owners of California Hall to cancel the dance. The ministers had to intervene. Then on the night of the dance the police stationed photographers at the entrance to the hall to photograph each person arriving. They repeatedly interrupted the dance, using the excuse of inspecting for fire code violations. At one point a partygoer tripped over a chair, and police took him into custody, charging him with trying to kiss another man. Three attorneys and a housewife were also arrested on the trumped-up charge of trying to block the entrance to California Hall.

The episode was eye-opening for the ministers and their wives—already sympathetic—who had heard gays talk about harassment but had never actually witnessed it firsthand. The next day seven members of the coalition called a press conference to denounce the behavior of the police. The *Chronicle* carried a page one story and photograph of the ministers on January 3, 1964, headlined ANGRY MINISTERS RIP POLICE. "That was when we got newspapers, TV, and radio on our side," remembered Harold Call, one of the organizers. "The police were so brutal. And with some respectable clergymen on our side, that was a turning point."[11]

But the Mattachine Society itself was self-destructing. Internecine squabbling erupted when the New York chapter surpassed San Francisco in membership. New York members began to resent having to pay dues that brought no tangible benefits. In March 1961 an exasperated board of directors had dissolved the national structure, leaving the local chapters to fend for themselves. The San Francisco and Los Angeles chapters grew stronger. The Chicago chapter weakened but managed to survive for a while. The group in Philadelphia reorganized and eventually formed a similar group, the Janus Society. Chapters in Denver and Boston collapsed. The group's leaders realized that for a national organization to survive, it would need national exposure in the news media that would help build a solid membership base. But most editors and publishers were unwilling to provide such coverage, fearing accusations of promoting not only the Mattachine Society, but homosexuality.

TV GETS SERIOUS

While the doors of the national Mattachine Society were shut in 1961, freelance television producer John W. Reavis had convinced Jonathan Rice, a founder of San Francisco public television station KQED, to allow him to produce a program that was initially to be called "The Gay Ones." By the fall of 1961 Reavis's project had already been rejected by the major networks in New York, but KQED was in a better position because it was free of advertising pressures to avoid controversial topics. Rice approved the program (which was renamed "The Rejected") despite a resignation threat from a member of the station's board of directors. "The Rejected" became the nation's first television documentary on homosexuals when it aired on September 11, 1961.

Working with a budget of less than $100, Reavis and coproducer Irving Saraf shot all the footage in the KQED studios, except one sequence that they shot at the Black Cat, the most popular gay bar in San Francisco. The program began with renowned anthropologist Margaret Mead, who set a tolerant tone by describing the historical role homosexuals had played in a variety of civilizations, including those of ancient Greece, the South Sea islands, the Arctic, and Native Americans. She explained, "It's society that patterns homosexual behavior. It's society that tells young children that these are possible roles, and it's society that treats the practices of homosexuality, or the identification of an individual as only interested in playing a particular homosexual role. It's society that treats these as sacred or profane, as preferred, or as criminal."[12]

The documentary then delved into various aspects of homosexuality in separate segments, including law, religion, public health, psychiatry, and the homosexual perspective from three gay men. Bishop James A. Pike of the Episcopal Diocese of California commented, "The person who is in this situation is like anyone else with an illness, and should be cared for as such, with love and concern and interest; not casting them aside; not labeling them as evil, any more than we would do so these days with the alcoholic who is in a compulsive drinking situation."

Karl Bowman, a San Francisco psychiatrist, expressed an exceptionally liberal view for his era, avoiding the harsh condemnations that dominated descriptions used by much of his profession. "The attitude of some people is to try to treat it in an entirely punitive way, with the idea that the more severe the punishment and disgrace, the less likely that the condition will occur at least as far as overt behavior is concerned," he said. Bowman pointed out that many other countries have no cultural taboos against homosexuality, and he cited communist Europe, West Germany, and Great Britain as the only countries in which homosexual conduct was a crime.

Harold Call, Don Lucas, and Les Fisher spoke as openly gay men. "In the Mattachine we are seeking acceptance of the homosexual in society, whether we approve of his type of conduct or not—the fact is, he is in our midst, and in large numbers." Called explained. "We hope that, by acceptance, he may be spared much of the derision that society now points toward him, and that he may thereby be able to assume his full and equal place as a human being in the community."[13]

Reavis had carefully constructed the program so that it would raise a homosexual stereotype and then contradict it with a compelling interview. "The viewer should be left, if anything, with a feeling he is confused and that society as a whole is confused about homosexuality," he wrote in his original proposal for the program.[14]

Even before it aired the documentary attracted more than one hundred requests for transcripts. Afterward the station was flooded with another four hundred requests.[15] Dwight Newton, the *San Francisco Examiner*'s TV columnist, wrote, "KQED handled the subject soberly, calmly and in great depth." The *Chronicle*'s TV writer, Terrance O'Flaherty, called it "courageous." A reporter for the *Palo Alto Times* observed, "The often-mentioned but seldom seen Mattachine Society seemed less sinister."[16] Between 1961 and 1963 the program was broadcast by public TV stations in a number of cities, including New York and Los Angeles.

Typically, as with most media exposure, "The Rejected" did not include lesbians. But in 1962, as the Daughters of Bilitis held its national convention in Los Angeles, the program *Confidential File* contacted the organization, inviting a lesbian to appear. This was the same program on which host Paul Coates had interviewed Curtis White, Mattachine Society treasurer, in 1954 in the first known television interview with a homosexual.

A thirty-eight-year-old college graduate, who appeared under the name of Terry and ran a grooming parlor for poodles, explained to Coates that she had agreed to appear because she was "the least vulnerable" among DOB's members. When he asked her how many women belonged to her organization she responded, "Between one hundred twenty-five and one hundred fifty." Coates was clearly caught off guard by her response because many people assumed that both the Daughters of Bilitis and the Mattachine Society were huge. So when his guest told him DOB had only 125 to 150 members, Coates naively asked, "Don't you mean thousand?"[17]

MEDIA BREAKTHROUGH

Although increasing numbers of gays were living openly on the East Coast, the eastern media carried far less coverage than media outlets on the West Coast, where both national organizations had originated. The large dailies in Washington, D.C., virtually ignored the subject until the summer of 1963 when the Mattachine Society of Washington burst into the headlines of the *Washington Post* and the Washington *Evening Star*, creating an uproar beneath the Capitol dome.

When conservative members of Congress learned that a local gay organization had been founded, they immediately proposed legislation intended to shut it down by crippling the group's ability to raise money. During congressional hearings on the matter, Franklin Kameny, a founder of the Washington group, was called to testify, and he made certain the media were apprised. Kameny had been a government astronomer until 1957 when he was accused of being a homosexual and fired. Unable to find a lawyer who would represent him, he conducted his own campaign for reinstatement. A lengthy series of court cases ended in bitter defeat when the Supreme Court refused to hear his appeal. A short time later he and fellow Washington, D.C., activist Jack Nichols founded the Mattachine Society of Washington. The national organization no longer existed, but several former chapters retained the name Mattachine. Kameny had urged the group to choose a different name, but he was outvoted.

The general public was largely unaware of the Washington group until the congressional hearings in August 1963 questioned the right of the organization to solicit money. Representative John Dowdy, a Texas Democrat who had introduced anti-Mattachine legislation, used the hearings as a soapbox to rail against bestiality, incest, and homosexual orgies. "Down in my country if you call a man a 'queer' or a 'fairy' the least you can expect is a black eye," Dowdy said. When Kameny pointed out that Texas also had homosexuals, Dowdy responded, "Maybe, but I never heard anyone brag about it."[18] After the American Civil Liberties Union and several family services agencies testified against the bill (H.R. 5990), it died and the Mattachine Society of Washington faded into obscurity.

Meanwhile the Mattachine Society of New York was beginning to break through the ambivalence that characterized much of that city's news media. With the exception of Lerner's two series in the *New York Post* a decade earlier, New York newspapers had virtually ignored that city's large homosexual subculture.

On December 17, 1963, the *New York Times* carried an especially uncharacteristic article on its front page about a recent rash of routine police raids on gay bars. Typically, the *Times* avoided stories that might appear sensational, but the raids provided an opportunity for the paper to disclose to its readers that homosexuals had become a serious problem facing the city. Under the headline GROWTH OF OVERT HOMOSEXUALITY IN CITY PROVOKES WIDE CONCERN the *Times* story began,

> The problem of homosexuality in New York became the focus yesterday of increased attention by the State Liquor Authority and the Police Department. The liquor authority announced the revocation of the liquor licenses of two more homosexual haunts that had been repeatedly raided by the police. . . . The city's most sensitive open secret—the presence of what is probably the greatest homosexual population in the world and its increasing openness—has become the subject of growing concern of psychiatrists, religious leaders and the police.[19]

The story appeared on page one because A. M. Rosenthal, the *Times's* new metropolitan editor, wanted to make a point. After eight years abroad he had abandoned an exemplary career as a foreign correspondent to reinvigorate the paper's city section, which had been plagued by reporting problems since the early 1950s.

Not long after Rosenthal arrived in the city, he and his wife were apartment hunting in the East Fifties and wandered into a notorious cruising area for gay men that ran for several blocks along Third Avenue. The couple were startled to see male couples openly holding hands. Several building directories listed pairs of men who were sharing apartments. Although New York's gay subculture dated to at least the turn of the century, Rosenthal had not spent much time in the city during the 1950s, a period in which large numbers of gays had settled there rather than return to the confines of their small hometowns after World War II.

When Rosenthal returned to the *Times* newsroom, he breathlessly described what he had seen to his assistant metropolitan editor, Arthur Gelb. Gelb responded, "That's an old story." "Not to me," Rosenthal retorted. Several department heads thought Rosenthal had lost his mind. "There was a certain amount of nervousness because it just wasn't the sort of thing the *Times* did," remembered Harrison Salisbury, then the managing editor. "That was the general attitude toward homosexuality. It wasn't conscious, but it wasn't brought up and talked about."[20]

Rosenthal assigned the story to Robert Doty, a veteran international correspondent who had recently returned to the city after getting into a spat with Turner Catledge, the executive editor. Doty had barely begun on the story when he found a press release from the Homosexual League of New York. The group identified its press contact as Randolfe Wicker and listed his telephone number.

A clean-cut blond in his mid-twenties, Wicker had grown up in Texas where he had spent time as a civil rights activist. In the summer of 1958 he visited New York and attended his first meeting of the Mattachine Society. Wicker, a promoter by nature, publicized the organization's discussion groups by distributing posters to stores on Manhattan's West Side. As a result attendance at meetings tripled, with some drawing as many as nine hundred people until Wicker returned to the University of Texas. Other members of the group felt that taking signs to the stores was not safe.

After he finished college in 1961, Wicker returned to New York and resumed his public relations duties. But his activism had not sat well with his father, Charles Hayden, for whom he had been named. When his father learned of his son's publicity drive for the Mattachine Society, he asked him to stop using his name. "He gave me the name with one hand and took it away with the other," Wicker remarked to friends. So he chose the name Randolfe Wicker, using the odd spelling of *Randolph* to avoid objections from others who might have the same name.

Trying to drum up publicity that would boost membership, Wicker began contacting reporters and editors at newspapers and radio and television stations with information about the organization's public lectures and discussions. But trouble was brewing among the old guard of the Mattachine Society. With memories of the terrifying witch-hunts of the McCarthy era still vivid, they worried that Wicker's campaign would create more problems than it could solve. Said Curtis Dewees, "Randy was very young and wild-eyed. He was very radical and did things that the rest of us didn't have the guts to do. Many of the people in our group were professionals, and I think they thought Randy was moving too fast. We weren't sure things were ready for someone like him yet. But he certainly made us sit up and take notice."[21]

As pressure to scale back mounted, Wicker created his own organization, the Homosexual League of New York. As its sole member, he elected himself director of public relations, which he spelled out on a new set of business cards. Whenever members of the Mattachine Society balked at his publicity stunts, Wicker would simply claim that he represented his own organization.

One of his first opportunities came in July 1962 after WBAI, a listener-supported FM radio station, carried "The Homosexual in America," an hourlong program that featured a panel of psychiatrists who painted homosexuals as sick individuals who could be cured if only they would seek help. The next morning Wicker marched into the station and demanded that gays be allowed to speak for themselves. The startled station manager agreed to air a second program, provided Wicker would assemble a panel of homosexual guests.

When news of the arrangement reached Hearst's *Journal-American*, radio-TV writer Jack O'Brien lashed out at the idea, suggesting in his column that the station change its call letters to WSICK and that it had been duped by an "arrogant card-carrying swish"—a reference to the flamboyant Wicker and his newly printed business cards. O'Brien wrote, "We've heard of silly situations in broadcasting, but FM station WBAI wins our top prize for scraping the sickly barrel-bottom. WBAI announced, a bit proudly, it will give 'eight young homosexuals' equal time to tell their perverted side of the admittedly sad but certainly sinful story because WBAI believes 'in the right of minorities to be heard.'"[22]

One week later, on July 16, 1962, radio listeners heard Wicker and six other gay men talk for ninety minutes about what it was like to be homosexual. Their sometimes rambling conversation touched on promiscuity, police harassment, social responsibilities of gays and nongays, and their careers. The next morning favorable comments appeared in several newspapers, including the New York *Herald Tribune*, the entertainment newspaper *Variety*, and the *New York Times*, where TV columnist Jack Gould called the show "the most extensive consideration of the subject to be heard on American radio." *Newsweek* described it as "96 minutes of intriguing, if intellectually inconclusive, listening."[23] But the positive reviews did not discourage a group of listeners from challenging the station's broadcast license at the Federal Communications Commission (FCC). In the end the case set an important precedent among broadcasters because the FCC rejected the complaint. The agency told the disgruntled challengers that if it prevented provocative programs by denying broadcast licenses, then "only the wholly inoffensive, the bland, could gain access to the radio microphone or TV camera." In essence the decision sent a message to the rest of the radio and television industry that homosexuality was an acceptable topic for broadcast, at least as far as the FCC was concerned.

By late 1962 gays and lesbians were beginning to make important strides in gaining media coverage. At a panel discussion on the subject in December 1962 Curtis Dewees, New York Mattachine president, suggested that gays emphasize the positive aspects of homosexuality. "The negative side will come out in due time anyway," he told his audience. Author-journalist Jess Stearn, author of a 1961 exposé on gay life that became a best-seller, suggested that in order for lesbians to be palatable to the public they "must appear to be as normal as 'the girl next door.'" Although Stearn was considered an authority on the subject, Wicker quickly took issue with him. "All types of homosexuals should be represented, from the most respectable to the most flamboyantly disrespectful." The only woman on the panel, a DOB member who used the pseudonym Meredith Grey, suggested that homosexuals should emphasize that "it is wrong to compel others to comply with one's own standards of sexual morality."[24] Many ideas put forth in the panel discussion would come to form the basis of the modern gay rights movement.

A CALL FROM THE *TIMES*

The publicity drive by New York's Mattachine Society had received only passing attention from the New York media when Robert Doty contacted Randy Wicker in November 1963 to ask for help with his story on homosexuals for the *New York Times*. The reporter told him that he knew little about homosexuals but acknowledged that he and his wife had several gay friends. Wicker offered to take Doty on a "field trip" to see the city's gay subculture firsthand. He arranged for several of his friends to meet them at an East Side bar called Regent's Row. As Wicker recalled it, "I told him, 'Look, I understand that the majority opinion in the psychiatric community says that homosexuality is a disorder and that these people are out claiming they can change people. All I want is equal treatment. At least give some exposure to the minority voices that say homosexuality is not necessarily pathology.'"[25]

Wicker handed Doty an article from *One* about Evelyn Hooker, a professor of psychology at the University of California at Los Angeles. Hooker had produced a series of papers in 1953 that challenged the widely held theory that homosexuals were sick.[26] The study had been largely ignored by her colleagues and the press. Wicker hoped Doty's article would provide the attention Hooker's work had been denied for nearly a decade.

On December 17, 1963, Doty's article appeared, breaking the decade-long silence among New York newspapers. Describing "the city's most sensitive open secret," it said,

> Sexual inverts have colonized three areas of the city. The city's homosexual community acts as a lodestar, attracting others from all over the country. More than a thousand inverts are arrested here annually for public misdeeds. Yet the old idea, assiduously propagated by homosexuals, that homosexuality is an inborn, incurable disease, has been exploded by modern psychiatry in the opinion of many experts. It can be both prevented and cured, these experts say.[27]

As Wicker read the article, he quickly realized that it was not the sympathetic story he had envisioned. Instead, it was an alarmist portrayal of homosexuals as a serious threat to the city. Once again it was a case of "experts" assuring a reporter that homosexuals were a problem that was only getting worse. "This matter is of constant concern to us in our efforts to preserve the peace and protect the rights of all the people," Doty quoted the police commissioner as saying. "It has been given and will continue to be given special attention." That assessment was confirmed by several clergy, a public health official, and two psychiatrists who described homosexuality as a pathological disease.

The article included the findings of a nine-year investigation of homosexuality conducted by Irving Bieber, an associate clinical professor of psychiatry at New York Medical College. Using information from more than seventy

Growth of Overt Homosexuality
In City Provokes Wide Concern

By ROBERT C. DOTY

The problem of homosex- and restaurants that cater to uality in New York became the the homosexual trade. Com- focus yesterday of increased menting yesterday on the sit- attention by the State Liquor uation. Police Commissioner Authority and the Police De- Michael J. Murphy said: partment.

The liquor authority an- one of the many problems con- nounced the revocation of the fronting law enforcement in liquor licenses of two more this city. However the under-

"Homosexuality is another

New York Times, December 17, 1963 (© New York Times, used with permission)

psychiatrists about than one hundred homosexual patients, Bieber explained that his team attributed homosexuality to some combination of a "close-binding, intimate mother and/or a hostile, detached or unrespected father" in almost every case. In a separate study, Bieber's wife, psychologist Toby Bieber, claimed to have found similar patterns among lesbians.

Bieber's research was supported by Charles Socarides, another New York psychiatrist also quoted in the article. Unlike many of their predecessors— including Freud—Socarides and Bieber maintained that homosexuality was a learned behavior that was based on fear of the opposite sex. "The homosexual is ill," Socarides warned in the *Times* article, "and anything that tends to hide that fact reduces his chances of seeking and obtaining treatment."

When the *Times* story appeared, Socarides and Bieber were well on their way to becoming the public enemy number one and number two for gay Americans. Through books, lectures, and interviews in the news media, the two psychiatrists promoted the notion that homosexuals were a social menace. Few questioned the reliability of their studies—although that was easily accomplished by showing that their views were based entirely on studying homosexuals who were either undergoing psychiatric treatment or serving prison terms, not exactly a representative population.[28]

Wicker, perhaps naively, thought that by showing Doty that homosexuals were like everyone else, except for their same-sex lovers, the *Times* would portray gays and lesbians accurately. But the story became a lesson in how the supposed objectivity of the media is often selective in what it includes and what it ignores. "I thought it was a terrible betrayal because he was a man I had given all this information to and when it came out it was disgusting," Wicker recalled. "He didn't give any mention—not one mention—that there was a division among the psychiatrists—not one word. It was all based on the 'best kept secret' in New York. But at the same time the *Times* had a tradition of intelligent reporting and for that day [era], it was intelligent reporting."[29]

The Ladder contended that the story frightened readers by giving them the false impression that homosexuals were flooding into New York and "threatening to engulf the normals." *Newsweek*, on the other hand, thought the article was terrific and signaled a new direction at the *Times*. It said, "While straining for objectivity, a *Times* trademark, Doty nevertheless tried to explode a favorite myth propagated by some homosexuals that their condition is incurable and innate."[30]

FROM FAD TO FRENZY

Despite the negative tone of the *Times* article, Randy Wicker became something of a media celebrity. News reporters and producers of radio and TV programs clamored for interviews. In what may have been the first interview of an open homosexual on American television, Wicker appeared on the *Les Crane Show,* a popular New York television talk show.[31]

But the *Times* article became a guidepost for other media. Reporters and editors at other publications, who had been uncertain how to cover the subject, found they could more easily do so now by pointing to the *Times*. The nation's magazines carried more stories about homosexuals in 1964 than in the previous three years combined. The number was even greater for 1965, and the trend continued into 1966. Much coverage reflected the information used in the *Times*, citing psychiatrists, police, and other official sources as experts on the subject.[32]

In the spring of 1964 the *New York Times* again showed its penchant for relying on official sources in a front page story headlined HOMOSEXUALS PROUD OF DEVIANCY, MEDICAL ACADEMY STUDY FINDS. The basis of the story was a newly released study by the prestigious New York Academy of Medicine that declared homosexuality "an 'illness' that can be treated successfully in 'some cases' but is more easily dealt with by early preventive measures."

The article went on to explain, "The study takes strong issue with the contention of spokesmen for homosexuals that their aberration makes them merely 'a different kind of people leading an acceptable way of life.'"[33]

Although much coverage during the early 1960s was either negative or inept, the flurry of articles stirred a surge of interest in the homophile movement among homosexuals who had never heard of the Mattachine Society or Daughters of Bilitis. Some had gotten into trouble with police or had been discharged from the military and needed help. The caseload of complaints received by the Mattachine Society about veterans benefits, employment discrimination, and arrests climbed to more than three thousand in late 1964, stretching the resources of the group to its limits.[34] If for no other reason, the organization had incentive to seek more publicity.

One of the most remarkable and most sensational of the articles was a fourteen-page spread in the June 26, 1964, issue of *Life*, the quintessential family magazine. The opening page announced, "A secret world grows open and bolder. Society is forced to look at it—and try to understand it." The headline—HOMOSEXUALITY IN AMERICA—was bolstered by a two-page photograph showing the silhouette of leather-clad men standing in a crowded San Francisco gay bar, their faces obscured in the dark smoky leatherman motif. Although the scene represented only a small segment of the gay subculture, *Life* spotlighted it as typical. The article began, "These brawny young men in their leather caps, shirts, jackets and pants are practicing homosexuals, men who turn to other men for affection and sexual satisfaction. They are part of what they call the 'gay world,' which is actually a sad and often sordid world."[35]

The day *Life* reporter Paul Welch and photographer Bill Eppridge walked into Don Slater's office at *One* in Los Angeles, the volunteer staff practically dived under their desks in fear of being exposed in a national magazine. But Slater was far from apologetic about his homosexuality; in fact, he was the antithesis of sad and sordid. Not only did he agree to allow *Life* to interview him for the article, but he agreed to allow the magazine to use his photograph. In addition, he served as a guide for the reporter and his photographer, showing them the gayest sections of Los Angeles. Slater recalled,

> Welch didn't know anything. He spent a week here, and we introduced him to the bar scene and the street scene. We took him along Selma and showed him the hustlers. His photographer must have snapped a million pictures. I felt a little guilty exposing that particular scene. He would never have found it by himself. I had introduced him to more "garden variety" homosexuals, including one gay couple in the Hollywood Hills who ran a business, but he didn't use anything about them.[36]

The article was the most in-depth look at homosexuals ever featured in an American magazine, but the descriptive phrases and lengthy quotes from police, politicians, and psychiatrists that characterized most of the coverage in this era left much to be desired. Even so, the homophile press was ecstatic. The *Mattachine Review* called the story "a presentation unlike anything ever done on the subject in modern mass media." *One* magazine called it "a milestone in journalism." Although the article completely ignored lesbians, *The Ladder* described it as "surprisingly objective and far-ranging." But the editors also noted that "homosexuals who are quiet-living, constructive people get short shrift."[37]

In October 1964 East Coast homophile organizations held a convention in Washington, D.C., to discuss discrimination against homosexuals and invited the media to a press conference afterward. Several reporters attended, including Jean White of the *Washington Post*. The next day the *Post* reported, "The fact that the four participating organizations can hold a public conference in a big-city hotel is considered a significant accomplishment in itself by the organization's leaders."[38]

Between late 1964 and 1966 media interest shifted from psychiatric studies to laws that regulated homosexual behavior. To a large extent the shift was fueled by the October 1964 arrest of Walter Jenkins, a presidential adviser, in the men's room of the Washington YMCA. When word leaked to the press that he had been arrested on morals charges, the story became front page news across the nation, although President Lyndon Johnson had tried to keep it secret. PRESIDENT'S AIDE QUITS ON REPORT OF MORALS CASE, Max Frankel reported on the front page of the *New York Times*.[39]

The summer after the Jenkins affair, the British parliament put homosexuality back into the news when its members gave serious consideration to repealing the Labouchiere Amendment, the law under which playwright Oscar Wilde was convicted in 1895 of gross indecency with another male and sentenced to two years in prison. Legalization of homosexuality in Great Britain had been introduced in 1957 but had languished until the House of Lords approved the measure in July 1965. But it bogged down again when it reached the House of Commons and was not adopted for another year.

In the meantime the American news media focused on a bill that had been introduced in the New York legislature. Like the measure that had been adopted in Illinois four years earlier, the bill was based on a model code developed by the prestigious American Law Institute, an organization composed of lawyers and legal scholars. The model code was supposed to serve as a guide for state legislatures that wanted to modernize their criminal statutes.

When Illinois adopted the model in 1961, many legislators may not have realized that they had repealed the state's sodomy law. The New York legislature, however, knew exactly what it was considering in 1965. After debate steeped in melodrama, legislators deleted the sections that reduced the penalties involving homosexuals before approving the balance of the revisions.

The debate stirred considerable attention in the media, including a *Life* editorial on June 11, 1965, that warned readers that other states might follow the lead of Illinois and legalize homosexuality. The editorial railed against any attempts to relax sodomy laws, claiming that homosexuality "can and does break up families, and the protection of the family is a legitimate area for legislation. Repeal would imply an indifference that society cannot afford." But as a writer in *One* magazine pointed out, "There are no facts to prove homosexuality a threat to the family. Statistics show mothers-in-law to be a far more frequent cause of divorce."[40] But *One*, of course, had no hope of reaching a readership the size of *Life*'s.

Life's sister publication, *Time*, took a similar swipe at gays in a two-page essay on January 21, 1966, THE HOMOSEXUAL IN AMERICA. It was one of the most vehement attacks to appear in the media since the McCarthy witch-hunts. It defined homosexuality as "a pathetic little second-rate substitute for reality, a pitiable flight from life. As such it deserves fairness, compassion, understanding and, when possible, treatment. But it deserves no encouragement, no glamorization, no rationalization, no fake status as minority martyrdom, no sophistry about simple differences in taste—and, above all, no pretense that it is anything but a pernicious sickness."[41]

The Ladder reacted by saying, "Items that are neutral or favorable to homosexuality are snidely put down or followed by counter-statements. . . . *Time* rolls religious, psychiatric, and plain bourgeois prejudice into one big mud-ball which it slings about, hoping to blacken homosexuality forever." The magazine also questioned the motivation behind the essay: "If they are not ignorant, the editors of this essay are intellectually dishonest, motivated by prejudice, and guilty of deliberate omission and distortion."[42]

The tone of the *Time* article was especially harsh because some *Time* editors knew personally a promising young gay reporter who worked in the magazine's Los Angeles bureau and who reflected none of its description of homosexuals. They had learned about reporter Andrew Kopkind after he was entrapped by police, who had arrested him on morals charges and notified the magazine in 1963. Instead of firing him, *Time* agreed to keep him on the payroll if he consented to undergo psychiatric counseling. Kopkind found a gay-friendly psychiatrist in San Francisco and negotiated an agreement that the magazine would pay for his weekly excursions to San Francisco for treatment.[43]

GAY RIGHTS TURNS MILITANT

In 1964 radical elements of the homophile movement in New York, Washington, and Philadelphia began to adopt confrontational tactics employed by the New Left, the counterculture movement of the 1960s. One of the first such actions came on September 19, 1964, when Randy Wicker and Craig Rodwell, another member of the New York Mattachine Society, led a ten-member picket line in front of the army's huge Whitehall Street Induction Center in Manhattan. Wicker contacted several reporters, but none responded, and nothing about the protest appeared in the next day's news.

In Washington, D.C., the media ignored the first picketing by gays outside the White House in April 1965. Reacting to news that Marxist dictator Fidel Castro had banished homosexuals to work camps in Cuba, Jack Nichols convinced Franklin Kameny and other members of the Mattachine Society of Washington that Castro's tactics and the antigay policies of the federal government differed little.[44] Despite the uncertain consequences, the activists notified the city's police and news media that they would mount a picket line in front of the White House. A camera crew from a Washington TV station (WTOP) filmed the event, but the footage did not make the evening news. A brief article in the *Washington Afro-American* was the only coverage.[45]

But the Mattachine Society's persistence paid off. When the group held its second White House protest the next month, stories went out over the major wire services—Associated Press, United Press International, the French news agency Agence France Presse. The wire reports generated brief articles in the *New York Times* and the *Washington Star*. In addition, a camera crew from ABC filmed the picket line and distributed pictures to local affiliates in at least nine states.

What the public saw was a neatly dressed group of nine men and three women holding hand-lettered signs protesting government discrimination. Kameny insisted that the women wear skirts and the men coats and ties, believing that if they were going to protest employment practices, they had better look employable.

The media coverage was exhilarating for the small group, which then turned its attention to the Civil Service Commission, the federal agency that set hiring policies for the federal government. The Mattachine Society learned that the commission had recently reviewed its ban against open homosexuals working for the government and had decided not to change it.

When officials refused to meet with members of the group, the group set up a picket outside the commission's downtown offices. By now the line had grown from the twelve people who picketed the White House to forty-five. Immediately after the protest officials from the commission agreed to a meeting, the first time government officials ever had to try to justify publicly their exclusion of homosexuals from federal employment.[46]

In the months that followed gays staged protests at a variety of government buildings, including the Pentagon and the State Department. Gay New Yorkers picketed the United Nations. Protesters from various East Coast groups picketed Independence Hall in Philadelphia on the Fourth of July, which became the date of an annual gay rights rally in the city until 1969. Kameny justified the public confrontations on the grounds that the antihomosexual policies of the government set the tone for private employers and reinforced prejudice throughout society. But more conservative members angrily denounced Kameny, contending that the protests were counterproductive. He responded that the demonstrations produced far more media attention than polite letters requesting coverage.

The confrontational style was affecting media coverage and beginning to change the mind-set among gays accustomed to hiding. Through their activism, gays and lesbians willing to confront prejudice publicly became symbols of the growing resistance to invisibility and silence as a way of life.

3

BECOMING FRONT-PAGE NEWS

As the news media became aware of the large clusters of homosexuals who had settled in various cities, several major papers attempted to explain the phenomenon with lengthy stories. However, the explanations rarely reached beyond superficial descriptions of homosexuals based on psychiatric observations. The coverage invariably concluded that homosexuality was a growing social problem.

One of the earliest in-depth feature articles appeared in January 1966 in the *Washington Post*. Reporter Jean White wrote a five-part series, THOSE OTHERS: A REPORT ON HOMOSEXUALITY, that examined nearly every facet of the issue. The first installment appeared on the front page, telling readers, "This series of articles would not have been written five years ago. Then, a frank and open discussion of homosexuality would have been impossible. The conspiracy of the past nurtured myths, misconceptions, false stereotypes and feelings of disgust and revulsion. They still cloud any discussion of homosexuality. But more and more, recognition has come of a need to reappraise our laws—and our attitudes."[1]

Each installment was constructed around the framework used by Robert Doty in the *New York Times* two years earlier. The *Post* reporter concentrated on comments from police, psychiatrists, health officials, and clergy. However, she included quotes from several members of the Mattachine Society of Washington, D.C., who noted that homosexuals had served with distinction in the government and the military. The series was particularly unusual because it was one of the first to try to describe everyday conflicts faced by homosexuals. *The Ladder* described the series as "the most astute as well as most extensive coverage so far in U.S. papers."[2] An abbreviated version appeared in newspapers in several other cities, including the *Post*'s sister newspaper, the *Providence Sun-Journal* in Rhode Island, and the *Sun-Times* in Chicago.

More typically, major newspapers responded to the emergence of the nation's homosexual subculture in a tone that bordered on hysteria. "MILITANT MINORITY" POSES SERIOUS PROBLEM FOR SOCIETY, the *Denver Post* reported in February 1965. The editor introduced each of the six installments with a disclaimer that read, "Homosexuality is a topic which is at all times distasteful for public discussion. But when it reaches the proportions that raise it from the individual to the community level, calling for thought and action from our citizens and public officials, the *Post* believes the topic must be openly considered."[3] Part two was titled TROUBLE AT THE YMCA.

A few days later the *Post* underscored the alarm sounded in its series with an editorial urging city officials to "make certain that the Denver homosexual community is contained and restricted, that Denver does not become known as a haven for homosexuals. This will probably necessitate putting more men on the police force, but we are certain that, in this case, this is an expense the citizens of the community would gladly bear."[4]

Despite the negative tone, the coverage was an affirming recognition for homosexuals who had never seen public acknowledgment of their existence outside the crime pages. "You are to be commended for undertaking this project on which there is so much need for public enlightenment," a member of the New York Mattachine Society wrote the editor of the *Denver Post*. "The series does show a genuine endeavor on your part to be objective and fair."[5]

'Militant Minority' Poses Serious Problem for Society

Denver Post, February 14, 1965 (© Denver Post, used with permission)

In January 1966 the *Atlanta Constitution* carried a seven-part series by reporter Dick Hebert headlined ATLANTA'S LONELY 'GAY' WORLD. "The homosexual is an unhappy person," one section began. "His emotions stopped growing up at an early age. No matter what he says, he wants to change his ways. He just isn't convinced it can be done." Hebert based the description on his interview with an Atlanta psychiatrist who had worked extensively with homosexuals for more than a decade. The second installment of the series explained how DETECTIVES WATCH HANGOUTS AND CURB SOME OF ACTIVITY. An Atlanta police officer explained, "We know where they hang out, the places we get a lot of complaints on. As soon as we get touched by one we book him for assault and battery and disorderly conduct." "We keep a file on them," another officer added. "We have a pretty extensive file."[6] Three months earlier Atlanta police had arrested ninety-seven men in a raid on Halloween night—a traditionally festive occasion among drag queens.

In New York members of the Mattachine Society began to build contacts with various press outlets after police launched a crackdown on "undesirables" before the opening of the 1964 World's Fair. The organization had been unable to convince the press that the surge in arrests of gay men was politically motivated until late 1965 when Randy Wicker and Leitsch, New York Mattachine president, persuaded *New York Post* reporter Joseph Kahn to come to the society's office to listen to telephone calls from men who had been lured into police traps. Kahn listened for three nights as calls flooded into the office and for the first time began to grasp the magnitude of the harassment.

On December 30, 1965, the *Post* printed Kahn's examination of abusive police practices in a series entitled OUR PENAL CODE. Two installments were based on Kahn's visit to the Mattachine Society's office. "It is well known that the vice cop will make fast arrests when he is falling behind his quota," Kahn wrote.[7]

Soon after John Lindsay became mayor in 1966, the city launched Operation New Broom, which set off another wave of entrapments and bar closings in Times Square and Greenwich Village. In an attempt to draw media attention to the increase in entrapments, Clarence Tripp, a psychologist who served as an adviser to the Mattachine Society, took one of his patients to meet James A. Wechsler, the *New York Post*'s editorial page editor. The visit resulted in an editorial headlined ENTRAPMENT INC. in which Wechsler described the antigay crusade as grotesque and called on the chief police inspector to abandon the quota system. "At a moment when the city cries out for protection against crimes of violence, a squad of grown robust police officers dedicates itself to the pursuit and entrapment of men suspected of preferring men to women," wrote Wechsler in an extremely rare display of support. "Technically the police are enforcing archaic pre-Kinsey statutes that the legislature has refused to modify."[8]

The entrapment complaints did not become front page news in the *New York Times* until the American Civil Liberties Union (ACLU) joined the growing chorus of critics a month later. And even then the city's chief police inspector continued to deny allegations that his force was using questionable tactics. Instead, he tried to shift the emphasis of the coverage by calling on the public to report evidence of unethical police conduct to him. "It's alarming to think that the chief inspector doesn't know that a large number of police spend their duty hours dressed in tight pants, sneakers and polo sweaters . . . to bring about solicitations," an ACLU official told the *Times* in response.[9]

Three days later the *Post* responded to the police in a second editorial. "The Chief Inspector's expressed attitude is welcome," it said. "But it is clearly his responsibility, not the public's, to get the word to the plain-clothesmen and to review the 'quota' system under which the cops feel obliged to make arrests."[10]

The Mattachine Society successfully persuaded the media to stoke the fires of the entrapment controversy when several members decided to challenge the city's blatantly discriminatory liquor policies in a similar fashion. Although it was not against the law to serve homosexual customers, the state liquor authority consistently denied liquor licenses to gay and lesbian bars. Inspectors routinely revoked the licenses of bars that knowingly allowed gays to congregate, citing city statutes against "indecent behavior."[11]

As a result, frightened bar owners either refused to serve gays and lesbians or asked them to leave.[12] The few gay bars that managed to stay open were shabby holes in the wall, most owned or operated by the Mafia, which bribed police officers for protection. Certain precincts were widely known to accept Mafia payoffs.

In the spring of 1966 four members of the Mattachine Society contacted reporters at the *Times*, the *Village Voice*, and the *New York Post* and said that they planned to stage a "sip-in" at a Village bar in order to provoke a crackdown that they could then challenge in court. The delegation included Mattachine president Dick Leitsch and members Craig Rodwell and John Timmons. Four reporters and a photographer from the *Voice* agreed to meet the activists outside the Ukrainian American Bar in Greenwich Village, one of several with signs over their doors that read IF YOU ARE GAY, PLEASE STAY AWAY.

As Leitsch recalled,

> The reporters got there ahead of us, and when they asked the manager about the demonstration he closed the place before we got there. There we were in the middle of the street, wondering what we were going to do, when the reporter for the *Times* asked if we knew of another place. Howard Johnson's on Sixth Avenue also had a sign so we went over there. But the owner realized what we were doing and agreed to serve us. By that point, we were ready to go home when one of the reporters said, "No, come on, rack your brains, think of a place." So we went to Julius's. We didn't want to cause any trouble for Julius, but the reporters felt like they had been on a wild goose chase and wanted a story out of this thing. The bartender refused to serve us and we claimed the bar had violated our free speech.[13]

While the Mattachine Society prepared its complaint, reporters besieged the state liquor authority with calls asking about its policy against gays. Stories appeared in the *Times* and the *Post* in which the head of the liquor authority denied that bar owners or bartenders had ever been told not to serve homosexuals. The May 5 edition of the *Voice* carried an article headlined THREE HOMOSEXUALS IN SEARCH OF A DRINK and included a photograph of the gay foursome standing at the bar in Julius's. Reporter Lucy Komisar wrote, "It was a Greek scene in more ways than one. Three heroes in search of justice trudged from place to place. On the other hand, it was a highly contemporary maneuver. It was a challenge to one of the remaining citadels of bias, and a citadel of bias backed up by law, at that."[14]

After the news articles appeared, the chairman of New York City's Human Rights Commission threatened to cite the liquor authority for discrimination. For a brief period bar raids subsided. But the human rights commission soon realized it had no authority to deal with antigay discrimination, and bar raids returned to their previous levels.[15]

In Chicago the newly formed Mattachine Midwest made its first attempt to attract publicity in November 1965 by holding a four-day conference, The Homophile Movement in America. The notices the society sent the media brought an invitation from *Kup's Show*, a talk show on WBKB hosted by Irv Kupcinet, the popular *Sun-Times* columnist. *Daily News* city editor Bob Rose found the gays' bowling league more fascinating than the conference and included a brief reference in his daily column. He described the Mattachine organization as "the boys-will-be-girls group." In response, Paul Goldman, a Chicago attorney who worked with Mattachine Midwest, wrote a letter to the editor that appeared a few days later. In his letter Goldman asked, "How can responsible journalism justify and present that type of characterization. . . . The meeting centered about Dr. Franklin Kameny's presentation. The theme of his address was just contrary to (Bob Rose's) reference."[16] The biggest break in the Chicago media came in the summer of 1966 when Lois Wille, a *Chicago Daily News* reporter, contacted Mattachine Midwest about a series she was writing. Wille recalled that

> I wanted to see what a gay bar was like. I had heard about them, and the Mattachine Society gave me a list of locations. When I told my city editor what I was going to do, he suggested that I take along an escort and asked the crime reporter to go with me. On the night we were to go, he arrived to pick me up wearing an old dirty, ragged T-shirt and a dingy old pair of pants—he looked really awful. I realized that he was trying to avoid having anyone make a pass at him, but when we got to the first bar, they wouldn't let him in because he wasn't wearing a coat and tie—the bar was quite tasteful. The same thing happened at the second bar. This reporter spent his entire evening waiting for me outside these bars while I went in to see what they were like.[17]

Wille's four-part series, CHICAGO'S TWILIGHT WORLD, began on June 20, 1966, and presented newspaper readers in Chicago with their first in-depth coverage of the subject. The first installment, THE HOMOSEXUALS—A GROWING PROBLEM, was accompanied on the second front page (page three) by a stereotypical photograph of the backs of three transvestites, in floor-length evening gowns and with carefully sculpted wigs piled high on their heads, en route to the city's annual Artists & Models Ball. "Big cities act as lodestars," the article explained, "drawing homosexuals who can't hide their deviancy in small towns."

Wille pointed out that although Illinois had repealed its sodomy laws five years earlier, police had failed to recognize the change. She quoted police officers who had made mass arrests of homosexuals who called themselves "hair fairies." Another explained, "Our detectives pretend they're queer, or a straight (nonhomosexual) out for a one-night fling. They go into one of the fag bars and order a drink. . . . There are a lot of notes passed back and forth. Some just say 'fruit,' or 'freak.' They seem to get a kick out of that." After a little conversation, he went on to explain, his detectives often arrested the bar manager and the patron for prostitution. "When they sit in bars and kiss and pet and fondle, this is an act of public indecency," he said.

Throughout the sixties and into the early seventies, newspapers in Chicago and other cities routinely printed the names, addresses, and occupations of men and women who were arrested in bar raids. In one 1964 case reported in Wille's series, after Chicago newspapers ran the names of 103 men who were arrested for disorderly conduct at a popular night spot near O'Hare Airport, 30 of them lost their jobs—even though the charges were later dismissed.[18]

Although newspapers readily publicized bar raids and arrests, they were reticent about mentioning homosexuals in any other context. Chicago newspapers routinely rejected any press materials Mattachine Midwest sent them, including advertisements. In September 1966 a small group of gays responded by picketing both the *Chicago Tribune* and the *Sun-Times*. "We've had demonstrations and protests for almost every conceivable cause, but here's an eye opener: Mattachine Midwest, an organization to aid homosexuals, will demonstrate on Wacker Drive Saturday," Kupcinet noted in his *Sun-Times* gossip column. He introduced his next item: "And quickly changing the topic—." But he neglected to tell his readers that the protest was directed at his newspaper. The *Tribune* printed nothing.[19]

Although the visibility of gays had reached historic levels in much of the nation's news media, almost none of it reflected the everyday life of homosexuals. The media focused on the extreme stereotypes, ignoring anyone who contradicted them. From reading the newspapers, the average American would have no way of knowing that lesbians existed. "The word 'homosexual' is being thrown around as never before in the mass media," *The Ladder* complained, "and almost always it refers to the male of the species. The male has become socially 'visible,' but the lesbian is the invisible woman."[20]

GAYS IN PRINT LEADS TO GAYS ON TV

By the early sixties, television was rapidly replacing newspapers as the public's preferred source of information. Manufacturers could barely stay ahead of the demand for TV sets as sales doubled to eleven million between 1960 and 1968.

For lesbians and gay men television offered opportunities that were unavailable in the print media. They could speak for themselves without having their words subjected to the filters of reporters and editors who determined how they would be portrayed. In city after city homosexuality became a topic of discussion on some of the most popular radio and television shows, including *The Jerry Williams Show* in Chicago and *The Steve Frederick Show* in Boston, *The Lewis Lomax Show* and Fred Anderson's *Kaleidoscope* in Los Angeles, *The Arnold Zenker Show* in Baltimore, *Off the Cuff* and Ronnie Barrett's *Chicago* in the Windy City, and several segments on David Susskind's television show beginning in the mid-1960s and extending well into the seventies. WBAI, the listener-supported New York radio station that broadcast the 1962 program featuring Randy Wicker, had a weekly program on the subject beginning in 1968.[21]

Although the size of the nation's homosexual population ranged from two million estimated by psychiatrists to fifteen million cited by gay activists, only about a dozen were brave enough to acknowledge themselves in the public spotlight.[22] DOB cofounders Del Martin and Phyllis Lyon responded to an increasing number of requests on the West Coast, including one from the producer of a TV show in Los Angeles. Lyon recalled that one clearly:

> I spent hours on the phone with this person talking about lesbians, and I sent him piles of materials—such as there was in those days. Then, when I got on the program, the first question this guy asked me was, "All right, how are you different physiologically from other women?" I couldn't believe it. My mouth dropped to the floor. I looked at him and I really don't really remember what I said. But I do recall thinking, "I don't believe this is happening to me."[23]

The few who dared to appear on radio and television recognized these appearances as rare opportunities to counter the popular stereotypes of homosexuals. They were prepared to deliver a message no matter how the interviewer responded to them because they wanted to be seen by closeted homosexuals who needed some sign of hope. Returning to her office after her TV appearance in Los Angeles, Phyllis Lyon was greeted by a barrage of telephone calls. Some simply wanted to know more about Daughters of Bilitis. Others were from heterosexual women upset with their husbands or wanting to know how they could change their lives for the better. Lyon listened to these women patiently and then assured them, "That's not on our agenda."[24]

Some appearances took a heavy personal toll. After a radio appearance in New York, DOB chapter president Ruth Simpson was told by a woman friend, "Ruth, I'm going to have to ask you not to speak to me."[25] Likewise, Franklin Kameny and Jack Nichols were stunned during an appearance on a television program in Baltimore when host Dennis Richards turned on them, pounding his fist on a desk, waving his arms in the air, and shouting insults. "Get off of my stage!" he screamed at the two gay men. "Get out of my studio, you vicious perverts! You lecherous people! You make me want to vomit!"[26] Kameny and Nichols sat in a dazed silence. The audience was equally flabbergasted. One viewer called to ask whether the host was homosexual. "No, I'm not; they are!" responded Richards, pointing to Kameny and Nichols.[27] As a precaution the men began asking Lilli Vincenz, one of the women members of the Mattachine Society, to join them. Her femininity, warmth, and intelligence ran counter to the prevailing mannish image of lesbians and put show hosts on their best behavior.

By the mid-1960s Kameny and Nichols were firmly established as the leaders of a radical wing of the homophile movement. They had introduced picketing as an acceptable form of protest for homosexuals, and they had dared to take on the powerful psychiatric profession. In 1963 Nichols had approached the board of directors of the Mattachine Society of Washington, urging it to adopt an official statement denouncing the standard psychiatric view that homosexuality was a mental illness.[28] He and Kameny were among the first to point out that the widely accepted clinical studies on homosexuality were flawed because they were based on unrepresentative data drawn from psychiatric patients and inmates who had been incarcerated for sex crimes.

The psychiatrists were passing the information off as scientific, but it failed to stand up under scrutiny. "I see nothing wrong with homosexuality, nothing to be ashamed of," Kameny routinely told interviewers. When he appeared on *Off the Cuff* on WBKB in Chicago on April 4, 1964, he informed the audience, "It is not a disease, a pathology, a sickness, a malfunction, or disorder of any kind." Kameny described the psychiatric theories as "theological positions" that had been thinly veiled as science. "Underlying all of these theories is the subtle suggestion that it is undesirable," he would tell journalists and talk show hosts. "Homosexuals are entitled to their rights—promptly!" he would shout during interviews at ear-splitting decibels.[29]

But to Kameny's dismay some homosexuals had accepted the psychiatrists' explanations by internalizing the homophobia that surrounded them. To them Kameny's tirades against psychiatry were nothing short of heresy. The two camps fought numerous heated battles over the subject for nearly a decade.

By 1966 the novelty of media exposure was wearing thin. Homosexuals had a growing awareness that more media coverage was not necessarily better coverage. The media barrier that had kept them invisible had been breached, but the preoccupation with the causes of homosexuality continued unabated. "Society has finally focused its attention on the lavender world, but always with the same predictable results," said a 1966 article in *Vector*, the magazine of the Society for Individual Rights, a San Francisco–based organization that had broken away from the conservatism of the other homophile organizations and had surpassed both the Mattachine Society and Daughters of Bilitis in membership. The article went on to suggest that perhaps the time had come "for the bewildered homosexual to arise from the church altar or the analyst's couch and shape the environment and his destiny by his own will and actions."[30]

TROUBLE AT THE *TIMES*

The public paranoia that homosexuals represented an invisible enemy had not been forgotten as the nation moved from the postwar 1950s into the cold war 1960s. Increasingly, concerns arose that a "homosexual mafia" was mounting a surreptitious propaganda campaign to promote homosexuality through the arts and the media.

Time addressed these concerns in its 1966 essay, THE HOMOSEXUAL IN AMERICA, claiming that in the theater, dance, and music worlds "deviates are so widespread that they sometimes seem to be running a kind of closed shop." It said the influence of homosexuals on Broadway was so great that it would be difficult to find a production in which homosexuals did not play important parts. Homosexuals working in the entertainment industry were so numerous, "you have to scrape them off the ceiling," said Broadway producer David Merrick.[31]

According to *Time*, *Life*, and several other publications, gay writers were undermining the nation's social values by mocking American women, marriage, and society. The clamor had risen to such levels among the New York theater elite by the middle sixties that theater critic Stanley Kauffmann addressed it in the *New York Times*. Postwar drama had presented "a badly distorted picture of American women, marriage and society in general," he wrote in his January 23, 1966, article headlined HOMOSEXUAL DRAMA AND ITS DISGUISES. Rather than single out homosexuals, however, he laid much of the blame on heterosexuals who had created an atmosphere that kept gay dramatists closeted:

> I do not argue for increased homosexual influence in our theater. It is precisely because I, like many others, am weary of disguised homosexual influence that I raise the matter. We have all had much more than enough of the materials so often presented by the three writers in question: the viciousness toward women, the lurid violence that seems a sublimation of social hatreds, the transvestite sexual exhibitionism that has the same sneering exploitation of its audience that every club stripper has behind her smile.[32]

Although Kauffmann did not single out any playwrights specifically, he mentioned that "three of the most successful American playwrights of the last twenty years are (reputed) to be homosexual." At the time of the article's publication Edward Albee was opening a Broadway show based on the James Purdy novel *Malcolm*, leaving little question about Kauffmann's target. Albee's *Who's Afraid of Virginia Woolf?* had premiered four years earlier, followed by *Tiny Alice* in 1965. Albee, who would come out publicly in the 1970s, was quickly becoming a "boy wonder" among the theater crowd as his characters gave eloquent expression to social topics other writers did not dare to address.

Although the message may have been too obscure for many readers, Kauffmann's article generated an overwhelming response.[33] Some letter writers ignored the points raised by Kauffmann and launched into tirades against homosexuals. One suggested that society prohibit homosexuals from writing about heterosexuals. "How long will we have to suffer from sick literature and theater?" he asked. On the other hand, several writers suggested that audiences judge a play on its merits alone.

Kauffmann used the letters as the basis for another article. Like the first, the second was prominently displayed on the front page of the Culture section. The large headline read ON THE ACCEPTABILITY OF THE HOMOSEXUAL. In it Kauffmann repeated his thesis: "The homosexual dramatist ought to have the same freedom that the heterosexual has. While we deny him that freedom, we have no grounds for complaint when he uses disguises in order to write.

Further, to deny him that freedom is to encourage a somewhat precious esthetics that, out of understandable vindictiveness, is hostile to the mainstream of culture."[34]

Even before the *Times* reached newsstands, trouble was brewing behind the scenes. Iphigene Sulzberger picked up her copy and nearly had a fit when she saw the headline. Although she had no direct authority over the day-to-day operations of the newsroom, she was the daughter and only child of the newspaper's founder, the wife of its second publisher, the chairwoman of the *Times*'s board of directors, and the mother of the man who became publisher in 1963, Arthur Ochs ("Punch") Sulzberger. Staff members described her as a hidden force who "put her stamp on the paper in endless subtle and not so subtle ways."[35]

She hurriedly fired off a sharply worded protest to her son the publisher:

Feb. 5, 1966

Dearest Punch:

I thought that you agreed with me that while Homosexuality, like prostitution and social diseases, was now legitimate news, it should not be played on the front page of a section. Mr. Kauffmann's second article on the homosexuals in section 2 of tomorrow's paper came as a shock. I am sure many parents and grandparents must object to their children, who turn to this section for television and movie news, being confronted with all this talk about perversions. Why not put the article on an inside page with a headline not saying "acceptability of the homosexuals?" Haven't we enough troubles with the young without giving them this encouragement? Your old mother who still likes virtue and normality but has compassion for others.

Love from Mother.[36]

The letter landed on Sulzberger's desk with the force of a grenade. He immediately summoned his executive editor, Turner Catledge, and informed him that his cadre of editors and copy editors had made a bad decision. Although he was probably unaware of the Kauffmann article until he read it in the paper, Catledge shouldered overall responsibility for everything that appeared in the *Times*.

It was not uncommon for publishers to nudge the staff from time to time when they took exception to something they saw in their newspaper, particularly in the partisan days of the penny press before the turn of the century. But even after much of the press erected Chinese walls in the 1930s and 1940s to carefully separate editorial decision making from business interests, some publishers were legendary for breaching them. Walter Annenberg, owner of the *Philadelphia Inquirer*, routinely prohibited his editors from mentioning the names of people he disliked, including people who usually would be considered newsworthy. The du Pont family altered news coverage in its Delaware newspapers according to how it affected family interests. The censorship was so blatant, according to newspaper veteran Ben Bagdikian, that one distinguished editor resigned rather than comply.[37]

At the *New York Times*, however, meddling was known to be infrequent and far less blatant than at other newspapers. In his 1971 memoir Catledge wrote that while Arthur Hays Sulzberger was publisher between 1935 and 1961, Catledge would receive blue notes—so called because of the color of the paper on which they were written. If a blue note contained praise for a reporter's work, Catledge sent it on to the reporter. "If it was critical, and I thought the criticism valid, I would pass it on to the reporter as my own comment, for insofar as possible I wanted our reporters and editors to do their work without feeling that the publisher was constantly looking over their shoulders," Catledge wrote.[38]

The reality of the news business is that comments and criticisms from publishers become unwritten policy that affects how people and events are portrayed—or not portrayed—in the news. The ways in which publishers set policies and their editors implement those policies carry powerful implications for what readers do and do not see. Journalists like John Brannon Albright, who remembers the flap over the Kauffmann articles, learned to recognize such signals and avoid trouble by censoring themselves: "How does the staff know what's going on? That's like asking how people at *Time* know that they were supposed to take a conservative approach. You just know who you were working for."[39]

Iphigene Sulzberger's letter may have been nothing more than a well-intentioned expression of concern, but it carried the weight of a directive. Kauffmann was fired after just eight months on the job because Arthur Hays Sulzberger had grown increasingly uncomfortable with complaints from Broadway producers who objected to Kauffmann's habit of reviewing preview performances of new Broadway plays and musicals—which later became standard practice.

Although he had passed control of the newspaper to Arthur Ochs Sulzberger, the elder Sulzberger continued to take a personal interest in the operation of the paper and its contents. "If the *Times* looked silly," Catledge explained, "he felt that he looked silly." Kauffmann was offered a reassignment, but he declined. All he has ever said about the incident publicly was that the *Times* "dealt with me irresponsibly."[40]

HOMOSEXUAL VISIBILITY REACHES NETWORK TELEVISION

The masses got their first look at homosexuality on national television when CBS broadcast the first network documentary on the subject on March 7, 1967. Titled "The Homosexuals," the program was produced by *CBS Reports*, an award-winning series that grew out of the 1959 quiz show scandal. When it became known that television producers had rigged quiz shows, Frank Stanton, president of CBS, had announced a series of bold documentaries to restore the prestige of the network and the entire television industry. For its executive producer he chose Fred Friendly, the television veteran who had worked with TV legend Edward R. Murrow during the 1950s and was perhaps the industry's most talented documentary producer.

Friendly's mandate was to delve into social issues that were too controversial for most programs, including abortion, drug abuse, and integration. By the mid-sixties the program had covered many burning social issues of that era. One day Friendly turned to a producer and asked for a program on homosexuals. "I thought they ought to have a chance to talk about their life and about what it was like to live in a world where they were laughed at," Friendly recalled. "It was an 'upstream' idea because the American people didn't want a program about that in the mid-sixties. It was a difficult program to do and it was difficult getting it on the air. We weren't certain how to do it."[41]

To produce the hourlong program Friendly chose William Peters, who had joined *CBS Reports* in 1962 after ten years as a freelance writer, magazine editor, and author. Having written on a wide variety of subjects, including medicine, psychology, politics, and crime, Peters had developed a specialty in race relations. His book *The Southern Temper* (1959) was a highly praised report on the racial crisis in the South. When CBS recognized that civil rights was looming as one of the most important continuing stories of the sixties, it hired Peters to track it.

After Friendly assigned the project, Peters began reading books about homosexuals, contacting experts in various fields, and identifying locations for filming elements of the program. He reported to Friendly that although the idea was feasible, a single hour was insufficient to cover both gays and lesbians. He recommended lesbians be left for a separate show. After Friendly agreed, Peters flew to San Francisco to begin filming at the home of Don Lucas, the secretary of the Mattachine Society there.

To show the diversity among homosexuals Peters had arranged to interview a variety of men, including a sailor, a truck driver, a bartender, a rodeo rider, and a female impersonator. During a four-hour session he asked each one to describe his first realization that he was homosexual and proceeded to ask a number of questions about their lives. "Because the program would expose most of our audience to its first factual knowledge of the subject," Peters recalled, "I felt we had a responsibility to touch on all aspects of it with compete candor."[42] From San Francisco Peters and his CBS camera crew shifted to Los Angeles, Philadelphia, Charlotte, and New York City for additional filming. When they returned to their offices, they had amassed thirty hours of raw film that would have to be edited down to one hour.

After Peters assembled a rough cut of the program, he asked CBS correspondent Mike Wallace if he would serve as the on-camera reporter. Peters recalled that Wallace's "immediate reaction was negative. He told me he wanted no part of a 'pity the poor homosexual' show. I told him I wouldn't either and that my documentary was an honest straightforward examination of male homosexuality, and he agreed to take a look. When the lights went on, Mike had tears in his eyes. 'My God,' he said, 'I never realized what kind of a life they lead. Hell, yes, I'll do it.'"[43]

In the meantime Friendly had been promoted to president of CBS News, become embroiled in a flap over the network's coverage of the Vietnam War, and had quit, all in rapid succession. Richard Salant, a special assistant to Stanton, was named to replace Friendly. The choice of the cost-conscious lawyer sent ripples of concern throughout the news division, especially at *CBS Reports*, where Friendly's absence spelled an uncertain future.

Even more uncertain was the outlook for the documentary on homosexuals. In the middle of the turmoil William Peters left CBS to help produce a four-hour television documentary about Africa for ABC. When he returned to New York, he learned that Salant had killed the gay documentary. Mike

Wallace told Peters that Salant considered the documentary "*Daily News* journalism"—a way of saying the film smacked of sensationalism. "I don't know what's going to happen," Peters quoted Wallace as saying. "I don't think he's going to put it on the air." At that point the documentary would have been forgotten had not articles about it begun to appear in the television trade press. As a result killing it outright would have been more embarrassing than going forward.[44]

In mid-1965 Salant asked Harry Morgan, a *CBS Reports* producer, to finish the documentary. Instead of returning to San Francisco, Morgan and his staff contacted the Mattachine Society of New York, which put them in touch with Clarence Tripp, the psychologist who was a Mattachine adviser. Tripp led them to one of his patients, handsome young Lars Larson. Everything about the clean-cut blond defied the gay stereotype:

> I was not a militant, and I wasn't out to convert the world to homosexuality, but I knew this was the first opportunity offered to homosexuals to speak directly to the people of America. I was there to speak to other men and women who happened to be gay and say there's nothing wrong with it. Mike Wallace had his own agenda and it was not necessarily kind to gays. On the other hand, he had integrity and honesty so he came straight to the point. At the end of it he said he had never met a homosexual that was as well adjusted.[45]

At the Mattachine Society of Washington, D.C., Morgan found Jack Nichols, the handsome, athletic-looking twenty-eight-year-old cofounder of the organization. Nichols was direct and confrontational. He had a sharp edge to his voice and an intensity in his eyes that contrasted with the calm relaxed manner of Larson. He agreed to be interviewed, provided he would be identified as Warren Adkins, a pseudonym he used to distinguish himself from his father, a twenty-five-year FBI veteran of the same name.

Nichols carefully rehearsed his responses with Franklin Kameny, Washington Mattachine president, to avoid "unscientific leaps into briar patches." Wallace arrived a few days later to conduct the grueling ninety-minute interview from which he would select only a few seconds for the documentary. Nichols recalled that

> after we finished and the camera was turned off, Mike Wallace sat down with me and talked for about half an hour. He said, "You know, you answered all of my questions capably, but I have a feeling that you don't really believe that homosex-

uality is as acceptable as you make it sound." I asked him why he would say that. "Because," he said, "in your heart I think you know it's wrong." It was infuriating. I told him I thought that being gay was just fine, but that in his heart *he* thought it was wrong.[46]

At ten o'clock on Tuesday night, March 7, 1967, viewers across the nation watched as the first open homosexuals appeared on network television. One sign of the controversial nature of the program was that commercial breaks were filled with public service spots—the network's sales force had been unable to find sponsors.

Lars Larson appeared first, explaining what it was like for him to step out of the closet. "What you're asking is, why am I a homosexual?" the program began. "And the question is not that simple. There're a great number of reasons, and what they are, I couldn't even begin to tell you."

A second man was shown lying on an analyst's couch, his face unrecognizable, as he explained to his psychiatrist the anguish felt by his family when he told them he was gay. "They were sorry for me as though I had some . . . were some wounded animal that they were going to send to the vet so they got me a psychiatrist real quick." Next, Mike Wallace was heard asking Jack Nichols, "What do you think caused your sexual orientation?" "I have thought about it, but it really doesn't concern me much," Nichols responded, explaining that he had no more guilt about his homosexuality than about his blond hair or light skin.

Much of the program featured psychiatrists Charles Socarides and Irving Bieber. Filmed as he lectured to a group of medical students at the Albert Einstein School of Medicine, where he taught, Socarides was especially dramatic and convincing. The segment was set up to look as though he was responding to spontaneous questions. "I was wondering if you think that there are any 'happy homosexuals' for whom homosexuality would be in a way their best adjustment to life?" a woman student inquired. "The fact that somebody's homosexual—a true obligatory homosexual—automatically rules out the possibility that he will remain happy for long, in my opinion," Socarides said, characterizing happiness among homosexuals as "a mythology."

In the next sequence Bieber told Wallace, "I do not believe it is possible to produce a homosexual if the father is a warm, good, supportive, constructive father to his son." The comments from Bieber and Socarides were underscored by a fourth homosexual, a closeted gay man whose face was obscured by a potted plant that left haunting shadows across his face. "I know that inside now I'm sick," he told Wallace. "I'm not sick just sexually. I'm sick in a lot of ways . . . immature, childlike, and the sex is a symptom . . . like a tooth ache is a symptom of who knows what."[47]

Long after Larson and Nichols were forgotten, the man behind the plant would be remembered. In his 1981 book *The Celluloid Closet* Vito Russo wrote that "all the homosexuals interviewed by Mike Wallace on 'CBS Presents: The Homosexuals' [sic] in 1967 were seated behind potted palm trees, the leaves obscuring their faces." Russo was not alone. In a 1981 edition of *TV Guide* Richard M. Levine wrote about a CBS documentary that brought homosexuals out of the closet and "into the leafy shadows behind potted palm trees where interviewees were questioned, to protect their identities, as though they were mob informers in Miami." And in his Media Watch column in the *New York Native*, David Rothenberg said in 1981 that "no one over 30 will forget Mike Wallace's interview of a shame-filled homosexual hiding in the shadows of a potted plant."[48]

Even more memorable was Wallace offering one of the most damning descriptions of homosexuality ever heard on television:

> The average homosexual, if there be such, is promiscuous. He is not interested in nor capable of a lasting relationship like that of a heterosexual marriage. His sex life—his 'love life'—consists of chance encounters at the clubs and bars he inhab- its, and even on the streets of the city. The pickup—the one-night stand—these are characteristic of the homosexual relationship. And the homosexual prostitute has become a fixture on the downtown streets at night.[49]

"Well, I said it," Wallace responded when asked about the segment years later. "That is—God help us—what our understanding was of the homosex- ual lifestyle a mere twenty-five years ago because nobody was out of the closet and because that's what we heard from doctors—that's what Socarides told us, it was a matter of shame."[50]

Audience estimates showed the program had been seen by about forty million viewers. The *Washington Star* called it enlightening and frequently moving. The *New York Times* described it as an "intelligent discussion of a grow- ing social problem that only recently has reached the public forum." In the meantime the original version by William Peters sat locked securely inside the CBS network archives, never seen by the public. Clay Gowran, a TV writer for the *Chicago Tribune*, wrote, "Last night, the Columbia Broadcasting system finally presented an hour-long documentary on homosexuality in America which it has been talking about telecasting for almost a year. CBS would have done better to have scrapped the program and written off its cost." Under the headline of TV NO SPOT TO UNLOAD GARBAGE, Gowran went on to point out that he thought "CBS performed not a service for its viewers but a definite disservice to them—particularly to the younger, most impressionable, most easily influenced members of the audience." In contrast, Dean Gysel, a TV writer at the *Chicago Daily News*, wrote, "It took CBS two years to get 'The Homosexuals' on television, but the program did get on the air Tuesday night and that is an achievement in itself. . . . CBS deserves a hand for ventilating the subject."[51]

Jack Nichols had been a sales manager for a Washington hotel when the program aired. When he arrived at work the next day, he was fired. Lars Larson was no happier than Nichols's boss with the documentary. He fired off a letter to CBS withdrawing his consent for the interview and demanding that the network not re-air it.

"They had some rather nasty, angry antigay people on there who were treated as professionals. I had no problem with Harry Morgan or Mike Wallace because they were thorough," Larson recalled. "But obviously others in the decision-making process were truly upset with homosexuality. They saw it as a threat to the human race and were out to kill as best they could."[52]

"I should have known better," Mike Wallace commented in 1992. "Two of my best friends at that time were homosexual, and they had been living together forever. But I found them—at that moment—to be the exception that proves the rule. I simply did not know about long-lasting homosexual relationships; I was in the dark along with the vast majority of Americans."[53]

Wallace's ethic was neither unusual nor inappropriate but expected under the journalists' code of objectivity. As a matter of course, reporters put aside their personal observations when they conflict with an expert's. In hard news stories journalists' thoughts are considered biased, whereas the sources' information is fact—which is how "facts" in the news can overshadow the truth.[54]

DEFINING HOMOSEXUALITY IN THE NEWS

In June 1968 Charles Socarides published his book *The Overt Homosexual* and became one of the most widely quoted authorities on the subject. That same month the American Medical Association invited him to speak to its annual meeting in San Francisco, where he described homosexuality as "a dread dysfunction, malignant in character, which has risen to epidemic proportions."[55] Claiming that homosexuals in America outnumbered sufferers of any other form of mental illness, heart disease, or arthritis, Socarides proposed the creation of a government-sponsored sexual rehabilitation center.

Reporter David Perlman's story on the speech appeared the next day on page one of the *San Francisco Chronicle*. The long-time science writer for the *Chronicle* knew almost nothing about the psychological or medical aspect of the subject, so he was impressed that Socarides had described homosexuals as sick but curable, as opposed to bad people who were hopeless. As far as Perlman knew, Socarides was a reasonable and compassionate authority on the subject:

> It sounded to me like a guy who was being very humane—that's how naive I was.
> I didn't conduct a survey, but I suspect people like me in newspaper work at that
> time must have thought that saying anything other than 'homosexuality is an evil
> choice'—any other explanation of homosexuality or any other discussion of it—
> was better than saying these are bad people. I remember a lot of people who knew
> much more than I about homosexuality said I was listening to a guy who was full
> of bull shit.[56]

Gay and lesbian activists were already concerned about the convention, handing out two thousand leaflets to participants as they arrived. After reading Perlman's article, the Daughters of Bilitis and the Society for Individual Rights called a press conference to denounce Socarides and his proposed center for rehabilitation.

To the gays the centers sounded like modern concentration camps.

They were joined at the press conference by members of San Francisco's Council on Religion and the Homosexual, the coalition of Protestant ministers that had sponsored the ill-fated New Year's Eve dance for gays in 1965. The next day news of their rebuke to Socarides was featured prominently in the *Chronicle* and the *Examiner*. The *Chronicle* began its front page story by saying, "Spokesmen for the Nation's homosexuals—variously estimated at from four to six million—took a verbal swipe here yesterday at one of their leading medical critics. Dr. Charles W. Socarides, they contend, didn't know what he was talking about when he told an American Medical Association meeting this week that homosexuals as a group are 'mentally ill' with a disease that entails 'massive suffering.'"[57]

San Francisco was one of the few places in the nation where gays and lesbians could effectively confront the media because their population had
become so big that they felt relatively safe in speaking up. Elsewhere, however, the psychiatric framework that portrayed homosexuals as sad, sick, and
pitiful had become well entrenched in the news media, as well as in books,
plays, and films.

That portrayal had its desired effect. A 1966 public opinion poll showed
that nearly three out of four Americans viewed homosexuality as an illness.
Three years later another poll found that more than half the population considered homosexuals "harmful to American life."[58] By 1968 homosexual
stereotypes had become fashionable in the entertainment industry. Bitchy
queens were the focal point of Martin Crowley's stage hit *The Boys in the
Band*, prompting *Time* to report, "Unashamedly queer characters are everywhere. . . . Hollywood has suddenly discovered homosexuality, and the 'third
sex' is making a determined bid for first place at the box office."[59]

The following November *Life* described *The Killing of Sister George* as "the
most explicit and sensational of a flock of films on lesbians." It went on to say
the film gave its audiences a good sense of what lesbian characters share with
"fags, prostitutes and even lower-echelon show folk. It is tacky, tawdry,
repellent—and true." Hollywood could see little beyond stereotypical nelly
queens and butch dykes who were sadists, psychopaths, or buffoons. There
was no in-between. *Time* suggested that producers may have turned to homosexuals because "Hollywood has run out of conventional bad guys."[60]

In February 1969 the *New York Times* carried an unusual article: WHY CAN'T
"WE" LIVE HAPPILY EVER AFTER, TOO? The author was Donn Teal, a gay writer in
New York who had grown weary of the images he was seeing in the media.
"A plethora of plagues is upon us!" he wrote, using the pseudonym Ronald
Forsythe. Citing numerous examples of characters and plots in motion pic-
tures and plays, he wrote: "We seem to have to commit suicide, murder one
another (or be murdered, as in *The Detective*), die à la Camille, or at least
break off the relationship lest insanity be the result."[61]

Teal sent the unsolicited article to the *Times* as a lark. When an editor
called to ask permission to print it, Teal was ecstatic. For the first time the
New York Times was allowing a gay to speak for himself, albeit under a pseudonym. The story got prominent display on the front page of the February 23,
1969, Culture section.

That summer Teal heard from the *Times* again—would he write a second
article to coincide with the June 1 release of the original cast album of *The*

Boys in the Band? This time he used his own name and explained that he had been the author of the earlier piece. "Self-hate and a feeling of guilt are not typical of today's homosexual," he wrote, "though it has been a labor to shake these leftovers of Judaeo-Christian puritanism, and many of us are still wrestling with the inferiority complex which society has been only too glad to foist upon us." Referring to the album, Teal cautioned that "the heterosexual buyer may not realize that 'The Boys in the Band' presents a distorted picture of a subculture about which he may know merely a trifle."[62]

After the article appeared, Teal found himself shut out of the pages of the *Times*. "They said they had received instructions from on high that I was to write nothing further in the nature of a gay protest article," he said. "I had been outlawed from the pages of the *New York Times*."[63]

NEWS OF THEIR OWN

It wasn't until the late 1960s that American gays began to cover their own community in publications that reached well beyond their organizational newsletter and small-circulation magazines.[64] The publications of the homophile movement had been an essential platform for homosexuals in the early years, but in-fighting undermined *One* and it collapsed in 1967. Declining membership in the Mattachine Society forced the *Mattachine Review* to shut down a year later. *The Ladder* continued to be an important publication for women, but its emphasis broadened and shifted from lesbians to the feminist movement.

Although each of the early publications carried important information that informed and enlightened, much of their contents read like literary journals. None was truly a source of unbiased news about the homosexual subculture, nor were they supposed to be. But that was about to change. The first stirrings of a gay press came in 1967 when two Los Angeles men took over a newsletter from a floundering organization that had formed to combat police harassment of the city's gay bars. Publisher Dick Michaels had a personal interest in sounding an alarm over illegal police activities, having been arrested several years earlier in a bar raid on Melrose Avenue. Michaels's lover, Bill Rand, who became the editor, recognized the need for an effective way to warn other gays of danger.[65]

In September 1967 Michaels and Rand put together the first issue of the *Los Angeles Advocate* on their dining room table. They surreptitiously printed three hundred copies in the basement print shop at the Los Angeles studios of ABC television where Rand worked part time while he finished college. The two had no intention of turning the small publishing enterprise into a business. They only wanted to fill the void created by the refusal of the *Los Angeles Times* and a blatantly homophobic tabloid called the *Hollywood Citizen-News* to cover their community. But they faced two major problems. First and foremost, magazine distributors refused to touch a publication for homosexuals. So Michaels created a crude sales network through gay bars, which explains why much of the *Advocate*'s content focused on gay men. (Although lesbian bars existed, lesbians typically relied much more on private social clubs to meet one another.) Moreover, Michaels insisted on charging for his newspaper, believing that "people don't respect anything they get for free."[66]

The second problem was advertising. Because the newspaper was not affiliated with an organization, it was completely dependent on ad sales. As a marketing ploy the next year Michaels created an annual Groovy Guy contest in which handsome young men competed to be featured shirtless in a photo spread. Within only a few months sales leaped to three thousand copies.

Michaels expanded the paper to tabloid size later that year (1968), boosted the number of pages from twelve to thirty-two, and shortened its name to the *Advocate*. He hired its first ad salesman and moved the layout tables out of his dining room and into a three-room office above a bar on Western Avenue in Hollywood. In addition, Michaels hired an independent audit firm to verify the circulation and sales figures in hopes of one day attracting major advertisers. Finally, he quit his $15,000-a-year job as a writer at a chemical association to work full time on the paper, dreaming of a day when it would be sold openly on newsstands in New York, Chicago, San Francisco, Minneapolis, and Atlanta.[67]

By 1970 the *Advocate* had become a critical lifeline for the scattered homosexual subculture and was beginning to show a small profit. Rob Cole, an editor at the *Dallas Times-Herald* for fifteen years, became the first news editor and increased its frequency from monthly to biweekly:

> Dick insisted on an absolute separation between advertising and news because he really wanted a news publication. It was already a credible national publication when I joined it in the sense that anyone who was interested in gay activism was dependent on it for news. When people in other parts of the country saw the

Advocate and saw what it was doing, they began to try similar things in their areas. This is what really started the gay newspaper movement in this country.[68]

By the late 1960s there were signs of a gay press in several East Coast cities. Lilli Vincenz and several other members of the Mattachine Society of Washington, D.C., organized a community services committee and almost immediately tried to create a newspaper. In October 1969 she and a small group of men and women met in the basement of a Connecticut Avenue building to work on the first issue of the *Gay Blade*. It contained three columns of news, community notices, and a small advertisement for someone who wanted to sell a car. By distributing copies at the city's gay and lesbian bars they quickly established the *Blade* as a source of valuable information that was not available from any other source.

According to Nancy Tucker, the editor, they printed the "things that we thought were important to the mental health and social welfare of other people like us. Periodically, we ran warnings of blackmailers who hung around Dupont Circle or the gay bars. We wrote about rough cops. There were plenty of military and government workers who were undergoing some type of security investigation, and all of these people needed to know about their rights. These were a heavy orientation for us."[69]

The *Gay Blade*, later renamed the *Washington Blade*, was one of the first of a new generation of gay papers that included *Gay Community News* in Boston, *NewsWest* in Los Angeles, *Gay News* in Pittsburgh, and *GayLife* in Chicago. Unlike the early homophile press, which stressed identity and cooperation, this second generation concentrated almost solely on political change and resistance.

4

COVERING STONEWALL

Gays in New York could have expected a police crackdown in 1969. It was an election year, and the city had a long history of heightened police activity aimed at gays at election time. But the crackdown in 1969 came early.

POLICE BEGIN TIMES SQ. CLEANUP AFTER NIGHT WORKERS COMPLAIN, the *New York Times* informed readers on an inside page in the February 6 edition. "The police began a crackdown on drunks, homosexuals, loiterers and other undesirables in the Times Square area last night, although the cold weather apparently kept many of them away," the article explained. It said police promised to "saturate the area with patrolmen" after a meeting with union and management representatives at the *Times* at which employees complained of being attacked as they left work.[1]

That week police arrested 292 people on a variety of charges. A *Times* editorial on February 17 commended the police and urged them to continue putting pressure on "muggers and degenerates." "Every street in the city should be safe at every hour of day or night," it said. "The police and the courts both had a part to play in achieving that goal."[2]

Gays were outraged that the *Times* in particular would lump homosexuals into a laundry list of undesirables that included drunks and prostitutes. Marty Robinson of the Mattachine Society fired off a complaint to Theodore Bernstein, assistant managing editor of the *Times*. "You may have a point," Bernstein responded in a letter to Robinson. "Undoubtedly, the reporter obtained the component of the undesirable group from the police and merely included it in that way in his story. The point you make has been called to the attention of our metropolitan desk and other editors involved in the organization so that there will not be a repetition of such a stigmatizing statement."[3]

Bernstein apparently investigated Robinson's complaint and determined that in 1968 the American Psychiatric Association had officially reclassified homosexuality, listing it as the same type of "non-psychotic" disorder as fetishism, pedophilia, transvestitism, exhibitionism, voyeurism, sadism, and masochism.[4] Bernstein, the well-known stickler on language, recognized that the *Times* had been inaccurate. A few days after he sent a directive to the *Times* staff, a copy of his memo ended up in the hands of *San Francisco Chronicle* columnist Herb Caen, who wrote: "ANOTHER BREAKTHROUGH: Such sentences as 'Police rounded up narcotics addicts, drunks, panhandlers, homosexuals, and drifters' won't be seen again in the impudent N.Y. *Times*. 'Homosexual is no longer universally considered a term of opprobrium,' reads an editor's memo to the staff. 'If you mean "soliciting homosexuals" or "homosexual prostitutes," say it that way.'"[5]

In the summer police shifted their resources to Greenwich Village. One indication of the change came on June 3 when a convoy of fifteen police wagons swept down on a notorious rendezvous on the West Side near the docks, and police arrested nearly everyone in sight. Only days later police raided five Village gay bars and charged the owners with serving alcohol without a license.

Instead of hauling all the customers off to jail, as had once been standard procedure, police were more likely to arrest only the bartenders, destroy the liquor supply, and order the customers to line up along a wall where they would be asked to produce proper identification. Most customers would be released. But because city law required everyone to wear a minimum of three articles of clothing appropriate to one's gender, police paid particular attention to drag queens to gauge whether they complied with the law. Police were also rough on butch lesbians. "You think you're a man?" they would sometimes taunt the women. "Let's see what you've got in your pants" they might say, reaching down the women's pants to humiliate them.[6]

By 1969 a young and angry breed of gays had become increasingly visible in the Village. They were fearless, with a cocky, defiant attitude. They included Jerry Hoose, who had come out to his family in early 1964 when he was only nineteen. After he saw Randy Wicker interviewed on the *Les Crane Show,* Hoose decided it was time to move to the Village:

> New York was one of the worst cities in the world for gay people in the middle sixties. We never felt safe. We could not stand in the street and talk to each other or cruise or do anything without the police 'shooing' us along and jabbing us with their nightsticks. In the main area—Christopher Street at Greenwich Avenue—we literally couldn't stand on the sidewalks without the police walking up with the nightsticks to chase us off. We were treated like we were lower than dirt.[7]

On June 28, 1969, under a full moon, six plainclothes New York City police officers arrived at the door of the dilapidated bar for the second raid that week. When they walked through the door at approximately 11 P.M., the bar was packed with a weekend crowd of nearly four hundred gay men. Many were in a particularly contrary mood, having stood outside a midtown funeral home earlier that day to view the funeral procession for Judy Garland. For a vast number of gay men the actress-singer had been an icon. Her suicide was a devastating loss.[8]

Since it opened in 1967, the Stonewall Inn had become the largest and one of the most popular gay bars in the city despite its dirty, deplorable condition. It was as hot as a sauna during the summer and as cold as a tomb in the winter. The owners charged exorbitant prices for watered-down drinks, but the bar drew a huge crowd because it was one of the few bars where gays could drink and dance.

As raids went, the one at the Stonewall Inn was routine until Betty Badge—as the gays referred to the police—began to escort a group of men to a waiting police wagon. Some customers who had been released were watching from the park across the street at Sheridan Square, along with a large group of kids and drag queens who hung out there most nights. As police moved toward the wagon, the crowd began to whistle, jeer, and throw pennies. Someone threw a beer bottle that smashed against a light pole just above the head of a young cop. "Who threw that?" he barked. "We all did," came the ominous response. By then the crowd had swelled to nearly one thousand.[9]

Tensions escalated as the police tried to load a woman into a patrol car. She began screaming and slid across the seat and out the opposite door. A nearby policeman caught her, slammed her in the head with a nightstick, and threw her back into the car. The crowd roared with anger. Some began to rock the police wagon from side to side, while others started pelting the police with cocktail glasses, shoes, rocks, sticks from the park, and a trash can. "Gay power!" they chanted in unison, "Gay power!"[10]

Several startled policemen ducked back into the bar to escape, only to find the situation deteriorating further. Someone was using an old parking meter as a battering ram to break down the door. Outside they could hear the crowd chanting, "Kill the cops!" Then someone squirted lighter fluid through a broken window and tossed in a match, sparking a fire the police quickly doused with a hose from behind the bar. They were on the verge of firing on the crowd but heard sirens wailing. The Tactical Patrol Force, the city's crack police unit that specialized in civil disturbances, had arrived.[11]

Distinctive because they wore visored helmets and carried wooden clubs, the heavily armed squad members moved up Christopher Street in a Roman flying-wedge formation to clear the street. In the past gays had run at the first sign of trouble. Not this time. They held their ground as the police broke ranks and surged into the crowd, smashing their clubs against anyone in their path. Heads were cracked, ribs bruised, and faces bloodied as the police charged, swinging their batons wildly as the gays kicked, bit, and slapped back. High heels suddenly became dangerous weapons in the hands of angry drag queens. After two hours of fighting the mêlée ended. Police arrested thirteen people; an untold number were injured. Miraculously, no one was killed.[12]

Word of the rioting reached the metropolitan news desk at the *Times* only minutes after the fighting began. Just as Albin Krebs and several other rewrite men returned to the newsroom from their dinner break, they heard a telephone ring on the city editor's desk. On the other end was Phillip "Philly" Mehar, a "legman" whose job was to monitor the police and fire department at night.

Krebs watched as an assistant took the information from Mehar and handed it to George Barrett, the night editor on the metropolitan desk.

Barrett directed an assistant to call the police and find out about it. A few minutes later the information was confirmed, and Barrett turned to a clean-cut young writer named Jim Sikes and told him to hustle down to Sheridan Square.

A tall lanky Texan, Sikes had worked at the *Times* for six years after graduating magna cum laude from Harvard. He had attended law school for a while but dropped out before the end of his first year. He joined the *Times*, starting as a junior member of the rewrite desk, where most new people began their careers. By the time he arrived at Sheridan Square, the street brawl had become a full-blown riot. People were smashing windows along the front of the Stonewall Inn as the tactical force was trying to clear the streets by pushing, shoving, and clubbing people to the ground. Sikes ran to a nearby telephone booth to call the rewrite desk.[13]

Back at the *Times* newsroom Krebs was fascinated by the unfolding drama. He watched Barrett wrestle with how to handle the story. There was plenty of time to get it into the next morning's edition. But Krebs watched with disbelief as Barrett talked on the telephone and then put the story aside. "I'm going to recommend that we look into it tomorrow," he told his assistants.[14]

According to Krebs,

> He was just uncomfortable; he was old-fashioned. He said a lot of stuff happened—it was night and reporters couldn't get there and get in-depth interviews and so forth—so they would do a follow-up the next day, but I don't believe much of anything was done. At the time, Stonewall was not the great big historic thing that it became later—I suppose Bunker Hill was that way too. I remember I wanted very much to say something, but at that time you didn't say anything if you wanted to keep your job. I don't think they would have fired me over it, but anyone who was "suspect" would be marooned to the Family Style section, the women's news page, or to Culture Gulch—the arts section—places where people couldn't cause trouble.[15]

The six-paragraph, single-column story ran on page thirty-three of the *Times* on Sunday, June 29. It carried no byline, indicating that the author was a junior writer. The small article was classic *New York Times*. In sterile language it described the clash in terms of the problems faced by the police. It mentioned nothing about the recent rash of arrests at gay bars or the history of police harassment. Readers were left to figure out for themselves the reasons for the uprising. The story began,

4 POLICEMEN HURT IN 'VILLAGE' RAID
MELEE NEAR SHERIDAN SQUARE FOLLOWS ACTION AT BAR

Hundreds of young men went on a rampage in Greenwich Village shortly after 3
A.M. yesterday after a force of plainclothes men raided a bar that police said was
well known for its homosexual clientele. Thirteen persons were arrested and four
policemen were injured. The young men threw bricks, bottles, garbage, pennies
and a parking meter at the policemen, who had a search warrant authorizing them
to investigate reports that liquor was sold illegally at the bar, the Stonewall Inn,
53 Christopher Street, just off Sheridan Square.

The tone of the article and its placement deep inside the newspaper came
as no surprise to homosexuals. "I didn't expect it to be on the front page
because the *Times* didn't cover gay stuff," recalled Martha Shelley, then president of the New York chapter of Daughters of Bilitis. "I knew that if there
had been that many black people rioting in Manhattan, the story would have
been front page news."[16]

Reporter Dennis Eskow took a similar approach in his story in the *New York
Daily News*, 3 COPS HURT AS BAR RAID RILES CROWD. It was accompanied by a
three-column photograph showing police talking to a group of smiling young
men outside the bar. Like the *Times* story, Eskow's was buried on page thirty.
It began, "A predawn police raid on a reputed Greenwich Village homosexual hangout, the second raid within a week, touched off a two-hour melee
yesterday as customers and villagers swarmed over the plainclothes cops.
Before order was restored, the cops were the targets of thrown coins, cob-
blestones and uprooted parking meters, windows were smashed, a police van
was nearly overturned and the front of the raided bar, the Stonewall Inn, was
fire-bombed."[17]

Despite extensive damage, the Stonewall Inn reopened the night after the
riots as customers stopped by for a free soda and exchanged stories about the
riot. By 9 P.M. the crowd outside had grown larger and more boisterous than
the one inside. Several people blocked the path of a bus on Eighth Avenue,
banging on the windshield and chanting, "Christopher Street belongs to the
queens!" A ranking police officer who arrived to investigate was greeted by
a sack of garbage that careened through his passenger window, slapping him
in the face with a ball of wet coffee grounds as it broke open. Another police
cruiser was met by a concrete block that landed squarely on the hood, Eskow
reported.

Arms linked and batons extended horizontally to clear the street, the tactical force returned. This time the squad were greeted by the "Stonewall Girls"—a campy rendition of the Rockettes, the precision dance team at Radio City Music Hall. The young straightlaced cops had never seen anything like it. But the scene quickly turned ugly again when police charged into the crowd, chasing people with their clubs and knocking them to the ground. By some accounts the Saturday night riot was more violent than the previous night's and again included thirteen arrests. Smaller skirmishes continued on Sunday night and again the following Wednesday as groups of gay men roamed the streets, setting fire to trash cans and breaking windows.[18]

The *Times* reported the Saturay night outbreak in a second article. Again, the single column, ten-paragraph article was buried on page twenty-two. It began,

POLICE AGAIN ROUT "VILLAGE" YOUTHS

Heavy police reinforcements cleared the Sheridan Square area of Greenwich Village again yesterday morning when large crowds of young men, angered by a police raid on an inn frequented by homosexuals, swept through the area. . . . A number of people who did not retreat fast enough were pushed and shoved along, and at least two men were clubbed to the ground.[19]

Only reporter Jay Levin of the *New York Post* was able to put the uprising in a context that would enable the average reader to understand the events, despite the condescending tone of the article. His story ran on July 8, more than a week after the riots erupted. Headlined THE GAY ANGER BEHIND THE RIOTS, the story began,

"People are beginning to realize," said the doorman at the Stonewall Inn, "that no matter how 'Nelly' or how 'fem' a homosexual is, you can only push them so far." With a battle cry of "gay power," the Nellies, fems, gay boys, queens—all those who flaunt their homosexuality—have been demonstrating that they have indeed been pushed too far.[20]

Although most of the city's newspapers underplayed the riots, two others sensationalized them beyond extremes. The worst offender was the *Daily News*, the irreverent paper of the city's working class. Headlined HOMO NEST RAIDED,

Homo Nest Raided, Queen Bees Are Stinging Mad

By JERRY LISKER

She sat there with her legs crossed, the lashes of her mascara-coated eyes beating like the wings of a humming-bird. She was angry. She was so upset she hadn't bothered to shave. A day old stubble was beginning to push through the pancake makeup. She was a he. A queen of Christopher Street.

Last weekend the queens had turned commandos and stood bra-strap to bra strap against an invasion of the helmeted Tactical Patrol Force. The elite police squad had shut down one of their private gay clubs, the Stonewall Inn at 57 Christopher St., in the heart of a three-block homosexual community in Greenwich Village.

Queen Power reared its bleached blonde head in revolt. New York City experienced its first homosexual riot.

"We may have lost the battle, sweets, but the war is far from over," lisped an unofficial lady-in-waiting from the court of the Queens. . . . .

little girls do when they get together.

The thick glass shut out the outside world of the street. Inside, the Stonewall bathed in wild, bright psychedelic lights, while the patrons writhed to the sounds of a juke box on a square dance floor surrounded by booths and tables. The bar did a good business, and the waiters, or waitresses were always kept busy, as they snaked their way around the dancing customers to the booths and tables. For nearly two years, peace and tranquility reigned supreme for the Alice in Wonderland clientele.

The Raid Last Friday

with cheers of encouragement from the gallery.

The whole proceedings took on the aura of a homosexual Academy Awards Night. The Queens pranced out to the street blowing kisses and waving to the crowd. A beauty of a specimen named Stella wailed uncontrollably while being led to the sidewalk in front of the Stonewall by a cop. She later confessed that she didn't protest the manhandling by the officer, it was just that her hair was in curlers and she was afraid her new beau might be in the crowd and spot her. She didn't want him to see her this way, she wept.

Queen Power

The crowd began to get out of hand, eye witnesses said. Then, without warning, Queen Power exploded with all the fury of a gay atomic bomb. Queens, princesses and ladies-in-waiting began hurling anything they could lay their polished, mani-

pranced around like Wonder Woman, while several Florence Nightingales administered first aid to the fallen warriors. There were some assorted scratches and bruises, but nothing serious was suffered by these honeys turned Madwomen of Chaillot.

Official reports listed four injured policemen with 13 arrests. The War of the Roses lasted about two hours from about midnight to 2 a.m. There was a return bout Wednesday night.

Two veterans recently recalled the battle and issued a warning to the cops. "If they close up all the gay joints in this area there is going to be all out war."

Bruce and Nan

Both said they were refugees from Indiana and had come to New York where they could live together happily ever after. They were in their early 20's. They preferred to be called by their married names, Bruce and Nan. "I don't like your paper," lisped matter-of-factly. "It's anti-

New York Daily News, July 6, 1969 (© New York Daily News, L.P., used with permission)

QUEEN BEES ARE STINGING MAD, the article by Jerry Lisker appeared on July 6, nearly a week after the riots, on the first page of the local news section:

> She sat there with her legs crossed, the lashes of her mascara-coated eyes beating like the wings of a humming bird. She was angry. She was so upset she hadn't bothered to shave. A day old stubble was beginning to push through the pancake makeup. She was a he. A queen of Christopher Street. Last weekend the queens had turned commandos and stood bra-strap-to-bra-strap against an invasion of the helmeted Tactical Patrol Force. The elite police squad had shut down one of their private gay clubs, the Stonewall Inn at 57 Christopher St., in the heart of a three-block homosexual community in Greenwich Village.[21]

In mocking, denigrating descriptions that ran throughout the article, Lisker described gays as "Queen Bees," "princesses and ladies-in-waiting," "Florence Nightingales," and "honeys turned Madwomen of Chaillot." "Queen power reared its bleached blonde head in revolt," the article said. He referred to the Stonewall Inn as "a gay mecca" and a "homosexual beachhead." In one section he wrote,

> The whole proceedings took on the aura of a homosexual Academy Awards Night. The Queens pranced out to the street blowing kisses and waving to the crowd. A beauty of a specimen named Stella wailed uncontrollably while being led to the sidewalk in front of the Stonewall by a cop. She later confessed that she didn't protest the manhandling by the officer, it was just that her hair was in curlers and

she was afraid her new beau might be in the crowd and spot her. She didn't want
him to see her this way, she wept.[22]

Written in an entertaining and dramatic fashion, the story evoked the days
of yellow journalism, when newspapers put a premium on telling a story
rather than finding the facts—or providing the truth.

The July 3 edition of the *Village Voice* struck a similar tone in two front
page articles that provided the most extensive coverage of all. By coincidence
the *Voice*'s editorial offices were located on Christopher Street, only a few
doors from the Stonewall Inn. When the riot began on the first night, reporter Lucian Truscott IV was in the Lion's Head, a favorite drinking spot for
journalists, and darted outside to see what had happened. As a result he
wrote GAY POWER COMES TO SHERIDAN SQUARE, the lead article on the front
page of the next edition:

> Sheridan Square this weekend looked like something from a William Burroughs
> novel as the sudden specter of "gay power" erected its brazen head and spat out a
> fairy tale the likes of which the area has never seen. The forces of faggotry, spurred
> by a Friday night raid on one of the city's largest, most popular, and longest lived
> gay bars, the Stonewall Inn, rallied Saturday night in an unprecedented protest
> against the raid and continued Sunday night to assert presence, possibility, and
> pride until the early hours of Monday morning.

Like the article in the *Daily News*, Truscott's contained a liberal dose of
prejudiced characterizations ranging from "fags" to "blatant queens." "The
stars were in their element," he wrote, capturing the drama of the moment
but ignoring and trivializing legitimate complaints about oppressive police
tactics. He referred to the "limp wrists and primed hair" of the gays but
described the police as "the city's finest."

There was a certain irony in Truscott's having written the primary article
chronicling the launch of the gay liberation movement. A West Point graduate, he came from a long line of military brass—his father and his grandfather
were colonels in the army and his other grandfather was a four-star general.
While he attended West Point, he wrote articles in his spare time that he
mailed to the *Voice*, which he could count on to print his conservative essays.[23]

In June 1969 the twenty-two-year-old army lieutenant was on a two-
month leave before he had to report for duty at the huge army base at Fort
Benning, Georgia. He filled his idle time by taking a job at the *Voice* as a part-

time writer. It was sheer coincidence that he happened to be there the night of the Stonewall. As he wrote his article, Truscott could not have imagined that it would one day become a symbol of journalistic homophobia. In a 1993 interview, Truscott recalled,

> I wasn't used to using the term *gay*; to me they were just a bunch of fags in the street. I also thought that the demonstration was rather humorous—it wasn't humorous that they got beaten up—but the idea of a bunch of gay kids causing this huge problem, drag queens getting in lines and doing Rockettes routines in front of the cops, was hilarious. I thought the alliterative business was cute—the "forces of faggotry"—but I shouldn't have done it, and they shouldn't have published it. But there weren't any rules about what was right to say and what wasn't right to say. We did it and we weren't thinking.[24]

Despite the shallowness and indifference of the stories, sections of them managed to capture the deeper significance of the outbursts. Truscott closed his article with comments from Allen Ginsberg as the openly gay Beat generation poet surveyed the aftermath outside the Stonewall Inn. "Gay power! Isn't that great!" Ginsberg said. "We're one of the largest minorities in the country—10 percent, you know. It's about time we did something to assert ourselves." "Watch out," Truscott concluded, "the liberation is under way."

The second *Voice* article was written by Howard Smith who arrived at the Stonewall Inn during the first raid just as police were losing control of the crowd. When the rioting erupted and Deputy Inspector Seymour Pine and the other officers ducked inside the bar for safety, Smith went in with them and wrote his article from his unusual vantage point. "I found myself on the wrong side of the blue line," he wrote. "It was very, very scary."[25]

In the weeks following the riots young gay militants organized protests outside the closed bar and in front of the Greenwich Village police station. These news events merited stories in the *Village Voice* but were ignored by the *Times* and the other major dailies.

In comparison to ghetto riots that summer in Los Angeles, Detroit, and Newark, the Stonewall riots seemed minor. In those cities people were killed and entire city blocks destroyed. The higher profile of the race riots may have contributed to the invisibility of Stonewall. It was only in time that Stonewall would take on the mythical importance for homosexuals that the Alamo holds for Texans, representing bravery in the face of insurmountable odds. Because of the media's ignorance about gays and lesbians the press could not have understoond Stonewall's significance. But those who had closely watched the change in the gay psyche closely during the sixties recognized the importance immediately.

Once again the gay press played an important role by allowing gays to report on gays. FIRST GAY RIOT, read a headline on the cover of the *Advocate*, trumpeting a story written by Dick Leitsch for the New York Mattachine Society newsletter. Calling the Stonewall fracas "the first gay riots in history," Leitsch provided a detailed account. "The police behaved, as is usually the case, with bad grace, and were reproached by 'straight' onlookers," he wrote. Although some of the Mattachine Society's old guard was angered and embarrassed that a group of drag queens would fight with police rather than quietly work through the hard-fought channels their organization had established with city officials, Leitsch took a more activist stand. In a leaflet Leitsch referred to the riots as "the hairpin drop heard around the world."[26]

The second insightful article appeared in *Screw*, the avant-garde New York newspaper of the sexual revolution. Jack Nichols served as managing editor after he was fired from his job in Washington for appearing on *CBS Reports*. At *Screw* Nichols and his lover, Lige Clarke, wrote a regular column, Homosexual Citizen. They were out of town when the first night's riots erupted but returned Sunday and gathered details of the uproar. In reaction they composed what amounted to a homosexual call to arms that, ironically, appeared in *Screw*, the granddaddy of heterosexual sex tabloids:

> The revolution in Sheridan Square must step beyond its present boundaries. The homosexual revolution is only a part of a larger revolution sweeping through all segments of society. We hope that "Gay Power" will not become a call for separation, but for sexual integration, and that the young activists will read, study, and make themselves acquainted with all of the facts which will help them to carry the sexual revolt triumphantly into the councils of the U.S. Government, into the anti-homosexual churches, into the offices of anti-homosexual psychiatrists, into the city government, and into the state legislatures which make our manner of love-making a crime. It is time to push the homosexual revolution to its logical conclusion. We must crush tyranny wherever it exists and join forces with those who would assist in the utter destruction of the puritanical, repressive, anti-sexual Establishment.[27]

On Sunday, July 27, one month after the riots, three hundred to four hundred gays and lesbians held their first organized protest against police harassment. The rally signaled a second era of gay politics, known as the gay liberation movement, which sought to liberate homosexuals from society's oppression. "Gay power" became their battle cry. Gay Liberation Front (GLF) became their banner. The name was chosen to reflect the resurgence of the fighting armies of the National Liberation Front of communist North Vietnam.

GLF quickly became the movement's dominant force, relying on a confrontational style that for the most part the Mattachine Society and the Daughters of Bilitis had strenuously avoided throughout the fifties and the sixties. Young militants like Michael Brown and Martha Shelley would not concern themselves with decorum as their predecessors had. Gay liberationists were not the type to arrive at a protest wearing coats and ties or dresses. Although they may not have felt their militancy to any greater degree than the homophiles did, they were decidedly larger in number and considerably louder.

In August 1969 GLF tried to place two innocuous notices in the free Bulletin Board section of the *Village Voice* to promote its fundraising activities. But the newspaper's advertising staff deleted the references to *gay*, despite the newspaper's willingness to accept apartment ads that specified No Gays. Ironically, the *Voice* was a liberal—if not the most liberal—newspaper in the nation. Founded in October 1955 by Ed Fancher and Dan Wolf, two former GIs who had fought in World War II, the paper quickly established itself as an avant-garde counterculture journal that matched the bohemian atmosphere of Greenwich Village. Not only would it become the forerunner of the fledgling alternative press, it set the standard for similar newspapers that sprang up in San Francisco, Philadelphia, Berkeley, Boston, New Haven, Washington, D.C., and other cities.

In its early days the *Voice* attracted a stable of talented journalists willing to submit articles gratis in return for the wide latitude they were given to express themselves. From its inception the newspaper reflected a head-on, first-person, advocacy style of journalism that was unmatched by any mainstream publication. The writers could say whatever they wanted in whatever space they wanted, without worrying about having to conform to the accepted practices of journalism or the wishes of a meddling editor.[28] But the editorial freedoms that allowed *Voice* writers to describe gays as fags, coupled with its restrictive advertising policy, brought gay and lesbian picketers to its doors on September 12, 1969, at 9 A.M. It was the first protest by the newly organized Gay Liberation Front aimed at the media.

Picketing continued throughout the day as publisher Fancher sternly refused to meet. One protester tried to break the stalemate in the late afternoon by placing a small classified ad that read, "The Gay Liberation Front sends love to all Gay men and women in the homosexual community." The ad was refused, but a short time later Howard Smith, one of the reporters who had covered the riots, came to the door amid a chorus of boos and invited three representatives inside to meet with Fancher.

The meeting was stormy. Fancher staunchly defended the right of his writers to use derogatory language, calling it an expression of free speech and a free press. But in a concession, he agreed to rescind the ban on using the words *gay* and *homosexual*. GLF member Lois Hart stepped over to one window and flashed a V sign to the crowd below, setting off a roar of cheering.

At the same time Nichols and Clarke were about to turn their column into a full-fledged newspaper, the first to be established by gays on the East Coast. *Screw* publisher Al Goldstein bankrolled the two men so they could launch *Gay* in November 1969.[29] It quickly became a newspaper of record for New York's gay community and provided a cohesive element for the gay liberation movement in its early years. Regular contributors included John Paul Hudson, Vito Russo, Kay Tobin, Leo Skir, Randy Wicker, Arthur Bell, John LeRoy, Pete Fisher, and Dr. George Weinberg—all of whom wrote or went on to write books. "*Gay* provided a forum for the likes of me," Hudson said. "It would be impossible to measure its impact on raising the gay consciousness on a mass scale."[30]

TAKING AIM AT THE PRESS

The radicalism of GLF rapidly caught on in cities throughout the nation. Similar groups formed in Berkeley, Los Angeles, Chicago, and San Francisco. Like the New York group, their attention soon turned to the media.

One of the earliest targets was Hearst's *San Francisco Examiner* for a series of articles about the city's seedy late-night "breakfast clubs," a euphemism for after-hours clubs that sold low-grade liquor without a license. "Trouble is the principal item on their menus," one police officer explained to the *Examiner*.[31]

Although most of Robert Patterson's series concerned straight clubs, his installment on October 24 called attention to the clubs for gays. Headlined THE DREARY REVELS OF S.F. "GAY" CLUBS, it began by saying,

San Francisco has more than a fair share of "gay" breakfast clubs. The "gay" clubs are gay in name only. Actually, they are sad, dreary after-hours traps where homosexuals and weird "straight" types gather for their sick, sad revels. . . . Take the Corral at 1535 Folsom Street. . . . Here the virile, ultra-male is wined and dined and wooed by other semi-males with flexible wrists and hips, and bona fide females have a strictly zero rating. The bar and outlying tables are occupied by types who undulate and wriggle, whose voices are an octave higher or lower than they should be, and whose manual contacts with their associates are lingering and tender.[32]

The article referred to the clubs as "deviate establishments" and "postmidnight sororities." Folsom Street, where many of the clubs were located, was called "Queer Street." Transvestites were "drag-darlings," "the pseudo fair sex," "hybrid blossoms," "women who aren't exactly women," and the epitome of "counterfeit femininity."

At noon on October 31, sixty members of GLF and the Society for Individual Rights (SIR) picketed the *Examiner* building, demanding that the newspaper fire the offending reporter. For about an hour Larry Littlejohn and the other protesters picketed peacefully until someone inside the building opened a window on the third floor and dumped a bag of purple printer's ink on the protesters below. Not to be outdone, the gays blotted their ink-drenched hands on the building's freshly painted white facade, leaving their purple palm prints dotting the windows and walls along the front of the building. Several smeared the wall with the words *Gay Power!*

Littlejohn, then the president of SIR, recalled,

At that point, the tactical squad arrived—not to get the employees who dumped the ink, but to arrest the demonstrators who were the victims. The police could have surrounded the Examiner building and found out who did it but, no, they went after the gays. It was just incredible how stupid the police could be. Somebody could have been hurt if that ink had gotten in their eyes, but the police came racing in with their clubs swinging, knocking people to the ground. It was unbelievable.[33]

The scuffle between the gays and the police quickly turned bloody as baton-wielding officers charged into the crowd. Two officers threw a lesbian to the pavement and then arrested her for obstructing traffic. Gushing blood from head wounds, several gay men were knocked to the curb. Another's teeth were knocked out when police threw him into a police wagon. The clash came to be known in San Francisco as Bloody Friday of the Purple Hand.[34]

Gays were also ready to confront the media in Los Angeles where the *Los Angeles Times* had ignored a long history of police brutality aimed at gays. The newspaper also overlooked the formation of the first gay church, the Metropolitan Community Church, which was incorporated by Rev. Troy Perry in October 1968. Soon after Morris Kight organized the Los Angeles chapter of GLF in September 1969, the *Times* became one of the group's first targets. According to Kight, gays in Los Angeles saw

> society [as] a monolith against us. We were treated as either unconvicted or unapprehended criminals. Churches considered us of such poor spiritual worth that they didn't even bother to send missionaries to save us. Police spied on us, raided our homes, arrested us, harassed us, and, in some cases, even killed us—I'm not exaggerating. Socialists treated us as bad credit risks, unemployable, or as employable at only mid-level or low-level jobs. Communists considered us the result of bourgeois decadence—that riding around in stretch limousines and all those credit cards were bound to leave some defect in character. So why wouldn't the press reflect this too?[35]

In late October, after the *Los Angeles Times* rejected an advertisement for a series of public lectures on homosexuality, GLF flew into action. The ad had been requested by Don Slater, the former editor of *One* who had since founded *Tangents* magazine and the Homosexual Information Center (HIC), a community education organization. But the *Times* advertising staff notified the group that the term *homosexual* was unacceptable.

Joining forces, Slater and Morris Kight met with officials of the paper but with little success. "They showed us a list that contained child molesters, rapists, axe murderers, homosexuals, and so forth," Kight said. "We asked why we were on that list; we weren't part of that. And they stood up and told us we could either accept it or not."[36]

After the ad had been rejected twice, twenty-five GLF picketers and HIC arrived at the paper's front door on November 5, 1968, to launch a boycott of both the paper and its advertisers. The protest attracted so much attention from the city's other media, eager to embarrass their competitor, that reporters outnumbered demonstrators. By late in the afternoon the executive editor, Robert D. Nelson, had issued a statement, telling the demonstrators, "The *Times* cannot accept advertisements which, in our judgment, fail to meet the standards of acceptability which we have established and which apply to all advertising copy. We feel that it must be our responsibility to make the final decisions as to what is acceptable for publication."[37]

Rather than risk arrests and even injury, the activists ended their demonstration. The following April, without any announcement or fanfare, the *Times* ran an advertisement for the film *Song of the Loon* that described it as "a homosexual classic" in big bold type. It turned out that the *Times* had changed its policy after Slater, who had learned that the *Times* planned to buy a newspaper and a television station in Dallas, threatened to organize a letter-writing campaign to the Federal Communications Commission to block the sale.

THE SPOTLIGHT SHIFTS

The new confrontational mood of gay and lesbian radicals in the wake of Stonewall and the formation of GLF set off another flurry of stories in a variety of publications, including one entitled UNDERSTANDING HOMOSEXUALITY in the July 1969 issue of the young women's magazine *Seventeen*. And the December issue of *Esquire* carried a feature titled THE NEW HOMOSEXUALITY.

The *Washington Post* was among the first major daily newspapers to detect the new mood among gays in a feature article, HOMOSEXUAL REVOLUTION, which ran on the front page of its Style section in October 1969, four months after the riots. Reporter Nancy Ross recounted the gay uprising and the GLF protest outside the *Village Voice*. In addition, the article delved into the political gains achieved by homosexuals in San Francisco and Los Angeles, calling it a "total social upheaval currently taking place in this country." Perhaps more significant, she concluded the article with one of the most astute observations to appear in the mainstream media: "What is more important than the changes themselves is the attitude toward them, both on the part of homosexuals and the world at large. Therein lies the revolution, of which the new militancy and openness are merely the methods."[38]

Simultaneously, the media began to include lesbians in their coverage of women's issues and the emerging women's liberation movement. The *New York Times* reported on THE WOMAN HOMOSEXUAL: MORE ASSERTIVE, LESS WILLING TO HIDE, accompanied by a photo of lesbian picketers in a Mattachine Society protest the previous July 4 in Washington, D.C. "The young homosexual woman, to an increasing degree, is refusing to live with the limitations and restrictions imposed by society and is showing a sense of active resentment and rebellion at a condemnation she considers unwarranted and unjust," the lengthy story began.[39]

Although the coverage reflected a deep understanding of gay-related issues, it relied on some of the old clichés. The *Times* turned to psychiatrist Charles Socarides who used terms such as *ill* to explain that homosexuality stemmed from "despair, disappointment, or fright." Although the article was buried in the paper's Food, Fashions, Family, Furnishings section, it provided important recognition for women who had long been ignored in print.

In July 1969 the *San Francisco Chronicle* reported on HOW DOES GIRL MEET GIRL? In a series of stories reporter Julie Smith described the budding romance between "Bonnie" and "Jane," telling readers, "Lesbians say they meet each other through friends, in bars, in the military, at the YWCA, in organizations, even, one woman said, 'in my labor union.'" The articles won accolades from lesbian readers. *The Ladder* declared it "the first time a major newspaper has profiled a lesbian marriage with no more and no less emphasis than they might describe a heterosexual marriage. This series is recommended reading for all."[40]

Even personal advice columns, which had long served as a platform for the psychiatric point of view, seemed to be showing a new openness. In November 1969 a reader of *McCall's* wrote to ask, "Could you explain lesbianism? I have had psychiatric treatment, but my therapists seemed unsure and ill at ease." In an unusually nonjudgmental tone, psychiatrist Gerald Caplan responded by saying, "A fundamental problem for a lesbian is how to preserve self-respect and a satisfying set of enduring personal relationships in a society that rejects her as a deviant. . . . I hope that our society will eventually gain a deeper understanding of lesbians and a greater tolerance for their human condition. Your life will become easier; but until then, I am afraid you will continue to have a hard struggle."[41]

A December 1969 issue of the *Chicago Sun-Times* carried two stories in its magazine section. Although the articles provided Mattachine Midwest with some much-needed exposure, one—THE HOMOSEXUALS: A NEWLY VISIBLE MINORITY—centered on a group of psychiatrists who tried to explain the "cause-and-cure" and concluded by noting a surge in the Chicago area in sex-change operations. The second article, THREE SPEAK OUT ON HARASSMENT, PARENTS, ANALYSTS AND GIRLS, featured interviews with three gay men, each of whom was identified by his pseudonym.[42]

Although signs of a new accommodating editorial policy were appearing in a variety of publications, the nation's top newsmagazines took a more negative tack. *Policing the Third Sex*, read an October 1969 headline in *Newsweek*. The article described several clashes between police and gays, including the Stonewall riots four months earlier. "When we rode herd on the fags, they stayed with their own kind in their own places," lamented one police inspector. "They didn't bug people and the people didn't bug them." *Newsweek* referred to a "détente" between the gays and police and called it tenuous at best.[43]

Time carried a seven-page cover story by Christopher Cory, THE HOMO-SEXUAL: NEWLY VISIBLE, NEWLY UNDERSTOOD. In the front of the magazine the editors explained that the article would "knock down many of the stereotypes." But it began by describing gay men in drag: "An exclusive formal ball will mark Halloween in San Francisco this week. In couturier gowns and elaborately confected masquerades, the couples will whisk around the floor until 2 A.M., while the judges award prizes for the best costumes and the participants elect an 'Empress.' By then the swirling belles will sound more and more deep-voiced, and in the early morning hours dark stubble will sprout irrepressibly through their Pan-Cake Make-up."[44]

In a strained attempt to maintain "balance," *Time* included extensive comments from Dick Leitsch and Franklin Kameny to represent gays, as well as quotes from psychiatrist Socarides and a man who claimed that after psychiatric treatment, "Women arouse me now."

Although the views of antigay psychiatrists may have been acceptable to old-line conservative homosexuals in the past, many had become concerned about the negative coverage. The new breed of radicals that comprised the Gay Liberation Front no longer saw any need for the media to include "experts" who questioned their mental state and morals. GLF members were particularly angry at *Time* because they had cooperated with the writer, only to find that he had emphasized the effeminate side of homosexuality to the exclusion of everyone else. "They didn't come out and call us queers, but it was a very patronizing article," said GLF member Bob Kohler.[45]

On November 12, 1969, protesters arrived outside the Time-Life Building in New York to picket and hand out leaflets that succinctly stated their objections. "In characteristic tight-assed fashion, *Time* has attempted to dictate sexual boundaries for the American public and to define what is healthy, moral, fun, and good on the basis of its own narrow, out-dated, warped, perverted, and repressed sexual bias," read the leaflets.[46]

Organizers had hoped to attract thousands of protesters, but cold snowy weather cut the number to fewer than thirty. "We had the long-hairs from

GLF and some middle-aged women from Daughters of Bilitis who came really dressed up—some had never really worn heels, but they struggled into them," Kohler recalled. "So it was a very strange-looking group that made a lot of noise and made a lot of people very uncomfortable. Basically, if we could do that in those days, we were happy."[47]

The most attention they attracted came from a group of construction workers across the street who jeered and threw eggs at them from seventeen floors above. "When you get pelted with eggs from seventeen floors, they hurt," Kohler said. When he challenged the bullies to "come down and fight like a man," the police moved in and threatened to arrest him for inciting a riot. The only media coverage of the protest was a brief film clip on the local ABC network affiliate that night.

PART 2

PROGRESS AND BACKLASH, 1970–1980

SEPTEMBER 1961   50 cents

mattachine REVIEW

TELEVISION SPOTLIGHT ON A 'TABOO' SUBJECT: "THE REJECTED"

Dr. Karl M. Bowman, a San Francisco psychiatrist, was one of several experts on homosexuality interviewed on the 1961 KQED special "The Rejected," television's first documentary on the subject. Bowman explained that the 1948 Kinsey study found homosexuality to be more prevalent in American society than anyone had previously believed.

(PHOTO: PHILIP GREENE; COURTESY KQED)

Harold Call (right), executive director, and Don Lucas, secretary, of the Mattachine Society were interviewed on "The Rejected." Produced by San Francisco public station KQED in 1961, the hourlong documentary was the first television special on homosexuality. (PHOTO: PHILIP GREENE; COURTESY KQED)

Don Slater (at the filing cabinet), the first editor of *One* magazine, works with some of the volunteer staff members in the editorial office in Los Angeles. (COURTESY HOMOSEXUAL INFORMATION CENTER LIBRARY)

Barbara Gittings was editor of the *The Ladder: A Lesbian Review*, the magazine of the Daughters of Bilitis, from 1963 through 1966. Gittings, pictured here in the early 1960s, was one of only a few lesbians in the nation who was willing to speak openly about homosexuality in interviews with print and broadcast media. (PHOTO KAY TOBIN LAHUSEN)

During the hourlong call-in show in 1964 Wicker responded to questions from viewers of *The Les Crane Show*. It was unusual for the media to carry an interview with a homosexual in the 1960s because most would not speak openly. As a result many media interviews involved psychiatrists who described homosexuality as a mental illness. (COURTESY RANDY WICKER)

The news media initially ignored White House picketing by Dr. Franklin Kameny and members of the Mattachine Society of Washington, D.C., in April 1965, but reporters began to cover the activists a month later. (COURTESY FRANKLIN KAMENY)

Randy Wicker, posing with a *New York Post* delivery truck, arranged for a *Post* reporter to interview gay men in December 1965 for a special series. (COURTESY RANDY WICKER)

Dick Michaels founded the *Advocate* in Los Angeles in September 1967 with his lover, Bill Rand. It became the nation's largest gay newspaper before it switched to a magazine format. (PHOTO: KAY TOBIN LAHUSEN)

Gays and lesbians picketed the *Village Voice* in the aftermath of the 1969 Stonewall riots when the newspaper rejected an advertisement from the Gay Liberation Front for its newspaper, *Come Out!* The newspaper's advertising department considered gay and homosexual ads obscene. (FROM *COME OUT!* COURTESY GAY AND LESBIAN INFORMATION CENTER—NEW YORK PUBLIC LIBRARY)

Village Voice columnist Jill Johnston, shown here in 1983, was an early advocate of lesbian and women's rights. From 1970 to 1974 she turned her weekly dance column in the *Voice* into a personal diary that chronicled her coming out as a lesbian feminist. (PHOTO: PETER HUJAR)

Arthur Bell (at center, wearing beads), one of the founders of New York's Gay Activists Alliance, wrote for the *Village Voice* and *Gay*, a New York gay newspaper, in the early 1970s. He became a staff writer at the *Voice* in 1974. Other GAA founders pictured here, from left to right, are Arthur Evans, Fred Cabellero, (unidentified), Kay Tobin, Marty Robinson, and Tom Doerr. (PHOTO: FRED N. ORLANSKY)

Time magazine was picketed by New York's Gay Liberation Front and Daughters of Bilitis after it ran its 1969 feature, NEWLY VISIBLE, NEWLY UNDERSTOOD, the first national newsmagazine cover story about homosexuality. The two organizations objected to derogatory comments in the article by antigay psychiatrists. (PHOTO: DIANA DAVIES; COURTESY DIANA DAVIES COLLECTION/NEW YORK PUBLIC LIBRARY)

Gay men and lesbians picketed the *New York Daily News* in April 1972 after the newspaper published an antigay editorial. Several of them were arrested, including Arthur Bell, who claimed he was covering the protest for the *Village Voice*. (PHOTO: BETTYE LANE)

Gay activists Jack Nichols and Lige Clarke were interviewed by Geraldo Rivera in November 1972. Nichols and Clarke founded the New York newspaper *Gay* and were among the small number of open gays in the nation willing to be interviewed. (PHOTO: LINDA ROMANO; COURTESY JACK NICHOLS)

Eighteen-year-old gay activist Mark Segal zapped *The Mike Douglas Show* in May 1973, handcuffing himself to the studio camera to protest negative portrayals of gays and lesbians on television. Douglas, an unidentified stagehand, singer Tony Bennett, and actress Helen Hayes watched. (PHOTO: HARRY R. EBERLIN)

Mark Segal discussed his media campaign in an interview on Philadelphia television station WCAU. (PHOTO: HARRY R. EBERLIN)

Ronald Gold became a major force behind gays' organized campaign against network television portrayal of gays in the early 1970s. Seated at far left in the front row, Gold is shown at the 1973 New York press conference announcing formation of the Gay Task Force. Other founders of the task force were (front row, from left to right) Howard Brown, Bruce Voeller, and Nathalie Rockhill; in the back row, from left to right, were Martin Duberman, Barbara Gittings, and Dr. Franklin Kameny. The organization was later renamed the Gay and Lesbian Task Force (GLTF). (PHOTO: BETTYE LANE)

Morris Kight, founder of the Los Angeles Gay Liberation Front in 1970, became a major spokesman for gays and lesbians. He founded the Los Angeles Gay Community Center and established Christopher Street West, a West Hollywood observance of the Stonewall riots. (COURTESY INTERNATIONAL GAY AND LESBIAN ARCHIVES, LOS ANGELES)

Gay activists picketed the New York headquarters of ABC-TV following the airing of "The Outrage," a 1974 episode of *Marcus Welby, M.D.* The plot involved a schoolteacher accused of raping one of his male students. After gays protested in Los Angeles, Philadelphia, Washington, and other cities, several of the show's sponsors withdrew their advertising from the controversial episode. (PHOTO: BETTYE LANE)

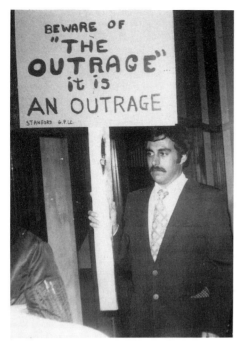

ABC's San Francisco affiliate, KGO, is picketed over the *Marcus Welby, M.D.* episode "The Outrage" in October 1974. Frank Fitch of Stanford University's Gay Community of Concern is shown leading the picket line. (COURTESY INTERNATIONAL GAY AND LESBIAN ARCHIVES, LOS ANGELES)

Gays and lesbians emerged from their October 1974 meeting with officials of the *Los Angeles Times* claiming victory in the protest of the newspaper's coverage. Led by Rev. Bob Sirico (center, in beard and mustache) of the Los Angeles Metropolitan Community Church and veteran activist Morris Kight (wearing glasses), the group had staged a sit-in at the newspaper's headquarters. (PHOTO: PAT ROCCO; COURTESY INTERNATIONAL GAY AND LESBIAN ARCHIVES, LOS ANGELES)

Members of Lesbian Feminist Liberation (LFL) picket NBC headquarters at Rockefeller Center in New York in May 1975 after the network's broadcast of an episode of *Police Woman*, "Flowers of Evil." LFL member Eleanor Cooper is shown with activist lawyer Florence Kennedy, an LFL supporter. (PHOTO: BETTYE LANE)

More than five hundred demonstrators protest in front of the *New York Post* in December 1985, calling the newspaper a yellow rag because of its inflammatory coverage of the AIDS epidemic. The protest was the first coordinated by the group of gays and lesbians that later became known as Gay and Lesbian Alliance Against Defamation (GLAAD). (PHOTO: STEVE ZIFFER)

In one of several ill-fated attempts to organize a boycott of the *New York Times* the Coalition for Lesbian and Gay Rights picketed the newspaper in 1983 because of its ban of the term *gay*. The picketers included (from left to right) Eleanor Cooper, Allen Roskoff, Steve Ault, and Jimmy Flowers. The man carrying the sign could not be identified. (PHOTO: STEVE ZIFFER)

Emmy Award–winning television journalist Paul Wynne gave the AIDS epidemic a face for thousands of viewers in San Francisco in his seven-month series on KGO-TV from January through July 1990. As his illness progressed, Wynne taped his weekly segments from his hospital bed. (PHOTO: KGO-TV; COURTESY ESTATE OF PAUL WYNNE)

Former *Advocate* reporter Randy Shilts became the first openly gay reporter to be hired by a major daily newspaper when he joined the *San Francisco Chronicle* in 1981. Shown with Supervisor Harvey Milk on election night 1978, Shilts later covered Milk's assassination by former supervisor Dan White at city hall. (PHOTO: STEVE SAVAGE)

Journalist Robert O'Boyle chronicled his battle with AIDS for more than eighteen months in the *Seattle Times*. His weekly column, "Living with AIDS," ran from June 1990 until his death in February 1992. (PHOTO: JEFF HORNER AT THE WALLA WALLA *UNION-BULLETIN*. COURTESY REGINA A. O'BOYLE)

Carl Griffin Jr., a reporter who joined the *Minneapolis Tribune* in 1972, may have been the first openly gay journalist at a mainstream newspaper. In addition to his reporting duties the newspaper, Griffin, shown here in 1980, wrote freelance articles for the *Advocate* under his own byline until he left the *Tribune* and journalism in 1980. (COURTESY CARL GRIFFIN JR.)

CNN anchorman and financial correspondent Tom Cassidy was diagnosed with AIDS in October 1987 and went public with his illness in magazine and television reports. He chronicled his battle against the disease until his death in June 1991. (COURTESY CNN)

New York Times editor Jeffrey
Schmalz began his newspaper
career at the *Times* as a copyboy in
1973 and rose through the ranks
of the newspaper to become
deputy national editor in 1990.
After suffering a brain seizure at
his desk in the *Times* newsroom in
late 1990, he was diagnosed with
AIDS. When he returned to work
in 1991, he began covering AIDS
and gays as the first such beat at
the *Times* and continued to do so
until his death in 1993. (PHOTO:
MARC ASNIN /SABA, REPRINTED
WITH PERMISSION)

Deb Price, Washington editor of the *Detroit News*,
made history when she began writing the first
newspaper column dealing exclusively with gay and
lesbian issues in May 1992. By 1996 her syndicated
column was going to more than one hundred
newspapers nationwide. (COURTESY *DETROIT NEWS*)

Essence magazine's senior editor Linda Villarosa
revealed to readers that she is a lesbian when she
coauthored with her mother a May 1991 article about
coming out. The article prompted more mail than
any in the publication's history. In August 1994
Essence named her executive editor.

5

GAY NEWS, STRAIGHT MEDIA

The Gay Liberation Front challenged homophobia with the confrontational tactics that the conservative homophile movement had studiously avoided. The radicals believed that the only hope for reversing antigay bias was to apply shock therapy to society. The radical core of GLF saw the organization as a partner in the realignment of American society, allying with other radical New Left organizations such as the Black Panthers, Students for a Democratic Society, and the Student Nonviolent Coordinating Committee.

But like the Communist party of the fifties, the social revolutionaries of the sixties failed to embrace the rights of homosexuals. Radical members of the New Left were as likely as the communists a decade earlier to attack GLF members as fags. Panther leader Eldridge Cleaver once denounced homosexuality as an evil as great as being the chairman of General Motors.

In November 1969, shortly after the Stonewall riots, a group of disgruntled GLF members met to form Gay Activists Alliance (GAA).[1] By January 1970 the small group had adopted a constitution. Unlike the GLF, GAA would confine itself to the single issue of winning legal protections against discrimination for gays and lesbians. Jim Owles and Marty Robinson, two young gay men who had been activists in the antiwar movement, were the visionaries who laid out a strategy that focused on achieving antidiscrimination protections, the repeal of state sodomy laws, and an end to police entrapment and harassment.

In only five months GAA was catapulted to the forefront of New York's gay movement. Its regular Thursday night meetings at a member's Village apartment overflowed week after week. Action included picketing police stations and "zaps"—members would occupy the mayor's office or disrupt city council meetings with noisy outbursts. The least provocation instantly became an opportunity for GAA to assert itself at the vanguard of gay liberation and attract press coverage.

One of the first zaps outside Greenwich Village was aimed at the *New York Post* in mid-January 1970. Writers Pete Hamill and Harriett Van Horne had both included derogatory comments about gays in their editorial page columns. Hamill called a GLF contingent in an antiwar demonstration "slim-waisted freakcreeps." Van Horne included the Oscar Wilde Memorial Bookshop in a tirade against pornography.[2] (The Greenwich Village bookshop was the first in the nation to specialize in gay-themed literature, but it did not handle pornography. In fact, Craig Rodwell, founder and owner of the bookstore, stridently avoided sex magazines that he considered exploitative, despite enormous pressure from distributors and occasional smashed windows.[3])

After picketing noisily outside the newspaper for a short time, seven protesters broke ranks and marched into the lobby to demand a meeting with James Wechsler, the editorial page editor. Listening sympathetically to their concerns, Wechsler defended the editorial freedom of his writers, blaming their prejudice on ignorance about gay life.[4] For a time, though, reporting in the *Post* began to include stories about major GAA political protests and several minor demonstrations. The paper even ran an editorial on antigay job discrimination.

Six weeks later, in March 1970, Deputy Inspector Seymour Pine, the same officer who had led the Stonewall raid, raided another popular gay bar, the Snake Pit, where he and his officers arrested 167 customers on charges of disorderly conduct. One man, Diego Vinales, a distraught twenty-three-year-old Argentine national who feared that his arrest would result in deportation, panicked and jumped from a second-floor window of the police precinct, landing on a fourteen-inch spike on a fence below. Rescue workers brought in an electric saw to cut him free so he could be taken to a hospital.

The *Daily News* carried graphic front page pictures, but the incident failed to attract much attention from the *New York Post* and the *New York Times*. The *Times* buried a story on page twenty-nine, HOMOSEXUALS HOLD PROTEST IN 'VILLAGE' AFTER RAID NETS 176. The impaled man, who miraculously survived, was relegated to the sixth paragraph.[5]

The next big burst of coverage came in June 1970 when a crowd of several thousand marched from Greenwich Village to Central Park for the Christopher Street Liberation Day celebration to mark the first anniversary of the Stonewall riots. Crowd estimates varied from 1,000 (the police) to 20,000 (gay activists). Although the *New York Times* had taken a full year to explain to its readers the significance of the riots at the Stonewall Inn, reporter Lacey Fosburgh, who covered the commemoration, provided what may have been the most balanced news story. Her work was particularly unusual because she quoted three gays, including GLF founder Michael Brown. "We're probably the most harassed, persecuted minority group in history," Brown had told the reporter, "but we'll never have the freedom and civil rights we deserve as human beings unless we stop hiding in the closets and in the shelter of anonymity." The *Times*'s coverage included two photographs on an inside page and put the crowd at 1,000 to 20,000. The *Daily News* gave the march a single paragraph and estimated the crowd at 10,000.[6]

The first indication that the *Times* recognized the significance of gay liberation came on August 24 in a front page headline: HOMOSEXUALS IN REVOLT. The article described "a new mood now taking hold among the nation's homosexuals" and then quoted psychiatrists warning of the dangers they posed. "Homosexuality is a psychiatric or emotional illness," one psychiatrist said. "It's possible that this movement could consolidate the illness in some people, especially among young people who are teetering on the brink."[7]

BACK TO BACKLASH

By September 1970 evidence of a media backlash was clear. The first sign was the cover of *Harper's*, which featured a photograph of a tightly framed male torso, arm flexed to accentuate his overly inflated biceps and chest to dramatize the headline: HOMO/HETERO: THE STRUGGLE FOR SEXUAL IDENTITY. Written by literary critic Joseph Epstein, the essay concerned his personal "confusion, revulsion, and fear" over homosexuality. Describing gays and lesbians as cursed, he characterized their lives as a living hell. But Epstein saved his most cutting comment for the conclusion:

> If I had the power to do so, I would wish homosexuality off the face of this earth. I would do so because I think that it brings infinitely more pain than pleasure to those who are forced to live with it; because I think there is no resolution for this pain in our lifetime, only, for the overwhelming majority of homosexuals, more pain and various degrees of exacerbating adjustment; and because, wholly selfishly, I find myself completely incapable of coming to terms with it.[8]

The essay sparked an uproar among members of the Gay Activists Alliance, who fired off a hastily written letter to Editor in Chief Willie Morris to demand a comparable article told from their viewpoint. Although Morris claimed to be open to the idea, he rejected each draft submitted. Even when the gays offered to hire a professional writer, Morris refused to cooperate.

Finally, at nine o'clock on Tuesday morning, October 27, forty activists, wearing overcoats to conceal dark blue T-shirts emblazoned with GAA's gold lambda insignia, quietly made their way into the building to the eighteenth-floor *Harper's* offices. They had already alerted the media, and WOR sent a camera crew to follow them inside. As they barged through the door to the reception area, several announced to the startled receptionist, "Hello, I'm a homosexual. I'm here to show you what homosexuals are really like."[9]

In the reception area one group set up a table with coffee and donuts, while another contingent distributed leaflets throughout the staff's private offices. As the startled workers arrived for the day, the gays welcomed each with a handshake and refreshments. GAA borrowed the idea from a protest of media coverage by the women's movement in the spring of 1970. Nearly one hundred women had seized the offices of *Ladies' Home Journal* for eleven hours, eventually convincing the male editor to devote a forthcoming issue to women's liberation.

"We were very aware that if we could make something visually amusing or find some way to get the press in on it—preferably TV—that was what we had to do," GAA's Peter Fisher said. "One of the main thrusts was to show ourselves as individual human beings—the man or the woman next door or a coworker."[10]

The drama escalated when the men located the office of Midge Decter, the editor of the Epstein article.[11] There Arthur Evans, GAA president, immediately erupted into a tirade that was captured by a radio reporter who played it on an afternoon broadcast:

> You knew that article would contribute to the suffering of homosexuals! You knew that! And if you didn't know that, you're inexcusably naive and should not be an editor. If you know that those views contribute to the oppression of homosexuals, then damn you for publishing it, and we have a right to come here and hold you politically and morally responsible for doing that. You are a bigot, and you are to be held responsible for that moral and political act![12]

Decter argued to no avail that the article was misread. Although she could have called the police to have the protesters arrested, she chose instead to debate. "It does not reinforce antihomosexual prejudice," she insisted. "The question of changing the minds and hearts of men is a complicated one that does not yield to political demands."[13]

As the two vented their anger at each other, tape recorders captured every word. New York's WOR used its film in a three-part series on the broader issue of gay liberation that incorporated interviews with GAA stalwart Arthur Bell and Barbara Gittings, founder of New York DOB. News director Lem Tucker later boasted that the series boosted his ratings by nearly five points.[14]

MERLE MILLER COMES OUT

Although the *Harper's* article was one of the most insulting to appear in the media, it galvanized gays and lesbians who had never become involved in gay liberation at a public level. Among them was Merle Miller, a writer known for his novels and his biographies of presidents Harry Truman and Lyndon Johnson and a former managing editor of *Harper's*.

A soft-spoken man who kept to himself, Miller helped GAA plan its *Harper's* zap. Although a prior commitment prevented him from attending, he sent a strongly worded letter to the magazine's editors to voice his concerns. He wrote,

Mr. Epstein's piece would have been deplorable in the 1930s; in 1970 it is frightening, aggressive, inaccurate, silly, but above all, dangerous. I am told a number
of thinking people feel the way Mr. Epstein does. I cannot believe, however, that
Harper's would have printed such an attack on any other minority group in
America.[15]

Epstein's article continued to nag at Miller. This was clear to two *New York
Times* editors when they met Miller for lunch to discuss an article he was
writing on an unrelated topic for the *Times* magazine. Victor Navasky, one of
the editors, arrived at the restaurant, and found Miller and *Times* editor
Gerald Walker discussing the *Harper's* article, which Navasky had shown to
Walker a few days earlier. Walker had just finished writing *Cruising*, a novel
that some considered homophobic because its plot revolved around a serial
killer who prowled gay bars for victims.

Navasky reconstructed the ensuing discussion:

MILLER: I understand you told Gerry to read the article. Well, you
know it's—

NAVASKY: (interrupting): Yeah, it's a powerful article, but it's disturbing, there's an oddness.

MILLER: I'll tell you what's wrong with it—it's not that way.

NAVASKY: What's not that way?

MILLER: Epstein is saying that he regards homosexuality as being
crippled. It's not that way.[16]

Navasky recalled that Miller's comments set off a discussion about what it
was like to be gay, and Miller acknowledged, "This is the first time that I'm
telling somebody that I'm gay—that I'm telling a straight person that I am
gay." (Miller described the discussion as more heated, recalling that he told
the editor, "Look, goddamn it, I'm homosexual, and most of my best friends
are Jewish homosexuals, and some of my friends are black homosexuals, and
I'm sick and tired of reading and hearing such goddamn demeaning, degrading bullshit about me and my friends.")

Miller was at the *Times* a few days later to use the library when Navasky
asked whether he would be willing to write an article about what he'd said
at lunch. Miller was intrigued but skeptical that the *Times* would actually
print what he had to say. "In my mind, I suspect on everybody's, including
Miller's [mind], it was almost unthinkable that the *Times* would print the

piece that we were discussing," Navasky said. "It was long before people would be coming out in that way, and it was certainly long before the *New York Times* was ready to do anything like that. So, we said, there's only one way to find out."[17]

The magazine section of the *Times* had long operated almost as a separate publication, with its own staff and an editor who reported directly to the newspaper's executive editor. Unlike the general news sections of the paper, which adhered to a strict standard of objectivity, the magazine allowed writers some latitude to express their personal opinions and served as a showcase for in-depth features. Even so, Miller's was one of the most controversial subjects the magazine could tackle.

Miller agreed to write the piece but the idea still needed the approval of Gabe Schwartz, editor of the magazine. As Navasky and Walker discussed how they would approach Schwartz, Walker grew concerned that his involvement might be misinterpreted. With his gay-themed novel about to come out, Walker was afraid Schwartz and others would think he was promoting the subject. Navasky agreed that he would present the idea at the magazine's next editorial meeting.

A few days later Navasky presented the idea to Schwartz and the other editors. He described it as Miller's account of the changing attitude toward homosexuality, including his own. At the end of the long meeting Schwartz consented but warned that the article still might run into trouble with the newspaper's hierarchy. Navasky called Miller to tell him and, reflecting Schwartz's concern, told him, "You won't advocate in it, will you?" Miller assured him there were two things he was not about to recruit for: homosexuality and the army.[18]

GAY TIMES

As Merle Miller worked on his groundbreaking essay, GAA tried to generate publicity for the movement by asking candidates for political office in New York City in 1970 to endorse a gay rights platform. Many political insiders considered such a stance political suicide. Nonetheless, it represented the first attempt to harness gays and lesbians into a mainstream political force. Surprisingly, GAA won support from three candidates and set out to make sure the accomplishment was noted by the news media. Arthur Bell and Marc Rubin hand-carried press releases to newspapers and broadcast stations throughout the city. A reporter at the *New York Times* gave them the impression that a story would run on the front page the following Monday. But when the papers arrived on Monday morning, neither the *Times* nor the *Post* mentioned the endorsements.

When the story did appear on October 27—the next day—it was far from the cymbal-crashing announcement GAA had anticipated. 3 CANDIDATES SUPPORT RIGHTS OF HOMOSEXUALS was the headline above three short paragraphs at the bottom of page thirty-six. The *Times* also downplayed the introduction of the first gay rights legislation in the nation when it came before the New York City Council in January 1971. The *Times* devoted a considerably longer story to the rejection of GAA's application to incorporate as a nonprofit organization. The state comptroller claimed the organization could not use the term *gay* in its name.[19]

Convinced that the *Times* would only portray gays as villains or ignore them, Jim Owles, the charismatic twenty-three-year-old president of GAA, and five others from the organization took their complaints to Marvin Siegel, an assistant metropolitan editor who met with them on January 12, 1971. For close to an hour Siegel listened politely to their complaints of a media "brownout" but made no promises that coverage would change.

By March it was clear that the pattern would continue. That was especially apparent to gay and lesbian activists following a March 14, 1971, rally at the state capitol in Albany to support the state's first gay rights bill. The rally on the steps of the State Assembly drew a crowd of more than twenty-five hundred. In comparison, before the Stonewall riots in 1969, activists would have been lucky to draw fifty. Although the demonstration was the largest ever held by homosexuals, the *Times* ignored the outpouring of support and concentrated instead on the defeat of the proposal, which lost by a surprisingly close vote of 85–60.

COMING OUT IN THE *TIMES*

Merle Miller labored over his essay for the *Times* throughout the fall of 1970 at his home in Brewster, a quiet town just north of New York City. He found it difficult to organize his thoughts. Never before had he delved so deeply into his psyche. Although he was not eager to mount a personal crusade for gay rights or reveal his private thoughts, he was determined to respond to the hatred Epstein had expressed in *Harper's*.

One morning in November 1970 Miller read a front page article in the *Times* describing how British writer E. M. Forster had withheld publication of his great gay novel *Maurice* until after his death.[20] Having admired Forster both as a writer and as man, Miller read about the writer's closeted life and was spurred to rethink his own. Two days later he submitted his essay to Navasky.

"I remember the day it came in," Navasky said. "Articles were routinely photocopied, and people read them simultaneously—even though the copies moved from desk to desk—and there was a unanimous, immediate consensus that this was something very special and it had to be published. There was also a feeling that it should be published earlier rather than later. And that's what happened."[21]

WHAT IT MEANS TO BE A HOMOSEXUAL appeared on Sunday, January 17, 1971, with only minor changes to fit space limitations. Miller movingly described the pain of growing up gay—aware but hiding the fact—in his native Iowa. He explained how he had spent his entire life trying to avoid being called sissy. As city editor of his college newspaper, the *Daily Iowan*, he had modeled himself after a character in *The Front Page*. He wore his hat indoors, spoke out of the corner of his mouth—never without a cigarette—maintained a cozy relationship with the cops, and denounced "queers" regularly, all in an effort to hide his true identity.[22]

Miller continued his ruse during a tour in the army and later when he served as an editor at *Time*. At one point he even sought unsuccessful psychiatric treatment to convert to heterosexuality. In a book published the same year he wrote: "It took me almost fifty years to come out of the closet, to stop pretending to be something I was not, most of the time fooling nobody. . . . I dislike being despised, unless I have done something despicable, realizing that the simple fact of being homosexual is all by itself despicable to many people, maybe, as Mr. Epstein says, to everybody who is straight. Assuming anybody is ever totally one thing sexually."[23]

Miller's article became a landmark. Neither the *Times* nor any other mainstream newspaper had ever published an article by a person who publicly acknowledged his homosexuality. For closeted gays who had never read—or even heard—about the experience of coming out, Miller's description of coming to terms with his sexuality was particularly enlightening.

After it appeared on newsstands, stacks of letters poured in to the *Times* mail room—more than fifteen hundred in the first six weeks alone. The number eventually climbed to nearly five thousand, about 95 percent from homosexuals expressing their appreciation for Miller's candor. They wrote from his home state of Iowa, from prisons, and from as far away as Southeast Asia. "How do we teach this at Larchmont High?" one teacher wanted to know.

Not all readers appreciated Miller's candor, however. The reaction of anti-gay psychiatrists bordered on the hysterical. "I'll take you into therapy for free, but since you're too old, there's really not much point," wrote one. Another said, "It is clear that you still have not adjusted to your affliction or to the society in which we live, and while it may be too late . . . for your own peace of mind, I think you should submit yourself to psychiatric treatment."[24]

Some of Miller's friends responded in a similar manner. Apparently fearing guilt by association, two announced that they would no longer see him. His mother briefly disinherited him. ABC Television canceled his contract to write a program. Even some gay activists criticized his article as a "middle-aged sob story."[25] But Miller knew he had taken an important first step, not just for his own life but for honest and accurate press coverage of the lives of gays and lesbians.

BACKLASH AT THE *TIMES*

Two weeks after Miller's article appeared, the *Times* ran a February 10 article headlined HOMOSEXUALITY: PARENTS AREN'T ALWAYS TO BLAME, by Jane Brody, an award-winning science writer at the *Times* who was well on her way to becoming a national authority on health and nutrition.

For her article on homosexuals Brody focused on new research conducted by New York psychiatrist Lawrence Hatterer into the cause of homosexuality. "Dr. Hatterer believes that environmental and cultural factors are becoming increasingly important contributors to the development of homosexuality," Brody wrote. "Psychiatrists agree that it is by no means easy to turn a child into a homosexual, and most children seem able to resist even the worst combination of influences."[26]

Two weeks later Brody wrote an even more extensive article that ran on the front page, MORE HOMOSEXUALS AIDED TO BECOME HETEROSEXUAL. In this one Brody used Martin Crowley's off-Broadway play *The Boys in the Band* as her peg for a story about claims by psychiatrists that they could "cure" many homosexuals. It began, "The widely held view that once a homosexual always a homosexual, expressed in Mr. Crowley's drama, is being challenged by specialists around the country. Therapists, using a variety of psychological approaches, have found that the young homosexual who is strongly motivated to change his sexual orientation has an excellent chance of success." Relying exclusively on information provided by psychiatrists and excluding the views of homosexuals, the article was a throwback to a decade earlier.[27]

But Stuart Byron, a gay film critic for the *Village Voice*, was concerned about Brody's interest in the psychiatric angle because the "homosexuals are sick" theme had not appeared in the *Times* for seven years. According to an account he wrote for the *Voice*, Brody's editors had long rejected her attempts to write about homosexuals. But when Miller's article appeared, Byron claimed that Brody used it as leverage to convince the editors she should be allowed to tell the "other side of the story."[28]

A similar instance of the *Times*'s journalistic balancing appeared on March 28 when Judy Klemesrud wrote an in-depth story about the New York chapter of the Daughters of Bilitis. DOB had risen to a new level of recognition after Kate Millett, one of the chief architects of the women's liberation movement, told a meeting of DOB that she was bisexual. The disclosure revealed a deep schism between heterosexuals and lesbians in the women's movement. *Time* put Millett on its cover in a story about the rift.

While covering the story for the *New York Times*, Klemesrud mentioned to Ruth Simpson, then president of the New York DOB chapter, that she was interested in doing an in-depth article on the organization. Recognizing the story as a rare opportunity for publicity, Simpson agreed to be interviewed. But when the article appeared in print, it was riddled with antigay comments from several sources. Harvey E. Kaye, for example, was described as a Manhattan psychiatrist who had headed a 1967 study for the Society of Medical Psychoanalysts that defined lesbianism. "I consider lesbianism an inhibitory aspect of the heterosexual drive," Kaye attested in the *Times* article. "If you want to treat an inhibition, you can treat it. But you don't have to treat it. It's like arthritis; if someone has an arthritic finger, you can treat it if you want to."[29]

Protest letters poured in to the newspaper from members of both DOB and GAA. Gay and lesbian activists were particularly concerned that the article might jeopardize gay rights bills that were pending in both the New York state legislature and the city council. On April 16 Klemesrud, responding in a letter to GAA president Jim Owles, confirmed what the activists had long suspected. "You say I had to 'balance' this with psychiatric statements," she wrote. "You are right. It was done at the request of the editors. I did not agree with them, but I thought the piece was worth saving so I did it."[30]

As a result GAA hastily assembled a small committee to retaliate, hoping it could draw enough attention to embarrass the *Times*, its editors, and publisher. To kick off the campaign the organization invited fifty reporters to a press conference. Only six attended—three freelance writers and one each from ABC Radio, *Women's Wear Daily*, and a popular magazine, *Coronet*. Reporters were outnumbered by activists three to one. The *Times* sent no one.

GAA's Eben Clark blasted the media for "refusing to print news contrary to the American image." He complained that the media were eager to publish shock stories while ignoring news of a healthier nature. He was particularly critical of the "laundry list," in which homosexuals were often categorized alongside drug addicts, prostitutes, and child molesters.[31]

As a next step GAA threatened a boycott of the *Times* if its coverage of gays did not improve. The group erected posters at subway entrances and passed out flyers outside the newspaper's offices that read, "The N.Y. Times may think it's making up for its lack of reporting of homosexual political news by permitting occasional opinion pieces. But New Yorkers have a right to know the real news when it happens. WE ACCUSE the management of the Times of creating debates about the sanity of homosexuals while censoring out political news. WE ACCUSE the Times of attempting to muzzle and suppress the reality of a movement of which they do not approve."[32]

A few weeks later the activists stepped up their protest with a strongly worded letter directed to every employee on the *Times* staff. It said,

> Every Gay who's worked in the media knows the special problems. Any reporter, Gay or straight, who takes an unusual interest in Gay news or understands its meaning or who doesn't temper it with bigoted inaccuracies is immediately suspect. . . . It is time for at least some Gays on the *Times* to come out of the closet. Not only to help your editors evaluate Gay news when it happens, but also to act as viable barriers against bigotry and the perpetuation of myths by straight reporters and editors.[33]

Although gay activists were urging gay journalists to come out, everything about the culture of the newsroom told them not to do it. "So far as I can discover no gays emerged as a result of the GAA letter," Merle Miller wrote in *More*, the journalism review, "although there are surely as many covert gays in the editorial offices of the *Times* as in any other organization of similar size." Miller described a closeted gay writer in the cultural news department who resigned when he failed to win a promotion to a better job. Apparently someone questioned whether a homosexual was "emotionally stable enough to handle the job."[34] This was the atmosphere that dominated the industry.

Although the letter failed to empty the closets of gays in the *Times* newsroom, it caught the attention of other journalists, including reporter Joseph Lelyveld, who, according to Merle Miller, told colleagues it was valid criticism. The following June Lelyveld was assigned to write a preview of the second annual Christopher Street Liberation Day observance of the Stonewall riots. MILITANT HOMOSEXUALS TO STAGE MARCH TO CENTRAL PARK TODAY provided an overview of the concerns and accomplishments of the gay liberation movement and marked the first time the newspaper had reported on gays without including comments from antigay psychiatrists.[35]

LOIS LANE IS A LESBIAN

Jill Johnston emerged from the media closet incrementally through several articles in the *Village Voice*, beginning with one that appeared six months before Miller's. It did not attract thousands of letters from readers, but it did attract considerable attention among lesbian readers.

An art and dance critic, Johnston had never heard of the *Voice* until an editor contacted her in 1959 about writing a column. The fledgling newspaper was only four years old and seeking writers who would contribute articles without pay until it could build a readership among the eclectic Village crowd. For young writers like Johnston, who was writing for *Art News*, the *Voice* offered an opportunity to hone their writing skills in an atmosphere that encouraged experimentation and individuality.

After her marriage ended in 1962 and Johnston was unable to care for her two children alone, she went through a period she described as "a tumultuous kind of breakdown" in 1965. In the aftermath she felt as though she was on a slow burn back into the reality of Earth as virtually everything about her life changed. Her dance column reflected the upheaval and became an anecdotal account of her transformation.

In the mid-1960s Johnston became more interested in herself and less interested in criticism. She wrote about anything that struck her as interesting. Sometimes she incorporated the graffiti she saw in women's restrooms. When she traveled, she wrote about her adventures in whatever city or town she happened to be in. The articles became so fascinating that few noticed that she seldom mentioned dance. "Who gave you permission to start writing your autobiography?" barked Editor Dan Wolf when he finally realized the change. But by then the column was a fait accompli, and it had become popular in the art world.

"Around 1969, I found out that men ran the world, and that I was a member of quite a few minorities," she wrote years later.[36] Her first venture out of the closet and into print came on July 2, 1970, in an article that marked the first anniversary of the Stonewall riots. Entitled OF THIS PURE BUT IRREGULAR PASSION, it began,

> In support of the gay movement on the occasion of the gay celebration week: I guess yes I've been saying it in this column for a year and a half now, but always fragmentarily in the context of literary exercises. So this will be straight on. I don't recall any decision to declare my sexuality, in print, as though it should necessarily have interested anybody in any case. . . . Gradually the life became the theater became the column: The life being everything of course included everything. Sex was especially interesting since I was in love with a beautiful girl.[37]

Johnston's obscure brand of prose evolved from her immersion in the art world and the aesthetic consciousness of the sixties. Her message may have seemed confused to many readers, but it resonated among lesbians. "Have you read anything like this lately?" *The Ladder* asked. "This woman has a column called 'Dance Journal' which appears regularly in *The Village Voice*, discussing everything but dance. . . . The dance this lady discusses is of vital importance to all of us." When Lois Hart and some other women in GLF discovered Johnston's writing, they set out to recruit her for the liberation movement. "I can't say I became convinced of anything right away," Johnston said of that period, "but obviously, from July 1970, this had already happened and I was beginning to become militant."[38]

In the fall of 1970 Johnston drove from New York to California and used the trip as fodder for her columns. For one of them the *Voice* carried a front page headline that catapulted her sexuality into the open: LOIS LANE IS A LESBIAN—PAGE 8.

The March 4, 1971, article described Johnston's fury over the discrimination faced by a group of lesbians she had met in Texas. "I was starting to put it into my column because I didn't know how not to tell the truth, and I was traveling with a lover I was absolutely wild about and this was seeping into my columns," she said. "There was an incredible sense that the whole world was going to come out." In stream-of-consciousness prose she described the beginning of her militant feminism: "Polymorphous perversity is the norm. There is no norm. Unless it's [Norman] Mailer, who perfectly embodies the heterosexual problem. I think all of us are authorities on the heterosexual problem. Knowledge on the subject is instantly available, in case you've missed out, in every daily newspaper with their front page accounts of the Wars. We are bored with the news from the heterosexual fronts. We want to hear from the lesbians and the homosexuals now."[39]

The response to the article was startling even for Johnston, who quickly found herself at the epicenter of a controversy over lesbianism and feminism. "Jill Johnston, who has made her Lesbianism patently clear to all but the most obtuse in past *Village Voice* columns on the dance of life," said *The Ladder*, "now publicly states that fact for us in this column. Unfortunately, she also introduces a conglomeration of theoretical philosophy that will confuse anyone who is not thoroughly familiar with Lesbian literature."[40]

By August 1970 Johnston was beginning to look more like a meteor than a rising star. The high point came at a fundraiser for the women's movement at the Hamptons estate of Ethel Scull, who was married to a wealthy taxicab magnate. The crowd included celebrities and reporters from a host of publications such as the *New York Times*, *Time*, *Newsweek*, and the Associated Press. During a talk by Gloria Steinem the crowd suddenly realized that a woman had stripped off her shirt and jeans and was swimming barebreasted in the pool. It was Jill Johnston. One spectator speculated that she was protesting members of the movement who disliked lesbians. Betty Friedan, watching the incident, muttered, "One of the biggest enemies of the movement." *Times* society writer Charlotte Curtis overheard the comment and printed it.[41]

The schism between the feminists and the lesbians only widened the next spring, and again Johnston found herself standing at the fault line that separated the two factions. In late April 1971 she was invited to appear on a panel at what was billed as "Town Hall, A Dialogue on Women's Liberation." The other panelists were Germaine Greer (author of *The Female Eunuch*), Jacqueline Ceballos (president of the New York chapter of the National Organization for Women), Diana Trilling (literary and social critic), and moderator Norman Mailer, who had just written *The Prisoner of Sex*. Tension was already running high in the capacity crowd when Johnston took to the dais and launched into a prose diatribe. The text of her comments later appeared in its entirety in her *Voice* column in the same breathless, single-paragraph poetic style in which she had delivered it at the "Town Hall":

> All women are lesbians except those who don't know it naturally they are but don't know it yet I am a woman who is a lesbian because I am a woman and a woman who loves herself naturally who is other women is a lesbian a woman who loves women loves herself naturally this is the case that a woman is herself is all woman is a natural born lesbian so we don't mind using the name like any name it is quite meaningless.[42]

After fifteen minutes Mailer attempted to cut her off, a prearranged cue for two other women to leap onto the stage and begin caressing and embracing Johnston as they rolled on the floor to simulate a lesbian orgy. For many in the audience it was theater of the absurd. For Johnston it was the exclamation point that punctuated her monologue. The theater erupted, with women and men heckling, shouting, and hissing at Johnston and the other panelists. "It was the night that turned my hair gray," Mailer later commented.[43] A writer for the *Village Voice* compared it with a graduation exercise in which "the brightest pupils in the school recite their verbal calisthenics to an auditorium of seat-induced paraplegics."[44]

Johnston became more widely known in 1973 with the publication of *Lesbian Nation: The Feminist Solution*, a collection of essays, many of which had appeared in her column, that spelled out her separatist lesbian-feminist philosophy. "We had a powerful illusion that we really were going to institute something called Lesbian Nation," Johnston recalled. But she had been trying to understand herself in the midst of a schism in the women's movement. Friedan and her followers feared that the lesbians—Jill Johnston in particular—were going to scare off the suburbanites. To Friedan and others Johnston represented everything that was undesirable about lesbianism. Johnston became the target of a media backlash. One reviewer said of *Lesbian Nation*, "What's sad is that in her zeal Ms. Johnston demeans her own cause."[45]

In the spring of 1974 a group of investors that included Clay Felker, editor of *New York* magazine, bought the *Voice* and cleaned house. Johnston was one of his first targets. He criticized her writing style, which avoided most forms of punctuation and syntax. She felt that conventional rules of grammar masculinized her work. Felker called it "elitist in the extreme." "I agree that what she has to say is important, that she is original and a unique mind, an important contribution, but it isn't a contribution if nobody can read it," he remarked.[46]

Johnston was cut adrift from her newspaper and for several months found no writing assignments at all. "To the right of me," she later recalled, "the establishment said no, they would not support me any longer in my outrages; to the left of me, the radicals whose causes I adopted and championed said no, they would not rescue me from the establishment."[47]

Naively, perhaps, Johnston thought that she could use her credibility at the *Voice* to ride the notoriety forever. But with her column killed and her role in the women's movement damaged, she faded from public view, leaving the media without a crucial lesbian voice. She was an individualist who was propelled by her knowledge of the art world and an almost desperate yearning to be a writer. In 1983 she published *Mother Bound*, followed by *Paper Daughter* in 1985. She also concentrated on writing criticism for *Art in America* and book reviews for the *New York Times*. "The revolution was over," she said. Her mother had died, she was becoming a grandmother, and she had settled down with another woman. In reflecting on her evolution as a lesbian activist, she commented, "I didn't understand how society works, that there were these people in the background who own and run the media who use people up front to act out for them because they are angry about one thing or another. I didn't see myself being used in that way. People said I was heroic but I never saw that."[48]

6

BECOMING VISIBLE

While some journalists were slowly emerging from newsroom closets in the early 1970s, Arthur Bell burst out. He had decided that when gay liberation arrived, so had he. Long fascinated by news, Bell had no formal journalistic training. He took a publicist's job at Random House, where he wrote promotional copy for children's books.

In his off hours Bell hung out with friends in an off-off-Broadway theater crowd at the popular Café Cino. It was not exclusively gay, but the cafe exemplified the type of freedom Bell yearned for. "The Cino group made me want to assert my own gayness to the world, no matter what the world said was wrong," he later wrote.[1]

During this period of 1965 Bell's sexual orientation became known among his coworkers at Random House. After one of them happened to see him kiss his boyfriend at a subway station, word circulated that "little Arthur's a faggot." Bell took the incident in stride. After spending several "high-falutin' years" in a monogamous relationship with a closeted interior decorator, he quipped that "the stigma was a blessing." In late 1968 Bell became interested in political activism when he came across feminist literature that pioneering feminists Robin Morgan and Ti-Grace Atkinson were handing out to Random House employees. "My secretary would talk about how she demanded equal rights," he once wrote, "and I'd think to myself, 'Baby, you are not alone.'"[2]

Bell was out of town when gays rioted outside the Stonewall Inn. After his return he started attending Gay Liberation Front (GLF) meetings. But the meetings tended to be chaotic. Born of the same socialist philosophy as the student antiwar movement, GLF had no elected leaders. Its business was conducted by consensus. Many meetings deteriorated into loud screaming matches that in only a few weeks began to frustrate some of the more moderate members.

In December 1969 Bell and several other activists fled the chaos and created their own organization, Gay Activists Alliance (GAA), committing themselves to gay liberation and to a strict organizational discipline based on *Robert's Rules of Order*. Bell became GAA's publicity chairman and at the same time expressed his activism through articles he wrote for *Gay Power*, a left-wing newspaper owned by the *East Village Other*, that later turned pornographic.[3] After Jack Nichols and Lige Clarke started *Gay* shortly after the Stonewall riots, Bell left *Gay Power* and became a regular contributor to *Gay*.

But Bell continued to push for more and better coverage from publications with an established readership, particularly the *Village Voice*. His incessant cajoling to cover the fledgling gay movement wore thin in August 1970. "If it's so important," City Editor Mary Nichols snapped at him one day, "why don't you go and cover it yourself?" That was all the invitation Bell needed, and he began to submit articles.

In his first he wrote about a GAA zap at Rockefeller for Governor campaign headquarters, and the story, GAY IS POLITICAL AND DEMOCRATS AGREE, appeared on the front page of the August 13, 1970, issue. "Gay did not die after Gay Pride Week—it just lay dormant for a month," it began. "It sprang back full force last week with a couple of actions that reached out beyond New York's homosexual community to the political arenas of both the Democratic and Republican parties."

Later that year rumors began to circulate that Vice President Spiro Agnew's twenty-four-year-old son Randy had separated from his wife and was having an affair with Buddy Hash, a Baltimore hairdresser. Bell convinced the editors at *Gay* and the *Voice* to split the cost of sending him to investigate. "Buddy Hash is a businessman," young Agnew explained to Bell during an interview. "He spends long hours at his shop. What he does after hours, I don't know." Bell concluded that his investigation had yielded "delicious non-stories" for the two publications. Agnew was heterosexual. After his story appeared in the *Voice*, a producer at NBC canceled Bell's scheduled appearance on the *Today Show* as a GAA representative. But four months later the producers rebooked him for January 13, 1971, to discuss gay liberation. The network received more than five hundred letters, most of them negative. One asked whether the producers also planned to have rapists and murderers on their program.[4]

Bell saw no conflict in his alternating roles of activist and journalist. He considered it merely taking off one hat and putting on another. (Soon after he joined GAA Bell left Random House to become a full-time activist and freelance writer. His first book, *Dancing the Gay Lib Blues*, one of the earliest chronicles of GAA's first year, was published in 1971.) In April 1972 Bell instigated GAA's largest media protest at the *New York Daily News* after the U.S. Supreme Court refused to hear the case of Mike McConnell, a young gay man who had been fired by the University of Minnesota after he and his male lover applied for a marriage license. Bell and others recognized that the decision had allowed the government to continue its McCarthy-era practice of firing people because they were homosexual. The *Daily News* had applauded the Court's decision in a homophobic editorial titled ANY OLD JOBS FOR HOMOS? The editorial included this passage:

> Herewith, a cheer for the U.S. Supreme Court's ruling Monday (with Justice W. O. Douglas dissenting—but you knew that) that state governments have a right to refuse employment to homosexuals. Fairies, nances, swishes, fags, lezzes—call 'em what you please—should of course be permitted to earn honest livings in nonsensitive jobs. But government, from federal on down, should have full freedom to bar them from jobs in which their peculiarities would make them security or other risks. It is to be hoped that this Supreme Court decision will stand for the foreseeable future.[5]

A few days later Bell led a protest by 250 gays and lesbians from a dozen

ANY OLD JOBS FOR HOMOS?

Herewith, a cheer for the U.S. Supreme Court's ruling Monday (with Justice W. O. Douglas dissenting—but you knew that) that state governments have a right to refuse employment to homosexuals.

Fairies, nances, swishes, fags, lezzes—call 'em what you please—should of course be permitted to earn honest livings in nonsensitive jobs.

But government, from federal on down, should have

New York Daily News, April 5, 1972 (© New York Daily News, L.P., used with permission)

gay organizations outside the *Daily News*. SPELL IT RIGHT: LESBIANS, NOT LEZZES, several signs read. The protest attracted little attention until about fifty demonstrators burst through the front doors and climbed the stairs to the newspaper's seventh-floor newsroom. Pandemonium erupted when an employee attacked the contingent, knocking the glasses off the face of one protester. While a member of the Daughters of Bilitis was trying to make a call from a newsroom telephone, an employee walked up and slapped her. She shoved him against a wall and forced him to tell her his name, which she yelled to reporters to jot down. When police arrived, four demonstrators were taken to jail, including Bell who tried to avoid the charges by claiming he was covering the story for the *Voice*. But the judge rejected his claim and ruled that all had trespassed, a misdemeanor that carried a maximum fine of $250 and fifteen days in jail. The judge suspended the sentence of each who agreed not to trespass again.

Although Bell's zapping days were effectively over because he could not risk another arrest, other GAA members staged one of their largest and most disruptive zaps in the spring of 1972. The target was the fiftieth annual Inner Circle Dinner, a roast sponsored by political journalists. Members of GAA learned that one skit planned for the dinner show contained derogatory comments about the gay rights bill that had been killed by a city council committee. During an intermission in the show a GAA group charged into the banquet hall and moved from table to table, passing out leaflets and shouting at the journalists and their guests, including Mayor John Lindsay.

When the uproar died down and the activists began leaving the hall, several men suddenly attacked some of the activists on the hotel escalator. They brutally punched and kicked the demonstrators, severely injuring GAA member Morty Manford. Although the hall was filled with journalists, the next day's *New York Times* and *Daily News* made no mention of the attack. Pete Hamill's column in the *Post* the following Monday referred to it in passing.

The media did take note three days later when GAA held a press conference to announce that Manford and several other members had been severely beaten and were filing assault charges against six men, including Michael J. Maye, a 210-pound former Golden Gloves heavyweight champion prizefighter who headed the eleven thousand–member Uniformed Firefighters Association of Greater New York. The fire fighters had been the most outspoken opponents of the proposed gay rights ordinance (along with the Catholic church). Maye told a grand jury that he never touched anyone except for a "golden-haired homosexual" who had grabbed his groin and torn his pants. He claimed he ejected the man from the ballroom after the man began shouting obscenities in front of Maye's wife and other women. The assault charges against Maye were later reduced to harassment and he was acquitted.[6]

In the meantime Arthur Bell and other GAA members recognized that zaps had lost their effectiveness. People simply did not shock as easily any more. And the zaps had become dangerous. Bell increasingly turned his attention to writing, particularly crime news. He had developed a strong rapport with many cops in the sixth precinct in the Village, the same precinct that had conducted the 1969 raid on the Stonewall Inn. In August 1972 those contacts paid off when he got an inside account of a bank robbery in Brooklyn in which the robber claimed he needed money for his lover's sex-change operation. The holdup and subsequent standoff with police became the basis of the 1975 movie *Dog Day Afternoon*.[7]

As the city council continued to refuse to enact a gay rights bill, he and some other activists grew increasingly disillusioned and slowly began to turn their attention to other interests. "Gay liberation as we knew it in 69–72 is dead," Bell told some of his friends. "People don't shock easily any more."[8]

Bell was also writing about entertainment, concentrating mostly on movies and movie stars. He and his friend Vito Russo routinely attacked Hollywood for its homophobic approach to homosexuality. "Let *Boys in the Band* die," he wrote in a 1973 op-ed piece for the *New York Times* after the Broadway play became a movie. "A steady diet of this fodder causes gay radicals to take up arms and gay inverts to stay in their closets and gay isolationists—with only the movies and television as nourishment—to consider suicide and gay activists to picket and make loud noises to stop this emotional destruction," he wrote.[9] His fascination with New York nightlife led to a regular column in the *Voice* in 1973. Called Bell Tells, the column provided him a unique platform from which to rave and rant, praise and cajole in his own style of gay liberation consciousness.

OUT AT THE *BOSTON GLOBE*

Reporter Kay Longcope knew of no openly gay journalists when she joined the *Record-Chronicle* of Denton, Texas, in the early 1960s. Longcope was fresh out of college and beginning her career. Soon she began to find disturbing little notes on her car. Some of them contained only one word: *Dyke!* The message, of course, was that someone in the newsroom had figured out that she was different and didn't like it.

After leaving the Texas newspaper, she accepted a job at the National Council of Churches in New York, where she coordinated the organization's national civil rights projects. But she soon realized that the council's idea of civil rights did not include gays. The personnel director called her into his office one day and asked, "Are you a lesbian?" Looking him straight in the eyes she responded, "How can you even think such a thing?" Her denial enabled her to keep her job, but it left an indelible mark on her psyche. "That was the first time and the last time that I would ever lie about who and what I am," she vowed.[10]

In November 1970 Longcope returned to newspaper work and became an urban affairs reporter for the highly regarded *Boston Globe*. She was one of a small number of women journalists. Census figures showed twice as many men as women working in the nation's newsrooms, and most of the women were confined to low-paying jobs in the lower echelons.[11]

Women were rare, but an openly lesbian reporter was virtually unimaginable. Lesbians knew that by revealing their sexual orientation they would only worsen the prejudice they already faced as women in the male-dominated news business. Only a few months after taking the job at the *Globe*, Longcope began to find antigay messages stuffed in her mail box. One was a postcard showing a group of bikini-clad women. Another time someone let the air out of her tires.

"There were rumors and I didn't do anything to counteract them," Longcope said. "The old guard was white Irishmen, who were straight and, of course, Roman Catholic—Boston being Boston. But I decided that I could work with anybody and that if I just did my job and did it to the best of my ability, no one could criticize me. I took a lot of static, and I know there were raises and bonuses I didn't get, but I broke a lot of news stories."[12]

In April 1973 Longcope faced her most difficult test yet. She received a telephone call from a source who informed her that a local Methodist minister was about to conduct a marriage ceremony for two Boston gay men. Because Longcope covered religion for the *Globe*, the story fell squarely within her beat. The next day a headline on a page five story read MINISTER MARRIES GAYS OVER BISHOP'S OBJECTION. Next to the headline was a photograph of two smiling, bearded, shaggy-haired men holding each other's hands at a church altar.[13]

It would have been easy for Longcope to drop the story at that point, but three weeks later she learned that the minister had been fired. She wrote a second story and then a third.

"No one in their right mind would have denied it was news—certainly not me. I wasn't trying to do advocacy journalism," she said, "I was just trying to report a community that is part of the general population. But one editor told me that all I did was the kinky stuff—like women, gays, and lesbians. But I didn't shun those issues because those were *the* issues facing the world of religion."[14]

As far as Longcope was concerned, allowing a story about gays to appear under her byline was tantamount to announcing that she was a lesbian. Her interest in the story and her willingness to suggest it to her editors spoke decibels about her personal life, regardless of whether that was her intention.

By making her sexuality known in 1973 Kay Longcope may well have been the first acknowledged lesbian on a major metropolitan daily. At that time psychiatrists still officially classified homosexuality as a chronic mental illness.

THE MIRACLE CURE

As GLF and later GAA were trying to knock down the media's barriers to covering gay news, the Mattachine Society of Washington was questioning the expertise of clinical psychiatrists by confronting them at public forums. One of the earliest and most widely publicized confrontations occurred at the American Medical Association convention in San Francisco in June 1968. The clash generated stories in the San Francisco dailies and raised the awareness of sympathetic factions of the medical profession. It also provided ample incentive for militant gays to step up their pressure.

In May 1970 militant members of Daughters of Bilitis (DOB) and the Society for Individual Rights (SIR) targeted the annual meeting of the American Psychiatric Association (APA), which was also held in San Francisco. During a session on "aversion therapy," the DOB and SIR members leaped from their seats and began shouting at the psychiatrists, arguing that their nauseating drugs and electroshock treatments were a form of torture. "You're a maniac!" one of the psychiatrists screamed in response to a gay protester. Another became so angry that he suggested that the police shoot the protesters.[15]

It was one of the few times that journalists from major news organizations had witnessed such a shocking display of the blatant bias of antigay psychiatrists.

Even so, when some reporters filed their stories, their editors were uncertain how to interpret them. "When I described the story to the editors, they weren't very excited about it," recalled the *Washington Post*'s Stuart Auerbach. "But when it came in to the newsroom, they recognized that it seemed to catch a spirit of national madness. I got a call at about five o'clock in the morning [Pacific Standard Time] from the general manager of the paper to say that after all of the dreary news we had had in the paper, here finally was a story that made him laugh." The *Post* and several other newspapers had been tipped by gay activists that they would try to disrupt the session on aversion therapy.[16]

Auerbach's page one story, GAYS AND DOLLS BATTLE SHRINKS, reported on May 15, 1970, that a distinguished Boston psychiatrist, Dr. Leo Alexander, had grabbed a feminist who was invited onto the stage. When she denounced his action from the podium, Alexander lunged on stage after her. He had to be restrained and led back to his front-row seat. The feminist, who identified herself as "Judy X," said, "This man wants to put his sadistic hands on me." Back in his seat Alexander, sixty-five, said, "This lack of discipline is disgusting. They should be thrown out." He added that he had arrived at the convention as a strong opponent of California governor Ronald Reagan but that the demonstration had changed his mind. Finally, he diagnosed Judy X as "a paranoid fool and a stupid bitch."[17]

Gay and lesbian activists continued their campaign against the psychiatrists for three more years. In 1970 they invaded the Behavioral Modification Conference at the Biltmore Hotel in Los Angeles while the participants were watching a film about shock therapy for homosexuals. They were unaware that GLF's Morris Kight and several other gay activists had slipped into the

Gays and Dolls
Battle the Shrinks

By Stuart Auerbach
Washington Post Staff Writer

SAN FRANCISCO, May 14—The Gay Liberation and their women allies out-

social behavior as anyone else.

One distinguished Boston

Washington Post, May 15, 1970 (© 1970 The Washington Post, reprinted with permission)

meeting until the activists began to shout, "Barbarism!" "Medieval torture!" and "This is disgusting!" "You must be responsible," Kight admonished the stunned psychiatrists. "With this kind of treatment you could make a Nazi!" The activists demanded that the psychiatrists turn their meeting into a dialogue that included homosexuals.[18]

Hoping to appease the activists, the psychiatrists the next year invited a panel of homosexuals to speak at their convention in Washington. The panel in May 1971 included Franklin Kameny and Lilli Vincenz of the Mattachine Society of Washington; Larry Littlejohn of SIR; Del Martin, a founder of the Daughters of Bilitis; and Jack Baker, the openly gay student body president at the University of Minnesota. Martin told the psychiatrists that they were "the most dangerous enemy of homosexuals in contemporary society." It was both the first panel discussion of the subject by homosexuals at an APA meeting and the first time gays were able to talk to the psychiatrists directly about changing the official designation of homosexuality as a disease.[19]

Despite their inclusion in the program, the activists were not convinced they had gotten their point across. Wearing forged credentials to gain access to the meeting hall, Kameny led a noisy group from the Gay Liberation Front into the convention hall, throwing the meeting into an uproar. "Psychiatry is the enemy incarnate," Kameny roared into a microphone. "Psychiatry has waged a relentless war of extermination against us. You may take this as a declaration of war against you." Although some psychiatrists shook their fists and compared the gays to Nazi storm troopers, others watched their colleagues in dismay.[20]

A schism was forming in the ranks of the psychiatrists; the split would become even more apparent at the American Psychiatric Association's May

1972 convention in Dallas. Kameny and Gittings were invited to attend and to appear on a panel moderated by Judd Marmor, the organization's vice president-elect. In addition, the panel included a masked gay psychiatrist who called himself "Dr. H. Anonymous." Gittings had contacted a half-dozen gay psychiatrists before she found one who agreed to appear but with the stipulation that he be allowed to wear a disguise.

Surprising many among the standing-room crowd of two hundred professionals, Dr. Anonymous described an informal group of closeted gay psychiatrists who attended the APA's annual conventions and met socially outside the organized program.

Calling themselves the "Gay PA," they held a secret dinner annually. Marmor sounded another controversial note when he told his colleagues, "There is nothing sick or unnatural about homosexuality except that it is socially condemned." A few days later the *Advocate* reported, "Psychiatry and the gay community may finally have reached a turning point."[21]

Kameny recognized that by participating in the convention he had a rare opportunity to integrate the event. He even attended the annual psychiatrists' ball. When the band struck up the music, Kameny grabbed Phil Johnson, a local Dallas gay activist, and the two men waltzed out onto the dance floor. The stunned psychiatrists and their spouses watched speechlessly, most of them pretending they were not seeing it.[22]

Later in 1972 gays staged what would later be seen as one of their most important demonstrations when they targeted the meeting of the Association for the Advancement of Behavior Therapy in New York. More than one hundred members of Gay Activists Alliance passed out flyers outside the hotel that read, "Torture Anyone?"[23] Inside, several GAA members had infiltrated the audience for a session on aversion therapy. "This is it!" shouted Ronald Gold, GAA's media director. "We're taking over!" Gold commandeered a microphone and demanded that the "sickness" label attached to homosexuality be removed from the psychiatrists' official diagnostic manual. Although much of the gays' campaign against the psychiatrists had been ignored by the media, this one was prominently featured in the next morning's *New York Times*.[24]

Meanwhile, a dramatic turn of events was shaping up behind the scenes at the APA. During the zap of the psychiatrists in May, one member of the audience had recognized Gold from having attended college with him and introduced him to Robert Spitzer, a member of the APA's Nomenclature Committee, which set the official classifications for illnesses. As a former reporter for the entertainment trade newspaper *Variety*, Gold instantly recognized the value of his new contact and began to lobby for a meeting of the Nomenclature Committee and representatives of GAA. Spitzer eventually agreed to set up the meeting, provided it was kept hush-hush. But after he agreed to the stipulation, Gold called Boyce Rensberger, a science writer at *New York Times*, who wrote a story for the February 9, 1973, edition, headlined PSYCHIATRISTS REVIEW STAND ON HOMOSEXUALS. Rensberger's lead said,

> A committee of the American Psychiatric Association yesterday began deliberating whether homosexuality should be considered a form of mental illness and whether it ought to be stricken from the association's official catalog of mental disorders. Gay organizations have contended that psychiatry's continued recognition of homosexuality as a mental disorder lends support to efforts to discriminate against homosexuals in business and government.[25]

"The article not only got attention far and wide once it was in the *Times* but put them on record," Gold remembered. The APA was furious over the leak, but the article practically assured the gay activists that the classification would be openly debated for the first time. Perhaps better than any activist, Gold understood that the essential value in the change was public relations. If the APA could be persuaded to remove homosexuality from the list of mental disorders, the "scientific" basis for the media and the general public to discriminate against homosexuals would be reduced. According to Gold,

> We gave them a scientific presentation on what was wrong with the theories of the Biebers, the Socarides, and presented them with Evelyn Hooker's material [which contradicted the sickness theory] and all of that. Spitzer was horrified to discover that Socarides said we were all psychotic, which, of course, nobody believed, except Socarides. I kept trying to show them that this stuff was absolute drivel and these people were supposed to be experts but were writing stuff that no sane person—including the people sitting in the room with us—could possibly believe. We showed them that everyone Bieber interviewed was in psychiatric treatment, so how could they represent us?[26]

The Nomenclature Committee stopped short of approving the change but invited Gold to make his case before the association's entire membership at its annual convention in Hawaii the following May. The convention would also hear presentations from four psychiatrists who were considered international experts on homosexuality, among them Charles Socarides and Irving Bieber.[27]

At the convention Gold stood at the lectern before a crowd of five thousand psychiatrists and explained that by labeling homosexuals as mentally ill, psychiatrists were perpetuating mental illness. He told them that by defining homosexuals as sick, they were making them sick. "Stop it," he told them. "You're making me sick."

Later that afternoon the Associated Press carried a story about the session, prompting coverage in newspapers across the nation. DOCTORS URGED NOT TO CALL HOMOSEXUALITY ILLNESS was the headline on the short AP story in the *New York Times* on May 10.[28]

Gold continued to pressure the psychiatric association. The following October Howard Brown, a ranking member of Mayor John Lindsay's administration, announced publicly that he was gay. Brown had secretly supported the Gay Activists Alliance with financial contributions. The forty-nine-year-old health commissioner had resigned and decided to go public the day after he learned that syndicated columnist Drew Pearson was planning to name homosexuals in the Lindsay administration.[29] Brown knew from a conversation with his brother-in-law, John Sibley, a reporter with the *New York Times*, that his homosexuality had been openly discussed among the newspaper's editors, and he was stunned to learn that his secret was so widely known.

Recognizing the public relations value of Brown's pending announcement, Gold arranged for him to be interviewed by a *New York Times* reporter. Even Gold was surprised when the story appeared on the newspaper's front page, headlined EX-CITY OFFICIAL SAYS HE'S HOMOSEXUAL. "[Brown's] decision to disclose his homosexuality was based in part on what he sees as a sharp decline in public hostility toward homosexuals," it said. Afterward Brown was startled to find himself under siege by a swarm of reporters for newspapers, magazines, and broadcast stations who were eager to interview him. "That my announcement would attract so much attention is a measure of how much more needs to be done," he later wrote.[30]

At about the same time several members of GAA who were in the throes of forming a breakaway organization asked Brown if he would chair the new group's board of directors. Ronald Gold became media director, and GAA president Bruce Voeller became president of the newly established National Gay Task Force (NGTF), the truly national gay organization that would have its own professional staff. Brown, a medical doctor, became an important ally in the negotiations with the psychiatric association.

In December 1973 newspapers and broadcast stations across the nation carried one of the most important stories homosexuals would ever see. The headline on the front page of the *New York Times* read PSYCHIATRISTS, IN A SHIFT, DECLARE HOMOSEXUALITY NO MENTAL ILLNESS. The story began,

> The American Psychiatric Association, altering a position it has held for nearly a century, decided today that homosexuality is not a mental disorder. The board of trustees of the 20,000-member organization approved a resolution that said in part, "by itself, homosexuality does not meet the criteria for being a psychiatric disorder." Persons who are troubled by their homosexuality, the trustees said, will be classified as having a "sexual orientation disturbance" should they come to a psychiatrist for help.[31]

In essence the decision meant that millions of homosexuals had been cured of mental illness overnight, triggering a flurry of news articles, many of them positive. The *New York Times Magazine* ran a long, in-depth piece on February 24, WHAT WE DON'T KNOW ABOUT HOMOSEXUALITY.[32] Written by Robert E. Gould, it may have been the fairest, most complete, and most balanced article to appear on the subject in the *Times* since the newspaper printed the Merle Miller essay three years earlier. THE EARTH IS ROUND, the Task Force proclaimed in its newsletter.

One month later the *New York Post* began a weeklong series, HOMOSEXUALS IN NEW YORK: THE GAY WORLD. Each installment carried a front page banner headline, a full inside page of text, and photographs. The articles resulted from the rapport GAA had developed with reporter Barbara Trecker, who at one point was considered for an honorary membership. Activists considered the series "positive and very constructive," despite one installment that was headlined IS IT NORMAL? Trecker explained that her editors insisted that she use one article to present "the other side," and she felt obligated to incorporate the antigay views of New York psychiatrist Charles Socarides.[33]

A few weeks later Arthur Bell wrote a three-part series on the state of the gay liberation movement for the *Village Voice*. In effect it was an obituary for GAA, which had lost much of its membership to the NGTF. Bell found the development disturbing because the new organization relied on a more conservative approach than GAA's or GLF's. "The end of the road may be liberation," he wrote, "but the route is back-room deals, selectivity, and elitism."[34]

Despite the criticism by Bell and efforts by Socarides to overturn the APA's decision, the reclassification became final on April 9 when a majority of the organization ratified it through secret ballot. Following the announcement, the prime movers—Ronald Gold, Franklin Kameny, Barbara Gittings, and Bruce Voeller—called a press conference, telling reporters that the vote removed "a cornerstone of homophobia." In their elation the activists underestimated just how ingrained the mental illness metaphor had become in American culture. A policy change alone could not reverse decades of reliance by the media on antigay psychiatrists.[35]

Even before the votes were counted, radio commentator Nicholas von Hoffman took a swipe at the proposal in his January 4, 1974, broadcast on CBS. "What's next?" he asked his listeners. "Do all the homicidal maniacs organize themselves to march on the American Psychiatric Association and picket the establishment until the doctors declare that they, too, are not abnormal?" Morty Manford, president of the GAA, demanded a chance to respond, but network officials told him that the federal equal time provisions applied only to political campaigns.[36]

Only days after the vote was counted, conservative *New York Times* columnist William Safire scolded the psychiatric association. After conceding that homosexuals should be given the legal means to combat social stigma, he wrote, "To be gay is to be abnormal, whether or not that abnormality extends to one-tenth of the population. To be gay is to be engaged in an activity that both moral absolutists and moral relativists would label 'immoral,' with both Scripture and sociological statistics on their side. The majority who consider homosexuality to be a mental problem to be corrected, or moral decision to be castigated, are not to be dismissed as a bunch of benighted bigots."[37]

Gay activists in Chicago picketed the *Daily News* after columnist Mike Royko ridiculed the gay liberation movement by comparing it with a fictitious Banana Lib Movement. The satirical article revolved around a political movement in which men demanded the right to fall in love with monkeys and win acceptance by "coming out of the cage." He wrote, "The movement gained momentum, of course, with the recent declaration by the North American Psychiatric Confederation that it has reversed its previous position and now considers monkey-man relationships to be normal."[38]

A week later fourteen members of the Chicago Gay Alliance set up a picket line. IT TAKES A MONKEY TO KNOW ONE, read one sign. Royko responded with indignation, writing in a second column, "There'll be no apology." To its credit the *Daily News* took the unusual step of pairing Royko's response with a separate news story about the protest.[39]

Even personal advice columnist Ann Landers joined the backlash.

"Granted some are sicker than others," she wrote, "but sick they are and all the fancy rhetoric of the American Psychiatric Association will not change it." On the other hand, Jane Brody, the *New York Times*'s personal health columnist, was noticeably silent until four years later when she wrote a July 9, 1978, article headlined STUDY FINDS SOME HOMOSEXUALS ARE HAPPIER THAN HETEROSEXUALS. The subject was a new study by the research institute founded by Dr. Alfred Kinsey in 1948. It began,

> A major new study on homosexuality concludes that many homosexual men and women lead stable lives without frenetic sexual activity and that some are considerably happier and better adjusted than heterosexuals as a whole. According to one of its authors, Dr. Alan P. Bell of the Institute for Sex Research at Indiana University, the study's findings contradict stereotypes about homosexuals. He said the study shows that "homosexuality is not ipso facto pathological and that all homosexuals cannot be lumped together."[40]

Brody's article was in marked contrast to her previous stories on the subject, although it stopped short of saying that her earlier stories were based on scientific methods that were statistically faulty. She did point out, however, that "previous studies of homosexuality had focused exclusively on special groups, including men in prisons, patients undergoing psychotherapy, or members of homophile organizations."

TROUBLE AT THE *LOS ANGELES TIMES*

While gays were winning significant improvement in coverage from East Coast media, tensions were growing in Los Angeles. Reporting in 1973 that a serial killer in Houston had slain twenty-seven boys and young men, the *Los Angeles Times* linked the gay community to male prostitution. GAY MOVEMENT FIGHTS STIGMA OF PROSTITUTION, read the October 28 headline. The story began,

> In Los Angeles they are called "California Golden Boys." In Dallas and San Diego they are simply known as "fellows." And in San Francisco and other major cities they may promote themselves as "male models," "escorts" or "masseurs." But the descriptions are nothing more than code names. The job is usually the same. They

are male prostitutes—"call boys"—servicing an increasingly vocal and visible homosexual community and mushrooming pornography industry.[41]

By failing to mention that prostitution was also a heterosexual phenomenon, the article left the impression that it was more widespread among gays—an idea gay activists angrily rejected. The negative framing of this and other articles touched off a series of noisy demonstrations outside the *L.A. Times* building throughout the fall of 1973, including a weeklong protest just before Christmas.[42]

In 1974 more than two hundred demonstrators tried to call attention to a police crackdown on gay bars in West Hollywood, but the *L.A. Times* ignored their protest. Later that summer a crowd estimated at more than two thousand turned out for the city's Christopher Street West, a gay pride parade down Hollywood Boulevard. Once again the *L.A. Times* was silent.

Four months later—in October 1974—the Los Angeles Metropolitan Community Church (MCC) raised money to buy a bus for a local children's home. The congregation had hoped to win some favorable publicity with its community service work. The *L.A. Times* showed no interest. On Sunday, October 20, Lee Carlton, an MCC minister, stood at his pulpit and announced to the congregation that the time had come to take on the *L.A. Times*.

The next day thirty protesters picketed the *L.A. Times* building again as reporters from the Associated Press, five local television stations, and several radio stations watched. *L.A. Times* executives thought the activists would leave peacefully at sundown, but when the staff tried to close the building for the night, some protesters barged through the doors, commandeering the vestibule at the front door. In a scene reminiscent of a high school pajama party several people spread blankets and sleeping bags, blocking the entrance to the building.

The activists escaped certain arrest when veteran activist Morris Kight told an *L.A. Times* executive that they would stage a hunger strike and, if they were taken to jail, the newspaper would be embarrassed even further. The next morning television cameras captured employees stepping across the protesters to reach elevators as they arrived for work. As the employees filed by, demonstrators stuffed notes in their pockets that said, "Come join us."[43]

By midmorning the entrance to the building looked like a battle zone, as gay protesters in their sleeping bags continued to block it. Finally, a tactful executive announced that the editorial board had agreed to meet with a small delegation of activists. The television cameras whirred as Kight led five others inside.

"They said we were absolutely right in our protest. They admitted they had dealt with us very badly and laid out a plan," Kight recalled. "They said we would disappear from their pages for about six months while they figured out what to do about us. We took them at their word on that. After that, they improved dramatically. In retrospect, our protest had been historic."[44]

In fact, the *L.A. Times*'s coverage of gays did improve between October 1974 and April 1975, until a review of an upcoming episode of *Barney Miller* referred to some of the characters as "faggots."[45]

Entertainment reporter Gregg Kilday read it in stunned silence. He realized that the writer probably had repeated the offensive term after hearing it used in the TV show, without realizing its significance. This was not the first instance Kilday had seen of such an inexcusable lapse in his newspaper. A similar indignity had appeared the previous summer in a front page feature about an all-night market in Hollywood, NIGHT SHOPPERS—FANTASY IN THE MARKET AISLES. The article began, "They come out of the darkness and into the markets like moths attracted to light, clustering around islands of life in the hours past midnight. They are old men who can't sleep and young men with no one to talk to. There are winos and pimps and fags and whores, freaks coming down off their lonely highs, old ladies who steal to eat."[46]

After reading the reference to faggots in the TV column, Kilday decided it was time to speak up. He turned to his typewriter and poured his anger into a polite but stern six-page memo to his editors. One part read,

> I appreciate what progress has been made, particularly since I have some sense of
> the deeply ingrained attitudes that often block the way. But as a homosexual, I find
> it troubling and frustrating to read a newspaper that on some of its pages treats
> homosexuals with interest and respect and on others dismisses them as faggots. .
> . . Speaking in all sincerity, it pains me to see homosexuals camped out in the
> *Times* lobby protesting lack of coverage. I think they are naive in their under-
> standing of how the media work. And I think they overlook what accomplish-
> ments have been made. As a journalist, I resent their pressure tactics. And yet I
> understand their frustration because I share it too.[47]

Kilday explained in the memo that so long as homosexuals could be referred to as faggots, gays and lesbians who worked in the newsroom would not feel free to come out and confront the prejudice that surrounded them.

Acknowledging that no simple formula existed, Kilday urged sensitivity, flexibility, and open discussion. He was putting his career on the line. One colleague read the memo and told him, "It's great! Don't send it." But it was too late.

Considering Kilday a busybody, some senior editors suggested that he "butt out." One refused to discuss the memo at a staff meeting, claiming it was an improper subject to discuss in front of women. Another colleague, however, sent a note of appreciation to Kilday. Editor in Chief Bill Thomas and City Editor Mark Murphy both read it in amazement.

"That word was commonly used in the newsroom," Murphy said. "I think editors and writers in the late sixties and early seventies didn't realize it was a bad word to put in the paper; I really don't think they knew. I used it as a young man and to me it meant gay; it didn't mean anything bad. We were ignorant. It took people like Gregg Kilday to open our eyes."[48]

DAVID GOODSTEIN AND THE *ADVOCATE*

The fledgling gay press was also undergoing major changes. In July 1973 Jack Nichols and Lige Clarke stopped publishing *Gay*. In less than four years it had become the second-largest gay newspaper in the nation. But Nichols and Clarke had tired of the routine and decided to move to Florida where they could turn their attention to book writing and other interests.

Burnout had also taken its toll on Dick Michaels and Bill Rand at the *Advocate*. In late 1974 they sold the paper to David Goodstein, a former Wall Street financial whiz virtually unknown to gay activists. He had originally moved to San Francisco to head the investment department of a large bank. But he was fired when one of his superiors realized he was gay. "I couldn't believe something so unfair could happen to me," he said later. "Since then, I've done everything I can to ensure that gay people need not accept second-class status in society."[49]

Beyond writing a few articles for *Vector*, the magazine of the Society for Individual Rights, the San Francisco–based gay rights group, Goodstein had little practical experience in publishing. At one point he tried to buy *After Dark*, a New York entertainment magazine that regularly featured handsome male actors and ballet dancers in underwear, in G-strings, or in the nude, but the editors denied it was designed to appeal to gay readers and refused to sell it to him.

After his ouster from the banking job Goodstein used some of his considerable wealth to purchase the *Advocate* for an estimated $300,000 and immediately breathed new life into the newspaper. He also earmarked $150,000 to promote the publication. He also introduced his own brand of advocacy journalism.

For an editor he turned to twenty-nine-year-old John Preston, a former seminarian whose background was primarily in sex counseling. In Minneapolis Preston had helped found Gay House in 1970, the first gay and lesbian community center in the nation. At the time he was studying sex education at the University of Minnesota's medical school and became certified as a sexual health consultant. Before joining the *Advocate* in 1975 he edited a newsletter for two years at the Sex Education Council of the United States in New York.

In addition to hiring Preston, Goodstein doubled the full-time staff of sixteen in order to make the paper less dependent on its loose network of poorly paid stringers and introduced a sleeker magazine format. He also shifted the editorial offices from Los Angeles to San Mateo, near San Francisco, in a move that symbolized Goodstein's determination to stop providing a soapbox for a small group of "self-appointed gay leaders," whom he described as "unemployable, unkempt and neurotic to the point of megalomania." He also introduced more professional journalistic standards. "We don't report news about organizations unless they do something," he said, responding to accusations that he was turning the *Advocate* into a "bully pulpit" to push his own agenda.[50]

Another factor behind the changes was the mainstream media's increasing coverage of gays and lesbians. As gays became more vocal and more visible in the media, Goodstein was forced to adapt to the reality that he no longer had a monopoly on coverage of homosexuality. Feature articles replaced much of the hard news; beefcake was out and lesbians were in. The magazine separated the explicit advertising for sexual devices, pornographic books and films, nude photos, and personal ads into a pull-out section that proved a lucrative source of income.

Goodstein ordered profiles of well-known gay people and stories about the views of famous straight people on gay rights. "We tried to follow the lead of other alternative publications—*Rolling Stone*, et al.—by forcing a magazine design into a tabloid format," Preston explained. "We also wanted something that spoke to our readers in a more complete way, not just a source for news."[51]

Within his first year as publisher Goodstein had boosted circulation by 50 percent. The *Wall Street Journal* took note of the accomplishment by featuring the *Advocate* in a front page article on November 3, 1975, A HOMOSEXUAL PAPER, THE ADVOCATE, WIDENS READERSHIP, INFLUENCE. The story began, "Many of the paper's 50,000 or so readers wouldn't be caught dead reading a copy in public. National advertisers shy away from it despite impressive demographics. Newsstands that carry it are few and far between, especially in America's heartland. Yet since its first issue was secretly printed in a Los Angeles basement eight years ago, The Advocate has grown in circulation, quality and influence as the only nationwide newspaper published by and for homosexuals."[52]

The article marked one of the first times the straight press had acknowledged in print the existence of a gay press, but the *Advocate* had not been recognized for its journalistic accomplishments. It was featured in the nation's leading business newspaper because it was making money.

7

TV BECOMES A BATTLEGROUND

By the early seventies television had become an inviting target for a variety of advocacy groups because they recognized it as a major cultural force in America. Ninety-five percent of the sixty million homes in the United States had a television, and more than a quarter of them had two or more.[1]

Television's influence went well beyond the print media for several reasons. Not only were its programs free but TV required no reading skills. It delivered information in an entertaining manner that appealed to a mass audience much larger than the print media's. But at the same time the seamless mix of truth, falsehood, accuracy, and distortion on television sometimes blurred people's ability to distinguish fantasy from reality.[2]

Although entertainment television was not governed by the same professional ethics and federal regulations as news reporters, television producers were not completely immune to pressures familiar to journalists, particularly when their subject matter was controversial. At times television producers can be even more sensitive to audience tastes than editors of newspapers and magazines because of the ratings system that determines the success or failure of programs.

By attracting large audiences networks and local affiliates are able to charge premium rates for commercial time. When television producers first approached the subject of homosexuality, they were especially cautious not to air anything that appeared to condone it. If they drove away viewers, they risked losing advertisers or offending local affiliates. Enough losses in either case would eventually cause a network to cancel the show. But derogatory comments about gays and lesbians were considered another matter altogether.

NBC's *Rowan and Martin's Laugh-In* was one of the first regular network shows to approach the delicate subject. A skit that ran on February 24, 1969, showed two men dressed in prison garb. "If you let your wife come in here," one said to the other, "we're through." In 1970 the show's producers developed a stereotypically effeminate character named Bruce who appeared on the program regularly. Even in his absence the mere mention of his name triggered spasms of canned laughter for a long string of antigay jokes. By late 1970 *Laugh-In* was averaging one joke per program about gay liberation.[3]

Gays made no attempt to confront a television network until October 1970 after comedian Mort Sahl appeared on ABC's *The Dick Cavett Show*.[4] Watching the episode in his New York apartment, Arthur Bell flew into an angry fit and, in his role as media director of the Gay Activists Alliance, fired off a letter to the network producer, demanding that the show provide equal time for homosexuals. Cavett's program director agreed to meet with Jim Owles and Marty Robinson, but nothing came of it. The request languished on the producer's desk for another six weeks, and gay activists became increasingly impatient.

On October 27 fifty protesters blended inconspicuously into a line of tourists waiting outside Cavett's television studio to see the taping of the show. They all carried whistles under their jackets, and at a signal they planned to disrupt the taping. Although the protest had been planned for a month, it fell on the same day as the zap at *Harper's* over the Joseph Epstein article. Somehow Cavett had seen coverage of the *Harper's* zap on television and grew suspicious. An usher was sent to inform the activists that the show was ready to negotiate.

In the meeting Cavett's producers invited Marty Robinson and Arthur Evans of GAA to appear on the program on November 26, one month later. After Dick Leitsch complained that the New York Mattachine Society had been left out, he was added to the group. GAA was reluctant to share the spotlight—the *Cavett Show* was the organization's first national exposure.

When the big night arrived, Cavett kicked off his program with comedian Phyllis Diller, followed by actor James Earl Jones. Then he turned to the camera to introduce his gay guests. "The subject of homosexuality still upsets some people," he began. "We will try to discuss it reasonably, but if it's going to give you apoplexy, for heaven's sake don't watch." The interview lasted forty minutes, touching on many of the most essential elements of being a homosexual in the early 1970s—albeit, a male homosexual. "If we deny our emotions and appear straight, then we have a career," Arthur Evans told Cavett. "But if we live openly and show our affections the way heterosexuals do and lead an open sexual life, then our careers are ended. We feel it is repressive, unfair, and unjust that we face that alternative."[5]

Cracking a dramatic series on television posed a much bigger challenge for the activists than gaining a voice on the public affairs programs. From 1968 to 1974 the dominant image of gay men on these programs was the limp-wristed effeminate drag queen who walked with a swish and talked in a high-pitched voice. Lesbians were alternately portrayed as Mack truck drivers or as serial killers.

In one episode of CBS's *Kojack*, for example, a gay man was portrayed as a child molester and was referred to as a "three-dollar bill." In an episode of the NBC dramatic series *The Bold Ones*, a young doctor dated a woman who turned out to be a lesbian. When he confided in a friend that he felt threatened, the friend told him, "I would hope you'd think of it as a threat to her femininity."[6] The list included many of the most popular programs on television—*M*A*S*H*, *Police Woman*, and *Hawaii Five-0*. "Who could blame the uneducated viewer who winds up thinking gays are a bunch of people who never work because they spend all their time in bars?" a writer asked in the *Advocate*. "Who could fault him for thinking that when gays aren't mincing around the streets, walking their poodles, and dropping the hankies, they're mercilessly killing and mutilating each other?"[7]

Television's most notable attempt to break away from the dominant gay male sissy stereotype came in the 1972 ABC made-for-TV movie *That Certain Summer*. The story concerned a father, played by actor Hal Holbrook, who was forced to explain his relationship with his live-in lover, played by Martin

Sheen, to his fourteen-year-old son. Richard Levinson and William Link, one of the most talented writer-producer teams in Hollywood, first proposed the film to NBC, which rejected it. "It was perfectly acceptable for Bob Hope or Johnny Carson to mince about the screen doing broad parodies of homosexual behavior," they later observed. "But anything else, anything not derisive or played for laughs, was out of the question."[8]

At ABC the script had caught the attention of Barry Diller, a young maverick executive who had created the tremendously successful *ABC Movie of the Week* as the head of the network's film unit.[9] The movie was particularly unusual for its time because it dared to show two gay men actually touching, and neither died at the end. But even with Diller's support ABC's standards and practices department—the division that functions as network censors—raised a red flag about a key exchange between the two lead characters.

"A lot of people—most people I guess—think it's wrong . . . they say it's a sickness . . . they said it's something that has to be cured," said the father. "Maybe they're right." Standards and practices wanted him to add: "I don't know, I *do* know that it isn't easy. If I had a choice, it's not something I'd pick for myself." Even with the changes affiliates in some cities refused to air it. ABC hired extra operators to stand by in major cities, but the deluge of angry telephone calls never materialized. The loudest complaints came from a small group of viewers who condemned the film as ungodly and indecent, and quoted the Bible. Levinson and Link described them as motivated by "a deep-seated distress . . . , a segment of the American viewing public that does not want to confront issues on the cutting edge of social change. For them, the purpose of television is to reinforce values that make them comfortable."[10]

The response from the gay community was mixed. A writer for the *Advocate* described *That Certain Summer* as "the most tasteful, sensitive, accurate, and compelling story on homosexuality to reach the screens thus far."[11] Others faulted it for not going further. Although the film would not raise the consciousness of an entire nation, it did raise the expectations of gay activists about their portrayal on television.

THE FIRST ASSAULT

Because broadcasters are required to hold licenses from the federal government, television and radio were more attractive as targets for activists than unregulated newspapers and magazines. Moreover, decision making at the networks was centralized in either New York or Los Angeles, whereas policy at most newspapers was set locally. By targeting broadcast executives in one or two cities, activists could influence what viewers across the nation saw on television.

When Ronald Gold became GAA's media director in 1973, he immediately began contacting programming executives at the three major television networks about their portrayal of gays. But before he could arrange meetings with them, someone at ABC leaked him a script for an upcoming episode of *Marcus Welby, M.D.* Titled, "The Other Martin Loring," the story depicted a divorced father who consulted Dr. Welby about his homosexual feelings. Welby told him he had "a serious illness" and urged him to suppress his desires. Homosexual "tendencies" were described as "degrading and loathsome."

Gold angrily denounced the episode as "medically unsound, filled with quackery, and defaming to homosexuals," but network officials ignored him. Four days before the air date two dozen activists picketed outside the network's headquarters in New York, and a second contingent entered the building. Using a detailed map acquired from someone within the network, thirty activists took over the thirty-ninth-floor offices of the network's two highest-ranking executives, board chairman Leonard Goldenson and Elton Rule, the network president.

"It was one of the first big actions we took," Gold said. "It was also one of the biggest mistakes we made. ABC offered to set up a meeting for two of us with their standards and practices person and the president of the network if the rest of us would go away. But we were afraid that we were going to get screwed over so we said no. That was very foolish because we didn't get to talk to anybody. They thought we were crazy—and to a certain extent we were. But we were also justifiably paranoid."[12]

Most demonstrators left peacefully when the police arrived, but six refused to leave and were arrested for trespassing. Gold came away from the incursion angry, feeling that the protest had failed. Not only had they missed their chance to influence the Welby program, but also they had forfeited an opportunity to establish a valuable dialogue with important network executives.

When the program aired on February 20, 1972, ABC had cut a reference to "homosexual tendencies" and a comment by the gay character that his homosexual longings "make my whole life a cheap and hollow fraud." Because the changes were far short of what they had demanded, the activists did not yet realize just how far they could push a major television network.

THE GAY RAIDERS AND THE TV ZAP

While gay activists were launching their initial assault on national network television, a gay teenager in Philadelphia was initiating a one-man war on a local television station. Nineteen-year-old Mark Segal was angry that he and a male friend had been thrown out of a television dance program one August afternoon in 1972 when the host of the program saw them dancing together. "Get out of here!" he began screaming at the pair.

A few days later Segal and several friends waited until the anchorman began to deliver the eleven o'clock news and barged into the studio of the ABC affiliate in Philadelphia, WPVI. "We have some grievances," viewers heard Segal tell Larry Kane, the startled anchorman. Then studio personnel wrestled Segal to the floor and tied his hands with a microphone cable. After a quick cut to a commercial, the weatherman came on the air, telling viewers, "I'm a little out of breath right now. Some of you know why, but I can't explain it on the air." Segal and his gay raiding party were arrested and taken to police headquarters for questioning.[13]

The next day the August 16 *Philadelphia Inquirer* carried a brief account of the incident on its front page. A day later the paper carried a more complete story quoting Segal as he decried the television station's "smirking" attitude toward gays in general.

His activism had been incubating for some time. One night in 1967, when he was sixteen, he watched *The David Susskind Show,* a popular late-night syndicated television program, when it broached homosexuality for the first time. The guests included antigay psychiatrist Lawrence Hatterer and Dick Leitsch, president of the New York Mattachine Society. "I remember getting my blanket and putting it over my TV and watching it because I was ashamed that anybody might hear or see me watching the show," said Segal, whose family lived in New York at the time. "Watching that program, I realized that people believed we were evil because they didn't know who we were."[14]

In late 1969 Segal began to attend Gay Liberation Front meetings in Greenwich Village. But he and other young members felt alienated from the older members and founded an independent organization, Gay Youth. The next year Segal's family relocated to Philadelphia, where gay liberation was only just beginning to catch on.

After accounts of Segal's zap appeared in the Philadelphia newspapers, a television producer who saw the coverage invited him to fly to Los Angeles and appear as a guest on the *Merv Griffin Show*. But soon after he arrived at the studio, he was told by the production staff that his appearance had been canceled; the reasons were never given.[15]

In Los Angeles with time on his hands Segal managed to get a ticket to sit in the audience of *The Tonight Show with Johnny Carson*. In the middle of the taping he leaped from his seat, handcuffed himself to the rail in front of him, and began complaining about the program's derogatory treatment of gays. According to the entertainment industry newspaper *Daily Variety*, the incident cost the network $40,000 in additional production expenses.[16] Even so, Carson's producer agreed to meet with Segal to discuss the young activist's concerns. Segal had prepared a list. He wanted the network to end its censorship of gay news, hire four gays (two men and two women) to serve on a review board, and produce two documentaries on the gay liberation movement to be aired in prime time.

On the day of his appointment he arrived at the NBC studios, only to learn that his meeting had been canceled. The producers were apparently unhappy that he had publicized the meeting by issuing a press release. Segal spied a marble table in the lobby, pulled out a set of his trusty handcuffs, and attached himself. Police were called to cut him loose and arrest him. Veteran activist Morris Kight, who was waiting in a car outside, had already arranged for an attorney and money for bail.[17] The charges were later dropped.

Segal struck again on May 7, 1973. After *The Mike Douglas Show* canceled two appearances by Troy Perry, founder of the Metropolitan Community Church, Segal barged into a taping session, handcuffed himself to a camera, and began shouting, "Mister Douglas, why have you and your show refused to let representatives from the gay movement in this country appear on your show?"The taping was halted as Douglas looked up and asked, "What are you talking about? We've had gay people on the show." Douglas returned to his guests, Tony Bennett and Helen Hayes, and Segal was carted off by the police civil disobedience squad.[18]

That fall Segal took action again because he took exception to an episode of NBC's *Sanford and Son* that depicted a parade of stereotypical queens in a gay bar. On October 26 viewers of the *Today Show* heard a commotion as newscaster Frank Blair read the morning news. Segal dashed through the studio shouting, "Gay people are sick and tired of NBC's bigotry toward us." Camera operators raced after him as television screens went blank. After the Associated Press ran several stories on Segal, newspapers across the nation followed suit. The *Philadelphia Inquirer*'s story was headlined GAY PHILADEL-PHIAN INVADES "TODAY" SET.[19]

Coincidentally, gay and lesbian activists had already scheduled a meeting with NBC brass. The meeting generated headlines when the executives surprised the delegation by acknowledging that the network had at times "dealt unfairly with homosexuals" and agreed to maintain a continuing liaison with homosexual organizations. "N.B.C. Acts After Complaints by Homosexual Organizations," announced the October 27 *New York Times*.[20]

Segal staged his last and most notorious zap on December 11, 1973. By posing as college students researching a term paper, he and his friend Harry Langhorne obtained passes to watch *The CBS Evening News with Walter Cronkite* from the studio. Midway through the newscast Cronkite began to read a story about Secretary of State Henry Kissinger. Segal darted in front of the camera with a sign that read GAYS PROTEST CBS BIGOTRY. "I sat on Cronkite's desk directly in front of him and held up the sign while the technicians furiously ran after me and wrestled me to the floor and wrapped me in wire—on camera," Segal said. "Then the network went black for six minutes while they took us out of the studio. They came back on the air and described what they knew had happened."[21]

In the dry emotionless tone that had become his trademark, Cronkite explained to his audience, "Well, a rather interesting development in the studio here—a protest demonstration right in the middle of the CBS News studio." After reading several other news stories, Cronkite returned to the incident and explained, "The young man was identified as a member of something called 'Gay Raiders,' an organization protesting, he said, CBS's alleged defamation of homosexuals on entertainment programs." Police charged Segal and Langhorne with trespassing, and stories about their escapade appeared in newspapers across the nation. "GAY RAIDERS" INVADE CRONKITE NEWS SHOW, read the headline in the *New York Times*.[22]

Cronkite may have been more startled several weeks later when Segal's attorney, Harold M. Weiner, tried to serve him with a subpoena to testify in the trespassing case. Incensed, CBS attorneys blocked repeated attempts to deliver the document. The industrious Weiner then informed network lawyers that he had found a little-used New York law that made photocopies of a subpoena as valid as an original. Weiner said he would make copies available to members of New York's Gay Activists Alliance and the Hells Angels, with a reward for anyone who managed to serve a copy on Cronkite. Faced with the prospect of having Cronkite stalked by gay activists and bikers, the

CBS lawyers quickly dropped their objections. Editors at newspapers across the nation were fascinated. "SUPERGAY" READY FOR CBS TRIAL, the *Des Moines Register* announced in a headline.

The trial began on April 23, 1974. Cronkite took the stand and said little. Each time Segal's lawyer asked him a question, the CBS lawyers jumped to their feet to object. Clearly impressed with the anchorman, the judge never required Cronkite to respond. But during a recess Segal felt a tap on his shoulder. "Why did you do that?" Cronkite asked him. "Your news censors," Segal responded. The anchorman was appalled that someone would accuse the most respected news organization in the world of censorship. "If I can prove censorship," Segal told him, "would you do something to change it?" He then gave the veteran newsman three examples, including CBS's report on the second rejection of a gay rights bill by the New York City Council. "Yes, I believe I wrote that story myself," Cronkite responded. "Well, why haven't you reported on the 23 other cities that have passed gay rights bills?" Segal asked. "That's censorship." Genuinely moved, Cronkite shook Segal's hand and thanked him.[23]

The judge convicted Segal and Langhorne of trespassing, slapping each with a $450 fine. His zaps had propelled gay rights into the headlines of newspapers across the nation, but Segal soon realized that his celebrity status was distracting from the central issue:

> I began to wonder if they were using me or I was using them—I was not quite sure. I was invited on all of the national talk shows. They invited me on not because they wanted to get information across to the public but because they wanted bigger numbers. Whenever I was on a talk show, the telephones lit up like nothing you can imagine. In that regard they were using me. But at the same time I was getting my message out to the public, so I was using them. But after the Cronkite zap the message began to get lost in the commotion. It began to look to me very unsavory.[24]

Segal's persistence soon paid dividends. His remark to Cronkite at the trial had hit home. On May 6, 1974, Cronkite featured a major segment on gay rights. "Part of the new morality of the 60s and 70s is a new attitude toward homosexuality," he told his audience. "The homosexual men and women have organized to fight for acceptance and respectability. They've succeeded in winning equal rights under the law in many communities. But in the nation's biggest city, the fight goes on with the city council due to vote on the matter again this week." Reports on the status of gay rights in New York, San Francisco, and Boulder followed, with one correspondent pointing out that ten cities had passed legal protections for gays and that similar laws were under consideration in at least four others.[25]

LOCAL BROADCASTS

While young Mark Segal was zapping the networks, Loretta Lotman was fashioning a markedly different technique in Boston.

As she was watching a documentary on the Boston CBS affiliate, WCVB, in April 1973, she became fascinated with media coverage of gays. While purporting to be unbiased news, the documentary ignored lesbians completely. Moreover, the gay men depicted in shadow-drenched interviews bore no resemblance to the people Lotman knew personally.

A Chicago native, Lotman had studied television production at the University of Illinois and moved to Boston in hopes of finding a job. But as many beginners learn, entry-level positions can be in short supply, especially in a major market. For a time she worked in the promotion department of Boston public television station WGBH and then at a production company that specialized in educational videos for the U.S. Army.

In March 1973 the production company laid her off; while she searched for another job, her friends urged her to take a role in "Come Out," a documentary play by gay historian Jonathan Ned Katz about gay liberation. "I never had a closet," she said. "I went from latency to activism overnight."[26]

When the WCVB documentary aired one month later, Lotman and the gay little theater group of which she was a member became the nucleus for one of the first local media advocacy groups in the nation. By late 1973 the group had adopted the name Ad Hoc Gay Committee for Truth in Broadcasting. Then it became Gay Media Watch, until its members settled on Gay Media Action. Whenever the Boston media covered homosexuals unjustly, Lotman was there:

> I told them that I was working within the gay community and that we had lots of groups and lots of speakers available. If they were doing bad news stories, I would call up and tell them that I represented Gay Media Action and we needed to talk because there were some problems with the story. I explained how embarrassing

it would be for several hundred gay activists to picket their organization and then I suggested that we should head that off. I didn't have activists ready to protest, but by bluffing I got meetings.[27]

Meanwhile, Ronald Gold was working furiously to position the National Gay Task Force as the primary gay watchdog of the national media. Network executives had already begun to turn to such organizations as the National Organization for Women, the National Education Association, the National Parent-Teacher Association, and African-American groups for advice on scripts. In the same manner ABC began to turn to Gold and the National Gay Task Force when the plots involved gays and lesbians.

One of the first consultations involved an upcoming segment of *Marcus Welby, M.D.* The plot centered on a junior high school boy forcibly raped by a male science teacher. Surprisingly graphic for the time, the script described the boy as suffering from intestinal damage and anal hemorrhaging after the attack. Gold saw the script as an attempt to dredge up the old stereotype that homosexuals prey on children. The episode, called "The Outrage," was scheduled to air on October 8, 1974. ABC claimed the segment involved pedophilia, not homosexuality.

Gold, who was also negotiating with the Nomenclature Committee of the American Psychiatric Association, was nearing his breaking point. He contacted Lotman in Boston to inform her that trouble was brewing at ABC. Quickly shifting her operations from Boston to New York, Lotman issued a distress call to some two hundred local gay and lesbian organizations that had sprung up since the Stonewall riots in 1969. "I told people how they should organize protests," Lotman said. "I also did workshops at all of the gay conferences on how to publicize them."[28]

Lotman's New York work marked an major turning point in the relationship between the television networks and gay activists. The battle could no longer be viewed as one New York–based gay rights organization versus the networks. In a dramatic show of power Lotman mobilized the first national grassroots campaign against a network that called upon dozens of local organizations.[29] While Gold concentrated on advertisers, Lotman coordinated some activities with the National Federation of Teachers, which also was concerned about the content of the program, and supplied detailed instructions to local gay and lesbian organizations about how to pressure their local ABC affiliates into dropping the segment:

Call the *General Manager* of the station and insist you speak with him (alas, few GMs are women). Explain the protest of the *Welby* script and the events in New York at the network; explain the repercussions to the gay population in the country and our civil rights movement; be articulate, concise and businesslike. Then, explain that if the program is aired nationally, militant gay action will be taken against the *local ABC affiliate*. Make this a very cold-blooded, un-emotional threat. Don't try nasty threats, as they will lessen your case. Be businesslike.[30]

In another section of the 1974 memo Lotman instructed them, "As few as 15 people can jam the phone lines of most major stations. You can find out for certain how many incoming phone lines a station has by having a woman call up as the 'phone company service representative' and have her question the head operator on the efficiency of her phone service, how many incoming trunk lines she has, and what changes she would like to see in service." She had sent the two-page set of instructions to be used for protests against *Marcus Welby, M.D.*, but Lotman pointed out that the same tactics could be used for any media problem in the future.

In another memo to the local activist groups Lotman explained the procedure they should use to book a guest on a radio or television program and provided a valuable set of pointers:

Check local program listings in your area and make a list of locally produced talk shows. Monitor them for format, content, approach, fairness of treatment. Call the stations and ask, "Who books the XYZ show?" Then, follow up with more phone calls. Be insistent and consistent. . . . Remember, most people are still afraid, ignorant or convinced we're sickies. When you appear on the air you are helping people change their opinions of us. Make a good impression. DON'T LOSE YOUR TEMPER.[31]

Gold and Lotman were aware that pressuring sponsors to demand changes in the script would be fruitless—sponsors had been prohibited from tampering with the content of television programs since the game show scandals of the fifties. Instead, Gold and Lotman sought to convince sponsors to pull their ads from the *Welby* episode, thereby sending ABC a costly message. What ABC didn't know was that an employee in its basement computer room was a member of GAA. Whenever an advertiser canceled, he would call Lotman and she would contact the media reporters at major newspapers and wire services. She knew the exact status of the network's advertising revenue and which companies had canceled their ads, even before some of the network vice presidents did.

By the night of the broadcast, October 8, seven major sponsors had pulled out, including Colgate-Palmolive, Lipton, Breck, and Gillette. Only Pet foods and Johnson Wax held firm to their commitment for a combined total of one minute of advertising. The network sales force scrambled to replace the defectors but managed to replace only some of them, signing up such names as Pizza Hut, Pfizer Drugs, Hanes, and Morton Foods. Gay activists staged noisy demonstrations outside television stations in Los Angeles, San Francisco, Chicago, Denver, and Washington, D.C., and in small towns in Ohio, Iowa, Mississippi, Texas, and Idaho. As a result seventeen ABC affiliates dropped the episode, including stations in Boston, Philadelphia, and Lafayette, Louisiana. Newspaper articles called it a first for major television stations to refuse an episode of a popular network series as the result of protests. "It was a bit like pre–civil rights movement treatment of blacks," remarked Bruce Voeller, executive director of NGTF. "They simply failed to hear the message, and now they were discovering that there was a new currency about the gay issue."[32]

But days later the entertainment industry newspaper *Hollywood Reporter*, in a story about a delay in the production of a segment of the NBC series *Police Woman*, disclosed that the plot of a segment titled "Flowers of Evil" revolved around three lesbians who methodically murdered residents of a retirement home. When lesbian and gay activists complained to the network, they were told that the episode had been sent back for changes. At one point an executive told them it had been canceled but later reversed himself. He explained that it would air but under a new title, "It's Only a Game," and without references to lesbians. But NBC broadcast the original episode on November 8, 1974, one week before the announced air date. *TV Guide* called it "the single most homophobic show to date."[33]

Two weeks later seventy-five members of the Lesbian Feminist Liberation arrived at NBC's New York headquarters.[34] After two hours of picketing, eleven women and three children found their way into the building and commandeered the office of the network's vice president in charge of standards and practices. They unfurled a red, white, and blue banner from his office window that read LESBIANS PROTEST NBC. News of the protest ran on local radio, independent television stations, the wire services, and in several newspapers. But NBC, ABC, and CBS made no mention of it. Organizers said people who answered the phones at the stations owned by the three networks kept hanging up. After several hours inside the offices the women realized the network was not going to have them arrested and they left.[35]

BECOMING A MEDIA RESOURCE

After the *Marcus Welby* and *Police Woman* protests Loretta Lotman succeeded Ronald Gold as the full-time media director at the National Gay Task Force in December 1974 and continued to monitor the networks, organize meetings with network brass, and build grassroots support. In addition, she coordinated NGTF's efforts with those of a loosely affiliated group known as the Gay Media Task Force in Los Angeles, which was essentially a one-man organization operated by Newton Deiter, a gay clinical psychologist who had written an advice column for the *Advocate*. He had been a screen writer earlier in his career and had developed contacts inside the vast entertainment industry.

In New York the National Gay Task Force was working to convince the networks that their programming executives on the West Coast should be submitting their scripts to Deiter for his review. But the networks considered that censorship and were reluctant to cooperate to that degree. Even so, Deiter obtained a host of manuscripts, often because they were slipped to him by gays or sympathetic straights who were working at the networks. In November 1974 producers at Mary Tyler Moore Productions (MTM), which was known for its sympathy toward homosexuals, asked Deiter to help with a script for *The Bob Crane Show* that had Crane learning that an old college friend was "a liberated gay." NBC rejected it until it was approved by Dieter, fearing it was "too controversial" and "might offend gay viewers."[36]

For Lotman the most significant developments came in February 1975 when she was invited to participate in a panel at the National Association of TV Program Executives (NATPE). It was the first time an openly gay person addressed the top programming executives of the television industry, including the presidents of all three major networks. Lotman told them gays considered television the most unfair of all of the media and pleaded with them not to portray gays and lesbians as clowns or psychopaths. "When you show only the stereotype of gays, you're telling lies," she told them. "No other minority is as abused, exploited, misrepresented or demeaned as gay people are."[37]

The symposium was the opportunity for which Lotman had been waiting. She was able to corner some of the highest-ranking executives in network television. Had they developed standards for the portrayal of gays? she asked. Would they portray homosexual relationships during prime time with the same openness and honesty as heterosexual ones? She then turned to network hiring practices:

> I asked them if they were going to adopt a nondiscrimination statement in their employment policies. NBC had agreed to this in a meeting, but it never became policy, so I asked all three if they would make that policy. At first they tried to fluff it off. But CBS network president Robert Wood said, "This is a reasonable woman who has asked a reasonable question and deserves a reasonable answer," and the others fell in line and reversed themselves in front of the audience of a thousand people. [38]

By the following summer Lotman had run out of energy. The almost constant battles with network executives, combined with the conflict that seemed endemic to gay rights organizations, had taken its toll. She called it quits after an exhausting ten months of nonstop activism. Moreover, the political agenda of the gays rights movement appeared to leave less and less time for media advocacy.

Lotman was succeeded by Ginny Vida, a founding board member who took on the communications duties from late 1975 through the end of 1979. She continued to pressure media executives in New York, while Dieter continued to work with Hollywood producers. In November 1975 NBC decided to repeat its made-for-TV movie *Born Innocent*. Starring Linda Blair as a fourteen-year-old delinquent, the film was set inside a juvenile detention center. In the most controversial scene Blair is attacked by several inmates who forcibly spread her legs and brutally raped her with a broom handle. When the film first aired in September 1974, it set off a national uproar that prompted congressional hearings into violence on television. The networks escaped mandated restrictions by voluntarily agreeing not to broadcast programs that were inappropriate for children until after 9 P.M.

Despite complaints from Vida and other activists, NBC decided to rerun *Born Innocent* but in a later time slot. Protests were held in San Diego, Fort Worth, Kansas City, Minneapolis, Boston, and Philadelphia. NBC affiliates in Minneapolis and Kansas City refused to broadcast it. The protests also convinced four sponsors to pull their ads. All this strengthened Vida's hand when she confronted each network's executives about how they were portraying lesbians. "We told the executives at ABC that they had never had one positive image of a lesbian on their network," she said. "The only thing any of them had shown was this horrible thing about lesbians. So I told them about a book that was about to come out about Mary Jo Risher, a lesbian mother who had lost custody of her children. One of the men assured me that if I could get hold of the manuscript he would look into it."[39]

It took ABC nearly three years to develop the script, but in late November 1978 ABC broadcast *A Question of Love*, starring Jane Alexander and Gena Rowlands. *New York Times* television critic John O'Connor pointed out that television seemed to be using homosexuality as a gimmick, but he concluded, "'A Question of Love' in some ways goes to the other extreme, becoming the lesbian equivalent of 'That Certain Summer,'" the breakthrough movie produced by the same network six years earlier.[40]

Much about television changed between 1976 and 1978. Positive gay characters were cropping up in prominent roles in network films and on three series—*Alice* on CBS and *Barney Miller* and *The Nancy Walker Show*, both on ABC.[41] Communications researcher Kathryn Montgomery determined that all but one demonstration by gay and lesbian activists resulted either in changes in a program or a shift in a broadcast schedule. She documented seven major hostile protests by gay and lesbian activists against the three major television networks from 1973 to 1978. In five of those protests she found evidence that the network changed the program content before it was broadcast. Programming executives at each network described gay activists as the most effective and well organized of all the special interest groups that lobbied the television industry.[42]

But the heightened visibility also resulted in more backlash. One of the most vicious examples came from conservative journalist Nicholas Von Hoffman, whose syndicated column appeared in a host of newspapers nationwide. "The old-style Chinese have the Year of the Tiger and the Year of the Pig," he wrote. "The new-style Americans are having the Year of the Fag."

> Is a new stereotype being born? Is network television about to kill off the bitchy, old-time, outrageous fruit and replace him with a new type homo? Perhaps the furry basso-profunda police sergeant who lives next door? ABC's Nancy Walker Show has a continuing major fag character whose representation is monitored by representatives of the Gay Task Force on the set when they're doing the runthroughs.[43]

With a liberal dose of such indignities as "fagolini," "flits," "faggots," "fruit," "homo," "faggotry," and "queer," the columnist's tirade was reminiscent of the sensational tone of news articles about gays at the Stonewall rebellion a decade earlier.

WORKING ON THE INSIDE

Although the lesbian and gay movement had made significant strides in network programming, it had done little to liberate gays and lesbians working in television newsrooms, although the activists had tried. "I'm speaking from my own pragmatic experience," Loretta Lotman explained to a gathering of journalists in 1974 in New York.[44]

Describing her pre-activist days as an aspiring journalist, Lotman told the gathering, "I couldn't even get an interview for a decent journalism job because I'm a known lesbian. If you're well-established, OK, but if you're on the lower levels, management will cut you quick." Lotman said she knew of forty gay and lesbian journalists in the Boston area "who can't come out" and nearly thirty who worked at television stations in New York.[45]

Merle Miller echoed Lotman's remarks at the same gathering: "Everyone knows that on the staffs of every newspaper and magazine in the United States there are many homosexuals, many closeted. Nobody wants to hear about it; it's really OK if you don't tell. If enough people came out—in the arts, media, everywhere—and said being gay is not so uncommon, the revolution would be underway."[46]

But gay and lesbian journalists had every reason to hide. For Burdette Bullock, a young reporter at a television station in Nashville, Tennessee, the danger became very real in the spring of 1977. One day after he finished an appearance on the noon news, he was called into the news director's office and told that his "lifestyle" was unacceptable.

"He told me the station was number two in the market and that it wanted to be number one and did not want anything to threaten that," Bullock said. "He handed me a paper to sign and asked me to resign. The resignation said we'd had creative differences and that I wanted to pursue my interests elsewhere. There was no mention of sexual preference."[47]

Bullock eventually arranged for a lawyer to help him work out a settlement that gave him enough money to move to Florida. After a period of unemployment he was hired by a television station there.

Garrett Glaser was another who found a subtle hostility toward gays in the television newsroom. He began his career in his hometown of New York City in 1976, fresh out of college and eager to take almost any entry-level position. By typing scripts for soap operas at CBS, Glaser hoped he would be noticed by influential network executives who would offer him a break into TV news.[48]

"The whole office knew I was gay," Glaser said, "because a group of little queens were coming in to look at me. I was twenty-something and new meat at 'Black Rock.' But when I became an associate producer at WCBS-TV, I became more closeted. I was open with my friends but not the people at CBS. I remember saying to myself that I was going to distinguish myself by being who I was, but no one at that time had done it by being openly gay."[49]

While working in the business office of *Readers' Digest* in the early seventies, Tom Cassidy decided that he wanted to become a reporter. He went on to earn graduate degrees in both journalism and business administration and began his TV career at a small station in Eugene, Oregon, in 1978, arriving one week after the city rescinded its gay rights ordinance.

"There was no gay life," Cassidy said. "It was a small town where discretion—especially for a TV news anchor—was very important. Oregon was a very progressive state in some ways but hadn't changed in other ways, and I wasn't prepared to be the pioneer at that juncture."[50]

At about the same time a young journalist named Hank Plante decided to switch from newspaper work to television in Washington, D.C. That his homosexuality could be used against him had been a primary factor in his decision not to make the change earlier in his career. But after friends urged him to apply for an opening at a television station in Norfolk, Virginia, he landed his first TV job in 1976. Two years later he became a TV reporter and anchorman in Houston, a much larger market.

"The general manager knew that I was gay because somebody told him before I got there," Plante said. "On the job interview he was like ice. But the news director wanted me, so I took the job anyway. The whole time I was there, the general manager was nothing but cold. Finally, when I was leaving to go to another station, he told the news director, 'You know, I was wrong about him—maybe I shouldn't have been that hard on him.'"[51]

8

WORKING IN NEWSPAPERS

When Perry Deane Young returned to New York in 1970 after two years of covering the Vietnam War for United Press International, he found a decidedly different social climate for gays than in 1968. Gay liberation was one of the hottest topics in the city.

But Young was facing his own personal postwar adjustment that overshadowed everything that was going on around him. Although he had escaped physical injury in Vietnam, the war had left deep psychological scars. He had lost his two closest friends, Sean Flynn, a photographer for CBS who was the only son of actor Errol Flynn, and Dana Stone, an Associated Press photographer. The two had disappeared on April 5, 1970, during an expedition in the Parrot's Beak area of South Vietnam near the Cambodian border.[1] When a search of the area failed to turn up any clue to their whereabouts, Young transmitted his resignation to UPI, hung up the dark green pants and jacket he had been issued by the military, and boarded the next plane out of Saigon.

"It was a survival instinct to get out of there," Young said. "But I'll never forget coming back and sitting at the Village Gate cabaret in Greenwich Village. I felt like all of my life was in the past; I didn't think there would ever be anything as exciting as that war. I also knew that part of me was pushing to come out of the closet—to get it all over. There's something about being so close to death. I think you say 'Fuck it! Why not be myself?'"[2]

He took a reporting job at the *New York Post*. He had brought with him a new attitude toward his work and a new openness about his sexuality. "If you don't know about me," he began saying to his new colleagues, "I want you to know that I'm gay." He soon found that the responses were more hospitable than he had expected. But the transition from wartime reporting to the routine news of New York became increasingly difficult and unfulfilling. Just before his thirtieth birthday in 1971 he left the *Post* to write a book about the war.

In 1975 Young finished *Two of the Missing*. The book was about his experience as a war correspondent, the loss of his buddies, and his first public acknowledgment that he was gay. "I decided that I wasn't going to live my life as a lie," he said. "I felt that being gay wasn't a sickness, but certainly the way we had to live it was sick."

But after the book was published, Young found that several magazine editors who had bought his articles in the past—some of them closeted homosexuals—now shunned him. Some refused to take his telephone calls. "You should realize that you are now a biased writer," one finally told him. "We'll let you know if we need opinion pieces on your subject."

Although some editors were concerned that his disclosure would expose him to criticism that he was biased, others were convinced that homosexuality was the only subject he *could* write about. The harsh reality was that by 1976 Young was out of the closet, out of work, and out of luck. "I'm not sorry I took that step, but I went a little crazy not being able to earn a living," Young said. "So I'm a little intolerant of people who talk about all they have to lose. I had it to lose and I lost it."

But Young would not be idle for long. During the Christmas season he spotted an article on the front page of the *Washington Star* about retired running back David Kopay of the Washington Redskins who had publicly acknowledged that he was gay. Young dashed off a note to *Star* reporter Lynn

Rosellini in the hope that she would pass it to Kopay. Young wanted to know whether he could help the sports figure write a book. The answer was yes.[3]

Young's book *The David Kopay Story* stayed on the *New York Times* best-seller list for nine weeks in 1977, making it the first book about a sports figure ever to appear on the list. It was Young's crowning accomplishment. He had finally melded his penchant for writing with his politics and expertise on homosexuality, and the public greeted it enthusiastically.

OUT IN MINNEAPOLIS

The gay former Washington Redskin was one of several high-profile individuals who shattered gay and lesbian stereotypes during the 1970s despite the risks of public acknowledgment. In 1971 Jack Baker, an openly gay law student at the University of Minnesota, made national headlines when he was elected student body president. In November 1974 Boston activist Elaine Noble was elected to the Massachusetts State House, becoming the first open homosexual elected to a state legislature in the nation's history. "I decided to run because I'm the most qualified for this damn job," she told newspapers.[4]

One month after Noble's election Minnesota state senator Allan Spear took a similar step by announcing his gayness in a front page story in the *Minneapolis Star*. Reporter Deborah Howell began the piece by citing numerous examples of Spear's accomplishments, saving the surprising news for the fifth paragraph. "Allan Spear also is a homosexual," she wrote. "And, as of today, he doesn't care who knows it."[5] Only a few months earlier the Minneapolis City Council had unanimously enacted one of the first gay rights ordinances in the nation. Neighboring St. Paul soon followed suit with a similar measure.

Minneapolis Tribune reporter Carl Griffin Jr. was following the reactions to these events with special interest. When he joined the newspaper in 1972, he knew he was the only black on the staff and suspected he was the only gay man until he ran into reporter Howard Ericson.

The two men had met several years earlier when Ericson covered a story in Griffin's hometown of Fargo, North Dakota. Ericson had suggested that Griffin apply for a job at the *Tribune* when he finished college. The two had worked together for nearly a year before each realized the other was gay. During a casual conversation one day Griffin mentioned he was buying a house in the heart of the city's gay district, an area known to locals as Homo

Heights. "I felt I needed to let him know that there was another person who was going to be buying this house with me," Griffin recalled. "He gave me a smile that indicated he knew lots of people who had done that."[6]

When Ericson left the *Tribune* several months later for a magazine job in Texas, he asked Griffin to take over his freelance work. For several years he had written for the *Advocate* under the pseudonym Lars Bjornson and had covered a number of important stories, including passage of gay rights ordinances in both Minneapolis and St. Paul. "Why not?" Griffin remembered saying. "I'll give it a try." In 1975, using his own name on his bylined articles, Griffin became a member of the small corps of stringers the editors had assembled to give the magazine a semblance of national coverage.

Griffin had done only a few stories for the *Advocate* when he realized that the *Tribune*'s readers ought to be getting some of the news running in the *Advocate*. One *Advocate* story announced that Betty Fairchild, the mother of a gay son, was the scheduled speaker for a conference of the Minnesota Committee on Gay Rights in September 1975. Three years earlier she had established a national organization called Parents of Gays. After the group in Minneapolis expressed an interest in forming a chapter, she arranged to fly in from her home in suburban Washington, D.C. Griffin suggested to his editor that he write a story for the *Tribune*.

"I don't think they knew I was gay," Griffin said. "I was a bit uncomfortable, but I always felt that they would hear me out. Also, being a black man, my hunch told me that I had even more credibility on human rights kinds of issues. The liberals were pretty liberal about a lot of things. I don't remember the slightest hesitation to my going out and covering that story."[7]

Headlined WOMAN DESCRIBES FORMING GROUP TO HELP PARENTS OF GAY CHILDREN, the article marked a personal turning point for Griffin. Although he was out to several friends in the newsroom, he had never before acknowledged his sexual preference to the entire staff. In so doing he may have become the first openly gay reporter at a mainstream daily newspaper to write about gay topics.[8]

Minnesota had long been a pocket of liberal politics, an attitude that may have stemmed from the Bavarian ancestry of the Germans, Swedes, and Norwegians who settled there. The live-and-let-live attitude that permeated the political and social climate was reflected in the *Minneapolis Tribune*. Old-timers attributed this to John Cowles, who demanded that all his newspapers treat *all* segments of their communities fairly.

But for all the newspaper's apparent sensitivity, Griffin was stunned when he overheard a group of copy editors laughing and joking about how repulsive homosexuals were. He listened to their cutting comments, which continued the following night. When a straight colleague pressed Griffin on why he seemed distraught, Griffin reluctantly described what he had heard.

A few days later the city editor asked if he could speak to Griffin privately.

> He told me he wanted to apologize for all of the crude remarks that were made in the newsroom. Now he wasn't even there, but he said he wanted to assure me that steps were being taken to address it and that it wouldn't happen again. He said all of those folks were told in no uncertain terms that the bigoted remarks were to end. I was completely taken aback. I asked him how he knew, and he said my friend had told him about it. That friend was a very impressive man, and they knew good and well he wasn't gay. So when it was another straight person brought it up, that cut all of the crap.[9]

During the next seven years that Griffin worked for the *Tribune*, he never again overheard antigay remarks. He left the newspaper and journalism in 1980 simply because he wanted to do something else with his life. He took a job at the local chapter of the Red Cross.

GAYS AND LESBIANS IN THE NEWS

Although the signals the media were sending on the issue were sometimes conflicted and inconsistent, clearly their attitude toward gays and lesbians was changing. By the mid-1970s the media and the public were more willing than ever to discuss homosexuality openly. One reason for this was that between 1972 and 1977 gays and lesbians had created a lot of news to cover. Activists had succeeding in having *sexual orientation* added to the antidiscrimination laws in thirty-six cities, ranging in size from East Lansing, Michigan, and Alfred, New York, to San Francisco, Detroit, and Seattle.

In July 1975 the Mattachine Society's Franklin Kameny won his decade-long battle with the federal government when the Civil Service Commission, under pressure from the courts, dropped its ban against civilian homosexuals in federal government jobs. GAY IS NOW OKAY IN 2.6 MILLION FEDERAL JOBS was the headline in the *Advocate*. A much smaller article appeared in the *New York Times* at the bottom of page forty-five: HOMOSEXUAL HIRING IS REVISED BY U.S.[10]

Later that year Air Force Technical Sergeant Leonard Matlovich set off a flurry of articles when the thirty-two-year-old acknowledged his homosexuality to his superiors. When *Time* learned of the disclosure, the magazine seized the opportunity to focus on the struggle for gay rights and featured Matlovich on its cover. When the September 8, 1975, issue appeared on newsstands across the nation and in many parts of the world, the cover showed Matlovich in a sparking blue air force uniform with a cluster of military ribbons prominently pinned to his shirt. I AM A HOMOSEXUAL, read the bold headline. In the article Matlovich explained that he had acknowledged his homosexuality to deliberately provoke a discharge in order to challenge the military's long-standing ban against homosexuals. Given his exemplary military record, his was seen as the perfect test case. The cover spread included a sidebar analyzing the accomplishments of the five-year-old gay rights movement.[11] It was only the second time that a national newsmagazine had dared a cover story about gays (the first, in 1969, also ran in *Time*).

But not all the coverage was so positive. Demonstrations erupted outside San Francisco station *KPIX* when the anchorman read a story about Matlovich and, thinking his microphone had been switched off, went on to say, "I was going to say a 'faggot flier' but I thought——" By the time a technician flipped the switch, it was too late.[12]

At the *New York Times* the new level of openness among gays and lesbians created an uneasy tension inside the newsroom. This was clear in the spring of 1975 after the newspaper ran an article in the Sunday Travel section about an unusual ocean cruise specifically for gay men and lesbians. Freelance writer Clifford Jahr had learned of the excursion the previous summer from the Islanders, the operators of a shuttle service that connected Manhattan and Fire Island and sponsored the cruise. Jahr was fascinated by the story he might get from spending seven days on a ship full of homosexual men and women.

The ship sailed from Florida to Guatemala, heading west to the Yucatán Peninsula before returning. In his article Jahr described the "six-course dining, pampered loafing and casual mating"—staples of more traditional heterosexual cruises. In one section he explained,

> Back home, even their friends were betting that any 300 gays together on a boat for one week would sink it with bitchery, pretension and bad manners. So they themselves were surprised when the week passed in a warm spirit of moderation and mutual respect. . . . A half dozen lesbian couples were on board, ranging from

a young dean of women at a small East Coast college, and necessarily in the closet, to Lois, in her late fifties, a blond ex-showgirl from Miami who assured us she had nothing to hide.[13]

Headlined THE ALL-GAY CRUISE: PREJUDICE AND PRIDE, the article was completely out of character for the *Times*. This was underscored by an earlier rejection of the article by the far more liberal *Village Voice*, where openly gay editor Richard Goldstein was convinced that publisher Clay Felker would never allow him to print it. Jahr took it to the *Times*'s newly appointed travel editor, Robert Stock, a clean-cut divorced man in his middle forties who was the father of teenage children. Jahr described Stock as looking like an "over-the-hill Clark Kent." Stock immediately recognized the story as an important footnote to the six-year-old gay liberation movement. "Nobody was writing about gay travel, and I thought we should write about it," he said.[14]

In sometimes sassy, dishy terms Jahr chronicled nearly every aspect of the trip, including the "sadomasochistic fashion show," down to the harnesses and G-strings and a tape recorder that played the moans and shrieks of someone feigning a savage whipping. He also described two chickens that someone mischievously brought aboard and primed with poppers, a stimulant used to enhance sexual pleasure, causing one of the birds to lay an egg while the other "engaged in a lust-crazed tussle with a Gucci carryall."

Times publisher Arthur Ochs Sulzberger was not amused. The next morning, according to one account, Sulzberger summoned his top editors to his office and announced, "You have offended my mother." He wanted to know how his editors could have been "sullied by such an article" and why they would want to print an account of "orgies by a bunch of faggots?"[15]

The publisher's office became the epicenter of an antigay tremor that rippled through the building in whispers. Sulzberger immediately issued an edict that banned "that word"—*gay*—from the *Times* forever. The only exception to his rule would be when the word was used in direct quotes or when it was part of the official name of an organization. The edict was later codified in the *Times*'s official style manual, the grammatical bible for the newspaper's reporters and editors. Sulzberger also "fired off a memo saying, in effect, that features of this sort were not fit to print," *New York* magazine reported in its gossip column.[16]

The incident became more embarrassing for the *Times* when rumors began to circulate that Sunday Editor Max Frankel had been fired during the confrontation with Sulzberger and then rehired a few hours later once tempers had cooled.[17] Although he probably knew nothing of the article before it appeared in print, Frankel, as the editor of the *Times*'s Sunday edition, was held accountable for its contents. Neither Stock nor Frankel would discuss the episode with Jahr or anyone else. "My inquiries around town," Jahr later wrote, "kept drawing references to Sulzberger's 1950's 10-pound Cordovan wing-tip shoes, an absurd detail but sadly relevant where so much power is concentrated."[18]

ABE ROSENTHAL AND THE *NEW YORK TIMES*

Although Jahr's article may have produced the most visible sign to date of the *Times*'s discomfort with the subject, homosexuality continued to give old Gray Lady the vapors. Two years later the culprit was one of the newspaper's own staff members, Grace Lichtenstein, chief of the *Times* bureau in Denver.

Lichtenstein read about Anita Bryant's campaign to overturn a Dade County, Florida, gay rights ordinance in 1977 and recognized that the issue had been underreported in the *Times*. She decided to write about its national ramifications. "I went to a gay night club in Tucson, I had some folks in the gay community take me around, and I got stringer reports from elsewhere, just to show that the notion of being openly gay was spreading across the country," she recalled. Headlined HOMOSEXUALS ARE MOVING TOWARD OPEN WAY OF LIFE AS TOLERANCE RISES AMONG THE GENERAL POPULATION, the story in the July 17, 1977, *Times* said, "Despite a successful anti-homosexual campaign in Miami that attracted nationwide attention last month, a spot check this week by The New York Times indicated widespread outward tolerance of homosexuals, although some backlash generated by the Florida campaign was evident. These findings seemed to be supported by the most recent Gallup Poll, which shows that a slim majority of Americans approve of equal-job rights for homosexuals."[19]

By coincidence, soon after the article appeared Lichtenstein was transferred back to New York. After settling in as a reporter on the metropolitan staff, she asked whether she could cover gays as a beat. "There were just millions of stories out there," she said. "Gay liberation, the sense of the gay community, was really exploding in the late 1970s in the same way that the women's movement was."[20]

Lichtenstein suspected that the main reason gay liberation had been underreported by the *Times* was that the newspaper's gay reporters were fearful of telling editors they were gay. She became even more suspicious when she learned that her request to cover gays had gotten an icy reception from the newsroom hierarchy. "Forget it," she was told. "Abe's not going to approve that." "Abe" was Abe Rosenthal, the newspaper's executive editor, who had gained a reputation for homophobia.

Nonetheless, three months later Lichtenstein wrote a series of three in-depth articles about the state of the gay rights movement. She described gay life in unusual detail, including the diversity of gay life; the series described the networks of gay professionals that existed in New York and other cities. Her editor was impressed, and Lichtenstein thought the series merited a slot on the newspaper's the front page. After a few days, however, the stories were dropped back on her desk with instructions from Rosenthal to reduce them to a single article. He apparently thought the subject was not worthy of so much detail.[21]

Lichtenstein's single article, HOMOSEXUALS IN NEW YORK FIND NEW PRIDE, appeared on the front of the Metropolitan section on October 25, 1977, describing what was believed to be the first gay synagogue in the nation. "It was Yom Kippur at Congregation Beth Simchat Torah, Manhattan's four-year-old self-proclaimed 'gay synagogue,' and the temple facilities in Westbeth Apartments in Greenwich Village were overflowing with more than 350 worshipers," the story began.[22] Its author later remembered:

> I knew it was a story that would touch a nerve so I deliberately began it with the synagogue and the Yom Kippur services to bring the point home. I did it deliberately. I thought the people who read the New York Times—not to mention the people who publish the Times and very many New York Jews, including a homophobic Jewish editor—should have their eyes opened. And I got a lot of phone calls and response from people saying, "Thank you, that was a great story." I also got response from other reporters in the newsroom who told me they thought the story should have been on page one. It was just another example of the editor's prejudice.[23]

Lichtenstein's experience was hardly an isolated incident. Sports writer Dave Anderson found similar resistance to a column he wrote in 1976 about the book Perry Deane Young had written with David Kopay, the football player who had acknowledged his homosexuality a year earlier. When the column was killed by his editor, it was the first and only time one of the Pulitzer Prize winner's columns did not make it into print:

The sports editor took it to one of the assistant managing editors who said he didn't want me to write about the book unless I was reviewing it, and I wasn't. I was writing about the book's news value. I recognized that it was a touchy subject and felt that maybe they didn't want anybody writing about gays. I only had about an hour left before the deadline, so I just sat down and wrote another column about something else, and that was the end of it. I just kind of forgot about it.[24]

Times reporter Roger Wilkins had a similar experience in the midst of a 1978 debate over a gay rights bill that had languished in the New York City Council for seven years. Wilkins had been an assistant attorney general during the Johnson administration and then an editorial writer at the *Washington Post*, where he helped earn the paper a Pulitzer Prize for its coverage of Watergate. In 1974 Wilkins joined the *Times* as the first black member of the paper's editorial board. Two years later Rosenthal convinced him to join the metropolitan staff by offering him an opportunity to write a column on urban affairs.

When the city's gay rights bill resurfaced in the city council, Wilkins realized that he knew little about the issue. He contacted David Rothenberg, a prison reform activist who was gay, and asked if he could arrange a meeting with gay activists who could explain the significance of the bill from their perspective. Wilkins hoped to learn whether the proposed ordinance would actually make it possible for large numbers of people to come out of the closet, or whether other factors—such as rejection by their families—would continue to keep them closeted. After meeting with two lesbians, Wilkins wrote his column. But after he submitted it, his editor rejected it. Like Anderson, it was the first time Wilkins ever had one of his columns killed.

He [the editor] told me that I was supposed to be writing an urban affairs column and that gay rights was not urban affairs. Well, I couldn't imagine anything more urban affairs than writing about the impact of legislation pending before an urban legislature on a bunch of urban citizens— it was absolutely absurd. Obviously the piece was sympathetic to the legislation—it was a column, not a news story— and it was obviously sympathetic to the people I had interviewed. I was quite certain that it had been killed by either Abe Rosenthal or his deputy, Arthur Gelb.[25]

The message became even more pointed a week later when Wilkins submitted an expense report that included his lunch with the lesbians. "Mister Wilkins, do you really think Mister Sulzberger ought to pay for your having lunch with two lesbians?" asked an editor who questioned his expenses.

Pausing for a moment to collect his thoughts, Wilkins responded: "Well, let's put it this way: Mister Sulzberger has a much better chance of getting his money's worth if I'm having lunch with a lesbian than if I'm having lunch with a heterosexual woman." "That's a hell of a point!" the editor replied. The bill was paid.[26]

The message that gay coverage was unwelcome was reinforced through a variety of means. One ranking editor remembered Rosenthal's inquiring about the sexual orientation of a reporter who had left the *Times* for a West Coast newspaper. Rosenthal mentioned that he had heard the man was gay. "I knew what his question meant," the editor recalled. "It meant that if I had known and hadn't told him, then I had been disloyal. I told him I had known, that it wasn't a big deal, and that the reporter had done his work well." According to the editor, who requested anonymity, after a brief pause Rosenthal said, "Well, he'll never get hired here again."

Similarly, *Times* music critic Peter G. Davis recalls a day in 1978 when an editor asked Davis to take a walk with him. As they headed down Forty-third Street to Eleventh Avenue, the editor informed Davis that an important person in the opera world had been so offended by one of Davis's reviews that he had revealed the writer's homosexuality to the *Times* hierarchy. Apparently, *Times* executives were astonished to learn that homosexuals had "infiltrated" the newspaper. Davis was warned that his work would be closely monitored.

> Even after this editor talked to me—and he did it with great embarrassment and as a favor to me—his attitude was that he valued me and valued my work and that I had better be careful. That's what's so hard for me—I guess I'm so naive—I just couldn't believe that any adult person would have that kind of attitude. I always said the *New York Times* was my last disillusionment in the adult world. I was saying that all through my last five years there. I had finally grown up, and I couldn't believe in grown-up people anymore.[27]

Not long after the conversation Davis left the *Times* to become *New York* magazine's music critic. Rosenthal's personal and professional antagonism toward homosexuals continued to affect news coverage and personnel. "There's no question that Rosenthal hates homosexuals and is absolutely fanatic on the subject," remarked Charles Kaiser, a gay *Times* reporter who served as Rosenthal's clerk in the late 1970s. "But from time to time, his news judgment overcomes his homophobia."[28]

Others described news conferences in which Rosenthal referred to "fags," "queers," and "faggots." In his Media Watch column in June 1985 in the gay newspaper *New York Native*, David Rothenberg referred to this when he wrote, "At least one *Times* staffer who I talked to has heard Rosenthal refer to gays in the news as 'faggots.' It will take a brave soul to come out at the *Times*."[29] The atmosphere only worsened when a rumor circulated among gay employees that Rosenthal had asked for a list of gays on the staff. But when one of his department heads challenged the idea, Rosenthal apparently dropped it.

"Rosenthal never stood in the middle of the newsroom and said, 'I hate fags,' but the atmosphere led to defensive reporting and defensive editing," said Pulitzer Prize–winning *Times* reporter Nan Robertson, who wrote a book about discrimination practices against women at the newspaper. "We censored ourselves. We knew that if we wrote about certain subjects, the stories would probably not appear in the paper. It was very insidious."[30]

Peter Millones, who as metropolitan editor was one of Rosenthal's closest allies, characterized Rosenthal as reflecting an antigay bias typical of editors of his generation. "There wasn't any secret that he was typical of a great many people who were wary of that subject—who were uncomfortable with it," he recalled. "There was a flap over a series on gays in the late 1970s in which articles were killed [the Lichtenstein series that was cut to a single story], and that sent a message. There was an awareness that you had to be careful with the subject."[31]

GAYS, THE PRESS, AND ANITA BRYANT

For all the progress gays and lesbians had made by the mid-1970s, gay rights did not become a national issue until Anita Bryant launched her campaign to rescind the newly adopted Dade County [Florida] ordinance in 1977. The controversial ordinance generated a volume of coverage that gays and lesbians had been unable to generate on their own. Her status as a world-famous singer, former Miss Oklahoma, and runner-up for Miss America virtually assured national and international interest in her "Save the Children" campaign.

"As an entertainer, I have worked with homosexuals all my life, and my attitude has been live and let live," Bryant told the county commission. "Now, I believe it is time to realize the rights of the overwhelming number of Dade County constituents." Despite her emotional objections, the commission approved the extension of job protections to gays as Bryant vowed to overturn it. "I will not be moved," she told the Associated Press. "Even if my livelihood is stripped away from me."[32] Her announcement marked the beginning of her campaign to collect the fifty thousand signatures needed to take the issue to referendum in the primary election scheduled for June.

The following day, January 17, 1977, the controversy was spelled out on page seven of the *Miami Herald*: GROUP RAPS HOMOSEXUAL ORDINANCE.[33] The article prominently mentioned Bob Kunst, a 1970s antiwar activist who had engineered the adoption of the ordinance. Since 1972 Kunst and clinical psychologist Alan Rockway had hosted *Love Is*, one of the earliest radio programs anywhere in the nation to address sexual issues, including homosexuality. The program was an outgrowth of the Transperience Center, a well-regarded self-help counseling center the two men set up in 1976.

Kunst's efforts to persuade Miami officials to adopt a gay rights ordinance had begun in late 1976 when he, Rockway, and gay bathhouse owner Jack Campbell established an organization to spearhead the effort. Calling their organization the Dade County Coalition for the Humanistic Rights of Gays, the men wanted the county commission to expand existing housing and employment ordinances to include protections for "affectional and sexual preference." When area resident Anita Bryant learned of the proposal, she marched into the county commission meeting to lodge a protest, and Kunst quickly recognized that he was facing an opportunity to turn gay rights into a national issue. From his training in marketing he knew that he must define the conflict broadly in the press, focusing on the human rights aspect by stressing sexual freedom, not solely gay rights. From his radio program he knew that the Miami area was home to a sizable number of straights who chose to live outside traditional marriages. Kunst was certain that if they understood the issues, they could be counted on to support gay rights at the ballot box.

From January until the June 1977 primary election, Kunst concentrated on the news media, framing his arguments in terms of all Americans' having the right to live as they saw fit. To generate publicity he developed extensive mailing lists of media contacts across the nation, with special emphasis on the major wire services. But some of the more conservative members of his organization were uncomfortable with staging a high-profile fight.

Undeterred, Kunst and Rockway formed their own organization, naming it the Miami Victory Campaign. For months the new organization generated a steady flow of press releases. Their followers created media events by distributing large shopping bags outside the upscale stores along Washington Avenue that were inscribed TELL ANITA YOU'RE AGAINST DISCRIMINATION. The media captured pictures of people carrying the brightly lettered bags throughout the busiest shopping areas of Miami Beach. Kunst also hired a clipping service to keep track of how newspapers throughout the nation were portraying the battle with Bryant. Kunst recalled that

> Some publications were giving us support and some were beating us up. The ones that were supporting us were the ones located in some of the most conservative small towns. Big newspapers like the *Miami Herald*, the *San Francisco Examiner*, and others were ripping us to shreds. From that, we realized it was not a liberal-conservative issue the way it had been put out previously. We immediately changed tactics and aimed our to appeal to anyone who considered themselves sexually liberated—gay or straight.[34]

To generate even more publicity Kunst arranged for a short media tour along the Atlantic Coast. Members of his organization were photographed at the White House, with the Liberty Bell in Philadelphia, at the mayor's office in Trenton, New Jersey, and at the first-ever gay dance at the Waldorf-Astoria Hotel in New York City. Each stop brought more headlines. Kunst handed out bumper stickers and protest buttons that tied gay rights in Miami to the defeat of the Equal Rights Amendment in the Florida legislature. Although his strategy captured the attention of much of the mainstream media, its appeal to the gay press was limited. "I called the *Advocate* for coverage, and they said they'd come down in June for the vote," Kunst said. "We told them we'd be in the *New York Times* way before that."[35]

Kunst reaped stacks of sympathetic articles in newspapers and magazines nationally but not in Miami where the *Herald* sided with Bryant. "On balance . . . we believe the ordinance while well-intentioned is unnecessary to the protection of human rights and undesirable as an expression of public policy," said its June 5 editorial.[36] Two days later voters repealed the ordinance by a 2-to-1 margin. The victory brought Anita Bryant an outpouring of support.

> The repeal of the Dade County ordinance comes as a personal triumph for Miss Anita Bryant and as a refreshing manifestation of what one concerned citizen can accomplish.—*Cincinnati Enquirer* (June 10, 1977)

Anita Bryant . . . deserves the rank of First Class American Heroine for her determined and successful efforts in behalf of God and country.—*St. Louis Globe-Democrat* (June 9, 1977)

Miss Bryant's neck, which she stuck out a mile . . . is quite safe now. For her courage and staunchness, we salute her.—*Dallas Morning News* (June 9, 1977)

The defeat in Dade County set off an antigay backlash that rippled through the media in cities of all sizes. Commentator Tom Braden called on heterosexuals to reclaim ownership of the term *gay*. "They took a delightful word, one which we associated with brightness, liveliness, good cheer, flowers, color, pleasure, sometimes the spring of the year, and made it synonymous for a homosexual," he complained in his syndicated column.[37]

Gays also became the target of some liberal journalists who had traditionally supported other minority groups and the larger issue of human rights. Jeff Greenfield, the one-time aide to Robert F. Kennedy who later became the liberal voice of *CBS* News, was a case in point. As gay rights legislation foundered in the New York City Council for a seventh year, Greenfield compared gay rights to a shopping spree at Bloomingdale's in a front page article for the *Village Voice*: "Vuitton bags, digital watches, Bergdorf shopping bags trigger in me a strong sense of revulsion. This is probably unfair and may well be due as much to envy as to a deep-seated sense of social justice. And, certainly, I would have no right to attack these people or to deny them their civil and political rights. But if a member of this 'group' came to me for a job garbed in the uniform of the acquisitive, I would refuse out of hand, and I would have a right to refuse."[38]

In the fall of 1977 the *Atlanta Constitution* carried an article by Atlanta housewife Amy Larkin titled ENOUGH! ENOUGH! TV IS KILLING US WITH GAYS. "I don't hate homosexuals, or think their sex life is my business," she wrote. "But I'm tired of their coming out of the closet into my living room." Larkin was concerned that TV talk shows were inviting "one homosexual after another to talk about their sexual preference as casually as two women might discuss laundry detergents." "Now when I see one coming," she wrote, "off goes the set."[39]

The *News-Tribune* in Jefferson City, Missouri, carried an editorial on November 20, 1977, that announced, "FAG" DEMONSTRATION CALLED OFF. "A vast majority of Missourians will be happy to learn that the 'queers' will not be marching on the state capitol to demonstrate against Anita Bryant Monday," wrote newspaper publisher William H. Weldon.[40]

The backlash was also felt by network television. Soon after the Dade County ordinance was repealed, the networks began receiving complaints from religious groups. A primary target was *Adam andYves*, a proposed series loosely based on the 1980 gay-themed hit movie, *La Cage aux Folles*. More than 100,000 letters arrived at the programming department of ABC while the program was still in the development stage.

Many letters were generated by the American Christian Cause after its leader, Rev. Robert G. Grant, warned that "militant homosexuals may soon score a terrifying breakthrough in their war against the Christian family." After the network dropped the series, Grant's organization boasted to its constituents of routing "the campaign to force decent Americans not only to tolerate homosexuality, but to accept this perversion as a normal, even glamorous, lifestyle for our young people to follow."[41]

One result of the setbacks was that gays were in no mood to ignore even the slightest derogatory remark. In December 1977 a dozen protesters suddenly barged into the *Village Voice* to protest a headline above a small article about a cluster of unusually affectionate California sea gulls that read THE COAST IS QUEER. The screaming match that erupted in the newsroom between the angry activists and thirty busy staffers was particularly disturbing for Richard Goldstein, a *Voice* editor who was only beginning come to terms with his own homosexuality. "When those people seized the office and the editors started yelling about the First Amendment, I was mortified," he recalled.[42]

Not long after that, Goldstein gave the activists a copy of a homophobic article the newspaper was planning to print, and the leak almost cost him his job. "I had an editor calling me in to give me this huge diatribe about homosexuals and how she would see limousines outside gay bars stealing the souls of young boys," he recalled. "She kept asking, 'How can you do this, how can you do this?' Finally, I looked at her and said, 'If you were Jewish, and you were in Germany during the Weimar years, and your paper was about to publish some anti-Semitic garbage, what would you do?' Her eyes opened wide. She realized that I was gay."[43]

Gays were also a hotly debated topic in the newsroom of the *Wall Street Journal* after the newspaper ran a December 1978 article, SOME TOP CONCERNS RULE OUT JOB BIAS AGAINST GAY PEOPLE, which described how some of the nation's largest corporations had banned antigay discrimination. *Journal* editor Fred Taylor objected to the article with a memo to his staff that said, "They aren't gay to me and a lot of other people; they are homosexuals and should be so identified at all times, unless gay is in the title of the organization, or used in a quote. In short, gay is not a synonym for homosexual, no matter what the gays say."[44]

On a routine trip to meet with staff at the *Journal*'s San Francisco bureau, Taylor came under heavy criticism from several staff members, especially Bill Wong, a straight Asian-American reporter. Wong raised the subject during a staff dinner. "If blacks want to be blacks instead of Negroes," he told Taylor, "then that's what we ought to call them." The comment touched off an argument neither Taylor nor his staff would forget. "I told them, 'You don't call them gays, I don't call them fags,'" Taylor recalled. "I thought they were trying to gild the lily by trying to disguise what they were."[45] The ban remained in place until 1984 when Taylor's successor lifted it.

In the meantime gay activist Bob Kunst continued to generate headlines with his campaign to retain legal protections for gays in Dade County. Despite his loss at the ballot box, he was far from defeated. "We had gotten millions of people out of the closet as a result of this," he said. "Thousands of organizations formed as a result of this. The debate that resulted from this was our victory." By the end of the campaign Kunst had amassed more than fifty thousand news articles, which he described as "$100 million-worth of free media publicity."[46]

Within a few months of her victory in Dade County Anita Bryant set out on a tour to promote her campaign to jurisdictions across the nation. At the same time California state senator John Briggs introduced a ballot initiative seeking to prohibit gays and lesbians from teaching in California public schools. "One-third of San Francisco teachers are homosexuals," Briggs told the *San Francisco Examiner* in October 1978. "I assume most of them are seducing young boys in toilets." The *Los Angeles Times* described the measure as vicious, mean-spirited, and "repugnant to basic American freedoms."[47]

The Briggs initiative failed, but voters in several cities took the antigay crusades in California and Florida as a cue and reversed gay rights ordinances they had once approved. One of the earliest repeals came in April 1978 when the St. Paul (Minnesota) City Council rescinded the law it had enacted four years earlier. Wichita repealed its ordinance a month later by a 5-to-1 vote, followed a few days later by Eugene, Oregon.

In the meantime Kunst and his followers in Florida attempted to reinstate gay rights in Dade County by collecting eighteen thousand signatures to have the issue put back on the ballot. The measure restoring gay rights attracted only 42 percent of the vote, although that represented an increase from 31 percent a year earlier. (In November 1980 Kunst collected enough signatures to have gay rights put on a statewide ballot. This time it was approved by 60 percent of the electorate in Florida, including 62 percent of those who voted in Dade County. Moreover, it won approval in 63 of the state's 67 counties.)

Although much of the media reflected the antigay tone set by Briggs and Bryant, in late 1978 the *Examiner* published one of the earliest in-depth examinations of gay life ever carried by a major American newspaper. Features editor Pamela Brunger initially wanted someone on the newspaper's staff to write a series of articles, but she was uncomfortable broaching the subject because no one in the *Examiner*'s newsroom had ventured out of the closet, although the city had the first gay rights ordinance in the nation. Instead, she contacted the *Advocate*, which at the time was located in San Mateo, and editor Robert McQueen referred her to Lenny Giteck, a journalism student who had just graduated from San Francisco State University and who was earning his living by freelance writing. Giteck recalled,

> In the first installment it occurred to me that people probably didn't know what homosexuality was, in the sense that they always said, "What do they do in bed?" Very naïvely I thought we should tell them so people would know what we're talking about. So I had a list of things male homosexuals engage in and another list for lesbians—kind of a clinical list. Pam okayed it, but whoever was overseeing kind of blanched and said, "There's no way we can print this." So that part came out, but otherwise it went in as I wrote it.[48]

The series, GAYS AND THE CITY, began on October 30, 1978, and ran in installments for thirteen weeks. The first carried an editor's note explaining that the articles had been written by an openly gay reporter who would write about various facets of gay life—politics, religion, sexuality, social life, employment, and more. Giteck began one installment this way:

> John Briggs is by no means the first person to depict San Francisco as a latter-day Sodom and Gomorrah: The City has long had a reputation for being morally "loose." The Barbary Coast was notorious for prostitution and gambling, and as far back as the Gold Rush days, it was known as a haven for unconventional types. . . . In 1882, Oscar Wilde came to San Francisco. The English playwright had earlier been snubbed in Boston because of his effeminate, affected mannerisms, but he was received warmly here.[49]

For another installment Giteck had interviewed Harvey Milk, the first open gay on the San Francisco Board of Supervisors. After the interview, as the two talked casually, Milk told Giteck he had gotten a number of death threats and had a premonition that he was going to be killed. Initially, Giteck thought Milk was being melodramatic. "But the more he talked," Giteck recalled, "the more I realized he was sincere about it."[50] One month later former county supervisor Dan White walked into City Hall and gunned down Mayor George Moscone and Supervisor Milk, killing both.

GAYS REPORTING ON GAYS

Given the antigay hysteria in Florida, coupled with the Briggs initiative, news director George Ostercamp at San Francisco public television station KQED decided his nightly newscast needed a reporter with expertise to cover that city's large homosexual community. He hired Randy Shilts, the twenty-five-year-old West Coast writer for the *Advocate*, who had been writing about gays and lesbians for nearly two years.

Shilts had come out of the closet during college at the University of Oregon when he ran for student body president in 1972. In fact, his campaign buttons read COME OUT FOR SHILTS. As managing editor of the student newspaper he earned an impressive array of awards, but after graduating in 1975 he could not find a job. He knew why. He began writing freelance articles for the *Advocate*, beginning with WHAT'S HAPPENING WITH GAY STUDIES U.S.A? in the June 18, 1975, issue. In a sidebar to the article the editors introduced their new reporter as an example of "a new breed of gay people in America—the open young gay person trying to break into a profession."[51]

Within a year Shilts had moved into a full-time position with the *Advocate*, based in San Francisco (the magazine was reestablishing its headquarters in Los Angeles). The long hours barely brought in enough salary to cover his expenses. But the job gave him invaluable experience, including occasional trips for stories outside California. In 1976 he covered the Democratic National Convention in New York.

Shilts broke into the mainstream media one year later when Ostercamp hired him in February 1977 to report gay news one day a week for the nightly television newscast on KQED. The television station announced the arrangement in a press release. Shilts recalled that one newspaper printed the announcement under the headline HOMO HIRED TO BE TV REPORTER. His first story for the station described the candidacy of Harvey Milk. "The whole gay thing was just exploding on Castro Street," he later told *Rolling Stone.*[52]

Shilts continued to write for the *Advocate* for a year, until he quit after a tiff with publisher David Goodstein. Shilts was never comfortable with Goodstein's edicts on who could and could not be quoted in his magazine. Goodstein was adamant that his reporters not interview the old guard among gay leaders, such as Morris Kight in Los Angeles. Shilts considered Goodstein's demand an infringement on his journalistic freedom.

In November 1978 Shilts was reporting for KQED when White gunned down Milk and Moscone at City Hall. He covered White's trial in the spring of 1979 and the riots that erupted after the jury reached a verdict. Gays had expected the jury to find White guilty of first-degree murder, which could have carried the death penalty. Instead, the jury found him guilty on two counts of voluntary manslaughter, a lesser charge that carried a maximum sentence of eight years. Moreover, White would be eligible for parole in less than five years.

Disappointment and anger rippled through the city's gay community, touching off a riot in downtown San Francisco as nearly three thousand gays began smashing windows at City Hall and torching a dozen police cars. More than 160 people were injured in the mêlée, including 50 police officers. Damage estimates climbed to more than $1 million. Only hours after police quelled the riots, a group of officers attacked a bar in the city's gay enclave, shattering its windows and injuring several customers.

From 1979 to 1980 Shilts also reported on city politics and gay issues for KTVU in Oakland. In 1980 the Oakland station dropped him from its free-lance pool and, coincidentally, KQED canceled its newscast. Shilts immediately sent résumés to the *Chronicle*, the *Examiner*, and the city's local television stations, only to be told that nothing was available. His next stop was Washington, D.C., where he visited his friend Perry Deane Young, who had settled in Washington after leaving the *New York Post* in 1970.

Because gays had become headline news nationwide, Shilts applied for jobs at Washington television stations and newspapers, including the *Washington Post*, thinking he could prove a valuable resource to the newsroom. That was a pipe dream. "Nobody believed I was qualified to cover anything except gay stuff," Shilts said. "Of course, it was assumed that since I was homosexual, that's the only thing I would know how to cover. At the same time they didn't believe I was qualified to cover gay stuff either, because of course I would be shamelessly biased. The news director at one television station literally told me she wouldn't hire an openly gay person as a TV reporter because she was afraid people would change the channel."[53]

In an effort to stay in journalism Shilts began a book about the life of Harvey Milk. Fascinated by James Michener's use of characters to weave history and society in his book *Hawaii*, Shilts envisioned a book that described Milk's personal life, his public career, and his assassination in a context that both gay and general audiences could understand. The young writer lived on his unemployment checks through the end of 1980 while he worked on *The Mayor of Castro Street*.

GAYS IN THE NEWS

By the fall of 1979 the erosion of gay rights and the perpetuation of gay stereotypes in the media had galvanized lesbians and gays for their first national March on Washington. Organizers estimated the crowd at 100,000, but news media relied on the official figure released by local police, who put the crowd at only 25,000. The *New York Times*'s coverage consisted of a single article on its inside pages that included comments from a handful of born-again Christians who protested the march from the sidelines. Each of the three television networks ran stories, but nothing about the march ever appeared in the two major newsmagazines, *Time* and *Newsweek*, even though the march was the largest in Washington in more than a decade.[54]

Marion Tholander, a marcher from Boston, returned home expecting to see a front page story in the *Boston Globe* but found only a small article in the middle of the paper. Moreover, the *Globe* failed to report on the several thousand Massachusetts residents who took part. The snub made Tholander so angry that she called for a meeting of concerned lesbians and gays and advertised it in *Gay Community News*. The twenty-five people who responded drew up a list of demands that they presented to the *Globe*'s editors. In addition, they brought along a list of gay-related stories in the *Globe* during the previous six months and copies of articles about the march from forty-five other newspapers.

The editors agreed to establish a liaison with the gay community and urged the group to "keep in touch." The group, the Lesbian and Gay Media Advocates, went on to publish a book, *Talk Back* (1982), to try to teach gay and lesbian organizations nationwide how to gain coverage. In the book the authors noted the many changes that had begun to take place at the *Globe*.[55]

But as Christine Madsen would soon learn, the receptive atmosphere at the *Globe* would not influence another Boston newspaper, the *Christian Science Monitor*, the journalistically revered daily published by the Christian Science Church. When Madsen converted to Christian Science in college, she could not have imagined the day she would find herself embroiled in a controversy over her lesbianism.

"As I read the various Christian Science books I didn't see anything that was overtly antigay or antihomosexual," she said. "There was a great quotation that referred to the Amazons who conquered the invincibles, and that we must now look to their daughters to overcome our own allied armies of evil and save us from ourselves. I thought it showed lesbians led the way."[56]

When the *Monitor* criticized Anita Bryant's 1977 antigay campaign as "blatant discrimination," Madsen interpreted the editorial as evidence of the newspaper's tolerant attitude toward gays. The newspaper went so far as to praise laws that banned antigay discrimination, saying bias "cannot be tolerated."[57]

Madsen learned that the *Monitor* had a much different attitude when an editor asked to speak with Madsen privately. It was December 1981 and Madsen had been at the *Monitor* for seven years—she had started there as an assistant on the news desk and later became a reporter and an editor. She had no idea what the woman wanted and was astonished to learn she'd been accused of trying to seduce an employee's wife. After she denied the charge, the editor asked, "Are you a lesbian?"

"It was one of those moments when it felt like the top of my head had lifted," Madsen recalled. "Everything raced through my mind. I thought of the times I had said to myself that the most important thing to me was my integrity—being who I was—that if I was ever asked directly I was going to answer honestly. So, I said that since we were friends I would tell her. The answer was yes."[58]

The editor then told Madsen she had no choice but to inform the editor in chief. Madsen was furious. It no longer mattered that she was a highly regarded writer and a model employee. It didn't matter that she had been at the *Monitor* for more than seven years. None of the salary increases, bonuses, or performance appraisals counted. Suddenly, the only thing that mattered to anyone was that she was a lesbian. "I thought we were talking as friends, but I realized she had been sent to check out the rumors," she said. "It was an incredible betrayal; the woman I had worked with for years, my friend, turned me in."

After Christmas Madsen was summoned to a series of meetings to answer questions about the allegations. She felt each question coming at her like a dagger. "What were these rumors about?" they inquired. In rapid succession they asked why she had attended meetings with gay Christian Scientists. They asked why people were saying she had tried to seduce a manager's wife. They wanted to know why she had once changed her name. "Was it because of a broken homosexual marriage?" they asked. "Are you a lesbian?"[59]

Shortly after New Year's Day 1982 a female official of the newspaper summoned Madsen to her office and asked her to seek healing to cure her homosexuality. When Madsen refused, the woman said, "You should never have been allowed to work here for more than a month." With that, Madsen's career with the *Monitor* was over.

"I was alternately furious and hysterical," Madsen said. "I could have lied. I could have denied it. I could have saved my job by promising to seek healing, but I told them that I didn't see that was any kind of advantage—why was one worse than the other? I began saying goodbye to people—some were just finding out about it—and then I left. It was a dark, horrible day. That was my church, my friends, and my career—all gone. I went back to my apartment and locked myself inside."[60]

A deep believer in the church and the goodness of its people, Madsen was bewildered by her dismissal. The church had taught her that truth would overcome evil. Yet her truthfulness had jeopardized her career.

News of the firing had a chilling effect that went far beyond the *Monitor*. Gay and lesbian journalists across the nation learned what had happened to Madsen. Few had actually heard of a confirmed case of a journalist's being fired because of homosexuality. To these gay journalists Madsen's firing seemed especially odd at so well-respected a newspaper.

Madsen agonized over how to respond, taking eight months to recover from the shock of what had happened. Finally, out of desperation she contacted a local lawyer who explained that no state or local laws prevented discrimination against homosexuals. Federal civil rights protections applied only to blacks and women. The lawyer suggested that she contact a well-known lesbian attorney, Katherine Triantafillou.

"I'm not sure I was very optimistic," Triantafillou said, "because at that time so much of gay rights law was hopeless. Part of the strategy in the early days was to get the cases out there and attract some publicity to show what happens to gay people."[61] Both Triantafillou and Madsen knew the battle would not be an easy one, emotionally or financially. Because the *Monitor* was owned by a church, the fight would be even more complicated than otherwise—the First Amendment guarantee of religious freedom would make it extremely difficult to prove a discrimination case against a church. No one had ever won such a case, and rarely had anyone even been willing to carry the fight.

After Madsen had nearly exhausted her savings, a group of gay Christian Scientists in New York came to her rescue. One was veteran gay activist Craig Rodwell, the owner of the Oscar Wilde Memorial Bookstore in Greenwich Village, which he had patterned after the vast network of Christian Science reading rooms where the church sold literature in cities and towns across the nation. The only difference was that Rodwell's bookstore specialized in homosexual literature.

With the financial support of Rodwell and the legal expertise of Triantafillou, Madsen filed a fourteen-count, $1 million lawsuit against the *Monitor* in early 1983, charging the newspaper with discrimination, defamation of character, breach of contract, and violation of her constitutional rights. After Triantafillou called in a group of reporters to explain the significance of the case, stories went out over the wire services to newspapers and broadcast stations across the nation and Europe.

Stunned church officials hastily put together a response. "Someone who is living a gay lifestyle doesn't usually agree with the church's position that homosexuality calls for healing," they said in a press release. "So it doesn't make sense for a gay person to work at the church because they don't agree with the church's religious position on this subject."[62]

Coincidentally, in Washington and New York, executives at the Associated Press were rejecting a request from their employees' union to extend job protections to gays. They refused to discuss the issue with the union and representatives of the National Gay Task Force and then touted AP to prospective customers as "a better wire service" than UPI because it had refused to follow UPI's lead.[63]

The *Monitor* had offered no job protections for gay employees, but the early stages of Madsen's lawsuit were encouraging nonetheless. The *Monitor* asked a Superior Court judge in Suffolk County to throw the case out, but he refused. The newspaper appealed the decision but lost. When the *Monitor* appealed to the Massachusetts Supreme Court, the church-state argument proved more persuasive. The justices rules 4–1 that religious institutions had an absolute authority over hiring and firing. In their ruling the justices specifically cited Madsen's refusal to seek healing. But the decision left several aspects of the suit unresolved. As a result the case was returned to the same Boston court where it had begun three years earlier.

"What was so hard was that I never got to say a word while the lawyers were up there talking about me. The lowest moment came when their attorney stood up in front of the judge with his finger pointing at me, his thundering voice booming, '*Lesbian! Lesbian!*' over and over again. He made it sound like I was damned of the damned," she said.[64]

While the case moved through the courts, Madsen tried to find work in the newspaper business. She worked for a time at *Equal Times*, Boston's women's newspaper, but missed the frantic pace of daily journalism she had thrived on at the *Monitor*. Eventually, she quit journalism altogether as her lawsuit dragged through the courts. Its eighth birthday in 1989 triggered a state law that threw the case into mandatory arbitration. Reluctantly, Madsen agreed to a financial settlement that both sides pledged not to disclose.

"Sometimes I wonder if we should have pursued it," Madsen reflected. "I wonder if we should have refused the settlement and taken our chances in court. But we had the very distinct feeling that we wouldn't come out any further ahead. So after living with it for so many years, and playing it over and over again in my mind at night, I was finally able to put it to rest."[65]

9

GAY POWER, GAY POLITICS

After CBS's landmark documentary on homosexuals in 1967 the major television networks did not return to the subject until the December 1979 *ABC
News Close-Up*, "Homosexuals." In terms of allowing gays and lesbians to
speak for themselves, the hourlong documentary was unprecedented. The
content, however, was a stereotypical account of gay suicides, promiscuity,
and the lack of stable relationships.[1]

Financially the documentary was a disaster for ABC. Originally scheduled
for airing in October, it had to be delayed twice when the World Series went
into extra games. When it finally aired on December 18, 1979, at least fifteen affiliates refused to carry it. Moreover, the network failed to find a single sponsor for the program.[2]

The next major television report on the subject came on April 26, 1980, when *CBS Reports* presented "Gay Power, Gay Politics." Like the ABC documentary, CBS's followed a tumultuous time for gay politics. The antigay crusades in Florida and California had produced a string of setbacks for gay rights in several major cities. The assassination of Harvey Milk and a surge in gay bashing were the cruelest blows.

In October 1979 more than 100,000 gays gathered in Washington, D.C., for the first National Gay and Lesbian March. It was the largest demonstration for gay rights in history. At CBS the march caught the interest of producer George Crile. He had produced a eulogy to Milk for the network's afternoon program *CBS Magazine* and realized that the political climate for lesbians and gay men was shifting. Milk's assassination led Crile to believe that the gay politician's death was only part of a bigger, more important story. He asked CBS News to allow him and colleague Grace Diekhaus to produce a primetime documentary on the growing political clout of San Francisco's gay community. The two thought the topic might interest a national audience because San Francisco seemed to offer a microcosm of what was unfolding across the nation: political gains, followed by backlash, followed by a renewed determination.

With the exception of the documentary "Homosexuals" on ABC's *Close-Up* in December 1979, Crile's documentary would be the first since Mike Wallace introduced the controversial subject to network television twelve years earlier on *CBS Reports*. Although ABC's presentation proved to be groundbreaking in terms of allowing gays and lesbians to speak for themselves, it did not delve as deeply into the politics of homosexuality as Crile had hoped.

The program used as its focal point the 1979 mayoral race in San Francisco in which gay voters were playing a pivotal role. Former city supervisor Diane Feinstein, who was serving out the unexpired term of the late George Moscone, faced challenges from nine other candidates, including David Scott, who was a member of the board of supervisors and a gay businessman. Crile had a working premise that gay voters had become so powerful that successful candidates had to capitulate to their demands to win election. In his estimation San Francisco represented a trend in which gays— particularly gay men—used their political muscle to challenge traditional social values, intimidate the political establishment, and impose their lifestyle on others.

Filming began in the summer of 1979, as tensions heightened among the candidates for mayor. Crile and Diekhaus produced their film in several installments, dropping into San Francisco to shoot for a few days and then moving on to another assignment before returning to San Francisco to continue filming. The two used their substantial skills as journalists to mix, mingle, and charm their way deep into the confidence of the city's gay community.

Although they had only sketchy information about Crile and Diekhaus's intentions, most gay activists eagerly assisted them, thinking it was the gay community's opportunity to gain long overdue recognition for its accomplishments. The activists hoped to show that gays had reached the point where no one had to talk about their homosexuality from the shadows of potted plants, as in the 1967 CBS documentary. Those who expressed apprehension were assured by Crile and Diekhaus that the documentary would concentrate on politics, not morals.

But as filming progressed, some of those helping Crile—including Mayor Feinstein—grew suspicious of his motives, especially after he began his interview with Feinstein by asking, "How does it feel to be the mayor of Sodom and Gomorrah?" Feinstein stopped the interview and threw Crile and his camera crew out of her office.[3]

"We lesbians were very cautious," remembered activist Del Martin. "We didn't think they [Crile and Diekhaus] were for real." Sally Gearhart, a lesbian-feminist activist since 1969, agreed to be interviewed but later regretted it. An outspoken critic of the promiscuity that she considered rampant among the city's gay men, Gearhart sat under the TV spotlights for an interview that lasted almost four hours.

> I remember trying to say things in ways that could not be edited because I had become so mistrustful of George. I would lift my voice at a certain point so what I said could not be cut. He seemed to want me to vilify Diane Feinstein in some way and to set her in opposition to the gay community. There was a sense that she was homophobic on some issues, but she had also been supportive— certainly supportive of lesbians. During one of the breaks I told him that I didn't feel good about it because I wasn't saying what he wanted me to say; he was trying to make me say what he wanted me to say. I felt I had been twisted and manipulated.[4]

Although Gearhart had made powerful arguments that supported a central premise of the documentary—that sexual freedoms in San Francisco had gone too far—Crile eliminated her interview when he found it difficult to tell the story as convincingly and clearly as possible within the limits of a one-hour program, common practice for television producers faced with a dilemma involving time constraints or narrative flow.

THE DOCUMENTARY

After Diane Feinstein was elected in a December 1979 runoff, Crile and Diekhaus flew back to New York to finish the script and edit the hours of film they had shot from June through early November. The final edits were made the next spring, and the documentary was ready for airing.

"Gay Power, Gay Politics" flashed onto television screens on April 26, 1980, opening with a comment from gay activist Cleve Jones, who had been interviewed by Crile at the previous October's March on Washington.

> JONES: In San Francisco we can virtually bring the city to a stand-still but now we can move across the country and, by doing so, we make each other stronger.
>
> CRILE: So, what's the message today?
>
> JONES: The message is: Look out, here we come![5]

The next scene showed a sea of lesbians and gay men stretching from the Capitol to the White House. The march was the perfect metaphor, suggesting that gays could bring the nation's capitol to a standstill.

Veteran CBS correspondent Harry Reasoner provided star quality by appearing as the host at the beginning and end. He introduced the documentary by declaring,

> For someone of my generation, it sounds a bit preposterous. Political power for homosexuals? But those predictions are already coming true. In this report, we'll see how the gays of San Francisco are using the political process to further their own special interest, just like every other new minority group before them. . . . It's not a story about lifestyles or the average gay experience. What we'll see is the birth of a political movement and the troubling questions it raises for the eighties, not only for San Francisco, but for other cities throughout the country.[6]

In the vast national audience watching that night was openly gay reporter

Randy Alfred. In addition to producing and hosting a weekly public affairs program on San Francisco radio station KSAN, Alfred contributed to the *San Francisco Examiner* and the *Sentinel*, one of the city's two gay newspapers. As he watched "Gay Power, Gay Politics" unfold, Alfred was struck by the distortions of the everyday life he and other San Francisco gays were living. Alfred had covered many events shown in the documentary, and he had come away with an entirely different interpretation. As he watched the program, he kept thinking, "That's wrong! They're lying!"[7]

Unsure at that point whether he was merely having a negative reaction to a different viewpoint or the entire gay community had been slandered on network television, he called friends to compare notes. The next day he invited several of them to his apartment to discuss a response. By the end of the meeting he had volunteered to document the inaccuracies.

Alfred worked with a transcript of the program for the next ten weeks, comparing it to notes he had taken at the same events and with his own recordings of speeches by Feinstein and others. He talked with people who had been interviewed for the program. By July 10 Alfred had assembled a nine-thousand-word complaint filling twenty single-spaced typed pages and documenting forty-four allegations of misrepresentation and distortion by Crile's documentary. The program relied on a "systematic use of hearsay, oversights, exaggerations, distortions, inflammatory buzzwords, leading questions, and misleading and deceitful editing," resulting in "patterned distortion," Alfred said in the complaint.[8] He took the complaint to the National News Council, a short-lived media watchdog organization that provided a national forum for complaints of news bias.

"I filed it not as a gay activist who was worried about what the program was going to do to our image," Alfred said. "I filed it as a journalist saying that these practices brought the entire journalistic profession into disrepute. I felt that unless the News Council as an arbiter says to journalists, 'No, you can't do this; this is beyond the bounds,' we would all suffer as journalists because we would lose the trust of the public."[9]

"Gay Power, Gay Politics" was a classic example of how news can be based on facts yet fail to portray the truth. Rather than inform the public, it demonized homosexuals and frightened the viewers. For example, Crile took his camera to an S&M parlor where the sexual activities were described as "so dangerous that they have a gynecological table there with a doctor and nurse on hand to sew people up."[10] When Randy Alfred tried to verify the comment, he learned that Crile had gotten the information from the city coroner, who explained that it was based on hearsay. The caveat was dropped in the editing process.

Crile also proved to be a master at asking leading questions. When interviewing Mel Wald, described as an S&M consultant who taught classes to police and coroners, Crile asked, "You mean a lot of the S&M sex ends up in death?" Wald responded, "Not necessarily. There are some that do end up in either death or damage." Showing pictures of whips and handcuffs used in S&M bondage, Crile asked openly gay banker Burleigh Sutton, "What kind of people will use this sort of thing—the lunatic fringe of the gay community?" "No," Sutton tried to explain. "It's everybody. It's bankers, lawyers, doctors."[11]

Intentionally or not, Crile portrayed S&M as a phenomenon that was exclusive to homosexuals. But one month after the airing of "Gay Power, Gay Politics," San Francisco public television station KQED ran a one-hour documentary on the Bay area's S&M scene in which reporter Phil Bronstein reported that 90 percent of it occurred among straights. In fact, Bronstein recognized the mock torture chamber used in the CBS documentary as one located at The Chateau, an S&M parlor that catered almost entirely to a heterosexual clientele.[12]

The lapses were numerous. The documentary showed a vigil in downtown San Francisco for Harvey Milk and George Moscone and claimed that "until the night of the assassination, few people recognized the size and strength of the gay community."[13] Gay political strength had been well known for many years in San Francisco. Gays had played a key role in the election of Harvey Milk as the city's first openly gay supervisor in 1977, and Moscone had appointed Del Martin, Phyllis Lyons, and other activists to various city boards.

Because the mayoral race was central to the documentary's premise, one of the most important scenes was an appearance by Feinstein at a meeting of the Harvey Milk Democratic Club during the runoff. In order to win Feinstein would need the support of gays, so she turned to David Scott, the openly gay candidate who had lost in the general election but had managed to draw enough votes to force the runoff. Feinstein felt that she needed Scott's endorsement to assure herself a victory. To that end she had come to apologize for remarks she had made in an interview that ran in the March 1979 issue of *Ladies' Home Journal*. She had said that gays and lesbians must face the fact that some people would always find their lives offensive. "It's fine for us to live here respecting each other's lifestyles, but that doesn't mean imposing them on others," she had told the magazine.[14]

Crile's documentary showed the gays applauding wildly in response to Feinstein's apology, a scene that proved to be the smoking gun in Randy Alfred's search for evidence. A comparison of the documentary with Alfred's own audiotape of the event revealed that the applause had been taken out of sequence, making it appear that Feinstein was groveling to atone, as Crile described it, for her remarks in the magazine interview. Actually, the applause occurred when Feinstein condemned antigay violence and promised to appoint a lesbian or gay representative to the police commission.[15]

"I was both angry and happy at the same time. I thought, 'How could they have done that?' This wasn't just like a technical thing where you take out four seconds of silence before what comes next just to tighten the show," Alfred said. "They took the applause from somewhere else. It was clear that there was bias, but in terms of being able to find specific evidence, this was it."[16]

CBS officials had received complaints even before the documentary aired. As a result William Leonard, president of CBS News, sent Crile and Diekhaus to San Francisco for the broadcast. Immediately after the broadcast the city's CBS affiliate, KPIX, featured an interview with the two producers in which they acknowledged that they had chosen the material in the program to highlight what they found disturbing and controversial.[17]

One of the angriest viewers was Feinstein. "Certainly, to give the impression that 'glory holes,' S&M parlors, and bath houses, along with open-air sex in Buena Vista Park depicts the gay lifestyle accurately is unfair and false," she wrote the station manager of KPIX.[18] The San Francisco Board of Supervisors called it a "series of images of the 'darker practices of the gay community' intended to startle viewers and to show how gays are attacking traditional values and frighten heterosexuals."[19]

"It's shocking that CBS News, home of Walter Cronkite, would partake of such bigotry," wrote *San Francisco Examiner* columnist Jeff Jarvis. Media critic Terrence O'Flaherty wrote in the *San Francisco Chronicle*, "This dreadful little program is deadly for everyone it touches." Even more to the point was *Peninsula Times Tribune* television writer Michael Munzell, who wrote, "If blood is shed in San Francisco because of this program, CBS News will never be able to wash the stain from its hands." The day after the program aired, in fact, a gang of six teenagers attacked and beat a gay man in Buena Vista Park.[20]

THE RESPONSE FROM CBS

It took CBS executives two months to respond to Randy Alfred's forty-four allegations. Network vice president Robert Chandler characterized most of Alfred's criticism as "trivial, irrelevant or clearly represent[ing] matters of opinion or judgment." He wrote,

> In the opinion of our two journalists who had followed the campaign throughout, producer Grace Diekhaus and reporter George Crile, it was their news judgment that the community standards–apology issue was transcendent in the gay community, that it was the single issue that separated the two candidates, that it was the issue that was most important to the gays in determining their support. This was, of course, an editorial judgment, but based on months of reporting and close observation.[21]

On page two of Chandler's response, however, was a startling confession about the Feinstein scene. "Mr. Alfred is correct," the letter read. "The audience did not applaud at that moment, but shortly thereafter, following her reiteration of a promise of a gay police commissioner." Even so, the network denied that Crile had intended to distort the facts, explaining that he believed the audience was in fact applauding Feinstein's apology.

"Whatever the motivation," the network wrote, "it is clear that our producers indicated the applause out of its actual time sequence and therefore misled our viewers. This, then, constitutes an acknowledgment of error and an apology for a breach of our own journalistic standards." As for the other allegations in Alfred's complaint, Chandler staunchly defended the program: "We made it clear what our story was, and we reported that story as we found it, without bias or distortion."[22]

CBS'S DAY IN COURT

On September 18, 1980, the National News Council convened a panel at

Drake University in Des Moines, Iowa, to review the complaint against "Gay Power, Gay Politics."

After considering each of Randy Alfred's allegations, the council ruled unfounded the charge that Crile had distorted the mayoral race. Its members also decided that Alfred's criticism of the public park segment was unwarranted. For a time it appeared that the entire proceeding would go against Alfred. Then the council turned its attention to the sexual issues, including the scenes involving sadomasochism. In those cases the council sided with Randy Alfred by a 9–2 vote. "By concentrating on certain flamboyant examples of homosexual behavior the program tended to reinforce stereotypes," the members decided. "The program exaggerated political concessions to gays and made those concessions appear as threats to public morals and decency."[23]

Comments that several panelists added to the final report spoke volumes about the practice of news reporting. The three African-American members of the panel—Robert Maynard of the *Oakland Tribune*, James M. Lawson Jr., pastor of the Holman United Methodist Church in Los Angeles, and Franklin H. Williams, former ambassador to Ghana—sounded a message that went beyond "Gay Power, Gay Politics" by comparing coverage of gays and lesbians to portrayals of blacks during the civil rights era. "The interests of accuracy, fairness, and balance were more poorly served than the majority opinion would suggest," they wrote. "To the degree that CBS News failed those interests in this case, it failed all those it sought to serve."[24]

On the other hand, Jeffrey Bell, a board member of the American Conservative Union, voted to support CBS. "Despite some minor factual errors and the acknowledged major error of misplacing the applause, the documentary taken as a whole was, in my judgment, an effective examination of an unusually complex and troubling issue," he said. William Rusher, publisher of William F. Buckley Jr.'s conservative *National Review*, offered a similar argument. "I concur in The Council's careful and discriminating assessment of various aspects of this documentary. . . . But I disagree with the charge of 'unfairness' in regard to sexual topics—not because the documentary was a balanced presentation of homosexual life, but because it never pretended to be one."[25]

The most revealing comments came from Norman Isaac, chairman of the news council and a former president of the American Society of Newspaper Editors, and William Arthur, the council's executive director and a former editor of *Look*. Both remarked on how little they had known about homo-sexuals before reading the complaint and how much they had learned, con-cluding that CBS had wronged the gay community.[26]

The National News Council's rebuke caught Crile and Diekhaus by sur-prise. In a memo to their CBS colleagues dated October 21, 1980, they said, "In most instances it seems to us that the News Council was complaining more about the film they felt we should have made (that is to say, a compre-hensive, balanced look at the state of homosexuality in America today) rather than judging the film we did set out to do (that is, a look at gay power, gay politics as it is manifesting itself in the first city to have a serious homosex-ual movement)."[27]

As for the shift of applause, Crile was at a loss to explain it. "As strange as it may sound we simply did not realize that the two-second gap was there," their memo read. "Had we been conscious of it we would have corrected it and we would have been able to do so without any loss of impact to the sequence. But beyond this point where we can legitimately be criticized, we have no apologies to make." Crile later said his biggest regret was that he had not included his interview with Sally Gearhart:

> I think Sally would have made it easier for people to listen and consider the issue on its own merits rather than reacting against. When she talked about how fright-ened she was by the excesses of the gay men, she compared it with the bombing in Vietnam by people who just dropped these bombs from thousands of feet up and had no idea what was happening in the villages that were being struck. I think she broadened and legitimized, in some ways, the concerns about some of the excesses of the gay male sexual life in the city. And she articulated it tougher than anybody could have.[28]

On October 21, 1980, Randy Alfred's thirty-fifth birthday, he invited a group of friends to his apartment for cake and ice cream and to watch that night's *CBS Reports*. Near the end of the program everyone gathered around the TV as Alfred turned up the volume to hear the announcer read an apology.

"In a 9-to-2 ruling last month, the News Council dismissed as unwar-ranted those parts of the complaint charging CBS News with distortion in its reporting of the mayoral campaign itself. It also upheld CBS News's inclu-sion in the broadcast of a section dealing with public sex in one of the city's parks. But the News Council did find unfairness by CBS News in the presentation of four sexual issues," the announcer intoned. The narration named each of those segments and then turned to the shifting of the applause. "CBS News acknowledged that the complaint was accurate in that respect and that the insertion of applause was contrary to its own journalistic standards. CBS News regrets that error."[29]

Never before had gay activists managed to win an official apology from a major news organization. "The message to journalists throughout the United States will be clear," Randy Alfred later wrote. "Gay stories must be treated with the same absolute respect for the truth and for human dignity as would the subjects of any other inquiry."[30]

Despite the setback, Crile later submitted "Gay Power, Gay Politics" for several national journalistic awards. In each case Randy Alfred sent the awards committees telegrams, letters, and copies of the National News Council's decision. In the meantime copies of the program had begun to surface among right-wing religious groups. In Austin, Texas, for instance, a group of forty local ministers began circulating it in an attempt to warn residents of the results of extending legal protections to homosexuals.[31] Moderate Majority, the Canadian version of Jerry Falwell's Moral Majority, wrote in its newsletter,

> In case you haven't heard, the CBS special portrayed a San Francisco in the heinous grip of gay male voters who are forcing Mayor Dianne Feinstein to . . . kiss drag queens in order to be reelected; taking over parks and playgrounds in order to have sex there, and right in front of innocent children too; killing each other in S&M encounters; rioting and destroying public property; propagandizing for the gay life in the school system; threatening the life of any honest citizen brave enough to speak out against gays.[32]

Within the eight months of the documentary's broadcast the Committee United Against Violence, a group that tracked antigay violence, had found that attacks on gays and lesbians in San Francisco had risen by nearly 400 percent. At the same time, anger over the documentary had motivated activists in a number of cities to form local media watchdog groups that continued to function well after "Gay Power, Gay Politics." A protest by one of those groups, the Philadelphia Lesbian and Gay Task Force, prompted the *Philadelphia Daily News* to ban use of the term *faggot*.

WATCHING FROM THE NEWSROOM

As "Gay Power, Gay Politics" was setting off a furor among gay and lesbian activists nationwide, gay and lesbian journalists were beginning to make their presence known in network newsrooms. In contrast to Crile's perspective as an outsider, these journalists came to the topic as insiders who could separate homosexual stereotypes from the realities of gay life. Moreover, some network executives were beginning to realize that what these journalists offered was expertise, not bias.

Lesbian journalist Ann Northrop emerged from the closet at ABC soon after she joined the staff of *Good Morning America* in 1981. A gay friend had told her that each afternoon women staff members went to a nearby bar for "lesbian hour." On her first day Northrop turned to the person who had shown her around the office and asked, "Where's lesbian hour?" "Excuse me, but that has nothing to do with sexual orientation," the horrified woman responded. "It's just that the girls get together to chat in the afternoon. Some of us call it 'lesbian hour' as a joke."

Despite the jokes, Northrop persevered at *Good Morning America*. "When I came out in life that was it, I was out," she said. "I wasn't going back. It never really occurred to me to be closeted anymore. But at the same time I wanted to work in these mainstream jobs. So I just went about my business. There was a lot of talk behind my back at *Good Morning America*, and I was treated fairly nastily by a few people. But mostly those were fellow writers who had problems with the fact that I was being successful."[33]

Later that year the executive producer of the program scheduled a segment on runaway youth and assigned Northrop to write the questions and answers that would be used by then-host David Hartman. As she looked over the information the staff had put together, she realized that something was wrong. It told only part of the story. So she contacted a man who ran a shelter for runaway youth in San Francisco who talked about the large number of gay kids who were being thrown out of their homes with no place to go and ending up in shelters for runaways. This was a stunning revelation in 1981 and won accolades from the show's other producers. "The producers said it was one of the best segments we had ever done," she recalled.

A year later George Merlis, who had hired Northrop, left ABC to become the executive producer of the *CBS Morning News*. To help him with his new duties he invited Northrop and several staff members to join his staff at CBS. Although she was completely open about her lesbianism, it was clear that the network was not ready to use her as a resource on gay-related stories. According to Northrop,

> The producers wanted a week of segments on singles. "Alright," I said. "How are we going to integrate single gay people into this?" There was this silence until one of the producers said, "That's different." I said, "No, it isn't. We're single, we want to find someone, we go through the same things, or different things, or whatever. This is an issue for us too." Well, that was the last we ever heard about the segments on singles. Clearly, this was not something they were ready to do in 1984.[34]

Northrop proved to be extremely difficult for the network to ignore. Unlike the activists who had demanded fair treatment of gays by the television networks, she was a respected voice for equality from within the newsroom.

In the summer of 1984 the network began making plans to cover the Democratic National Convention from San Francisco. While working on a schedule of programs for the week, Northrop noticed something amiss. "Excuse me," she said to executive producer Jon Katz.[35] "I'm looking at this grid and I don't see anything here about gay people. We're going to SAN-FRAN-CIS-CO, get it? What's going on here?" "Maybe we should do something," Katz said, glancing at the schedule. "What should we do?" Northrop suggested that the program include a segment about straights and gays peacefully coexisting in the most heavily gay city in the nation. Katz agreed.

When Northrop arrived in San Francisco just before the convention, she found that another producer had already booked two straight people for the segment. "Thank God," she told the woman. "I had no idea where I was going to come up with straight people." The room full of producers burst into laughter. To complete the panel Northrop found a middle-aged, balding white gay man who owned an insurance company and a militant-looking black lesbian. The segment aired without a hitch. "Leave it to you, Northrop, to come up with two gay people who don't look gay," Katz told her after the show. "Excuse me?" she snapped. "You think you can pick all of us out by the way we look?" "Of course I can," Katz said.[36] While his comment may have been intended as a joke, it struck Northrop as yet another example of an attitude she had seen in newsroom heterosexuals. Northrup later commented,

> Journalists, I find, know less than most human beings on earth. This is a big secret that most of them haven't figured out yet. They're still going out there being arro-

gant—pretending they know everything—but it's shocking how little journalists know and how little they understand about real issues. When a story about lesbians and gays comes along, they assume they understand it all because they've absorbed attitudes since birth, and they're not aware of how their thinking has been shaped by the world around them. They are completely oblivious to it. And it's not all their fault. It took me forty years to figure it out.[37]

Northrop may have been the most forceful gay voice in a network television newsroom, but she was not the only gay voice. Joe Lovett began suggesting stories about homosexuals after he started at CBS in 1975 as a film editor. "As far as I knew I was the only open person on the staff," he recalled. "There were other people that I knew were gay and others that I assumed were gay, but I was the only one who was open about it."[38]

At the height of Anita Bryant's crusade against gay rights in Dade County in the fall of 1977, Lovett suggested a segment about a typical American family dealing with their child's homosexuality. The idea was debated in several production meetings before it was approved. The program aired in November 1977 on *CBS Magazine,* the same monthly daytime magazine program where George Crile worked before he moved to *CBS Reports* to work on "Gay Power, Gay Politics."

In his story Lovett included an interview with Judd Marmor, a psychiatrist who had been instrumental in persuading the American Psychiatric Association to reclassify homosexuality three years earlier. Lovett recalled,

> It was the first time homosexuality had been presented positively on television. I don't think we got one nasty letter. Homophobia is so extraordinarily pervasive—so ingrained in gays and straights—that gay people often find that they have a tremendous amount to risk being open about being gay. But as a gay man, I always felt that what I offered was a perspective that people paid attention to—maybe not at the moment I wanted them to—but there were a lot of stories that I would present that people wouldn't buy right off that were not necessarily about gays and lesbians.[39]

In 1979 Joe Lovett found that his openness about his homosexuality had not damaged his journalistic career. He was offered a producer's job at ABC's *20/20,* a promotion for Lovett because it was a primetime program and his first job as a full-fledged network producer. His first segment was about his childhood hero, James Baldwin, an African-American novelist who few knew to be openly gay. "Who wants to hear from a gay black has-been?" asked another producer. In another era closeted gays would have found such a comment chilling. But Lovett, who had been out for many years and had done gay-related stories in the past, saw the resistance as an isolated incident, not homophobia, and continued to push for accurate and fair stories about gays at *20/20* until he left the network to form his own production company in 1989.

PRESSURE FROM THE OUTSIDE

While journalists like Joe Lovett and Ann Northrop were beginning to influence television portrayals of gays and lesbians, religious fundamentalists were launching an effort to black out all mentions and treatments of gays and lesbians on television. Donald Wildmon, a fundamentalist Methodist minister in Tupelo, Mississippi, used opposition to homosexuality and other incendiary social issues as the basis of his political activities. Allying with Jerry Falwell, founder of the Moral Majority, Wildmon's 1977 campaign quickly gained national stature. Through the group's Coalition for Better Television and Clean Up TV, the conservative ministers threatened the networks with letter-writing campaigns and boycotts against advertisers. Partly as a result of their protests the number of gay-related programs in production fell from thirty in 1977 to only five in 1981.[40]

The first evidence of Wildmon's influence on network executives came in the fall of 1981 when NBC announced that Tony Randall would star in a new series, *Love, Sidney*, a situation comedy based on the made-for-TV movie *Sidney Shorr*. The plot of the movie involved an aging, middle-aged Jewish man named Sidney who had just broken up with his male lover. Sidney is snapped out of his depression by an energetic young single woman who moves in with him, eventually giving birth to a baby out of wedlock. Sydney, who talked his friend out of having an abortion, becomes the surrogate father. Sociologist Todd Gitlin described the show as an eighties version of *Father Knows Best.*

The television version was destined to be the most sympathetic treatment of homosexuality ever on network television, even though NBC never acknowledged that the lead character was gay. To protect the network from protest NBC officials claimed the series was not related to the movie and would be free of references to the character's sexuality. "A warm, poignant three-character comedy," said a press release from NBC. Randall, however, was determined to preserve the character's sexuality, even if it meant quitting the series. (He later received an award from the Alliance for Gay Artists for the role.) As descriptions of the plot leaked into entertainment magazines, religious fundamentalists launched a ferocious attack. The network canceled the show in 1983 because of low ratings. Even after it went off the air, NBC continued to deny that Sidney was gay.[41]

10

LESSONS FROM THE RAMROD

There was no reason for anyone to notice the white Cadillac when it pulled up to a row of dilapidated warehouses on New York's Lower West Side at shortly before 11 P.M. It was Wednesday, November 19, 1980, and the only sign of life was the pounding disco music coming from a small cluster of gay bars near the abandoned docks in Greenwich Village. Suddenly, the driver of the Cadillac turned the area outside the Ramrod bar into a shooting gallery.

He aimed his Uzi at a group of men standing in line outside the Ramrod bar and squeezed the trigger. Blood splattered against the wall and door as bullets ripped into one man's shoulder and another man's arm. In barely the time it takes to light a cigarette, forty rounds tore into the crowd, leaving five men in a pool of blood at the entrance to the bar. Twenty-four-year-old Jorg

Wenz died at St. Vincent's Hospital after doctors struggled for hours to save him. Twenty-one-year-old Vernon Koenig died a short time later.

As bullets sprayed the front windows of the bar, panic swept the crowd inside. Customers dropped to the floor. Several crawled to a stairway at the back of the building in a desperate attempt to survive. Grazed by a bullet, a bartender ducked behind the bar and held his bloody hand. Outside, the gunman strolled back to his car, made a u-turn across West Street and stopped again, pointed his weapon at the bar, and let rip once more before speeding off into the heart of the city's gay district.

At Washington Street he fired on an all-night delicatessen and wounded three more men. Not far away, he abandoned the car and ran off. Police found him hiding under a van in a parking lot. He was later identified as Ronald Crumpley, a thirty-eight-year-old former New York transit cop who was married and had two children. Investigators said he had stolen the car from his father a week earlier and had driven to Virginia where he bought the guns. At police headquarters he told detectives, "I'll kill them all—the gays—they ruin everything."[1]

When copies of the *New York Times* arrived at newsstands at dawn, the only mention of the shooting was on the bottom of page one, where a single-column box directed readers to page B1. In many newspapers mass murder would merit a banner headline. The *Times*, however, gave the story secondary priority and put the article by veteran crime reporter Josh Barbanel on the front of its local news section.[2]

"No one called up eighty-five editors and had a meeting about how the story was handled," Barbanel recalled. "This thing happened late in the evening. The deaths didn't happen all at once. It wasn't a finished, polished story that happened at five o'clock at night. These are factors that go into the eight million decisions that are made in the course of a night at a newspaper. It was put on page B-one, which is the second most prominent place in the paper."[3]

A candlelight vigil in Greenwich Village for victims of the shooting drew fifteen hundred mourners but failed to garner coverage in the *Times*. Just four months earlier the newspaper had given considerable attention to the closing of a public restroom in Westchester that had been used as a homosexual rendezvous.[4]

"From a news point of view, it looked like the victims were expendable," said David Rothenberg, who at the time was the only gay member of the New York City Human Rights Commission and a personal friend of one victim. "I wrote a piece for the *Village Voice* saying we should have a point system. If the victim is a white female in the East Fifties, the death is worth a plus five; a black drag queen in Crown Heights, a minus three."[5]

Rothenberg was not alone in his frustration. Assistant Metropolitan Editor Jeffrey Schmalz, who had not worked the night of the shooting, learned what had happened when he picked up the newspaper the next morning. Arriving at the *Times* newsroom, he began asking questions:

> It happened in the middle of the night, and my recollection is that when Metropolitan Editor Peter Millones was awakened and told of the story, he didn't see it as a page one story. The reason he didn't see it as a page one—although he would never say this—was that he knew that Abe Rosenthal was against anything gay. I remember being quite upset. Did I tell them I was upset? Yeah—not as someone who was openly gay but based simply on news judgment. I remember arguing that the story was worth a bigger display. Millones disagreed, and that was the end of it.[6]

Decisions about placement and length of stories are typically made by a committee of editors from several departments. Although no two newspapers are alike, most follow a similar decision-making routine. The top editor gathers the subeditors together in an editorial meeting at which each suggests stories for the front page. The competition among these editors is fierce, with each subeditor trying to impress the newsroom hierarchy by producing—and promoting—stories important enough to merit the front page.

When an important story breaks late at night, as the Ramrod shootings did, the metropolitan editor makes a determination about the story's importance. If this editor decides the story is sufficiently important, she or he would call the executive editor to make a pitch for front-page placement (at some papers the metropolitan editor makes this decision in conjunction with the news editor). Millones said he had no recollection of the Ramrod story. In fairness, the story would have been only one of thousands he oversaw during his tenure on the metropolitan desk.[7]

But at the *New York Post*, where crime stories were a staple of the news diet, the shootings consumed that newspaper's entire front page, under the headline BLOODBATH IN THE VILLAGE: WHY? WHY? WHY?

Post reporter Joe Nicholson was concerned that his newspaper's coverage implied that gays had done something to deserve the attack. One section of the story detailed the gunman's history of paying male hustlers for frequent sexual encounters.[8] Nicholson was angry that the paper failed to point out the homophobic motive for the crime.

At that point Nicholson, who had worked at the *Post* for ten years, had never openly discussed his sexuality with his colleagues. He had learned about the intolerance of the news business years earlier from his father, a twenty-three-year veteran of the Associated Press. When Nicholson, twenty-one and fresh out of the navy, took a summer job at AP in 1968, his father took him aside and warned him of what reporter he should avoid. "I have my suspicions about him," he confided. To Nicholson the message in the newsroom was as clear as it had been in the navy: avoid homosexuals. Two years later, when Nicholson became a reporter at the *Post*, one of his first stories was about the failure of a gay rights bill in the city council. "You better be careful," warned reporter Barbara Trecker. "People are going to wonder."[9]

In the late 1970s, after he had established himself as a talented reporter, Nicholson suggested that the Newspaper Guild push for an antidiscrimination clause in its contract negotiations with the *Post*. But the idea got a cool reception from liberal publisher Dorothy Schiff. Her negotiator reported her response: "The *Post* cannot be represented by reporters who are homosexual."[10]

By the time of the shootings in the Village Nicholson's sexual orientation was known to most of the reporting staff but not the editors. The day after the shootings he asked if he could answer the headline the newspaper had used on its front page: WHY? WHY? WHY?

"At that point I was angry, and it seemed that the best way to direct my anger was to come out and give them a chance to see that a homosexual was working there with them," Nicholson said. "I told the editor I was gay and offered to write him a first-person story about homophobia. I knew some of the editors knew I was gay, but they never said so. I think what surprised him was that I would tell him."[11]

The *New York Post* had built a reputation as one of the most liberal newspapers in the nation until 1976 when it was purchased by Australian media mogul Rupert Murdoch, who transformed it into a conservative bastion overnight. Murdoch brought in his own team of editors, including Metropolitan Editor Steve Dunleavy, who had a reputation as an ace reporter at Murdoch's Sydney *Mirror*. Known for his purple prose, his hard drinking, and his womanizing, Dunleavy personified the gruff, hard-driving stereotype of newspaper editors from the classic play *The Front Page* but with an Australian accent.

Dunleavy knew Nicholson had been a football player in high school and a navy officer. The reporter fit none of the gay stereotypes.

"You would describe what the homosexuals think?" he asked.

"No," replied Nicholson, "I would describe what I think."

"You, my dear boy?" Dunleavy asked. "You're letting us know a new dimension of yourself. . . . How long have you been gay?"

"I've considered myself gay for about ten years," Nicholson told him. Then Dunleavy asked whether Nicholson planned to use his name on the story.

"Yes," he responded, "you can use my picture too."

Nicholson sat down and wrote a lengthy article that described what he thought motivated people to hate—and even kill—homosexuals. At one point Dunleavy suggested that he might want to include how it felt to work with "a bunch of 'tough guys' in the newsroom."[12] When he finished, Nicholson handed the story to an editor who passed it to another editor, and another, and so on. But the story never appeared in print. When Nicholson was told that it was more of an op-ed piece than news, he submitted it to the editorial department, where it was rejected again.

A month later Nicholson gave his story to the *New York Native*, a new gay newspaper that had only just begun publishing. NEW YORK POST REPORTER COMES OUT! read the front page teaser for the newspaper's second issue.

"By and large, the bigoted only change fast enough to keep from looking ridiculous," Nicholson wrote. "For them it is easier to label one homosexual, such as myself, an exception rather than relinquish dearly held prejudices. More substantial change is likely to accompany the exodus of numbers of others from their closets, although at this point I'm not aware of any other gays among the hundred reporters at the city's three dailies."[13]

Nicholson was convinced that he had broken down a barrier and that after the article and a similar one for *Columbia Journalism Review*, others would step forward. But his articles were met by silence.[14] Eleven years later, during a late-night drinking session with one of his editors, Nicholson finally got a full account of why the *Post* had rejected his original article:

> They were afraid of what Murdoch would have said if they had run it. The article would have been saying that one of his *Post* reporters was homosexual at a time when the paper was saying homosexuals were basically sex deviates, and horrible, and their lifestyle was bringing down Western civilization, and that city council should not pass the gay rights bill. Saying that and then having a reporter writing a column saying he was gay wasn't what they perceived that Murdoch wanted.[15]

LEAPING THE BARRIERS

Even before Joe Nicholson make his gayness known at the *New York Post*, magazine typesetter Frank Perich was playing a similar role at *Life*. Perich had pushed for a nondiscrimination policy to include gays and lesbians for nearly a decade but had failed to gain the approval of the publisher, who claimed that a specific policy was unnecessary because there was no evidence of discrimination against gays.[16] After the Ramrod shootings in November 1980 Perich renewed his request in February 1981 and the company relented. It was a sweet victory for a man who had been thrown out of the military in the early sixties for "associating with homosexuals."[17]

Later in 1981 employees at the *Village Voice* convinced its owners to adopt a domestic partnership policy that included same-sex partners of employees. Openly gay restaurant critic Jeff Weinstein raised the idea after he learned that the paper had an unwritten agreement with the union that its health plan would cover unmarried opposite-sex partners. Weinstein raised his hand during a union meeting and asked why it didn't apply to same-sex couples. The union representative said she didn't know why, but it sounded okay. The provision was included in the next round of contract negotiations.

Weinstein said,

> It was difficult to negotiate because no one had ever done this before, and they were concerned about such things as cheating and how we would verify who a domestic partner was. We didn't even have a term. The management lawyer called it "spousal equivalent," and we went with that—although I hated the word *spouse*, but we didn't have any other way to do it. The other part that bothered me was that new hires would have to wait a year to qualify. I argued vigorously against that because when you get married, you don't have to wait a year.[18]

By adopting the idea, the *Voice* became the first employer in the nation to sanction benefits for same-sex partners. Several employees credited it with heading off a strike. "The most important thing for me was that the union shop decided to make this part of its contract negotiations," said openly gay editor Richard Goldstein. "Our straight colleagues came forward and said that it was so important that they are willing to sit back on other things and demand this front and center. That was a very moving moment for all of the gay people at the paper because it told us we really were a part of one big family."[19]

Later that summer, the *San Francisco Chronicle* became the nation's first major newspaper to seek out an openly gay reporter. Staff reporter Ron Moscowitz had paved the way for a gay beat in 1977 when he convinced City Editor Jerry Burns to allow him to cover the city's burgeoning gay population on a regular basis. A former assistant to California governor Edmund G. (Pat) Brown, Moscowitz was hired as a general assignment reporter by the *Chronicle* in 1968 and came out to his newsroom colleagues soon thereafter.

For nearly three years Moscowitz covered a variety of stories about the lesbian and gay community. Then, in 1979, he wrote articles revealing how the U.S. Immigration and Naturalization Service was prohibiting openly gay tourists from entering the country. Federal officials later changed the regulation and the San Francisco lesbian and gay community awarded him the coveted 1980 Cable Car Award for "outstanding achievement in news journalism." But a year later he suffered a debilitating heart attack, and on the advice of his doctors he retired from the *Chronicle* and from the stresses of daily journalism.

After Moscowitz's retirement, Burns circulated word that he was looking for someone to cover gay and lesbian news. When Randy Shilts applied for the job, Burns remembered that they had met during the Democratic National Convention in 1976, which Shilts had covered for the *Advocate*. Convinced that Shilts had the credentials, Burns hired him.

Under their agreement, Shilts would work nights as an assistant city editor so that he could use his days to finish writing *The Mayor of Castro Street*. After his workday ended at the newspaper at 1 A.M., Shilts would sleep for a while and then get up at sunrise to work on the book.

"The *Chronicle* was a very gentlemanly place, and people went out of the way to be very supportive," Shilts said. "They almost made it a point to show that they didn't care and that they weren't going to be biased, which surprised me. I thought of it as a conservative, stuffy newspaper. The editorial page was very Republican, and I thought I would have all sorts of horror stories. But everybody was great. I never had one bad thing happen."[20]

Asked whether a gay reporter could objectively cover news related to homosexuals, Burns told a writer for the *Columbia Journalism Review* that asking that question was like asking "whether a black reporter can cover black stories or a Jewish person a Jewish story. You want to build a staff composed of people of a variety of backgrounds."[21] Shilts and the *Chronicle* became beacons for other gay journalists across the country. The barrier against employing an openly gay journalist at a major daily newspaper had officially collapsed.

SHIFTING TONE AT THE *TIMES*

In 1981 Arthur Sulzberger Jr. began to have a series of private lunches with select reporters and editors at the *New York Times*. The son of publisher Arthur Ochs Sulzberger, Arthur Junior—as he was called—was being groomed to succeed his father by having him work in nearly every department of the newspaper.

The younger Sulzberger began his meetings with Jeffrey Schmalz, an editor Sulzberger had gotten to know while he worked as an assignments editor on the metropolitan desk. In the middle of the lunch, he startled Schmalz by asking, "When are you going to tell me you are gay?" "I am," Schmalz responded, "what do you want to know?" Sulzberger didn't want to know anything. He wanted to deliver a message that "things will get better" for gays and lesbians at the *Times*.

"I just thought it was the type of thing friends do when they sort of push each other a bit. I was tired of having this code of silence, and so I took the first step and made a series of lunches to get this behind us," Sulzberger said. "Theoretically, Jeff could have said, 'Oh, Arthur, that's very nice of you but by the way, I'm straight,' and if he had wanted to play it that way, I certainly would have backed off."[22]

Another name on Sulzberger's list was David Dunlap, a reporter who had joined the *Times* after his graduation from Yale in 1975. Dunlap was hired by the venerable James Reston to serve as his clerk in the Washington bureau. A year later he moved to New York, worked as the graphics editor for five years, and joined the metropolitan desk in 1981.

"I remember thinking I was embarking on a schizophrenic life," Dunlap said. "In my mind a person could either be a reporter for the *New York Times* or one could be gay. To be one I would have to sacrifice—or certainly subvert—the other. I didn't come out to a colleague at the *Times* until 1978. So for my first three years at the *Times*, not one person in there knew that I was gay—at least by my witness."[23]

Sulzberger broached the subject with Dunlap in much the same way he had with Schmalz, letting him know that being openly gay and working in the *Times* newsroom were no longer mutually exclusive. Putting Dunlap more at ease, Sulzberger joked that for some assignments it was probably a logistical advantage to send a single gay instead of a straight employee with family commitments. Dunlap was heartened by Sulzberger's effort to put him at ease and appreciated the gesture.[24]

A year after his lunch with Sulzberger, Dunlap found himself squarely in the middle of an ethical dilemma involving one of the most controversial gay-related stories at that time. The controversy arose after New York City Mayor Ed Koch ordered that outside contractors doing business with the city not discriminate against homosexuals. The announcement set off a storm of controversy, particularly from the Catholic Church, which had a multimillion dollar contract with the city to provide a variety of social services, including care for disabled and emotionally disturbed children.

Archbishop John J. O'Connor responded to the mayor's decree by announcing that the church would cancel its contracts rather than comply. Dunlap was assigned to the story:

> I thought about it for about ten seconds. I was already out to Arthur Junior, so I went back to the weekend assignment editor and told him that I knew there were probably plenty of rumors going around the newsroom, but I just wanted to make sure that he knew that I was gay. He sort of smiled sheepishly and said he knew, but that I was a professional reporter and that he expected the same good, objective job that I had done on other [stories]. It occurred to me that if there was a turning point for me, that was the moment.[25]

The next day, June 18, 1984, a headline on the front page of the *New York Times* read ARCHDIOCESE SEEKS ACCORD WITH CITY.[26]

A LESBIAN VOICE IN THE MAINSTREAM

The path out of the closet for reporter Lindsy Van Gelder was more circuitous than that followed by David Dunlap or Joe Nicholson. For her the process began at the Miss America Pageant in 1968 when she covered a protest by WITCH (Women's International Terrorist Conspiracy from Hell) whose members claimed the beauty competition exploited women. When *New York Post* editors read a press release announcing the protest, they assigned Van Gelder, who had just joined the staff, to cover it.

"My desk sent me because they thought it would be a funny," she recalled.

"But when I met these women, everything they said went click-click-click, and I said, 'Where can I join?' In fact, the group I joined was composed mostly of other women reporters and women in media who wanted to be reporters but had awful entry-level jobs, even though they had degrees from Ivy League schools. In a couple of cases, the women were married to reporters."[27]

"Atlantic City is a town with class; they raise your morals, and they judge your ass!" the women shouted as they picketed the Atlantic City convention hall, launching what would become the women's liberation movement. Van Gelder knew firsthand about discrimination against women journalists from her experience in applying for a job at the *Daily News* right out of college: "The man who interviewed me said I was more qualified than most of the applicants but that a pretty little thing like me ought to be at home having babies every year." Despite advice from her friends to ignore the incident, she decided to file a complaint with the New York Human Rights Commission. "If I had not been a feminist before, banging up against people in the news business would have made me one," she said.[28]

Eventually, Van Gelder landed a reporter's job in the New York bureau of United Press International, where she worked with Perry Deane Young. In 1968, after Young was assigned to cover the Vietnam War, Van Gelder left for a job at the *New York Post*. After she covered the women's protest against the Miss America Pageant, she began to meet open lesbians for the first time. "At this point, I was heterosexual—not bisexual," she said, "although it occurs to me that if we lived in a culture where this stuff was more spoken about, maybe I would have discovered that I was bisexual at a younger age."[29]

During her stint at the *Post*, she and her husband had two daughters, but her sexual identity continued to evolve. She divorced her husband, *New York Times* reporter Lawrence Van Gelder, and began to date women. Her coworkers remarked that she was going through "a cute little feminist phase" that wouldn't last.

Rupert Murdoch bought the *Post* in November 1976, and Van Gelder left the newspaper the next year and supported herself and her two daughters for two years by writing for *Ms.*, and selling freelance articles to newspapers in a variety of cities, including Philadelphia, Seattle, and San Jose. She also provided a regular commentary to WNEW, an independent television station in New York. For a short time in 1980 she returned to daily journalism as a feature writer for the *New York Daily News*. Meanwhile in her private life motherhood left her little time for activism, and she was becoming more deeply involved in her relationship with Pamela Brandt. "Her [Brandt's] friends, for a while, were very distrustful," Van Gelder remembered. "They thought I was some adventurous straight girl who would drop her."

Van Gelder reached a turning point two years later when she wrote an essay on bisexuality for *Ms.*, the feminist magazine founded in 1971 as the voice of the women's movement. What made it especially important was that it was the first article in which she would address her sex life. But there were complications. She had continued to use her married name and, when she contacted her ex-husband as a courtesy, he was adamant that she not use the name Lindsy Van Gelder on the article. In addition, the editors at *Ms.* feared a lawsuit if she ignored his objection. So to ease the concerns of her husband and her editors she agreed to use the pseudonym Orlando, which she borrowed from Virginia Woolf.

Van Gelder's second step toward coming out in print came a year later. In the summer of 1980 she wrote about her decision to stop attending straight weddings. Because legal constraints prevented her from having a wedding and marrying *her* lover of six years, she saw no need to support a ritual monopolized by heterosexuals. Her decision became the basis for an article for *Ms.* In it she spelled out the problems faced by same-sex couples who considered their relationships just as valid as heterosexual ones but were barred from the benefits of marriage, including income tax credits and health insurance benefits. More than any of the other articles she had written, this one was a transforming experience, personally and professionally. "I was placing myself smack in a gay activist position, telling people to go fuck themselves rather than asking for understanding," she said.[30]

Although *Ms.* was a champion of womens' rights, Van Gelder would soon find that, as in the mainstream press, the magazine had invisible boundaries in regard to articles about lesbians. Her story sat unpublished on the editor's desk for four years. In the meantime Van Gelder agreed to be interviewed by freelance writer Ransdell Pierson for a magazine article he was writing on how the straight press was covering gays. She also agreed that when it appeared in *Columbia Journalism Review* in March 1982, she would be identified as a lesbian.

When her article on gay marriage finally appeared in *Ms.* in February 1984, her acknowledgment that she was a lesbian was almost anticlimactic. "Writing the piece, as opposed to having it published, was the transforming experience," she recalled. "After that, I stopped accepting any assignments where my being queer could be an issue. I really can't write whiny articles for women's magazines about problems with my husband. But even when I was heterosexual, I found those articles a complete pain in the ass."[31]

PART 3

REQUIEM FOR THE MEDIA, 1981–1994

II

RESPONDING TO AIDS

Dr. Lawrence Mass did not immediately recognize the grave implications of the disease that was striking gay men in early 1981. Even as he wrote the first news report and then the first feature article published outside the medical press—both for the *New York Native*, a gay newspaper—he had no idea how rapidly the epidemic was growing. No one did. The outbreak had no official name, and its symptoms were only beginning to be identified. No one had yet figured out that the wildly varying symptoms might have a single cause. Medical journals were only beginning to understand that an epidemic was underway, whatever its cause.

As a gay physician and writer, Mass was in an ideal position to recognize the profoundly disturbing patterns that were escaping his colleagues. Mass's alarm first began to grow during a casual conversation with Brent Harris, an associate editor at the *Advocate*, for which Mass wrote a regular column on health issues. Although Harris had complained of feeling ill, he had never mentioned the exact nature of his illness. But over time he confided in Mass that he had been diagnosed with Kaposi's sarcoma (KS).

The disease sounded faintly familiar to the doctor. To refresh his memory, he turned to a medical dictionary, which said that it was a rare form of cancer that was generally confined to older Jewish and Mediterranean men. Because Harris, who was forty-two, fit neither category, Mass began calling health experts at the city health department and at the federal Centers for Disease Control (CDC) in Atlanta. After he was assured that rumors of a gay cancer were unfounded, he wrote an article about it that ran on page seven of the *New York Native*, titled DISEASE RUMORS LARGELY UNFOUNDED. The article in the May 18, 1981, edition was the first mention of the disease in any publication at all:

> Last week there were rumors that an exotic new disease had hit the gay community in New York. Here are the facts. From the New York City Department of Health, Dr. Steve Phillips explained that the rumors are for the most part unfounded. Each year, approximately 12 to 24 cases of infection with a protozoa-like organism, pneumocystis carinii, are reported in New York City area. The organism is not exotic; in fact, it's ubiquitous. But most of us have a natural or easily acquired immunity.[1]

Doctors across the nation would learn of the disease for the first time almost three weeks later, on June 5, 1981, when the CDC described it in *Morbidity and Mortality Weekly Report* (MMWR), a publication that acts as an early warning system for the nation's doctors and hospitals. The two Los Angeles physicians who wrote the article described their diagnosis of five young men who had contracted the rare form of pneumonia known as *Pneumocystis carinii*. They wrote, "Pneumocystis pneumonia in the United States is almost exclusively limited to severely immunosuppressed patients. The occurrence of pneumocystis in these 5 previously healthy individuals without a clinically underlying immunodeficiency is unusual. The fact that these patients were all homosexuals suggests an association between some aspect of a homosexual lifestyle or disease acquired through sexual contact . . . in this population."[2]

In effect, the *MMWR* article signaled the beginning of an epidemic. The shocking information went out to thousands of physicians who regularly receive the *MMWR* and to science and health writers at major daily newspapers and wire services who monitor the publication. After the news appeared on the Associated Press's June 4 wire report, the *Los Angeles Times* reported on page three the following day in an article by *Times* science writer Harry Nelson: OUTBREAK OF PNEUMONIA AMONG GAY MALES STUDIED, the first mention of the disease in the mainstream American media. But as the *L.A. Times* and others would quickly learn, the topic was riddled with uncertainty. "The best we can say is that somehow the pneumonia appears to be related to gay life style," a CDC epidemiologist working in Los Angeles told the paper.[3]

A day after the *L.A. Times* article the *San Francisco Chronicle* carried a similar story based on the wire service report under the headline A PNEUMONIA THAT STRIKES GAY MALES. Science writer David Perlman, who had covered the psychiatric debate over homosexuality in the 1960s, determined that the scope of the illness was far beyond anything he had ever covered before. On June 6, 1981, Perlman reported, "A mysterious outbreak of a sometimes fatal pneumonia among gay men has occurred in San Francisco and several other major cities, it was revealed yesterday. Researchers here and at the National Center for Disease Control who are investigating the outbreak do not know yet why the pneumonia . . . should strike generally healthy young men."[4]

In July 1981—more than a month after the *Chronicle* and the *Los Angeles Times*—the biweekly *Advocate* ran its first article about the illness, "GAY" PNEUMONIA? NOT REALLY, SAYS RESEARCHER. The short article showed the difficulties the gay press faced in trying to deliver reliable information to its readers without falling into the antigay traps of the mainstream press. The *Advocate*'s story said,

> Recent media reports have trumpeted a new form of pneumonia that supposedly attacks gay men, but Dr. Alexander Carden of the National Centers for Disease Control says it's not so. . . . Carden told the *Advocate* that all of the gay men tested thus far have had impaired immunity and this fact—not their homosexuality—made them vulnerable to the disease. Although gay sex might transmit the disease-causing organism, Carden believes the protozoa may simply be ubiquitous, leading to illness only in those with weakened resistance to the organism.[5]

The disease was especially complicated for mainstream media because it did not have an official name until the spring of 1982, after it had killed more than two hundred people. During the early stages of the disease medical experts often referred to the strange constellation of symptoms as "gay-related immune deficiency" (GRID), which gave the false impression that only homosexual men were at risk.

The gay press was in no better position to determine the exact nature of the disease. Gay publications barely were able to pay their rent, relying almost entirely on volunteer staff. Lacking reporters with scientific expertise, a luxury that only the big city dailies could afford, they often did a poor job of covering the immense medical complexity of the disease.

The Centers for Disease Control issued a second advisory on July 3, 1981, when the number of reported cases of Kaposi's sarcoma rose to twenty in New York and six in California. Six men had also been diagnosed with pneumocystis pneumonia. "It is not clear if or how the clustering of Kaposi's sarcoma, Pneumocystis and other serious diseases in homosexual men is related," the CDC article reported. "The occurrence of this number of KS cases during a 30-month period among young, homosexual men is considered highly unusual. No previous association between KS and sexual preference has been reported." But even more startling was the death toll: nearly fifty and climbing more rapidly than anyone thought possible.[6]

After the story appeared on the wire services, the *New York Times* ran its first story on July 3: RARE CANCER SEEN IN 41 HOMOSEXUALS. Medical writer Lawrence Altman, who is also a physician, noted that an investigation of the disease "could have as much scientific as public health importance because of what it may teach about determining the causes of more common types of cancer."[7] The article immediately caught the attention of playwright Larry Kramer, who had also read the small article by Lawrence Mass in the *Native*. Kramer knew people who had contracted KS, and the two articles convinced him that he was looking at a potential catastrophe. He suspected that everyone around him—including himself—was at high risk, if they had not unknowingly contracted this disease already.[8]

Kramer quickly summoned a group of friends to his apartment, including Mass and Alvin Friedman-Kien, a faculty member at the New York University Medical Center who had diagnosed the city's first cases. Some of Kramer's guests thought he was overreacting, while others shared his trepidation. In time, the group became the Gay Men's Health Crisis (GMHC), the first grassroots AIDS service organization in the nation. None had any way of knowing that some of them had already contracted the virus that researchers later identified as the cause and had only a short time to live.[9]

After creating GMHC, Kramer targeted the media. He wrote letters to key editors at a variety of media outlets throughout the city, including the *New*

York Times and the major television networks, but few showed any interest in the story. There were too many unanswered questions, they said, too much uncertainty. At that stage neither the media nor medical experts were anxious to trigger a public panic about a disease that still did not even have an official name. When Donald Francis, a CDC epidemiologist, failed to get federal funding for his research on the disease in 1982, he campaigned for news coverage by calling reporters who had interviewed him in the past about his pioneering work on smallpox and other medical advances. "They told me it wasn't a news story," he recalled.[10]

Mass, meanwhile, continued to sound the alarm by writing articles for the *New York Native*. His second article, CANCER IN THE GAY COMMUNITY, appeared on July 27, 1981, and filled the entire front page. The sprawling multipage analysis that contained interviews with leading researchers was the first feature article to appear. It speculated about multiple causes of what otherwise seemed like a single epidemic and why it was afflicting gay men. The article also made an appeal for a research foundation to study the epidemic.

The following month, Mass provided the *Native* with another first, an interview with a gay man diagnosed with KS in New York. For the same issue he wrote an article, *KS: Latest Development*, that brought together all the information he had collected from the city's public health department. He wrote, "I think that at this time it's appropriate to stress there's a lot we don't yet know. Epidemiologists are cautious by nature because in dealing with populations, they've learned that going from the generalized group to the specific individual or vice versa is fraught with complications."[11]

In addition to his steady stream of articles for the *Native*, Mass proved to be a reliable source of information for a string of gay publications throughout the summer and into the fall of 1981. In addition, he was a guest on what may have been the first television program about the epidemic, "The Gay Epidemic" on *The Lavender Connection,* a gay-themed production on the public access channel of the New York cable television system.[12] At the same time much of the mainstream media maintained their virtual silence on the subject.

NEWSROOM PREJUDICE

Although some media outlets produced exceptional coverage of the outbreak of AIDS—including the *Boston Globe*, *Newsday*, *Philadelphia Inquirer*, and National Public Radio—the bulk of the mainstream media responded poorly, if they responded at all. As late as 1992 journalism professor Joe Salzman at the University of Southern California found the media's AIDS coverage to be an illustration of "how the media are failing their readers, viewers and listeners . . . just when these citizens need an accurate, knowledgeable, and informative media the most."[13]

The seriousness of the disease was becoming increasingly clear by December 1981—the *New England Journal of Medicine* carried three articles and an editorial, signaling the preliminary recognition that an epidemic existed. Reporter Jerry Bishop, who had covered the medical beat for the *Wall Street Journal* since 1958, was one who immediately recognized the grave consequences implied by the articles. Only days later he wrote what may have been the most comprehensive article to date. He was confident that its urgency would put the story on the newspaper's front page, but he was wrong. Bishop's editors failed to see how a story about homosexuals and heroin addicts would appeal to their readers and killed it altogether. "They were uncomfortable with the connection with homosexuals," he remembered. "It was known that it had spread among homosexuals and that it involved homosexual sex activities."[14]

After a series of heated arguments with his editors, the article finally ran on December 10, 1981. Although the story, MYSTERIOUS AILMENT PLAGUES DRUG USERS, HOMOSEXUAL MALES, retained its urgency, the editors sliced it in half and buried it on page forty-one.

"A mysterious, often fatal illness is breaking out in epidemic proportions among young homosexual men and drug users," Bishop wrote. "More than 180 cases of the strange illness have been reported since last summer to the federal Center for Disease Control in Atlanta. As of last Friday, at least 74 of the victims had died. All the victims are men and 90% of them are either homosexual or bisexual. Many of the victims are drug users."[15]

Staying on top of the story, Bishop watched with dismay as the number of deaths climbed during the next two months. In late February he wrote a second story. He recognized that to secure a front-page slot, he would have to demonstrate that the danger extended beyond gays and drug addicts. He learned that doctors had also diagnosed several women and two dozen heterosexual men who were not intravenous drug users. That information formed the basis of his second story. But once again, Managing Editor Laurence O'Donnell balked, claiming the story was virtually identical to Bishop's first piece, except for the numbers.

Bishop again made a strong case for his story, pointing out that the death toll had climbed beyond the thirty-four who had died from Legionnaires' disease in 1976 and was higher than the eighty-four women who had died of toxic shock syndrome between 1979 and 1980—and both stories had received extensive coverage throughout the nation's news media, including the *Wall Street Journal*. Bishop said,

> The reason that the toxic shock and Legionnaires' diseases got so much coverage was that the editors felt both of those things threatened them and their families, and here AIDS did not—they didn't feel that it did, anyway. When editors don't feel threatened—when something doesn't threaten them, or their families, or the people they know—then it's not seen as a big story. Nobody ever said anything about the homosexual angle, but it was clear that they didn't know how to handle the intimation that it was being passed by sexual practices among gay men.[16]

Bishop's story, NEW, OFTEN-FATAL ILLNESS IN HOMOSEXUALS TURNS UP IN WOMEN, HETEROSEXUAL MEN, ran in the *Journal* on February 25, 1982. It pointed out that the epidemic, now in its eighth month, had spread to 250, with nearly 100 deaths. But the editors put it on page eight.

That summer Bishop received a telephone call from a corporate lawyer at the *Journal* who told him that his mother-in-law had been diagnosed with the illness—presumably contracted from a blood transfusion—and died. Surely, Bishop thought, a story about a seventy-year-old woman dying from the mysterious illness was front page news. Still, he could not explain the disease to readers without saying that it was spread primarily through unprotected sex between men. This time O'Donnell spiked it. Rather than quarrel for a third time, Bishop sold the story to the science magazine *Discover*, where it appeared in September 1982.[17] Bishop said,

> The delay in recognizing the AIDS epidemic was the responsibility of the health authorities, but if the press had been more alert to what was going on, the story would have been done much earlier. My editors were not reading anything about it in the local papers. I think they thought I was some maniac sitting back here in the newsroom because if it was as big and important as I claimed it was, it would be in the *Times*, and it wasn't there. What I was seeing was never reported in the *Times* or in the *Daily News*.[18]

Bishop was periodically reminded of the magnitude of the epidemic as he passed newsstands, where headlines blared from the cover of the *New York Native*. At about the same time Arthur Bell, the openly gay *Village Voice* columnist, began to note that the illness was taking its toll on his friends. Over the years he had successfully used his entertainment column to sound an alarm in the gay community about the latest crisis, including the spring 1979 protests against the movie *Cruising*, which was filming in Greenwich Village.[19] But by the time the health emergency arrived in 1981, Bell was in the fatal stages of diabetes and had grown too weak to rally the troops. Instead, he urged the *Voice* to commission Lawrence Mass to write an in-depth article to lay out the staggering new dimensions he had found. Both men recognized that information in the *Village Voice* would reach much larger numbers of gay men than if it appeared in the less well-established *Native*. Although Mass was fascinated by journalism, he was an inexperienced writer, and he struggled with the assignment. But his message was blunt: "If your physician has not yet heard about the epidemic of immunosuppression, you should probably consult another physician."

Mass had submitted his article to the *Voice* with a tentative headline: THE MOST IMPORTANT NEW PUBLIC HEALTH PROBLEM IN THE UNITED STATES.

"It was the most frightening headline that I could think of to shake people up and get them to pay attention," Mass said. "It was a direct quote from Doctor James Curran, head of the CDC AIDS Task Force. I wanted the media—the *Voice* in particular—to stop everything, to suspend their rules of journalism because this was an incredibly serious epidemic. It was clear to me that we needed to suspend the usual rules of style and format to get people to pay attention."[20]

But the article did not appear in the next issue of the *Voice* or in the issue after that. Mass's repeated efforts to contact editors were rebuffed for three weeks, when he finally was told that the story had been killed. "It's not a *Voice* piece," explained outspoken feminist Karen Durbin, who was a senior editor.[21] Mass then called the newspaper's openly gay executive editor, Richard Goldstein, who explained that he was not involved in the decision and had no power to change it. Goldstein would later come under severe criticism for the *Voice*'s lack of AIDS coverage.

On March 29, 1982, Mass's article, THE EPIDEMIC CONTINUES, appeared instead on the front page of the *New York Native*, where it would reach an estimated fourteen thousand readers, approximately 10 percent of the *Voice*'s readership (and 1 percent of the *Times*'s).[22] Many more would have seen it in the *Village Voice* and vastly more if the information had run in the *New York Times*.

News of the disease did not make the front page of an American newspaper until May 31, 1982, when the *Los Angeles Times* reported MYSTERIOUS FEVER NOW AN EPIDEMIC. Veteran medical writer Harry Nelson began his story by describing how the disease had been discovered by two Los Angeles physicians eighteen months earlier, that 145 had died since, and that new cases were being reported at a rate of one per day.[23] But most editors at newspapers nationwide did not consider gay deaths news.

As the death toll climbed, the San Francisco dailies carried several feature stories about the epidemic in September 1982. The *Examiner* carried its first page one story on the disease, NEW WORRY ABOUT A GAY DISEASE, on October 24, 1982. "The mystifying epidemic that has wrought serious illness, death and fear in the gay community is growing at a worrisome rate," it said. *Examiner* science writer Richard Saltus was one of the first reporters to delve beneath the numbers and the scientific jargon to include the perspective of gay men and the effects the disease was having on real people.[24]

By December 1982 Jerry Bishop still had not managed to get the story on the front page of the *Wall Street Journal*. Then he got a call from an epidemiologist at the CDC who told him that doctors had identified a two-year-old with the disease, apparently contracted from a blood transfusion. Further investigation by Bishop revealed twenty more children with symptoms. At the same time the official designation for the disease became AIDS (acquired immune deficiency syndrome).

On December 10, 1982, the *Wall Street Journal* published its first front-page story, LETHAL NEW AILMENT CLAIMS ANOTHER GROUP OF VICTIMS: CHILDREN. In it Bishop stated that the epidemic appeared to be "more lethal than such plagues of the past as smallpox." In the eighteen months it had taken him to win a page one slot, the death toll had more than tripled. More than three hundred had died, and eight hundred were infected.

Like print journalists, broadcast journalists encountered opposition to covering the disease. NBC News medical correspondent Robert Bazell said he was continually told, "Look, it ain't us. We don't want to hear stories about homosexuals . . . (and) drug addicts." Eventually, he convinced the network to carry the first national television news coverage of AIDS, on the June 17, 1982, edition of *NBC Nightly News*. But in all of 1982 the three major networks devoted a combined total of only thirteen minutes to the epidemic.[25]

AIDS AND THE GAY PRESS

In the initial stages of the epidemic, the small gay weeklies that had sprung up in major cities were nearly as slow as the mainstream media to pick up on the seriousness of the epidemic and for similar reasons. The little information that was available was conflicting and unclear—it would be confusing to readers, and editors were concerned that the public would be needlessly alarmed.

The gay press had traditionally paid little attention to health concerns, except for the occasional report on an outbreak of syphilis, gonorrhea, or hepatitis among gay men. The gay press was traditionally the only source of this type of information because mainstream media were reticent about reporting health stories that involved sexual activity. Often the gay press would rely on a local writer or physician to write articles or an advice column in response to questions from readers.

Much of the gay press faced the possibility that a rash of stories about death would offend advertisers, particularly gay bars and bathhouses, as promiscuity became a flash point for controversy. For its extensive early coverage the *New York Native* earned the reputation among some as "the AIDS paper." Its advertising revenues began to decline.

The gay press also was hampered by the deep division among gays themselves about how to respond to the epidemic. While Larry Kramer and others grew increasingly vocal in their condemnation of anonymous sexual activity, others were defensive, convinced that AIDS was being used as a guise for antigay moralizing. In a throwback to the sixties, homosexuality was once again being associated with illness. AIDS threatened to roll back most—if not all—of the gains of the gay rights movement of the seventies. Bitter divisions tore at the fabric of the gay community, and the gay press was caught in the middle.

From late 1981 through the spring of 1983, the *Native* stories by Larry Mass consistently provided the most reliable and informative material on the epidemic at a time when other New York publications were reluctant to print anything. Recognizing that only a small percentage of the nation's homosexual population was being reached through the few gay publications that were carrying AIDS-related stories, Mass argued in an August 1981 *New York Native* article that the bathhouses should be allowed to remain open in order to facilitate AIDS education and prevention. In his estimation, attempts to close the baths would backfire, making it difficult to distribute information on AIDS prevention to the people who needed it most.

In the summer of 1982, Mass wrote "Basic Questions and Answers About AIDS" for the newsletter of Larry Kramer's Gay Men's Health Crisis (GMHC), which mailed it to every gay newspaper in the country. Only Boston's left-wing *Gay Community News* ran the article, and even the editors there took almost two months to publish it.[26]

By the spring of 1983 the strain of the epidemic had proved to be too much for Mass, who plunged into a severe depression that forced him to quit his work at GMHC. In his stead Larry Kramer produced a stream of angry articles for the *Native*. The unforgettable front page headline of March 14, 1983, read 1,112 AND COUNTING. "If this article doesn't scare the shit out of you, we're in real trouble," Kramer began. "If this article doesn't rouse you to anger, fury, rage, and action, gay men may have no future on this earth. Our continued existence depends on just how angry you can get."

As late as 1983, three years into the epidemic, the editors of the *Advocate* still approached the epidemic cautiously, even as they watched editor Brent Harris become increasingly debilitated by KS. Features editor Mark Thompson remembers that no one, including Editor-in-Chief Robert McQueen, understood that Harris's death signaled danger for the rest of the gay community. Thompson said,

> Of course, we knew about AIDS, and we were very concerned about it, but I don't think that Robert [McQueen] knew what it was. He didn't want to just print speculative, screaming stuff—he wasn't that kind of man. He wanted to present a very careful, even assessment. If he was going to do something, he wanted to do it right. Maybe the paper erred on the side of caution. But it wasn't a willful rejection of the issue. It was more like, "What do we do with it?" and "How do we deal with this? What is it?"—and at the same time, Brent Harris, his best friend, was dying from it.[27]

The tone of the *Advocate* coverage changed in January 1983 with an article by freelance writer Ransdell Pierson about a meeting the previous October of a dozen medical experts in New York. It pointed out that while researchers had failed to identify a smoking-gun cause of the disease, "doctors are beginning to agree that AIDS may be sexually transmitted, and are cautioning the gay community in unambiguous terms to avoid anonymous sexual contact and to reduce to a minimum the overall numbers of sexual partners."[28]

The *Advocate* had carried its first cover feature on the epidemic in February 1982. That issue contained two articles, one by New York writer Nathan Fain, a founder of Gay Men's Health Crisis, and one by Larry Bush, the magazine's Washington correspondent. Fain wrote about the "state of the

epidemic" and drew together the broad range of theories on its cause, ranging from forms of herpes to intestinal parasites to recreational drug use,
including the inhalants known as poppers. His article also questioned the
effect the epidemic might have on sexual freedom in the gay community.

Bush focused on the paltry level of federal funding for combating the epidemic and then traced the gay community's response to the epidemic,
despite the lack of money. "The support systems that have grown up almost
overnight, the push to educate doctors on how to diagnose symptoms, the
grassroots funding for research projects—all this is very different from the
way Americans have traditionally responded to a new life-threatening illness," he wrote.

Soon after the cover story Fain began writing a regular health column for
the *Advocate*, concentrating almost exclusively on AIDS. In April 1983 it carried one of the earliest suggestions that gay men should use condoms during
intercourse. From 1981 through the spring of 1987, when he died of AIDS-
related causes, Fain had reported on the epidemic longer than anyone except
Randy Shilts at the *San Francisco Chronicle*.[29]

Although the gay press could offer its readers little definitive information
in the early days of the epidemic, it was light-years ahead of mainstream
media in terms of warning the public. As mainstream reporters and editors
continued to search for language that would be acceptable to a broad-based
readership, the gay press began describing the suspected methods of transmission in explicit terms, without relying on the vague euphemisms used in
daily newspapers and broadcast news.

As early as October 1982 the left-wing *Gay Community News* in Boston,
where the number of cases had grown exponentially, began to devote considerable attention to the epidemic. In the first five months of 1983 *GCN* carried a dozen stories about AIDS, including a February 26 article headlined ALL
ABOUT AIDS.[30] But its coverage was largely couched in the newspaper's suspicions about the motives of Mass, Larry Kramer, Nathan Fain, and others who
suggested that male promiscuity carried unknown dangers. "They were part
of the overall pattern of suspiciousness and failure to respond," according to
Mass. "Within the gay community, the call to arms and early work on the epidemic did not come from the left. It came mostly from the center."[31]

In March 1985 Lisa Keen, editor of the *Washington Blade*, produced an
eleven-part series that tracked a gay Washington lawyer with AIDS from his
diagnosis to his death the following August. The series was honored the next
year by the Washington chapter of Sigma Delta Chi, the professional journal-

ists' society. *Washington Post* reporter Susan Okie credited the story for helping to increase her newspaper's commitment to AIDS coverage. Gay newspapers in Miami, Minneapolis, Chicago, and Philadelphia also devoted considerable attention to the disease. Yet the epidemic continued to receive only scant coverage by prominent mainstream newspapers, like the *New York Times*.[32]

At the first International Conference on AIDS in Atlanta in 1985 Lawrence Mass, who had recovered from his depression and agreed to cover the conference for the *Native*, asked Lawrence Altman, who was covering the conference for the *Times*, why the *Times* hadn't devoted more attention to the epidemic. He pointed out that the *San Francisco Chronicle* had had twice as much coverage, even though San Francisco had half as many cases as New York. "Why hasn't the *Times?*" Mass asked rhetorically. "Because we are not an advocacy journal," Altman responded, according to Mass.[33]

REPORTING AIDS AT THE *TIMES*

Criticism of the *Times* reached a crescendo in April 1983, when Gay Men's Health Crisis booked the eleven-thousand-seat Madison Square Garden for a fundraiser featuring the Ringling Brothers and Barnum & Bailey Circus. New York City Mayor Ed Koch served as the honorary ringmaster, and Leonard Bernstein directed the Ringling band in a stirring rendition of the national anthem.

The *Times* mentioned the event in a small item in the Day by Day column, noting that it was the first sellout at Madison Square Garden in five years. Beyond that, there was no attempt by the New York media to publicize the fundraiser or to explain the seriousness of the epidemic.

On the night of the fundraiser, New York television stations carried stories on their eleven o'clock newscasts, and articles appeared the next day in the *Daily News*, the *Post*, and *Newsday*. After the Associated Press and United Press International carried stories on the wires, articles appeared in newspapers as far away as St. Louis and Louisville. The *Times*, however, was silent, symbolizing its larger failure to cover the epidemic.

"The *Times* was in a powerful position to make a difference," observed activist David Rothenberg. "It could have been instrumental in saving lives, in providing information, and in legitimizing the historic nature of a community creating its own health alternative because the establishment wasn't ready to deal with it."[34]

Rothenberg assembled a delegation to pressure the *Times*, including Virginia Apuzzo, then executive director of the National Gay Task Force; Richard Failla, an openly gay New York lawyer; and Andrew Humm, representing the New York Coalition for Lesbian and Gay Rights. This was no group of novices. Apuzzo was a political ally of Governor Mario Cuomo's and had become a ranking official in the state consumer protection agency. Failla later became the first openly gay man to be elected to the New York Supreme Court. Rothenberg was the head of a prison reform group and would later make a serious run for a seat on the New York City Council.

Unbeknown to the activists, the *Times*'s former food editor, Craig Claiborne, had already raised the subject with Managing Editor Arthur Gelb. "Someone showed me several articles from the *Village Voice* and asked me why the *Times* hadn't printed anything about AIDS while people were dying by the thousands. Before that, I'd never heard of AIDS," Claiborne said. "I went to Arthur Gelb and told him, 'You know, the *Times* should write about this disease.'"[35]

Not long after Claiborne's admonition, the *Times Magazine* carried a February 6, 1983, article, AIDS: A NEW DISEASE'S DEADLY ODYSSEY, by Robin Marantz Henig, a Baltimore-based freelance writer who first learned about AIDS from her brother, an intern at a New York hospital. As she listened to his harrowing description, she became both concerned and fascinated by the mystery of what she described as "the century's most virulent epidemic." Hers was the most in-depth article about the disease to appear in the *Times*. Although her story concentrated on the scientific/medical angle of the epidemic, it was an important breakthrough. She recalls that

> the article was tricky to write. I could say *homosexual* but I couldn't say *gay*. It had to be very coy about sex and about who put what where. I didn't know the *Times* had those kind of policies, and it struck me how out of date it was. Ed Klein, the editor of the magazine, asked me if I'd be interested in taking AIDS as a beat, to cover it as a freelance writer and get to know people in various labs and ingratiate myself so that when the cure was found, they could break it in the magazine. I didn't know what he was talking about because I didn't see that a cure would be found in the next couple of years, but that was definitely the way he was viewing it.[36]

In the meantime, David Rothenberg's group of gay activists sent a letter to *Times* publisher Sulzberger threatening to picket the newspaper unless he agreed to a meeting. Sulzberger assigned the task to his assistant, Sidney

Gruson, the publisher's chief troubleshooter. Armed with a list of complaints, Rothenberg pointed out to Gruson that his newspaper had covered much smaller fundraisers than the GMHC event in Madison Square Garden, including the Boy Scouts' Soapbox Derby and the annual banquets of the Daughters of the American Revolution. "We told him that they were ignoring the most important health story confronting the city and the nation," Rothenberg recalled. "It was no longer a sin of omission; the *Times* was now a contributing factor."[37]

The delegation also criticized the paper for its refusal to adopt the term *gay*, comparing the demand to an earlier era when blacks no longer wanted to be called *Negroes*. Gays had been asking the *Times* to modernize its terminology for twelve years without success whereas other newspapers—including the *New York Post* and the *New York Daily News*, and numerous other major newspapers, such as the *Minneapolis Tribune* and the *San Francisco Chronicle*—had used the term for years. When Gruson reached for a dictionary to describe the newspaper's position, he was startled to find an entry that described the word *gay* as the popular usage for homosexuals. Gruson could not unilaterally issue a new policy to lift the ban, but he did arrange a meeting with Executive Editor Abe Rosenthal.

Only days later the group met with Rosenthal and explained that gay-related stories were "crying to be told." They suggested that if the *Times* wanted to humanize and dramatize AIDS, it should do a story on the buddy system at GMHC. The group then confronted Rosenthal with the paper's failure to respond to AIDS, charging that it was the result of institutionalized homophobia. Rosenthal denied the charge.[38]

Rothenberg recalled,

> We said that given the gays and lesbians we knew on the *Times* staff, they didn't even need to go outside of the paper to find community expertise on what's happening in the gay community, but those resources were afraid they would be demoted to a correspondent in Cheyenne, Wyoming. We told him the atmosphere in his newsroom was stifling. He was surprised and defensive, but he admitted that not covering the circus was a mistake. He even said the *Times* had missed the boat on its coverage of AIDS.[39]

Gay Men's Health Crisis executives were shocked to receive a letter from Rosenthal several days after the meeting. "You are quite right that the *New York Times* should have covered the Madison Square Garden benefit," he wrote. "I really have no explanation for it except one of human error. . . . that's all I can say except to express my regrets."[40]

Boston-based reporter Dudley Clendinen knew nothing of the meeting between Rosenthal and the gay activists when he learned of a young college football player who had contracted AIDS. The athlete claimed that his only sexual experience had been oral sex with a transvestite who jumped out of the cake at a friend's bachelor party. Clendinen remembered,

> I had stumbled across a story that had not been written about or reported with the drama I was seeing. I called the national desk and explained that this seemed to be a powerful human story, and we were covering it only as a piece of science in the fourth section—and only occasionally. I pointed out that to him, that New York was the center of it, and while people were dying by the dozens, the *New York Times* had never played the story on the front page—which was inconceivable.[41]

Clendinen's editor, David Jones, had attended at least one meeting with David Rothenberg but had never mentioned that to Clendinen. Two weeks later Jones approved the story—but with a small catch. The metropolitan desk wanted to avoid the embarrassment of having a Boston correspondent report on a disease that was rampant in New York City, so metro reporter Michael Norman would write one story about New York and Clendinen would write with a national angle.

Clendinen immediately sent messages to the newspaper's network of stringers—nonstaff writers throughout the nation who contribute articles on assignment— asking each to supply an assessment of AIDS in the stringer's area. Most of all he wanted help in identifying people who could provide the human element that was missing from earlier stories. Because people with the disease were afraid to identify themselves, this was an especially difficult challenge. Clendinen warned the stringers that the story required an unusual degree of sensitivity and that he wanted to avoid reporting on "those people over there." It was not widely known that Clendinen was gay; to most of the world he was happily married with a young daughter.[42]

The *Times* printed the story by Michael Norman on June 16, 1983, HOMO-SEXUALS CONFRONTING A TIME OF CHANGE, the first in-depth feature on AIDS to appear on the newspaper's front page. At one point the story noted,

> Half of the cases nationwide have appeared in New York, and 71 percent of them have afflicted homosexual men. These numbers have done much more than just

sour the atmosphere in the bars, baths and private clubs, where some men travel a circuit of drugs, alcohol and anonymous sex. The epidemic has also created anxiety and caution in the homosexual community at large among those who lead a variety of life styles—individuals and couples whose lives are moored by work, home, family and friends. The concern generated by the disease has led many people to suggest that it may change basic patterns of male homosexual life. It has already renewed a debate about homosexual morality.

The following day the paper carried Clendinen's article, AIDS SPREADS PAIN AND FEAR AMONG ILL AND HEALTHY ALIKE, in a similar front page slot. Norman and Clendinen took their readers from their homes and offices into the world of people who had contracted AIDS. For the first time *Times* readers were shown the physical and social realities that confronted people with AIDS, in terms they could understand. Clendinen focused on a variety of graphic examples, including a man who accompanied his sick lover to his mother's home in New Orleans, only to have the pilot of the aircraft threaten to throw them off the plane. He described a woman in Denver who called the health department to find out how to fumigate an apartment she had bought from gay men. Then there was Chuck Morris, former publisher of the San Francisco gay newspaper the *Sentinel* who had endured three brain seizures in three months. Clendinen wrote,

Twice he has been forced out of his apartments, both times while in the hospital. The second eviction, he said, took the form of a phone call from one of his roommates, who called to tell Mr. Morris that he would kill him if he moved back. He moved out. "I was standing on Castro and 18th Street with a little plastic bag with all my possessions that I could grab, and all of a sudden the enormous horror of all this hit me," he says. "At that point I had been working for 25 years, and I felt that the year before I was a reasonably wealthy man. I had my own newspaper, and now here I was, standing on the street, homeless and broke, and I had no idea where I was going to stay. It was the first time that I realized that this had caused my whole world to crumble around me."

Of the dozens of stories Clendinen had written for the *Times*, this was his most frustrating, exhausting, and enlightening. He had learned not only about AIDS but about the gay community's intense antipathy toward the *Times*. When he first joined the newspaper in 1980, he was struck by the admiration readers had for it. He noticed that everyone wanted to talk to him simply because he wrote for the *Times*. He readily felt the respect people had for what he knew to be "the mystery and the majesty of the *Times*." While covering AIDS in 1983, he found that sense of admiration was gone: "I had never run into people who had mistrust, contempt or hatred for the *Times*. It was arresting—if not stunning—to find this very large colony of people in New York who saw the *Times* as an enemy. I still have the tearful letters sent to me from gay men who were outraged and felt stigmatized by the *Times*'s persistent use of *homosexuals*. It was the oddest feeling for a person who was homosexual himself."[43]

Indeed, the articles that June signaled a change at the *Times*. On December 5, 1983, the front of the metropolitan section carried a story by Maureen Dowd. Headlined FOR VICTIMS OF AIDS, SUPPORT IN LONELY SIEGE, it concerned the volunteer buddy system at GMHC. In one section she wrote, "The story of the organization reflects the dramatic changes that have recast life in the city's homosexual community in the years since AIDS emerged as a mysterious and frightening national epidemic. Fighting a siege of death and prejudice, the community that was once characterized by a carefree and freewheeling spirit has evolved into a more mature and politically savvy population."

The article was one of the several suggested by David Rothenberg and the other activists during their meeting with Abe Rosenthal seven months earlier.

ONE STEP FORWARD, ONE STEP BACKWARD

While Clendinen and Michael Norman were assembling their AIDS coverage in New York in the summer of 1983, Richard Meislin, the bureau chief for the *Times* in Mexico City, awakened one hot morning to find his legs crippled by a severe ache. The debilitating pain spread to joints throughout his body and lasted for weeks. Doctors who examined him had no idea what was causing it.

After joining the newspaper as a copyboy in July 1975, Meislin had risen through the ranks rapidly. He served as a clerk for Metropolitan Editor Abe Rosenthal until January 1977, when he was named a reporter and assigned to the *Times*'s Albany bureau. He later became the bureau chief at the age of twenty-five. He was certain his meteoric rise would not have occurred without Rosenthal's blessing.

In 1982 Meislin was selected for a prestigious slot on the international staff and assigned to cover Mexico. At about this same time Arthur Sulzberger

Jr., who was working on the *Times*'s metropolitan assignment desk as part of his grooming to become publisher, invited him to lunch. To Meislin's surprise the conversation quickly turned to Meislin's sexual orientation. Sulzberger told Meislin he knew he was gay and that it was inconsequential.

Meislin brought a male date to a New Year's Eve party thrown by Sulzberger in 1982. "My policy was that I didn't advertise it, but I wasn't going to lie to anyone who asked me," Meislin said.[44] It seemed to Meislin that his dream had come true. As far as he knew, he had attained a much sought-after foreign correspondent's slot as an openly gay man.

The mysterious pain began not long after he arrived in Mexico City, and his incapacitation stretched into months. Meislin eventually learned that an unfounded rumor was circulating in the New York newsroom that he was suffering from AIDS complications. Apparently, not everyone shared Sulzberger's view that his homosexuality was inconsequential to his career.

"I am told that the international editor was called in by Rosenthal and asked if he knew that I was gay," Meislin said. "He said he did, but it was not affecting my job; that I was a fine reporter. Rosenthal then wanted to know why no one had told him, and from that point on, whatever I did was never as good. No one ever said, 'You are being brought back from Mexico because you're gay,' but there was certainly a widespread belief in the newsroom that it was a factor—and not a small one."

Treated by a physician in New York, Meislin began to gradually recover. Hospital tests never determined the exact cause. By the end of 1984 he still had not recovered sufficiently to return to work.

"Several months after I was taken out of Mexico, I was flying from Washington back to New York when someone from the State Department told me the word around the State Department was that I was 'too gay for the *New York Times*,'" Meislin said. "I thought, gee if this has gotten to the State Department, I'd love to see what my file looks like. I never thought my sexuality would be an issue."[45]

Instead of returning Meislin to Mexico City or assigning him to another international post, the *Times* placed him in a lower-ranking position in the New York newsroom, which felt to Meislin like blatant homophobia. One editor advised him to lie low until Rosenthal's retirement. No one could say for certain why Meislin had been reassigned, but many in the newsroom, especially gays and lesbians who were fearful of Rosenthal's hostility toward them, had their suspicions.

Rosenthal retired in 1986, and publisher Arthur Ochs Sulzberger Jr.

named Max Frankel to succeed him. Frankel's career had carried him from the Washington bureau to Sunday editor and editorial page editor before being named executive editor.[46]

Shortly after he assumed command of the newspaper, Frankel set up an interdepartmental committee to examine how the *Times* had responded to the AIDS crisis. As a result the newspaper published a major four-part series about the effect of the epidemic on New York City, beginning in March 1987 with an article by reporter Jane Gross, headlined THE DEVASTATION OF AIDS: MANY DEAD, MORE DYING. Each of the four installments was prominently displayed on page one.[47] Under Frankel the *Times*'s approach to the epidemic was described as "some of the best, most wide-ranging AIDS coverage of any American newspaper."[48]

In the summer of 1987 Frankel took another step that influenced how gays and lesbians were portrayed in the pages of the nation's most influential newspaper. He lifted the newspaper's ban on the term *gay*. Exactly how it came about is something of a secret. At least one person claims to have seen a memo from Frankel to Arthur Sulzberger that said, "Punch, you're going to have to swallow hard on this one: We're going to start using the word 'gay.' "[49]

The reversal, however, was not so sudden as it appeared and may have been quietly engineered behind the scenes by Arthur Ochs Sulzberger Jr., who had become an assistant to his father at about the same time that Frankel became executive editor.

The young publisher won't say exactly what happened:

> I think suspicions are best left that way. They are much more exciting. I'm just going to let that one hang out there. The *Times* is slow. It's slow on words that have political meanings, and it's slow on words that don't have political meanings. There was political meaning to putting *Ms.* in front of a name, and we were slow to do that. My point is, it's not just *gay*. The *Times* is almost the last to change from one style to another style. But there was also a generational shift.[50]

Notice of the change went to the newspaper's reporters and editors in a June 15 memo from Assistant Managing Editor Allan Siegal: "Starting immediately, we will accept the word 'gay' as an adjective meaning homosexual. . . . Gay may refer to homosexual men, or more generically to homosexual men and women. In specific reference to women, lesbian is preferred. If we need to emphasize a distinction, we can write lesbians and gay men." But it cautioned against using *gay* as a noun. "We will write 'gay author' but not 'a gay' or similarly 'gay men' or 'homosexuals' but not 'gays.'"[51]

"GAY" FINALLY FIT TO PRINT was the front page headline in *Gay Community News*. THE NEW YORK TIMES FINALLY OKAYS USE OF GAY, the *Advocate* told its readers. A staffer at the *Times* commented, "The *Times* seems to be inching its way into the 20th Century."[52]

But routine practices that have guided a newspaper for nearly a century would not change easily or quickly. This was clear in early 1989 when the *Times* carried a feature that did not involve AIDS. The idea for the story, an article on lesbian parenthood, originated in a conversation between Urvashi Vaid, director of the National Gay and Lesbian Task Force, and Gina Kolata, a *Times* science writer. After discussing the status of the AIDS crisis, Vaid mentioned that several gay and lesbian organizations were addressing a number of other issues, naming parenting as an example. Kolata was fascinated and asked Vaid to arrange for her to talk with lesbian mothers.

LESBIAN PARTNERS FIND THE MEANS TO BE PARENTS appeared in the *Times* on January 30, 1989. In it a woman lawyer in Ohio described how she knew of at least thirty lesbians who had been inseminated and had become mothers. Richard Green, a psychiatry professor at the University of California at Los Angeles, offered a positive assessment, saying that children raised by homosexuals were no more likely to be gay than any other children.

To personalize the story Kolata described Kim Klausner and Debra Chasnoff, a lesbian couple in San Francisco, and their six-month-old son Noah. Klausner had been artificially inseminated with sperm from a gay friend. But overshadowing the positive aspects was a reference to some unnamed clinicians who speculated that in homes where children are raised by homosexual parents, "girls might have difficulty in intimate relationships with men, and boys might be uncomfortable with their role as males." Amplifying the concerns, the article quoted Sidney Callahan, a psychologist and ethicist at Mercy College in Dobbs Ferry, New York, who said she had "deep reservations." "You are getting a child that is totally different from all other children," she was quoted as saying. "Do you have the right to do that?"[53]

"I was extremely upset," Vaid later recalled. "I got on the phone and started calling people and asking them to call the *Times* and complain."[54] The story also appeared on the *Times* wire news service, which distributes articles to 600 newspapers and other subscribers worldwide, including 384 in the United States. When it began to appear in other newspapers, including the *San Francisco Chronicle*, Klausner and Chasnoff suddenly found them-selves on the defensive.

"We got calls from talk radio and television all over the country," Chasnoff recalled. "We were on at least ten radio shows and on *Good Morning America*. Of course, on every single show the interviewer would quote these unnamed critics in the article, and we were put in the position of having to respond to them. It was upsetting that such incredibly inaccurate information had been put out."[55]

Four days later, on February 3, the *Times* carried a small box on page two that was identified as an Editor's Note. In a highly unusual notice the *Times* acknowledged that the antigay quotes in the article had been added by edi-tors. The newspaper told its readers, "In the absence of evidence that hostil-ity toward men is common among lesbian parents, the reference to such hos-tility was unwarranted. The article should have given lesbian parents a chance to respond to the concerns raised by others."

The notice was the result of Kolata's pushing from inside the *Times* for a clar-ification, while Vaid, on the outside, called on her members to write and call the newspaper to complain. "I never could get to the bottom of why they did it," Vaid recalled. "My hunch was that it was a homophobic editor who could not believe that it didn't matter if you had gay parents or straight parents."

THE *CHRONICLE* AND AIDS

At the *San Francisco Chronicle* AIDS stories remained within the medical beat throughout 1981 and into the spring of 1982 while Randy Shilts finished his book, *The Mayor of Castro Street*. In April 1982 Shilts began to recognize the seriousness of the problem, as the number of cases rose to more than three hundred, about forty of them in San Francisco.

Shilts's first story looked at the Shanti Project, an umbrella group that organized and coordinated local support groups. The article languished on his editor's desk for three weeks. Rumors circulated that editors had joked about it at an editorial meeting.

Furious, Shilts searched the library for copies of articles the newspaper had printed on Legionnaires' disease and toxic shock syndrome. To drama-tize his point he created a third stack of articles on AIDS—all four of them. But before he could confront his editor, the newspaper printed his article, and Shilts moved on to his next assignment.

A month later Shilts wrote his first story that focused exclusively on the developing epidemic. THE STRANGE DEADLY DISEASES THAT STRIKE GAY MEN, read the May 13 headline. Shilts described a forty-five-year-old San Francisco man who had developed purple KS spots that covered his arms, face, and chest and who "contemplated the death sentence they might foreshadow."[56]

For several months after that Shilts's work was slowed by the release and promotion of his book and by an increasingly serious drinking problem. He did not write again about the growing epidemic until the next spring. When he returned to the *Chronicle* from his book leave in 1983, he was the only reporter among the mainstream media covering AIDS full time. In the first three and a half years of the epidemic the *San Francisco Chronicle* published more stories on AIDS than the *New York Times* and *Los Angeles Times* combined. David Perlman, the science editor, concentrated on the medical aspects, and Shilts wrote human interest stories about the epidemic.

Few reporters had focused on the federal AIDS policy in the early years of the epidemic. Shilts obtained memos revealing the deep divisions and conflicts that had stymied the Reagan administration's response. Although top federal health officials were telling Congress and the media that emergency funds were not needed for AIDS, they were exchanging memos within the administration that painted a far different story. "AIDS work cannot be undertaken because of the lack of available resources," said one memo Shilts obtained through a Freedom of Information Act request.

In March 1983 an aide to a powerful San Francisco Bay area congressman leaked a government report to Shilts that contained a shocking estimate: 1 in every 350 single men in sections of San Francisco with the heaviest concentrations of gays would have the disease by year's end. Shilts reported the story on March 23, STARTLING FINDING ON "GAY DISEASE." It brought a quick and harsh response from a number of the city's gay activists who feared it had established the city as a center of the AIDS crisis and because it pointed an accusing finger at the city's gay bathhouses. They feared losing the sexual freedom they had won in San Francisco, of which the bathhouses were a visible symbol. Labeling him a "gay Uncle Tom," activists accused Shilts of betrayal. "I had friends who wouldn't walk down Castro Street with me because so many people would come up and yell at me," he would later comment.[57]

The backlash only worsened as Shilts continued to hammer away at the danger the bathhouses posed to gay men. In the late spring of 1983 he quoted public health officials who were concerned that gay tourists at the annual Gay Pride festivities would unknowingly contract the disease and spread it nationwide. "There has been some pressure on me to close the bathhouses," acknowledged the city's top public health official, Mervyn Silverman.[58] Bathhouse owners accused Shilts of trying to wreck their businesses. Gays accused him of trying to enforce a heterosexual code of morality. Shilts continued to cover the controversy throughout 1983 and 1984. In October 1984 city health officials ordered the bathhouses closed. Activists blamed Shilts. Even some journalists questioned whether Shilts had crossed the line that distinguishes a detached journalist from an advocate.

AIDS IN THE NEWS AFTER ROCK HUDSON

The AIDS crisis took on a new significance in the news media in July 1985, when longstanding rumors that Rock Hudson had contracted the disease were confirmed. The news burst into headlines in newspapers worldwide. The number of AIDS stories in American newspapers jumped by an estimated 270 percent in the final six months of 1985.[59]

The *Los Angeles Times* carried three front-page articles speculating on Hudson's condition before it was disclosed. Once his illness was confirmed, the newspaper ran twenty-nine articles within only six months. Much of the media attention centered on a photograph that showed Hudson kissing actress Linda Evans only months before his illness became public.

Hudson's disclosure prompted President Reagan to mention AIDS publicly for the first time on September 17, 1985, when he expressed his empathy for parents who did not want their children in school with "kids with AIDS." The epidemic by then was in its fourth year, with more than twelve thousand cases and six thousand deaths.[60]

"The reason the President had never mentioned AIDS was nobody had asked him," observed Larry Bush, the *Advocate*'s Washington correspondent in the late 1970s. He was the first reporter for a gay publication to be admitted to the White House press corps.

> White House reporters can be as isolated from America as the president. At papers like the *Washington Post* and the *New York Times*, editors would sit down with the reporters before press conferences—they had so few of them—and work out what questions to ask. AIDS wasn't on anybody's agenda; just putting it on the agenda was what the gay movement was about. But there was this attitude that to write a story was to put it on the news agenda and to pander to gays. It got very bizarre.[61]

In early October 1985 Rock Hudson's spokesman, Dale Olsen, announced that the movie star was dead, and the number of stories about AIDS surged to new levels. In the *New York Times* alone the number of articles in 1985 jumped to 363, compared with just 70 in 1984. "Rock Hudson riveted America's attention upon this deadly new threat for the first time, and his diagnosis became a demarcation that would separate the history of America before AIDS from the history that came after," wrote Randy Shilts in *And The Band Played On*.[62]

Not only was there more coverage of AIDS after Hudson's death, much of it included more specific language. Earlier references to "body fluids" suggested that the disease could be spread through sweat. "Sexual contact" also left a lot of room for interpretation. In the summer of 1985 the news media began to mention condoms after United Press International reported on a grant given by the U.S. Conference of Mayors for a condom education campaign. Shortly after that a reporter for the *Washington Post* explained "safe sex" as "avoiding the exchange of body fluids—especially semen and blood, and to lesser extent saliva—which are implicated in the transmission of AIDS." The *New York Times* reached a new level of explicitness on September 13 in an article that drew together answers to some of the most often asked questions about the disease, FEARS ON AIDS TERMED LARGELY WITHOUT CAUSE.[63]

By late 1985 and throughout out much of 1986 tabloid newspapers increasingly characterized the disease as fitting punishment for homosexual behavior. The *New York Post* carried headlines that could be read from across a city street. Gay clubs were referred to as "AIDS dens" and "sex dens." Gay men were described as "desperate . . . without families . . . without real friends." For former GAA member Arnie Kantrowitz it was a flashback to another era: "Some of the newspapers were publishing pictures of people that were taken through the windows of their apartment. They had ghastly cartoons with AIDS dragons threatening children and so forth. There was a powerful sense of fear in the community that we were either all going to be locked away for some kind of quarantine or some type of crackdown. People were talking about it everywhere. It was like Berlin in the 1930s."[64]

In October 1985 *Christopher Street*, the literary sister magazine to the *New York Native*, carried an article headlined WAGING PEACE, in which two writers outlined a strategy for confronting homophobia in the media. "The gay revolution in America has failed," wrote Marshall K. Kirk and Erastes Pill. "There is still no nationwide appreciation of the gay community, nor sympathy for it, nor even much tolerance toward it." Predicting that the spread of

AIDS threatened the respectability of gays even further, the two writers called for a renewed drive toward media reform.[65]

The article, which the authors later expanded into the book *After the Ball*, became a rallying cry for a group of New York gay and lesbian writers. "We felt like there was never enough money being given to the research on AIDS, and there was a way of being presented by the media that was shifting how the public looked at us," said writer Jewelle Gomez. "But no one was talking about what controls the media had over how AIDS is portrayed in the media."[66]

A meeting of the group at gay writer Darryl Yates Rist's apartment in late 1985 led to the formation of the Gay and Lesbian Anti-Defamation League. But the new group almost immediately ran into trouble when the Anti-Defamation League of B'nai B'rith threatened to sue for copyright infringement over the name. After lengthy discussions the group became known as the Gay and Lesbian Alliance Against Defamation (GLAAD).[67]

On November 14, 1985, the group held a "town hall" meeting at a church in Greenwich Village, attracting a crowd of nearly seven hundred angry gays and lesbians, including some of the city's most energetic young activists. "Tonight is the final notice to the bigots!" bellowed Rist. "Tonight our tolerance has ended. We're no longer begging; we're no longer asking." Writer and film critic Vito Russo told them, "This community is being divided over a smokescreen for what's really going on, which is that the AIDS epidemic is being used by right-wing fanatics and yellow journalists to create a witchhunt mentality against lesbians and gay men in this city."[68]

The activists' anger heightened four months later when conservative commentators began calling for crackdowns on people with AIDS. Conservative journalist William F. Buckley Jr. was one of the first to broach the idea in a *New York Times* op-ed column on March 18, 1986, CRUCIAL STEPS IN COMBATING THE AIDS EPIDEMIC. Four months later political extremist Lyndon LaRouche called for mandatory tattooing in a statewide referendum in California, which lost by a wide margin in the following November's election.

On December 1 GLAAD lashed out at the media with a demonstration at the *New York Post*, in which five hundred demonstrators chanted, "The *Post* is a dirty rag!" as they pitched small yellow rags at the entrance. Television cameras captured the action. "This paper has published more than 20 op-ed pieces denigrating gay men and lesbians and associating us with every form of perversion known to man," Rist told the crowd.[69]

Watching from a newsroom above was Joe Nicholson, the paper's only openly gay journalist. It had been six years since he had acknowledged his homosexuality publicly in writing about the Ramrod shootings.

> I was pleased that the gay community was doing it, but I was also aware that the editors and the other reporters were very uncomfortable about me and didn't know quite what to say. They are already uptight about the situation, so they weren't going to make their problems worse by assigning their only openly gay reporter. I remember them saying, "Poor Margie Feinberg, she has to go down and cover this, and all the gays' anger and hatred will be aimed at her." That was the comfortable resting point. We sympathized with poor Margie who was four floors below in this gay mob.[70]

The protesters convinced the editors to meet with GLAAD about their grievances. It was their first victory.

In May 1987 the group organized a protest outside the *National Review* to protest Buckley's tattooing proposal. In response the columnist met with them and later agreed to write a column in which he disavowed his tattooing proposal and focused on the successes of safe-sex education.[71] GLAAD was quickly picking up the media advocacy role where the Gay Liberation Front, Gay Activists Alliance, and the National Gay Task Force had left off several years earlier.

News coverage shot up again in 1987 to an all-time high after a national debate flared over a short-lived proposal to require mandatory testing for AIDS antibodies. More articles appeared after the government approved use of AZT, the first drug licensed to fight human immunodeficiency virus (HIV), which causes AIDS. But after the 1987 surge, news coverage fell as editors worried about saturation. By 1989 the number of news stories had fallen by more than one third in the two years since the 1987 high.[72]

News editors were increasingly shunting stories about the epidemic to the back pages, if they ran any stories at all. Seven years after AIDS first appeared on the front page of an American newspaper, there was still no sign of a cure for the disease, and news decision-makers considered stories about it too routine and too depressing.

In 1987 Randy Shilts published his second book, *And the Band Played On*, which criticized the Reagan administration for its foot-dragging, the gay community for its denial of responsibility for taking preventative measures, and the media for ignoring the epidemic altogether. "Writing a book was the way to get over the heads of the *New York Times* and the other papers that weren't covering this issue," he later told an interviewer.[73]

Increasingly frustrated by the death rate, the illusive search for a cure, and declining public interest in the epidemic, gay and lesbian activists learned in January 1991 that the government was spending $1 billion a day to conduct a war in the Middle East. A total of $5 billion had been spent on AIDS research in the ten years of the epidemic. Television became the target. On January 22, three protesters from the militant group ACT UP crashed onto the live broadcast of the *CBS Evening News*, shouting "Fight AIDS, not Arabs." Visibly shaken, anchorman Dan Rather suddenly stopped the news as technicians switched to a commercial so they could escort the intruders from the studio. When he returned to the air, Rather explained, "I want to apologize to you for the way the program started. There were some rude people in the studio, but they were ejected."[74]

Almost simultaneously, seven protesters charged onto the set of the *MacNeil-Lehrer Newshour*. Several attempted to chain themselves to the desk and to New York anchorman Robert MacNeil. None of this was seen by viewers, however, because the cameras were focused on coanchor Jim Lehrer in Washington. Two other teams of demonstrators tried similar tactics at NBC and ABC but failed to slip past security guards. The activists called it their Day of Desperation.

The following summer a group of AIDS activists briefly disrupted CNN's *Headline News* when they barged into its Atlanta studio shouting, "Stop the AIDS panic!" The four men had been on a tour of the CNN complex but broke away and charged into the studio where the anchors were delivering the news.[75]

So scarce were stories about AIDS in the late 1980s and early 1990s that a September 24, 1991, headline in the weekly health supplement of the *Washington Post* asked WHATEVER HAPPENED TO AIDS?

"After 10 years, AIDS no longer captures as much attention," the article pointed out. "Yet the virus has spread to nearly every county in the U.S. So far, 118,411 are dead. One million more are estimated to be infected."[76]

12

THE EXPERIENCE OF AIDS

Most readers of the *Honolulu Star-Bulletin* knew Bill Cox only by his byline. But on September 2, 1986, when the newspaper printed his final story, they learned a great deal more about his private life. "I am going on the disability roll because of illness," he told them. "The illness is AIDS."[1]

For two years Cox had led a vigorous battle with city officials to open meetings and government records to the press. Once he developed AIDS, he suddenly had to confront his own lack of openness, which stemmed from his sense of privacy. To keep his illness a secret, he recognized, would only add to the fear, shame, and guilt that surrounded the disease.

His journalistic sense of candor prevailed. "By writing about AIDS, I am following a tradition of journalists who have written about their illnesses to help educate, and if blessed by finding the right words, to help others with the disease feel less alone," he wrote. "Most of all, I am writing to say if we don't want to be treated as a pariah, we have to stop acting like one." Cox died on May 19, 1988, at age thirty-nine.[2]

VOICES OF AIDS IN THE MEDIA

The staff of the *Walla Walla* (Washington) *Union-Bulletin* thought reporter Robert O'Boyle was on a weekend retreat in Mexico in February 1989. Instead, he was lying in a hospital bed across town, barely able to breathe.

"I had been in the hospital for three days before I could breathe well enough to call the personnel manager—a good friend—and tell her I had full-blown AIDS," he said. "There was just this stunned silence on the telephone. This was the first time anyone at the *Union-Bulletin* had gotten AIDS, and it had happened to one of their reporters."[3]

The newspaper staff was stunned by the sudden news, but it was not a complete surprise to O'Boyle. His first lover had died from the disease two years earlier, and he knew then that he might have been exposed to the human immunodeficiency virus (HIV). Then in early 1989 he began to feel fatigued, with swollen glands and low-grade fevers, but he attributed it to stress. His trip to the hospital was a jolt into reality.

After he recovered from pneumonia, one of his editors asked him to write an article about his diagnosis. The idea frightened his parents, the owners of a small paint business in Walla Walla who feared the publicity might drive off customers.

"I knew that some of the prisoners at the state penitentiary outside Walla Walla had contracted AIDS and were being flown to a hospital in Olympia for treatment. I also knew that some people with the disease had come to towns like Walla Walla to die—but nobody talked about it," O'Boyle said. "That's part of the reason people were afraid of AIDS—and it was part of the reason I was getting lousy medical care—so I decided it was time to let people know that AIDS was here."[4]

The article provided readers with their first indication that AIDS was not exclusive to large urban areas; in fact, the strange deadly disease had struck someone they knew—a reporter at the local newspaper. After the story's publication O'Boyle realized the disease had drained him of energy. Abandoning journalism, he moved to nearby Seattle in hopes of finding better medical care. He knew people in Walla Walla were afraid of him. He had been told that some nurses at the local hospital had refused to enter his room.

Soon after he settled into a Seattle apartment, O'Boyle contacted a local AIDS support group to learn about the disease and how to cope with it. During one meeting it suddenly dawned on him that he might be able to combine his new knowledge of the disease with his reporting experience. In the course of a conversation with Warren King, the health reporter at the *Seattle Times*, O'Boyle volunteered to write a column about his ongoing battle with AIDS.

By coincidence King had known O'Boyle's former lover, a well-known activist who had been quoted extensively by the Seattle media as he fought the disease. In addition, the *Union-Bulletin* had the same owners as the *Seattle Times*, so the editors were familiar with O'Boyle and his work. King suggested that O'Boyle write three sample columns; King would discuss the idea with his editors.

When the newspaper printed O'Boyle's columns in June 1990, they were the first of their kind. Just seven years earlier gays had denounced Seattle's major media to protest their characterization of AIDS as "the gay plague."[5] Now the state's leading newspaper was carrying a regular AIDS column.

"I'm seated alone, again, in the same melodramatic piano bar at the crest of Capitol Hill, reviewing flashbacks of the night before. In a flicker of clarity, between sips of my second brandy, the same vexing question I've been nursing all night repeats on me once more," O'Boyle wrote. "Why did my friend so abruptly withdraw his glass and cover the opening with his hand?"[6]

Each column was drawn from his experiences. As a columnist, freed from the constraints of objective reporting, he was able to put a human face on an otherwise strange and frightening disease.

O'Boyle wrote about the tests he was given and the drugs that were prescribed. One column detailed the wrenching process of adjusting to AZT, a highly toxic drug that was the only federally approved treatment. "I have a strong love-hate relationship with the blue-and-white capsules," he wrote. "The same drug that keeps me alive can open the floodgate on nausea."[7] O'Boyle said of that column,

> I wanted to raise people's compassion level. I'm not a scientist. I'm not a health
> reporter, so I wanted to stick with stories that were human because I am a human
> being just like everybody else. I was raised by decent, good parents—who are
> quoted all of the time in the column. I think we set an example for a lot of mid-

dle-class families who assume homosexuals are dirty, pedophiles, strange, or radical. No one had to be radical to be gay. We don't have to be outrageous or dress
in women's clothing. I think the column taught some people that for the first
time.[8]

O'Boyle's most powerful columns were about his family and their struggle to understand the disease. His parents had not always been comfortable
with his homosexuality. It had taken many years for them to accept it. AIDS
had made it more difficult. "We're all growing together on the subject," he
wrote. Perhaps the most disturbing column for his parents was one in
which he wrote that people with AIDS are still sexual beings despite their illness. "My parents nearly died," he said. "I didn't say we had to have *unsafe*
sex, but I said I'm still gay whether I have sex or not. I wanted people to
understand that people with AIDS still fall in love. But people in general
don't see us that way."

O'Boyle's column, Living with AIDS, ran biweekly for the next eighteen
months in both the *Seattle Times* and the *Union-Bulletin*. In December 1991
O'Boyle was hospitalized with another bout of pneumocystis pneumonia.
He died on January 6, 1992, at age thirty-two.

THE FACE OF AIDS

Paul Wynne served as an entertainment reporter for a San Francisco television station for many years. In 1984 the station decided not to renew his contract. Three years later, having been unable to find another television reporting job and living on unemployment, he tested HIV positive. By 1989 he had
lost fifty-five pounds and developed a nerve disease that left his legs numb.

Rather than surrender to the disease, Wynne proposed an AIDS segment
for a local radio station. But when the news director at KGO-TV heard the
idea, he contacted Wynne about doing the segment for his station's evening
newscast. On January 11, 1990, the first segment of the *Paul Wynne Journal*
aired during the six o'clock news.

The first episode opened with a film clip of Wynne early in his career. "I
had hair, I had a tan, I had—well, half a body," he narrated over the pictures,
"and here I am today. Only today I have something I would never have
dreamed about ten years ago. I have AIDS."[9] For some viewers the sight of a
gaunt, pale man whose blue eyes had sunk deep into their sockets was shock-

ing. But the segments gave life to the stark statistics that continued to climb at a rapid rate.

In later segments Wynne explained what it was like for a forty-seven-year-old to be so weak that a curb was a major obstacle. In subsequent episodes he took viewers on a tour of his medicine cabinet, explained his financial statement, told of rejection by family members, and displayed pictures of friends who had died too young.

"Hardened news reporters were in tears," the station news director told *New York Times* reporter Jane Gross. A reviewer for the *Oakland Tribune* wrote that he had been "personally isolated from this tragedy" until viewing *Paul Wynne's Journal*.[10] The audience responded warmly; one sent a hand-made afghan. By the summer of 1990 Wynne was taping his segments from his hospital bed. He told the viewers he was terribly sick and weak: "My life is very joyless and I'm very afraid." He died on July 5, 1990.

AIDS AT A NATIONAL NETWORK

Tom Cassidy, a correspondent for *CNN Financial News,* remembered October 19, 1987, as one of his darkest days. It was Black Monday,—the day the stock market crashed. It also was the day he learned that he had tested HIV positive. At first he failed to grasp the full significance. But he would find it increasingly difficult for him to keep his health problems and his personal life secret.

"Some people presumed I was gay but not many. Nobody mentioned it to me—ever—until I got sick. I guess I kept it secret because of a deep-seated fear that every gay person feels—that you're going to be rejected or discriminated against—because you get messages from society that this is bad, a controversial lifestyle," he said. "I was afraid of being penalized. I knew everyone liked me and they respected me, but in my gut there was still an insecurity."[11]

Cassidy had good reason to be insecure. Only two years earlier a camera crew at NBC had walked off an interview set rather than pin microphones on two men with AIDS. The guests had to attach their microphones and dispose of them afterward.[12]

When Cassidy joined Cable News Network in 1981, AIDS had yet to be named, and the disease was only beginning to be recognized as a potential health problem. After CNN hired him away from a financial radio network in Chicago, Cassidy took an apartment in Greenwich Village to be in the heart of the gayest neighborhood in the city. He had lived in New York years earlier while earning his master's degrees in journalism and business administration from Columbia University and dreaming of the day he could use those advanced degrees to specialize in financial news reporting.

In his third year with CNN he started *Pinnacle*, a weekly program that profiled business leaders. His guests were big-name executives who shied away from interviews but were relaxed with the easygoing Cassidy questioning them. When network executives tapped him to anchor financial segments, Cassidy quickly became one of CNN's rising stars.

Typically, when anyone showed any curiosity about Cassidy's private life, he fell silent, hoping to avoid raising suspicions. When he fell in love in the mid-1980s, he asked for a transfer back to Chicago. Almost immediately rumors began circulating that he had become serious about a woman and might soon marry. Cassidy never tried to correct the story because it was such an easy alibi. "I didn't start it, and I didn't stop it," he remarked to friends.

For about two years after his diagnosis in October 1987 Cassidy told none of his coworkers. In the summer of 1989 he developed full-blown AIDS, and his secret became impossible to hide. He had lost nearly twenty pounds. When he failed to show up for work at the CNN bureau, his coworkers became alarmed and called his sister in Boston. She panicked and called the police in New York. When they located him, Cassidy was in Mount Sinai Hospital, barely able to speak.

"That was frightening," he said. "I knew there was the distinct possibility that I might not be alive the next morning, and nobody knew where to find me. I had told two friends that I was in the hospital, but that's all. I told them. I had never been in a hospital before. I was an athlete—I was Mister Clean—and then suddenly, I was almost dying. I remember lying in that bed and thinking that I wasn't going to get to say goodbye to anybody."

As word of his illness circulated, a reporter for the local CBS station contacted him to ask him to consider doing an interview for a three-part series on AIDS. Cassidy asked for time to think it over. He wanted to discuss it with friends. For a man whose career in the limelight had kept him deeply closeted, this presented a bold step.

I think I shortchanged the straight world, frankly. I don't think I gave those people the credit they deserve. They weren't going to let that detail stand in the way. They have been incredibly supportive of me—remarkably. But you want the world to be upset about it. You want a solution and you want it now. I don't know if there will be a solution in time for me. AIDS has made a lot of people think about their lives. It is not doing anybody any favors. It's taking an awful lot of life out of life, because gay people contribute an awful lot of zest to the world. As we pass along, the world becomes a less interesting place.[13]

He agreed to do the TV interview, and then he gave an interview to *People* magazine and appeared on *Donahue*. On *The Dick Cavett Show* he talked about his success in television, his treatment for Kaposi's sarcoma, and his thoughts of taking his own life. "You know people assume that AIDS is a death sentence—which it very well may be," Cassidy remarked during one of his final interviews. "I'll let you know."[14] He died on Sunday, May 28, 1991. He was forty-one.

AIDS DENIAL

Charles Elder became a staff writer at the *Miami Herald* in January 1990, a welcome switch from the bitter winters of Washington, D.C., where he had worked for a short time at the *Washington Post* as an aide on the copy desk. By late summer the twenty-seven-year-old was lying in a bed at Miami's Jackson Memorial Hospital with a collapsed lung—and no one at the *Herald* knew he was dying of AIDS. He had kept secret from even his closest friends in the newsroom that he had tested HIV positive two years earlier.

"One weekend, I was coming into the paper," recalled *Herald* reporter Elinor Burkett, "and I hear that Charles, who I had met only once briefly because he was a bureau reporter, was in the hospital and that he had a weird kind of pneumonia." Burkett, who covered AIDS for the newspaper from 1989 through 1992, knew immediately. "Charles has AIDS," she told the staff.[15]

"Everybody said, 'How can you say that? That's a terrible thing to say.' I asked what floor of the hospital he was on, and they said, 'Three North.' I told them, 'That's the AIDS wing. He has AIDS! Say the A-word!'" For two weeks, until Charles Elder died, no one in the newsroom of the *Miami Herald* would say the A-word.[16]

When Elder died on August 31, 1990, some of his colleagues did not want the cause of death in his obituary to read AIDS. Others fought to print the truth in the hope it would chip away at the stigma that had forced him to retreat into silence.

No one was more stunned by the news than Charisse Grant, a *Herald* writer who was one of Elder's closest friends. Ten days after his death she wrote about the tragedy in an article for the *Herald*. In one section she wrote, "As we remember our friend, we also need to ask ourselves as people, and particularly as journalists, have we done enough to prove to those like Charles that we would be a ready ally in the fight against AIDS? Or did we send a message that we as an institution of social change would prefer not to use our power to influence public opinion out of fear of upsetting a complacent community with the harsher realities of life?"[17]

On September 12 the *Herald* held a brief memorial service. Among the speakers was the executive editor of the *Herald*, Janet Chusmir. "She got up at his memorial service," said Burkett, "and talked about our failure as a community and as journalists to have created an atmosphere in which Charles Elder would have been comfortable walking in to his editors when he was hired and saying, 'I have AIDS.' She talked about how that affected our newsroom but also what it meant in terms of coverage." The change in AIDS coverage was dramatic. Burkett soon found that she had far more latitude to choose stories and more time to pursue them than previously. Coworkers were openly talking about the disease. But the new atmosphere in the *Herald* newsroom did not extend beyond AIDS to include coverage of gays and lesbians overall. "There was no pressure for better coverage from the community and no pressure from the closeted gay and lesbian journalists inside," Burkett said.[18]

On December 22, three months after Charles Elder's death, Chusmir suddenly collapsed and died of a brain aneurysm. "When Chusmir died, that changed everything," Burkett recalled. "Her successor was not interested."[19] After Burkett left the *Herald* to write a book in the spring of 1992, she heard that several reporters had requested the AIDS beat but were refused. AIDS would be covered routinely as the need arose. In the two years after Elder died, AIDS claimed the lives of eight more *Herald* employees.

AIDS AWAKENS CHICAGO

Journalists take great pride in their ability to detach from the news. The media maintain an invisible boundary to keep the news at bay so they can maintain their objectivity. AIDS recognized no such boundaries. As journalists began to contract it, AIDS became increasingly difficult for the media to ignore.

When a young reporter at the *Chicago Tribune* died in March 1987, few of his coworkers knew the full story. His obituary did not mention AIDS, and there was nothing to acknowledge that he was gay. But reporter Jean Latz Griffin knew the unspoken truth. In the short time they had worked together, they had become close friends. Griffin never betrayed his trust by revealing his secret, yet she was deeply disturbed by his death and the silence that surrounded it.

A middle-aged mother of three who had been happily married for twenty-five years, Griffin knew nothing of her friend's sexual orientation until he contracted HIV and he told her. "I certainly had a strong interest in what was going on with gay people who had had to stay in the closet," Griffin said. "But also as a journalist I realized that this was an extremely fascinating community that was coming into much more highly visible areas that we weren't writing about at all."[20]

Only days after the man's death Griffin told the metropolitan editor of the *Tribune* that she wanted to write about AIDS as a beat. As she envisioned it, she would cover AIDS the same way other *Tribune* beat reporters covered the mayor, the police department, or business news.

To her surprise her editor responded, "Fine, go ahead and write some stories, and if they're good we'll put them in the paper." Handing her a stack of letters, he said, "While you're at it, you can go through these." The letters were from various gay organizations pointing out flaws in stories about the disease, things the newspaper had gotten wrong or missed. The names on the letters became Griffin's first contacts for her new beat.

"I called all of them to try and figure out what was going on and then developed the beat as anyone would develop any beat," she recalled. She asked them what happened to people who develop AIDS. What problems did they run into? What solutions were they finding? What was important to people who were gay? Each contact led to three more.

For much of the time Griffin had been with the *Tribune* she had been the newspaper's education writer. Her most extensive contact with the city's large gay community had come two years earlier, in 1985, when she had stumbled onto a story about gay teenagers and their experiences with the city schools.

Although Griffin's interest in AIDS was the primary catalyst for the gay beat, gay and lesbian activists had been pushing the city's newspapers for better coverage for several years. They were particularly incensed in 1982, when the *Tribune* reported on the murder of a former professor at Chicago's Loyola

University and his lover at their Georgia home. "Things at the house indicated they were involved in homosexual activity and devil worship," the story quoted a Georgia sheriff as saying. It went on to describe skulls, satanic altars, and "bizarre sexual instruments" that had been confiscated from the men's house. It described the professor's lover as his "servant," "his lackey," and "his boy."[21] It later turned out that the sheriff had lied. The *Tribune* had failed to check the facts in a wire service story that had taken the sheriff's claims at face value.

By the mid-eighties Al Wardell and Paul Varnell had become the gay community's unofficial watchdogs over the Chicago news media. They monitored coverage of gays and lesbians relentlessly and never hesitated to write or call local editors. But the editors of the city's dailies repeatedly refused to meet with them.

The hostilities only worsened in July 1986 when the city council resurrected a gay rights bill that had been in limbo since 1979, sparking a flurry of negative publicity about gays. The bill failed by six votes. Wardell and Varnell continued to push the papers to meet, and the *Tribune* editors relented. At the appointed hour the watchdogs arrived at the newspaper ready to document their charges. Varnell confronted them with the article about the professor's murder and the newspaper's coverage of serial killer John Wayne Gacy, the Chicago man who had confessed in 1979 to killing twenty-seven young men.

"They seemed to wonder why they should take our issues seriously," Varnell said of the editors. "They were not hostile or uncaring, but we constantly had to make our case. It was clear to us that none of what we were saying was significant to the managing editor, and he didn't seem to understand why it was so important to us."[22]

By the time the city council resurrected the gay rights bill yet again in the fall of 1988, the coverage had begun to improve. Griffin had been writing about AIDS and the gay community for several months, and some of her articles had delved deep into some everyday challenges facing Chicago gays, including discrimination and prejudice.

The gay rights ordinance passed 28–22, after a fifteen-year campaign. Activists claimed that Griffin's articles had played a decisive role by creating an enlightened atmosphere for the vote. "It was close," remembered Varnell. "But her coverage kept the issue alive and gave careful attention to the gay viewpoint." For the city's gay community a gay beat at one of the city's major daily newspapers was a dream come true. *Gay Chicago* magazine later featured Griffin in an article and named her an "honorary lesbian."

"Everybody was pretty supportive," Griffin said. "There were a few comments in the newsroom—as there always will be. A lot of people came up and said, 'Boy, you know, we really have not been covering these stories for a long time, and it's good to see this kind of stuff getting in the paper.' Some of the younger reporters said we were not doing nearly what we should. I told them, 'Yeah, you're right—we still don't. But, guess what? It's a lot better than it used to be.'"[23]

The effects of the change were obvious even across the street at the *Chicago Sun-Times*, of which gay activists had grown increasingly critical since late 1983, when it was purchased by media magnate Rupert Murdoch. He brought in his own cadre of editors to whip the newspaper into shape; coverage of gays and lesbians hit a low in January 1986 when the newspaper carried a string of antigay columns by syndicated columnist Joseph Sobran. In one, HOMOSEXUALITY ISN'T HEALTHY, he wrote: "Nobody really chooses to be homosexual, just as nobody chooses to be alcoholic. But my own hunch is that, making allowance for individual predispositions, both conditions result from a multitude of little choices that finally become habits. Like the alcoholic, the chain smoker and the fat man, the homosexual probably forms himself without fully realizing what he is doing until it has become hard to change."[24]

After Sobran endorsed tattooing as a means of identifying people who had contracted AIDS, gay activist Dan Layman fired off a strongly worded criticism to the editor of the *Sun-Times*. "Sobran wants to be a bigot, but he does not want anyone to call him a bigot," wrote Layman, who had succeeded Paul Varnell as the media committee chairman of the Illinois Gay and Lesbian Task Force.[25] The letter was addressed to Frank Devine, a right-wing former editor of Murdoch's *Australian* who had been an editor at *Reader's Digest* until Murdoch brought him to Chicago in 1984.

Although it is highly unusual for a reader to receive a direct reply from a newspaper, Layman found a letter in his mail box from the editor of the *Sun-Times*. "Since my task is to encourage free expression of opinion on all subjects," Devine wrote, "our goals are inimical to each other. So, to hell with you."[26]

Braving subfreezing weather, a small group of gay and lesbian picketers stood outside the *Sun-Times* offices and waved yellow rags at the staff to symbolize yellow journalism, prompting the publisher and his top editors to agree to a meeting. Wardell saw it as a chance to push the *Tribune*'s competitor to create a gay beat.[27] Coincidentally, the newspaper was undergoing a leveraged buyout in which management had arranged to purchase it from Murdoch.

By the summer of 1986 the new management was firmly in place, and Murdoch's lieutenants had been shifted to his other media holdings. That fall City Editor Mary Dedinsky passed a young reporter named Tom Brune in a hallway and casually informed him, "You are going to start covering AIDS." Dedinsky was one of the editors who had met with the gay protesters.

"They made a lot of sense. They were well-educated and their points were well taken," she said. "I knew that they brought a lot of points to the discussion that were worth listening to. I went back and talked to the editors on the city desk about being careful and being sensitive to the issues, and I also talked to them about increasing our coverage. Generally, a good newspaper covers and reflects what people in the community are saying, and here was a voice that was saying it wanted to be heard."[28]

Brune had just finished a long investigative assignment involving the Chicago Public Library when he got the word from Dedinsky. He was stunned. He knew almost nothing about gays or about AIDS. He welcomed a change of pace, but AIDS was not the break he had in mind.

"I was single and a lot of people thought I was probably gay," he said. "I didn't let them know one way or the other. If they had a problem with it, then they had a problem with it. If they didn't, well, fine. You can cover anything as long as you decide to do it."[29]

Since early in the epidemic medical writer Howard Wolinsky had covered the scientific aspects of AIDS. Brune would write about the human dimensions of the disease. Wolinsky suggested that Brune begin by contacting the Illinois Gay and Lesbian Task Force for background, which included a tour of Chicago's gay bars. A year earlier two task force volunteers had taken Jean Latz Griffin of the *Tribune* on a similar tour.

"I could call the task force and get the names of three or four people to call. They would even provide competing points of view," Brune said. "Their strength was in not playing politics with the sources. I learned a hell of a lot about gays that I never knew before; I learned a lot about AIDS. It was good for me." Brune's first gay-related article appeared on February 12, 1987. A sorority at Northwestern University (NU) had decided to hold an educational seminar on AIDS, but when a man with AIDS was invited to speak, some young women had balked.[30]

The prejudice Brune witnessed on the beat so impressed him that three months later he told his editors that he wanted to expand the beat beyond AIDS to include Chicago's gay community in general.

In 1992 both Brune and Jean Latz Griffin moved off their gay beats. Although both continued to write occasional gay-related stories, it was no longer their fulltime assignment. Both papers wanted to "mainstream" gay coverage into general news stories. A story on dating would include gay dating or a story on parenting would include same-sex parents. "I think that the stereotype is fading as more and more people come out and get into more visible positions," Griffin remarked. "I think that perhaps on both fronts, people were a little more willing to recognize the diversity that was out there."[31]

PUBLICIZING THE ANGER

In October 1987 gays and lesbians held their second National March on Washington and attracted prominent news coverage in national media and local outlets throughout the nation.

HUNDREDS OF THOUSANDS MARCH FOR GAY RIGHTS, read the front page headline in the *Washington Post*. THOUSANDS MARCH FOR GAY RIGHTS, reported the *Philadelphia Inquirer*. Although organizers estimated the crowd at 650,000, the news media routinely reported the 200,000 estimate distributed by the police. But even 200,000 dwarfed the estimated size of the previous march in 1979.

The urgency of the AIDS crisis was dramatized when the first two thousand panels of the Names Project, the AIDS memorial quilt, provided the news media with the first striking visual representation of the human tragedy of the epidemic. One day after the march activists coordinated a mass sit-in outside the U.S. Supreme Court to protest the decision in *Bowers v. Hardwick* a year earlier, when by a vote of 5–4 the justices had upheld the Georgia sodomy law.[32]

More than three thousand gays and lesbians turned out for the protest, which resulted in nearly six hundred arrests. The *Advocate* described it as the largest act of civil disobedience since the antiwar demonstrations of the 1960s and 1970s. The organizers had alerted the major media and had sent notices to newspapers throughout the nation that operated Washington news bureaus. Urvashi Vaid, media director of the National Gay and Lesbian Task Force, told the groups of protesters to carry signs that would identify which city and state they represented. This skillful tactic took advantage of the reporters' basic desire to find a local angle to please their hometown editors.

Vaid said, "I told the press they would see protesters from every corner of the nation, and when they held up their signs, the media swarmed all over them. It was the best. We gave the media what they wanted, and the people who got the coverage went on to be major spokespersons in their media at home."[33]

Yet the media response was spotty at best. Most startling was the decision by editors at each of the three national newsmagazines, *Newsweek*, *Time*, and *U.S. News &World Report*, not to cover the march at all. Veteran lesbian activist Barbara Gittings characterized it as "an appalling example of media blindness."[34]

AIDS AND THE *LOS ANGELES TIMES*

In April 1988 the Names Project quilt went on display at Pauley Pavilion on the UCLA campus as part of a twenty-city fundraising tour. Victor Zonana, a *Los Angeles Times* business reporter who had grown eager to get off the business beat in the paper's San Francisco bureau, happened to be in the city when the exhibit opened.

In six months the number of panels had grown to more than thirty-five hundred. Its size had outgrown arenas in several cities, and even at UCLA's sports facility it covered most of the floor. Some panels had to be hung from rafters and draped over bleachers. AIDS was snuffing out a life every twelve minutes in the United States.

As Zonana arrived, a campuswide power failure plunged the entire facility into darkness and forced a day's delay in the opening ceremony. He found *Times* reporter Laurie Becklund, who had been assigned to cover the ceremony, and they teamed up to cover the blackout. They wrote a second story when the display reopened the next day. Zonana wrote another piece, AIDS QUILT HELPS THOUSANDS REMEMBER, which was accompanied by photographs of people viewing the large quilt and sobbing in grief.[35]

Covering the quilt story reminded Zonana of the day he first joined the *L.A. Times* in 1985 from the *Wall Street Journal*. A colleague had given him a tour of the newsroom, pointing out the foreign, metropolitan, and sports desks. Turning to the new hire, he said, "This is the View section, or, as we call it, Fags and Hags." Zonana looked back with an icy stare and replied, "Then maybe I ought to ask for a transfer."[36]

As he wrote about the quilt three years later, Zonana found himself wrestling with whether to identify himself even more openly. The next week he went to Shelby Coffey III, the newly chosen top editor of the *L.A. Times*, with a proposal. "As a member of the gay community," Zonana told him, "I can do a better job writing about the epidemic than the people who are writing about it now." The coverage was adequate, but Zonana felt it could benefit from a reporter who could go beyond medical news and government policy. He explained to Coffey that he wanted to write about the political, social, and economic ramifications of the epidemic. His case was bolstered by the track record of Randy Shilts, who had been covering AIDS as a beat at the *San Francisco Chronicle* for six years and had broken numerous stories. Zonana's proposal also benefited from the release of Shilts's best-selling book, *And the Band Played On*, which had embarrassed some journalists by pointing out important aspects of the epidemic that they had missed (or were not aware of).

"I knew that I had a very persuasive case, but I didn't know what to expect," Zonana said. "Coffey was a young editor, and I think people of his generation are more comfortable with homosexuality and understand the story. He said he thought it might have been a good idea in 1983 or '84, but he wasn't sure it was an idea in 1988. Being a newsman, he challenged me to come up with ten story ideas before he would consider it. I did that and he was persuaded."[37]

With Coffey's blessing Zonana began covering AIDS full time from the San Francisco bureau, quickly becoming the most visible gay journalist among the thousand working on the *Times*'s news staff. One article provided the first chilling account of a Cuban quarantine center for people with AIDS. Another was a profile of Peter Staley, a twenty-eight-year-old bond trader who had left Wall Street to become a fundraiser for the activist organization ACT-UP.

Through his contact with AIDS activist Larry Kramer, Zonana was able to report in September 1991 on the death of Hollywood actor Brad Davis from AIDS and the actor's fears of discrimination. A former intravenous drug user, Davis had spelled out in a book proposal that he had felt compelled to keep his infection secret for six years lest he be blacklisted. Davis's widow had promised the actor that she would make the document public after his death and contacted Kramer, who turned it over to Zonana.

Zonana's page one story, PROFILE IN COURAGE, ANGER: BRAD DAVIS BATTLED AIDS, HOLLYWOOD, was a scathing indictment of the entertainment industry. "I make my money in an industry that professes to care very much about the fight against AIDS—that gives umpteen benefits and charity affairs with proceeds going to research and care," the story quoted Davis. "But in actual fact, if an actor is even rumored to have HIV, he gets no support on an individual basis. He does not work."[38]

The following year Zonana won a GLAAD media award for his work. In addition, Coffey submitted a collection of Zonana's articles for a Pulitzer Prize. The submission sent another powerful message to other staff members about being gay, being open in the *Times* newsroom, and being allowed to write stories that are important to gays and lesbians.[39]

A BOLD STEP AT THE *EXAMINER*

Although the quilt painted a graphic picture for millions of people whose lives had been untouched by the epidemic, the staff of the *San Francisco Examiner* had already gotten its jolt into the reality of the disease in June 1987 with the death of thirty-five-year-old Howard Taylor. A reporter with the newspaper for only three years, Taylor had quickly become a popular figure in the *Examiner* newsroom. His death instantly transformed AIDS into a personal loss for dozens of coworkers, most of whom had never lost a friend to the disease. "People were forced to confront things they didn't have to confront before."[40]

Two years later, in June 1989, many of his coworkers were among the sixty journalists at the newspaper who worked on the sixteen-part series, GAY IN AMERICA, the most exhaustive coverage of homosexuality ever to appear in an American newspaper. The idea for the series had come fourteen months earlier during a casual conversation between Ken Maley, an openly gay media consultant, and Greg Brock, the *Examiner*'s assistant managing editor, who is openly gay.

Aware that the twentieth anniversary of the Stonewall rebellion was approaching, Maley asked what the newspaper was doing to observe the event widely regarded as marking the birth of the modern gay liberation movement. With nothing in the works Brock asked him for ideas. Maley suggested that the *Examiner* pull out all the stops and publish a special section to show the emergence of a gay political presence in San Francisco and how it had spread throughout the nation. Brock invited Maley to meet with Managing Editor Frank McCulloch. "Of course we should do it," McCulloch responded. "There's no other newspaper in America that can do it."[41] Brock knew that McCulloch would be particularly receptive to the proposal because his son was openly gay and had contracted AIDS.

Editor in chief Larry Kramer (no relation to the playwright of the same name) suggested that Maley draw up a formal proposal to outline exactly what he thought the special section should contain. "I had been collecting topics and ideas for this, and I had begun to put it together over several months," Maley remembered. "They wanted to see if there was enough material to do this."[42]

The series was not the first in-depth coverage the *Examiner* had given gays and lesbians in San Francisco. In 1978 the newspaper had provided the most in-depth series on homosexuality that any newspaper had ever run.[43] Two decades later the *Examiner* was about to set another standard. Maley outlined his ideas at a meeting with the newspaper's editors. He handed them a thick packet that showed them exactly what he had in mind. As he envisioned it, the series would involve almost every department in the newspaper: politics, business, and even sports. By the time he finished his presentation, the editors had agreed that he should coordinate the huge project as a consultant to the paper.

But a few days later Maley found a much different tone among the *Examiner* editors. McCulloch explained to him that while they continued to be enthusiastic about the proposal, it had run into serious problems among the staff. "My heart went through the seat of my chair," Maley remembered. The primary objection came from the Newspaper Guild, the labor union that represented the reporters and editors. Union members objected to an outsider's serving as the project coordinator.

There were problems among the newspaper's older, well-established reporters and editors as well. "The typical reaction from people who had been there for a while was that we had done it all before," Brock said. "They even felt that way about AIDS, as though every story about the disease had already been reported."[44]

"The straight reporters in the newsroom argued a perfectly legitimate position," McCulloch recalled. "They wondered how we would handle calls for similar projects about Laotians, or Cambodians, or Latinos, or any other group in the city this way."[45]

The proposed series also created anxiety among gays and lesbians in the newsroom, many of whom were still not out to their colleagues. "I was writ-ing all of these stories about people coming out, but I still couldn't do it myself," recalled Lily Eng. "If I came out, I would be known not only as a les-bian but as a liar."[46]

Malley said,

> The whole topic brought an enormous upheaval in the paper because they had never discussed openly gay reporters or editors at the *Examiner*. It brought on a huge catharsis among the reporting and editorial staff as people decided which ones would become involved and who would be assigned to what story, who was out, who it would bring out, who it would focus attention on, and so forth. I would say it had more impact within the newsroom—among both management and editorial staff—than anything the paper had ever done.[47]

It was clear to the editors that in order to proceed, they would have to pay Maley a small development fee and remove him from the project. McCulloch designated Brock to oversee the project and formed a committee of staff members to develop specific story ideas. When the group met again a few days later, it had a list of thirty-four stories—twenty-eight of which involved AIDS. None was about lesbians. Brock asked Carol Ness to edit the project, because her journalistic skills and knowledge of the San Francisco gay and lesbian community would guide the rest of the staff toward stories that were interesting and unusual.

More than sixty journalists spent the next year working on the project, some as their fulltime assignment. Travel money was diverted from other stories so reporters could gather information and interviews across the nation. In addition, the newspaper paid for a public opinion poll that would compare public attitudes in San Francisco with the rest of the nation.

The articles ran from June 4 to June 25, 1989, concluding on the city's annual Gay Freedom Day. The daily installments ran under sections such as history, AIDS, and the media. Journalist Randy Alfred was asked to write a freelance article about how the *Examiner* had covered gays and lesbians since the 1960s. He was a particularly interesting choice for the assignment because it was he who had successfully challenged the CBS documentary "Gay Power, Gay Politics" nine years earlier.[48]

In an editorial in the first edition Editor and Publisher William R. Hearst III explained that the series was intended "to counter misinformation by exploring the myths and facts about this minority." He concluded,

A good newspaper must be a community newspaper. It must serve and enrich the place where it is published. And it must be willing to explore currents of change. GAY IN AMERICA is a journalistic examination of gay culture and its influence on the Bay Area and on American life during the past two decades. It is not intended to advocate a point of view, but to challenge assumptions. It's a slice of life, with stories about people, about families, about deeply felt feelings and about values. We will never be a community where everyone thinks or feels the same way, nor should we be, but neither should we become a community of strangers.[49]

In total, the series filled sixty-four open pages (free of advertising). The response from readers was mixed. "You have sunk to a new low in journalism," one man wrote. Wrote another, "Where are your priorities? I was amazed that the morning following such newsworthy, if not monumental events—the massacre in Beijing, the death of Ayatollah, and the train disaster in the Soviet Union—you still devoted nearly one-third of the Sunday front page to introducing Gay in America series. (OK, so accuse me of being 'homophobic.')" But there were also compliments. "Congratulations!" said one letter. "This is the most uplifting and emotionally charged journalism I have encountered in years."[50]

Perhaps the most unexpected response came from journalists at newspapers around the country who were in the closet. They wrote to say that by using the series as an example they thought they had been able to influence coverage at their own papers. An editor in Texas said it had given him the courage to face his own sexuality and come out.

Another sign of the changing attitude among newspapers appeared in a December 1992 edition of the Minneapolis *Star Tribune* when the newspaper published a special fourteen-page section, GROWING UP GAY: A CRISIS IN HIDING.[51] The idea for the section had originated three years earlier after openly lesbian staff photographer Rita Reed read a disturbing article about the high rate of attempted suicide among gay and lesbian youths. The story, in the local gay newspaper *Equal Times*, cited the findings of a federal study in which 30 percent of the five hundred youths interviewed said they had attempted suicide at least once. Reed prodded editors at the *Star Tribune* to report on how the Minneapolis–St. Paul area was responding to the needs of its gay teens, but the editors rebuffed the idea each time. "Some of them were skeptical that gay teenagers actually existed," she recalled. "They thought gay and lesbian teens were going through a phase and would come out the other side as heterosexual."[52]

In late 1990, after a murder-suicide involving a local gay youth, Reed again proposed a special report. Skeptical editors predicted she would be unable to convince young gays to talk openly. Editors also were concerned about gaining parental consent for interviews with and photographs of the teenagers. But Reed convinced them she could overcome the obstacles, and the editors agreed to let her try.

In January 1992 Reed began working with staff writer Kurt Chandler. "We wanted to know how these kids lived their lives," she recalled. "We wanted to know how and why the schools, the churches, and their families were failing them."[53] GROWING UP GAY appeared as a fourteen-page special section in the *Star Tribune* on December 6, 1992, with forty-four pictures shot by Reed and a lengthy text by Chandler.

Part of Chandler's story noted, "From the time they realize they're gay, kids are wounded, and you don't have to spend much time with them to see it. Despised for their sexual orientation, most of them become self-imposed exiles, suffering a bitter loneliness that shakes their identity and eats away at self-esteem. The most troubled ones drop out of school, run away from home, turn to prostitution, drugs or alcohol. Many try to kill themselves, and sometimes they succeed."[54]

The response was overwhelming. More than two thousand telephone calls poured into the newspaper. Only slightly more than half were supportive. But the response inside the newspaper was much warmer. The next year the editor of the *Star Tribune* submitted GROWING UP GAY for a Pulitzer Prize. Although it did not win, it had made a powerful statement about how the practice of journalism was shifting to a new set of rules.

GLAAD GROWS UP

By early 1987 the Gay and Lesbian Alliance Against Defamation (GLAAD) had made inroads with media in New York City but was unknown nationally. Its founders were eager to tap the anger among gays across the nation.

But some members were divided over whether GLAAD should be an AIDS organization or a media advocacy group. Their dilemma was solved in March, when a speech by playwright Larry Kramer at the New York Gay Community Center became the impetus for a new organization, AIDS Coalition to Unleash Power (ACT UP). Using Kramer's direct confrontational style as a model, ACT UP concentrated on the inadequate funding for AIDS research and the government's slowness to approve new drugs. ACT UP enabled GLAAD to concentrate on media and cultural advocacy and sidestep the dissension that had crippled similar groups in the past.

Still, festering personality conflicts on GLAAD's board of directors were beginning to paralyze the organization. In-fighting had broken out among members, who were accusing one another of being unfit to serve on the board. Tempers reached a new height in late 1986 when several cofounders began a race to see who could resign first. Survival of the fledgling organization looked bleak until the spring of 1987, when Craig Davidson agreed to become its first executive director.

A cum laude graduate of the Harvard Law School, Davidson had been a rising star at one of Wall Street's high-powered law firms. His diagnosis with AIDS had radicalized him, prompting him to abandon his promising career to become a gay activist. Davidson quickly became GLAAD's salvation. He managed to divert the members' attention from the bickering and provided the stability and credibility that was necessary to impress media heavyweights. Within only a few months GLAAD was beginning to attract its first substantial contributions. Donors were becoming more confident in the young organization and its more clearly defined goals.

Under Davidson's leadership GLAAD rented its first office. It hired its first two fulltime staff members, Davidson and assistant director Karin Schwartz. The two galvanized support by organizing GLAAD's second protest at the *New York Post*. The first in 1985 had attracted 700 demonstrators, giving the organization its first public identity. Davidson recognized the power of a public protest to marshal his forces and attract new members. Within three years membership in the New York area exploded from 500 to 5,000. The mailing list eventually surged to 10,000.

Davidson added substance to the GLAAD agenda by soliciting and writing columns that went out to gay newspapers nationwide. He also created a phone tree, a system in which members quickly notified each other of upcoming protests. He developed another procedure that had members respond to homophobia in the media with an avalanche of letters, postcards, and flyers.

GLAAD drew on the professional expertise of members, who ranged from Wall Street lawyers to graphic artists and writers. Ronald Gold, the former media director of the National Gay Task Force, spearheaded the production of "Media Guide to the Lesbian and Gay Community." Early organizers had talked about creating a national organization, but Davidson was laying the foundation required to achieve that objective. "There was a perception that we were either a large group of people or we could mobilize a lot of people," remembered Jane Hoffman, an early member who acted as the organization's legal adviser. "From the very beginning there was a professionalism about GLAAD."[55]

In May 1989 GLAAD representatives met with news executives at NBC to complain about the network's coverage of an explosion aboard the USS IOWA that unnamed navy sources speculated was the result of a "troubled homosexual" relationship between two sailors. The story was widely reported in the media, but GLAAD targeted NBC's story as the most speculative. (GLAAD's position was vindicated in October 1991. The navy exonerated the sailor, saying it lacked evidence, and apologized to the man's family.[56])

But the biggest flap of 1989 followed CBS News's December 20 retrospective of the year, which included an insensitive reference to AIDS by commentator Andy Rooney. In the cranky irreverent tone that was his trademark, he told his television audience, "There was some recognition of the fact that many of the ills that kill us are self-induced—too much alcohol, too much food, drugs, homosexual unions and cigarettes were all known to lead quite often to premature death."[57]

Rooney had made similar comments three months earlier in his syndicated newspaper column. Writing about the airlines' smoking ban on domestic flights, Rooney said, "I feel the same way about homosexuals as I do about cigarette smokers. I wouldn't want to spend much time in a small room with one, but they don't bother me otherwise."[58] That comment had been largely ignored. But after Rooney sounded off about AIDS on national television, GLAAD responded immediately and strongly.

"That's fundamentally incorrect," charged GLAAD's Karin Schwartz, who was quoted in *USA Today*. "AIDS is not caused by homosexuality. It's caused by a virus." The brouhaha set off a small ripple of headlines as GLAAD carried its complaint to CBS's top brass. *USA Today* reported that network news president David Burke promised the GLAAD representatives that Rooney's copy would be edited more closely and had urged Rooney to practice greater "sensitivity" in the future.[59]

The flap might have ended there, except that Rooney then tried to clarify his comments in an open letter to the gay community that he sent to the *Advocate* on January 30, 1990, at the request of the *Advocate*'s New York reporter, Chris Bull. In it he apologized for the remark and went on to explain his homespun philosophy of homosexuality in some detail: "AIDS is a largely preventable disease, and I expressed the opinion that there was a growing public resentment about being taxed to pay for the health care of people suffering from self-inflicted diseases. . . . With very little definitive medical or scientific evidence to go on, it seems to me that it is a behavioral aberration caused by some kind of trauma or caused when a male is born with an abnormal number of female genes, or vice versa."[60]

In one section of his letter Rooney explained that his closest relationship with a homosexual was his forty-year friendship with Merle Miller, the novelist and biographer who came out in the *New York Times* in 1971. "My friendship with Merle and a dozen other gay men taught me a lot about them and eliminated the know-nothing, all-American-boy kind of prejudice that I grew up surrounded by," he wrote. He concluded by saying he was genuinely sorry that homosexuals had taken offense at his broadcast and offered a backhanded apology. "It was not my intention to make their already difficult gay life any more difficult," he wrote. "I'll be more careful."[61]

But Rooney was not careful enough for CBS president David Burke, who got wind of the letter and ordered Rooney not to send it. It was too late; the letter was on its way to the most widely read gay magazine in the nation. To make matters even worse Rooney granted a telephone interview to Bull.

To Bull's surprise Rooney was extremely talkative. Asked about his comments on AIDS, he responded, "I know you people can't help yourselves, but it's crazy to go on engaging in this behavior in this day and age." When Bull asked whether he would broadcast similar unconventional remarks about other minority groups, including blacks, Rooney responded, "Don't be so sure. I've believed all along that most people are born with equal intelligence, but blacks have watered down their genes because the less intelligent ones are the ones that have the most children. They drop out of school early, do drugs, and get pregnant."[62]

Bull reported the comments in the *Advocate*'s February 27 issue. ANDY, WE HARDLY KNEW YE ran alongside Rooney's rambling letter. Almost immediately, wire services and newspapers jumped on the racist comments. Rooney denied making the comment and claimed Bull had taken his remarks out of context. Once news stories began to appear in the mainstream media, Burke summoned Rooney to his office and suspended him for three months from his $800,000-a-year job. Burke issued a statement that said, "I have made it clear that CBS News cannot tolerate such remarks or anything that approximates such comments, since they in no way reflect the views of this organization."[63]

Gay activists were apoplectic. The network had disciplined Rooney for making racist remarks but had ignored their calls for his suspension after his homophobic remarks nearly two months earlier. "The biggest issue to come from this series of events—aside from the Rooney suspension itself—is how dramatically biased against gays media coverage of the story was," wrote GLAAD's Craig Davidson, who called the news media to task for applying a double standard.[64]

Writers from mainstream newspapers tried to discredit Bull by repeatedly referring to his youth, as though it invalidated his credibility, and few questioned Rooney's credibility as a commentator on race and sexuality. When they learned that Bull had not taped the interview, the lack of recording became the center of controversy—as though it were damning evidence that supported Rooney's claim that he was misquoted. "They would ask, 'Why didn't you use a tape recorder?'" Bull recounted. "And I'd say, 'Are you taping this with a tape recorder?' And they'd say no. They didn't see a double standard operating."[65]

Several reporters began to investigate Bull's professional background, a tactic journalists usually reserve for errant politicians. He was particularly incensed when he learned that *Washington Post* reporter Roxanne Roberts was tracking down people he had cited in articles he had written at Boston's *Gay Community News*, where he had worked for three years before joining the *Advocate*. "If I were a journalist for the *Advocate*, I'd be furious if someone were to suggest that I couldn't do an objective job," Roberts recalled. "But there's enough very opinionated, editorial-like features to the magazine that it's difficult to distinguish between a feature or news article and an editorial-type article, so when you pick it up, it's almost impossible to know which person is coming from which perspective."[66]

Roberts's story never ran. Before she finished the research her editors switched her to another story, and by the time she returned to the one about Bull, it was considered stale. But *New York Post* editorial page editor Eric M. Breindel continued his investigation until he found two people who "insisted that they too had been misquoted by Bull." Writing in *Commentary*, Breindel sarcastically referred to Bull as a "neophyte who had been in journalism all of four months," comparing the young reporter's experience unfavorably with Rooney's forty years at *CBS*. Breindel and several other commentators suggested that the Rooney quote was suspect because it had appeared in a magazine for gays and lesbians.[67]

Bull was under fire from both ends of the political spectrum. Liberal syndicated columnist Nat Hentoff of the *Village Voice* cast some of the strongest aspersions when he berated gay and black leaders who "took the *Advocate* as gospel." *Washington Post* television writer John Carmody cited an incident in 1942 when Rooney was reportedly arrested and "briefly jailed in the then-segregated St. Augustine, Florida, when he had refused to move from a seat in the back of a segregated public bus" as evidence that Rooney was incapable of making prejudiced remarks about blacks.[68]

"They couldn't see that the gay press was part of the press," said Bull. "They saw it as nothing more than a propaganda machine. I wasn't interested in punishing Andy Rooney for his antigay comments. I didn't really care what his news subjects were. I just saw it as a good story. But the press saw it as me against Andy Rooney. Me, the young gay reporter, and whether I was fair and competent versus Andy Rooney, the doting commentator who was racist and homophobic. That distinction was unfair to both of us."[69]

After the clamor quieted, CBS rescinded the three-month suspension. "The message is clear," observed *Rolling Stone*. "Homophobia should be punished—unless the punishment leads to a huge drop in the ratings."[70]

CHANGES AT THE *NEW YORK TIMES*

Coverage of AIDS among the nation's major daily newspapers peaked in 1987 when the national debate about widespread testing for HIV antibodies more than doubled the number of AIDS stories run in 1986. The total number of deaths in the United States alone climbed to nearly twenty-eight thousand, with more than fifty-nine thousand cases reported. Yet a public opinion survey in 1989 showed that the average American still had no clear understanding of how HIV was transmitted. A large number believed they could contract the disease if they donated blood.[71]

The dimensions of the epidemic took on a new importance at the *New York Times* in December 1990. Deputy National Editor Jeffrey Schmalz had not felt well for several days when he noticed a problem with his vision and a sporadic twitching in his left eye, which he blamed on fatigue. But soon after he returned from lunch on December 21, he stood up from his computer terminal, took a few steps, and fell to the floor unconscious.

Reporters and editors rushed to his side, including medical writer Lawrence Altman, who is also a physician. When Schmalz went into a grand mal seizure, Altman called for an ambulance. It took a full month for doctors to complete their tests. When Schmalz learned he would require brain surgery, he also learned that he had already developed full-blown AIDS. Schmalz remembered that

> it took a month to figure it out. I met with [executive editor] Max Frankel and with [managing editor] Joe Lelyveld individually, and told them. They said it must come as a terrible shock and I said, "Well, when you're gay this is always in the back of your mind." I didn't say, "I'm gay," but in the course of my getting AIDS we just sort of talked as if everybody had always known I was gay. In fact, everybody had always known—there was no secret about it. I certainly never denied it, we'd just never talked about it that much. AIDS just sort of blew everything open.[72]

Schmalz's brain surgery was followed by a yearlong recuperation. When he returned to his duties as deputy national editor, it was clear that he could not afford the physical strain of the demanding job. Instead, the *Times* agreed to allow him to work on special projects. He would begin to cover lesbians and gays for the newspaper and write about AIDS as a beat.

13

THE CONSEQUENCES OF OUTING

On Friday morning, October 3, 1980, the *Washington Post* named a U.S. congressman who was having sex with other men. Although the news media generally considered such matters private, police had charged Representative Robert Bauman, R-Maryland, with having sex with a sixteen-year-old he had solicited at a Washington gay bar. But Bauman had crossed the media's invisible line. Once the allegation appeared on police records, Bauman became fair game. One investigator told the *Post*: "We don't want to go digging into someone's personal life, but when an allegation of involvement into soliciting is laid out in front of us, there's nothing to do but pursue it."[1]

Even before the morning newspapers began arriving at newsstands, news of the charges against Bauman appeared on the Associated Press and United

Press International wires. By dawn the story had been flashed to newsrooms throughout the capital and across the nation. His case was especially intriguing to reporters because of the stark contrast between the lives lived by Bauman the politician and Bauman the homosexual. A married Roman Catholic with four children, he was an ardent supporter of family issues in Congress and had strenuously fought such liberal issues as abortion, women's rights, and legal protections for gays.

Blaming the allegation on a period of "acute alcoholism," Bauman avoided facing a felony charge through a plea bargain. Prosecutors allowed him to plead innocent to a misdemeanor and agreed to drop the charge if he completed a rehabilitation program for first offenders. But his problems did not end. The news media would extract a heavier penalty by continuing to link the congressman with gay life in Washington and male prostitution. THE BOY-WHORE WORLD, read a front page *Washington Post* headline on October 7; accompanying it was a photograph of three young men standing outside a notorious hustler bar. The article began, "A misty rain dampens the sidewalk in front of the Naples Cafe on New York Avenue NW near 13th Street. Three hustlers standing on the street before the steaming rush-hour traffic draw the heated gaze of male motorists cruising through the tenderloin district."[2]

Only four months after the uproar over Bauman, police arrested Representative Jon Hinson with another man in a Capitol Hill restroom and charged him with sodomy. Like Bauman, Hinson was a champion of conservative causes and represented a vexing problem facing gay and lesbian activists. Although the activists were eager for gays to become more visible, they felt bound by a long-standing code of silence that protected the identities of closeted homosexuals at all costs. Gays were painfully aware that overzealous politicians had used exposure during the McCarthy era as a political weapon to silence their opponents. Although thirty years had passed, the unauthorized exposure of one gay person by another was still considered cruel and unusual punishment.[3]

Even so, the charges against Bauman and Hinson triggered a period of what gay journalist Larry Bush called "intense soul searching." Writing in the April 27, 1982, edition of the *Village Voice*, Bush posed this question: Should gays protect gays, as they had Bauman and Hinson, no matter how antigay their public politics? The hypocrisy was all too real for Bush, who lived in a city in which he could witness firsthand individuals who campaigned against gay rights by day but secretly sought gay sex at night.

For many years the details of a prominent person's sex life were off limits among the news media because, with few exceptions, divulging such information was considered an invasion of privacy. Reporters had known of closeted gays who held important positions in government and the entertainment industry long before the Bauman affair but never exposed them because of the unwritten code of silence. Reporters at the *Washington Post* and the *Boston Globe* had known for several years that Representative Barney Frank, D-Massachusetts, was gay. But it was not reported until Frank acknowledged it in an interview with the *Globe* in May 1987, shortly after the *Miami Herald* revealed Senator Gary Hart's extra marital affair with model Donna Rice, ruining his presidential aspirations.[4]

Although the media's rules also guarded the sex lives of high-profile heterosexuals, the restraint was enforced far more stringently with homosexuals. Typically a person's homosexuality became news only after it appeared in the public record books, and the record invariably was an arrest record for soliciting or having public sex. Because of this filtering process average homosexuals—those who never came in contact with the law—were invisible in the news media and thus to the general public. It would have been difficult—if not impossible—for the public to be aware of a prominent person's homosexuality unless he or she got into trouble.

The code was a standard practice among the news media that lasted until the outbreak of AIDS. As the epidemic worsened, gays began to question nearly everything. AIDS not only changed the tone of the debate over gay rights, it changed the debate itself. Gays could no longer toil within the system—quietly or otherwise—for recognition and acceptance, for their lives required that the larger society recognize them as part of the fabled American melting pot. They began to demand that their government dedicate tax dollars toward finding a cure for the disease. As patterns showed the epidemic worsening, gays understood all to well that this was a disease that would not be confined to a small segment of society, that soon its causes and its devastation would be everyone's problem. But their concerns could be addressed only through the mainstream press, holder of the keys to mass communication.

For the mainstream media AIDS meant having to confront issues that it would have preferred to ignore, from the sexuality of newsmakers to graphic descriptions of sexual practices to backlash from the religious right to how "survivors" would be listed in obituaries.

As the eighties wore on and the AIDS death toll mounted, gays in growing numbers began to question their own code of silence, to question whether it had become an anachronism that was now hurting their cause. A radical segment of the gay community decided it was time to break the silence about other gays' sexual orientation. In so doing they introduced a new word to the general lexicon: *outing*.

"Outing was adopted as a tactic in opposition to the tacit agreement by which gay private lives were granted an exemption from the public's 'right to know,' thus protecting the closets of the rich and famous and leaving unchallenged the distaste of the media—and the public—for facing the reality of lesbian and gay existence," wrote communications professor Larry Gross in his 1993 book *Contested Closets*. Randy Shilts told a writer for the *Washington Journalism Review* in 1990, "What bothers me is the media piously talking about private lives. They just find homosexuality distasteful and don't want to write about it. They don't have any problem lying about it; their problem is in telling the truth about it."[5]

Thus to gays outing meant being honest about the sexuality of newsmakers and celebrities who circulated within the gay community but were closeted to the rest of society. To the mainstream media outing meant publicizing the sexuality of gay people, whether they had chosen to publicly acknowledge it or not. So when gays spoke of outing, they meant honesty, but the mainstream media—and many in the established gay press—heard *exposure* and shuddered, envisioning lawsuits, readers' and viewers' complaints, and dried-up sources. Besides, how was the media to distinguish a homosexual who was out from someone who was closeted? And who wanted to have to talk to the bereaved Martha Jones about her son? She had spent twenty years denying that he might be gay, only to be confronted by a line in an obituary written by his friends: "He is survived by his longtime companion George Wilson."

OUTING IN THE MODERN ERA

The earliest known example of outing in the United States came in 1969 when author Josef Bush listed the names of suspected gays in the appendix of his gay travel book *The Homosexual Handbook*. Writing under the pseudonym Angelo d'Arcangelo, Bush assembled a list of individuals—living and dead—who were "generally thought to be gay."[6]

The show business newspaper *Variety* noted that although most of the names belonged to historical figures, the list included three dozen contemporary singers, actors, composers, writers, choreographers, producers, dancers, TV hosts, comedians, and several members of royalty. "The great majority of the names come as no surprise to knowledgeable tradesters, but there are a few bombshells," the article said. Among those named in the book were actors Rock Hudson, Tab Hunter, Richard Chamberlain, composer Leonard Bernstein, writers Truman Capote, Edward Albee, and James Baldwin, actor-dancer Fred Astaire, and author-columnist William F. Buckley Jr., but Bush offered no evidence that they were gay. *Variety* did not list any of the names in its article.

Variety returned to the subject six weeks later, on April 23, 1969, when it noted that the *New York Times* had rejected an advertisement for the book. "It gave as the reason that its medical panel had ruled the book's contents were not consistent with the purported title," *Variety* said. However, the editors of *Saturday Review* noted in a brief article in their June 14, 1969, issue that "the book, a paperback, intends to do for the homosexual what Dr. Spock has done for babies." A few weeks later the book's publisher yanked 7,000 copies off the shelves and had them destroyed. One can only speculate on the cause. When the revised edition of the book appeared on bookshelves, one name was missing: J. Edgar Hoover. The book eventually went into three printings, and by late 1970 it had sold nearly 250,000 copies, an enormous number for a gay travel book.[7]

Another early reference to the practice appeared in John Paul Hudson's 1972 travel book *The Gay Insider USA*. Writing under the pseudonym John Francis Hunter, he ended his book with a set of predictions about the future of gay liberation. It must have seemed outlandish at the time, but Hudson foresaw a secret militant gay organization that would promote the gay liberation movement by engaging in "ruthless exposure of celebrated men's private lives—substantiated by photographs, films, letters, tapes and testimonies."[8]

Outing stirred a much greater controversy in 1975 when Oliver Sipple earned national hero status by thwarting Sara Jane Moore's attempted assassination of President Gerald Ford. After the ex-marine saved Ford's life, gay activists who felt he had not gotten sufficient credit began telling the media about Sipple's homosexuality, despite his strenuous objections. According to Randy Shilts's *The Mayor of Castro Street*, Harvey Milk leaked the story to *San Francisco Chronicle* gossip columnist Herb Caen. Milk, in the midst of campaigning for city supervisor as an openly gay man, hoped the publicity would prompt the White House to formally recognize Sipple's act of heroism.

Once the story appeared on the wire services, it was picked up by newspapers throughout the nation, including three that identified Sipple as gay. Sipple's mother, a staunch Baptist who had not known of her son's sexual orientation, stopped talking to him. Angry at the media for invading his privacy, Sipple brought suit against the *Chronicle*, *Denver Post*, and *Chicago Sun-Times*— only to have a federal court dismiss the case, citing the First Amendment. According to some accounts, Sipple never fully recovered from the trauma. He died of pneumonia alone in his San Francisco apartment in 1989.

Outing was the source of a 1982 controversy in which author-journalist Perry Deane Young tackled the Christian right in his book *God's Bullies*. Among its revelations was the secret gay life of Terry Dolan, the head of the National Conservative Political Action Committee, a powerful PAC that opposed gay rights. Describing Dolan as a hypocrite, Young detailed how the closeted conservative fought political battles against gays by day but slept with them at night. Questioned about breaking the taboo of exposing another gay, Young said Dolan had "forfeited his right to privacy by advocating political measures inimical to the rights of his fellow closeted homosexuals."[9] (Dolan denied Young's characterization in an interview with the *New York Times* on August 19, 1982.) Young's standard would be adopted several years later by many gay activists.

SILENCE IN THE OBITUARIES

Nowhere have the media held so tightly to the code of silence about homosexuality than in obituaries. Although the dead cannot sue for libel or invasion of privacy, until the early 1990s journalists steadfastly avoided mention of a person's homosexuality even when the person had publicly acknowledged it.

But the even more contentious point between gay activists and the media was obituaries that neglected to list AIDS as the cause of death. Critics charged that by masking the number of deaths caused by AIDS, the media made it nearly impossible for the public to grasp the magnitude of the epidemic. Following the death of fashion designer Perry Ellis in May 1986, for instance, obituaries in the *Washington Post*, *USA Today*, *Newsday*, and *Newsweek* listed AIDS as the cause of death. But the *New York Times*, *Los Angeles Times*, and *Time* all failed to mention it. In many cases the gay newspaper in a city listed AIDS as the cause of death, whereas that person's obituary in the local daily gave another, false cause.

Many newspapers maintained that the reason for the inconsistency was that information in obituaries routinely comes from family members who sometimes withhold facts. Although most editors do not exempt obituaries from the same standards of accuracy that apply to news stories, they typically do not send reporters on the often intrusive mission of investigating the cause of every death. Some newspapers refused even to list AIDS unless it was specifically requested by the family or could be verified by a doctor or public record.

Media critic Edwin Diamond has compared the underreporting of AIDS in the 1980s with the underreporting of cancer during the 1970s. "Today, in many minds, AIDS registers an explicit, stronger aversion," he wrote in his book *Media Show*. "The obituary notice in our time has become a new battleground."[10] By 1988 journalists were already questioning the rules of privacy and confidentiality that were the basis for their silence. The AIDS epidemic, coupled with the debate over outing, intensified the pressure on many in the mainstream media to confront ethical questions they had long avoided.

At times the media carried the heterosexual facade to ridiculous extremes. The 1990 obituary for Aaron Copland in the *New York Times*, for example, referred to the composer as "a lifelong bachelor," even though it was well known that he was a gay man. After former New York City health administrator Harold Brown died in 1975, the *Times* mentioned that he had come out as a homosexual in its pages in 1973 but went on to describe him as a bachelor anyway.

More commonly newspapers refused to acknowledge a surviving gay spouse. After the death of novelist Merle Miller in June 1986, his *New York Times* obituary said, "There are no survivors." But Miller's obituary in Long Island's *Newsday* noted that Miller and writer David W. Elliot had been lovers for twenty-two years and that Miller had acknowledged his homosexuality fifteen years earlier in a celebrated article in the *New York Times Magazine*. In December 1986 the policy at the *Times* began to loosen somewhat. "We can mention a live-in companion of the same or the opposite sex in the course of the narrative," wrote Assistant Managing Editor Allan M. Siegal in a memo to the *Times* staff. "Generally we should mention an unmarried companion if associates of the deceased ask us to do so."[11]

The first evidence of the new policy came on May 8, 1987, when the *Times* ran the obituary of Paul Popham, a founder of the AIDS service group Gay Men's Health Crisis. The *Times* relied on the time-worn euphemism "longtime companion" to refer to his spouse, Richard Dulong.[12]

But other newspapers were slower to adapt. In July 1988 *Daily Variety* deleted the name of television producer Christopher Sands from the obituary of his lover of eleven years. *Variety*, like many newspapers and magazines, had a long-standing policy of listing "only those relatives who are blood relatives, adopted children, or a legally recognized spouse of the deceased." In an interview with the *Los Angeles Times*, a *Variety* executive further trivialized gay relationships by saying the policy "applies in all cases, whether someone is living with a man, a woman, a martian, or a cat." Outraged by the insensitivity, Sands bought and placed a half-page advertisement in *Daily Variety* to protest. "The grieving gay spouse [who is] left behind should not have the ugly boot of bigoted homophobia, unintentionally or not, pressed down hard against [his] throat," the ad said.[13]

OUTING IN THE ERA OF AIDS

But to the gay community at large there was more to the debate than compounding the grief of a loved one. By 1987 the AIDS epidemic had ravaged gay men, and gay activists were questioning their own code of silence more intensely than ever. SILENCE = DEATH became the grim motto of the AIDS activist group ACT UP (the AIDS Coalition to Unleash Power) as its members mounted a fierce campaign against public and government indifference to the mounting death toll. Outing was one of its first tactics.

In April 1989 the ACT UP chapter in Portland, Oregon, challenged the reelection campaign of Senator Mark Hatfield, who had a less-than-stellar record on AIDS legislation—although he was a leading supporter of gay rights—by painting across his downtown campaign billboards: HATFIELD, CLOSETED GAY: LIVING A LIE, VOTING TO OPPRESS. Work crews were quickly dispatched to remove one of the signs from public view, but the activists had taken pictures of the sign and sent copies to area newspapers and television stations.

Hatfield denied the group's contention, but stories about the billboards appeared in several newspapers, including the *Seattle Post-Intelligencer*, *Willamette Week*, and on at least two television stations. But other media outlets opted to ignore the incident, including the *Oregonian*, Portland's liberal daily, even though the story was unfolding in its own backyard.[14]

Chicago ACT UP used a similar tactic against Governor James Thompson of Illinois after he supported legislation to allow hospitals to test patients for HIV without their consent. AIDS activists passed out leaflets claiming that Thompson had been seen in the city's gay bars yet had a history of opposing gay rights and AIDS programs. Ignoring the claims about the governor's private life, Chicago newspapers reported only that the protest had taken place.[15]

At about the same time Michelangelo Signorile began attending ACT UP meetings in New York. He had joined a group of gay public relations professionals who were mapping out a strategy to put ACT UP and AIDS in the news. Signorile had earned a college degree in public communications at Syracuse University before moving to New York, where he landed a job at a public relations firm that specialized in getting clients mentioned in gossip columns.

As a Broadway press agent dealing with the top gossip columnists in the nation, Signorile had become increasingly aware of an anachronistic double standard in which these columnists routinely reported rumors of heterosexual love affairs but refused to report on homosexual ones. Even when they knew of a romance involving a closeted celebrity, these columnists either ignored it altogether or included details of a fabricated heterosexual romance that had been planted by the celebrity's press agent. Even when the gayness of a celebrity was known by many gays, they were abiding by the code of silence, so the open secret would never be publicly acknowledged.

In early 1989 Signorile met former keyboard player and party promoter Gabriel Rotello at an ACT UP meeting and listened as Rotello described his plans to start a new gay magazine. Signorile jumped at the opportunity to write for the new publication, creating the Gossip Watch column in which he would attack the practices of columnists he had fed in his earlier career as a Broadway press agent.

The first issue of *OutWeek* hit the newsstands on June 24, 1989, during New York's gay pride parade, the annual celebration of the Stonewall riots. The brash and irreverent new magazine was written in an inflammatory style. It reflected the deep anger and rage that fueled ACT UP—new chapters were beginning to spring up across the nation.

In August 1989 Signorile created a second column for *OutWeek*, Peek-A-Boo, which listed the names of more than sixty closeted celebrities, including syndicated gossip columnist Liz Smith, New York *Newsday* gossip columnist James Revson, and *New York Daily News* gossip columnist Billy Norwich. Although there was no explicit explanation for why the names appeared on the list, the message to closeted gay celebrities was clear. The next month Signorile's Peek-A-Boo listed the names of thirty more celebrities. He later acknowledged that his lists were highly speculative and left the magazine vulnerable to lawsuits. But Signorile enjoyed wide latitude from a group of wealthy investors who had bankrolled the renegade publication and were willing to take risks to put rich and famous closeted gays on notice that they would be held accountable to the gay community.[16]

Signorile stepped up his campaign throughout the late summer and fall of 1989, often prefacing additional names with such code words as *self-loathing* and *self-hating*. Magazine publisher Malcolm Forbes was subjected to relentless criticism for his seeming lack of commitment to the battle against AIDS, even though he had contributed millions to the cause. Signorile thought the billionaire should do more and began to attack Forbes and two other conservatives, former secretary of state Henry Kissinger and columnist William F. Buckley Jr. In his typical turgid prose with a liberal seasoning of capital letters and exclamation points, Signorile wrote, "What he can do is scream at his friends in Washington and in the media that THIS F—ING GOVERNMENT ISN'T DOING S—about an epidemic that has killed thousands of people, instead of kissing the asses of the murderous Kissingers and Buckleys."[17]

By January 1990 the controversy was spilling into the mainstream media. *Time* ran a feature on the phenomenon headlined FORCING GAYS OUT OF THE CLOSET. *Time*'s media critic, William Henry III, became the first to give a name to Signorile's tactic—*outing*—which he described as "the intentional exposure of secret gays by other gays." "Frustrated at the slow pace of gay civil rights legislation and what they consider government indifference to the AIDS epidemic, growing numbers of gay activists now claim a moral right to rip people out of the closet," wrote Henry, who also covered gays for the magazine as an unofficial beat. The rest of the media would not weigh in on the brewing controversy for several more months as Signorile continued his campaign to rip the doors off the closets of rich and famous homosexuals, including entertainment mogul David Geffen, who would eventually out himself several years later.[18]

As Signorile worked in *OutWeek*'s cramped office one afternoon in early March 1990, he heard a radio news report that magazine publisher Forbes had died. "I wondered how soon the media would start lying," he recalled. "I knew a truthful article about Forbes had to be written, right away."[19]

For years the media had fed a public perception that Forbes was a womanizing, globe-hopping eccentric. At his annual birthday bashes the billionaire would invite hundreds of celebrities to help him celebrate, posing with the most beautiful women while hordes of photographers snapped pictures that would appear in newspapers and magazines worldwide. A classic photo

showed him with actress Elizabeth Taylor riding one of his many motorcy-
cles, giving the impression that the two were inseparable.

Signorile began collecting information for a story about Forbes, contacting people who might have firsthand knowledge of the tycoon's secret social
life. The trail led him inside the New York club scene and to friends,
boyfriends, former employees, and people who had socialized with Forbes
on the gay party circuit. He found people who described how Forbes had
"sexually harassed and abused male employees."[20]

But before Signorile could finish his article, *USA Today* reported some of
the same rumors he was tracking about Forbes. "Once a taboo subject, a
celebrity's sexual proclivity now seems to be fair game," the article began.
Reporter Jeannie Williams mentioned the names of Richard Chamberlain,
John Travolta, David Bowie, and Mick Jagger, writing that they had also
encountered questions about their sexual orientation. The peg for the story
was Signorile's preparations for the *OutWeek* story on Forbes.[21]

A few days after Williams's story ran, *OutWeek* hit the newsstands with a
photograph of the smiling publisher mounted on one of his beloved Harley-
Davidsons and a headline that blared THE SECRET GAY LIFE OF MALCOLM
FORBES. Writing about it in 1995, *OutWeek* editor Gabriel Rotello called it
"the headline heard round the gay and lesbian world." Signorile began his
exposé by describing some of the prominent mourners at Forbes's funeral,
including former president Richard Nixon, author-columnist Buckley, and
media mogul Rupert Murdoch. "It was a splashy memorial service indeed,"
he wrote. "But did the homophobes know that they were coming to pay
homage to someone who embodied what they ultimately detested?"[22]

OutWeek tried to promote coverage of its exclusive story by sending
advance copies to news organizations. Although editors at New York's *Daily
News* and *Entertainment Tonight* showed interest, both outlets killed their stories at the last minute. After stories about it ran in several out-of-town
papers, the *New York Post* reported it, but criticized Signorile's tactic by comparing it with the anticommunist witch-hunts of Senator Joe McCarthy.
(Apparently it did not register with the *Post* writers that unlike the McCarthy
era, the exposure of Forbes was a case of gays exposing a gay, unless they
were referring to McCarthy's closeted aide Roy Cohn.) As controversy continued to build, stories appeared in the *Miami Herald*, the *San Francisco
Chronicle*, and the *Washington Post*. Supermarket tabloids had a field day, speculating (wrongly) that Forbes had died of AIDS.

Under attack from mainstream editors, Signorile retaliated in a *Village*

Voice article headlined GAYSTYLES OF THE RICH AND FAMOUS: HOW I BROUGHT OUT MALCOLM FORBES—AND THE MEDIA FLINCHED. "The Unwritten Rule must be broken—and I hurled the first stone. But instead of a resounding crash, all I heard was a modest thud. . . . The message to rich and famous queers is: come out while you can, because when you die you'll be thrown on the cover of a magazine and labeled a closet case. I may even bring you out alive."[23]

Newsweek weighed in on the issue in an April 30, 1990, article entitled OUTING: AN UNEXPECTED ASSAULT ON SEXUAL PRIVACY. "Feelings run high, especially among those selected for exposure," explained the article, which included a picture on *OutWeek*'s Forbes cover. "The issue is clearly riddled with booby traps," it concluded.[24]

Later that spring activists Michael Petrelis and Carl Goodman stoked the debate when they called a press conference on the steps of the Capitol to read the names of "twelve men and women in politics and music" whom they described as closeted gays. The tactic was so brazen that none of the gay and lesbian activist organizations would allow the pair to represent them. Six news organizations covered the event, but none reported the names.[25]

Another boost came the following summer in New York City when an anonymous gay vigilante group calling itself Outpost targeted celebrities by plastering the city with stylish posters that parodied Absolut vodka magazine advertisements. Each showed a celebrity's picture with a headline that read ABSOLUTELY QUEER or ABSOLUTELY HET. The poster campaign drew national attention, although the media typically would not show the photos on the posters.

When Cable News Network (CNN) contacted Outpost members about videotaping a story about their campaign, the vigilantes insisted that the celebrity photos be shown and that none of the Outpost members be identified. They knew that if they were recognized, they risked being sued for defamation. CNN rejected their terms and canceled the segment.[26]

When the supermarket tabloid *Globe* reported on the poster campaign, one of the targets, actor Tom Selleck, responded with a $20 million lawsuit. The suit was settled out of court a week later. Terms of the settlement were kept secret, but word later leaked out that the *Globe* had agreed to print a retraction and to pay Selleck the nominal sum of $5.[27]

While news editors in the gay and nongay press grappled with how to report on the growing number of exposures, the gay movement remained deeply divided on the tactic. "Our position is that individuals should make their own decision," said Urvashi Vaid, who served as executive director of the National Gay and Lesbian Task Force during the episode. Tom Stoddard, then head of the Lambda Legal Defense Fund, described outing as a "mean and nasty" tactic that was comparable to "rolling in the mud." Hilary Rosen, a board member of the Human Rights Campaign Fund, called it "useless and hostile."[28]

Most of the gay press opposed the practice. Don Michaels, publisher of the Washington, D.C., gay weekly *Washington Blade*, which was known for its high journalistic standards, expressed concerns that outing "reflected badly on the gay community." *Advocate* editor Richard Rouilard sounded a similar note, echoing a long-standing policy espoused by the magazine's late publisher David Goodstein. Writing in the *New York Times* and the men's fashion magazine *GQ*, gay journalist Randy Shilts expressed the strongest reservations: "When the threat of outing is employed to pressure a public official to vote a particular way, it amounts to nothing more than blackmail, plain and simple."[29]

Former CBS News president Fred Friendly condemned the practice in a *Washington Post* op-ed piece. "Whatever the advocates of outing may perceive as being in the best interest of their brothers and sisters in the gay world, however worthwhile, journalists cannot abridge or abdicate their historic commitment to fairness," he wrote in the *Post*.[30] (It was Friendly who had initiated the first network documentary about homosexuals for *CBS Reports* in 1967.)

Yet by the spring of 1990 it was clear that outing had prompted many to reevaluate their assumptions about the closet. "I used to think that 'dragging people out of the closet' was unacceptable under all circumstances," wrote gay film critic Stuart Byron in the *Advocate*. In his sobering analysis of outing Byron said the swirling controversy over it had moved him somewhat to the left: "I see the issue as presenting a tragic dilemma to the gay community and the gay press, and it is one for which every answer is equally troubling. No matter what position one takes, someone's going to get hurt."[31]

Outing had become news, but mainstream journalists considered the debate over the ethics of outing even bigger news. Stories appeared in *USA Today*, the *New York Times*, *New York* magazine, the *Washington Post*, and *Esquire*. The *Times* tried to report on the controversy without actually being drawn into the practice by describing the outing of Malcolm Forces as a story that named "a famous businessman who had recently died." Editors at the *Miami Herald* announced that they would approach outing cautiously but then proceeded to name several celebrities who had been outed by supermarket tabloids. The *Washington Post* took a similar tack after Signorile outed gossip columnist Liz Smith. The *Post* reported the story without naming Smith; its sister publication, *Newsweek*, named her. "I think a lot of us are confused as to what's going on in the gay community," said David Boyle of the *Boston Globe*, expressing the sentiment of his colleagues in the press.[32] "Are you gay, or are you queer? Is outing OK, or is it not? If you guys can't figure it out, how can we figure it out?" In *Mademoiselle*, writer Barbara Grizzuti Harrison asked an even more fundamental question: "How will it enhance the pride of any gay person to see someone dragged kicking and screaming out of the closet?"[33]

ABOUT FACE AT THE PENTAGON

Although outing proved to be an effective tool for AIDS activists during the late 1980s, AIDS was not the only political issue facing homosexuals. Because only a handful of states prohibited discrimination on the basis of sexual orientation, gays and lesbians continued to face a variety of forms of discrimination, especially in the military, where those who were identified continued to be ousted in large numbers.[34] Court challenges to the ban on gay and lesbian service members had failed, and the issue was quickly becoming a flash point for gay activism.

After the United States attacked the Iraqi army in Operation Desert Storm, the *New York Times* printed a profile of Pete Williams, an assistant to the secretary of defense and chief media spokesman for the Pentagon during the gulf war. With his daily—often televised—reports on the war Williams had quickly become a familiar face in many living rooms across the nation. Noting this, the article said, "Such is Mr. Williams's on-camera persona that when he acknowledged . . . that he was a bachelor, he was showered with letters from women who wanted to know if he wanted a date—or even marriage. But marriage, or even a social life, does not seem to be part of his agenda at the moment." The article quoted a member of the Defense Information staff as saying, "Pete is the epitome of the old military saying, 'Try to avoid working for a bachelor.'" Another person commented, "It would be nice to find him a wife, someone to take care of him." In addition, a woman friend from his hometown in Wyoming remarked, "Frankly, I've never seen him make room in his life for a woman." Although Williams had not acknowledged his homosexuality, it was an open secret among most of the reporters who covered the Pentagon.[35]

For Michelangelo Signorile and other gay activists Williams was a particularly appealing target for outing because the military had discharged gays
and lesbians by the tens of thousands under the ban against homosexual military personnel. Williams met the standard of hypocrisy that Perry Deane
Young had articulated a decade earlier. The news media's willingness to
countenance Williams's heterosexual facade made an even better target
because it raised the issue of dishonest reporting.

But as Signorile was preparing to pierce Williams's veil of secrecy,
OutWeek was collapsing, a victim of mounting debts and infighting among its
small group of owners. Although the publishers expressed hope that it would
reopen, privately they concluded the magazine was dead. Its offices were
padlocked on June 27, 1991.

The biggest story of Signorile's journalistic career was left without a
home. He turned to Richard Goldstein, the openly gay executive editor of
the *Village Voice*. Goldstein, who had worked at the *Voice* since the late '60s
when he was living in the closet as a married man, had edited Signorile's
piece on the press coverage of his Forbes outing story.

Goldstein, who opposed outing in principle, nonetheless recognized that
Pete Williams was an unusual case. After he discussed the idea with Editor in
Chief Jonathan Larsen, the *Voice*'s staff revolted. *Voice* editors quickly called a
general staff meeting to discuss the story.

Goldstein argued that the Pentagon official symbolized "the hypocrisy of
an institution that applies one standard to recruits and another to a man
close to the seat of power."[36] But he quickly learned that he was the only
gay staffer willing to support outing in this case. The vote to kill the piece
was overwhelming.

"That was one of those rare devastating moments," Signorile said. "I really
thought that was the only chance for the story getting out. Many people who
had worked on the military issue were set on that story having an effect on
the policy. I felt like I was letting down all of these people who had worked
on this issue and were so excited, even though it wasn't my fault."[37]

Signorile then turned to Richard Rouilard, the editor in chief of the Los
Angeles–based *Advocate*. A former editor at the Los Angeles *Herald Examiner*,
Rouilard recognized that the magazine needed to appeal to a new, younger
generation of gay readers. The flamboyant editor also saw it as an opportunity to fill the niche created by *OutWeek*'s demise. Although he had written
forcefully against outing, he agreed that the Williams story was an important
part of the national debate over the military ban.

The *Advocate* hit the newsstands at the end of August with a large photo of Williams on the cover. The headline appeared to be an attempt to anticipate the backlash from the magazine's older, more conservative readers: DID THIS MAN RUIN 2,000 LIVES? KNOW ABOUT THE SUICIDES? . . . WASTE TAXPAYERS' MILLIONS ON MILITARY WITCH-HUNTS? THE OUTING OF ASSISTANT SECRETARY OF DEFENSE PETE WILLIAMS.[38]

"We commit ourselves to this singular instance of outing in the name of the 12,966 soldiers who have been outed by the military since 1982," Rouilard explained in an editorial that accompanied Signorile's article.[39]

Even before the *Advocate* arrived at newsstands, syndicated columnist Jack Anderson jumped on the story after receiving a tip from members of Queer Nation, a militant gay group that had split off from ACT UP, about the forthcoming *Advocate* story. "Pete Williams, the lanky, bespectacled Pentagon spokesman who became a household face during the Persian Gulf War, is considering resigning because of accusations that he is a homosexual," Anderson reported in his column, which was carried by eight hundred newspapers. Anderson's six subscribing newspapers in Williams's home state of Wyoming published the column with Williams's name.

Although countless smaller newspapers printed the name in Anderson's column, the editors of several metropolitan papers decided to kill the column rather than compromise their ethical opposition to revealing a person's homosexuality without his permission. At some newspapers it was an agonizing decision. *Washington Post* media writer Howard Kurtz later referred to it as "the toughest decision I've ever faced on whether to write a story." In the end the *Post* did not carry the story. "Our policy is that we don't write about the personal lives of public officials unless the personal aspects begin influencing the way they perform their jobs," explained Karen DeYoung, an assistant managing editor at the *Post*. The *Post* was not alone. *New York Newsday*, the *New York Post*, *New York Times*, and *Los Angeles Times* ignored the story altogether. None of the four TV news networks used the name. The Associated Press carried a story about the uproar but without naming Williams. The *Detroit News*, the *Philadelphia Inquirer*, and *New York Daily News* printed Williams's name but only in their gossip columns.[40]

At the *San Francisco Chronicle* Executive Editor William German explained, "The paper's general policy is not to seek to point a finger at or 'out' a homosexual who had not chosen to declare himself."[41] Yet ten months later, in June 1992, the Sunday *Examiner* not only named Williams, it showed a copy of the *Advocate* with Williams's face on its cover.

ABC News correspondent Sam Donaldson added to the controversy when he brought the subject up in an interview with Defense Secretary Richard Cheney during *This Week With David Brinkley*. Donaldson asked Cheney how he could justify having a gay aide when the Pentagon maintained a ban on gays. Defending his aide, Cheney characterized the security rationale, which maintains that homosexuals are at high risk for blackmail, as "a bit of an old chestnut" he had inherited from previous administrations.[42] As Signorile and Rouilard had hoped, the debate shifted from the outing of Williams to the military ban itself. In editorials both the *New York Times* and the *Washington Post* denounced the gay ban in their most certain terms to date.

One of the most interesting commentaries on the ban appeared in an op-ed article in the February 1, 1993, *New York Times*, by Lucian Truscott IV, the former *Village Voice* writer who, in covering the 1969 Stonewall riots, had ridiculed gays as "forces of faggotry." By 1993 the views expressed by the former army lieutenant had mellowed considerably. "Discrimination and segregation based on sexual orientation is as unacceptable and plain stupid as the treatment of blacks before Truman," he wrote.[43]

Despite the demise of *OutWeek*, outing continued to flourish in the gay press. In June 1992 *Advocate* columnist Donna Minkowitz revealed that the newly appointed acting chair of the National Endowment of the Arts, Anne-Imelda Radice, "shares her condo with her long-time woman lover, a lawyer with the U.S. attorney general's office."[44] Minkowitz felt Radice met the hypocrisy test because she was enforcing the Bush administration ban on federal funding for most gay-themed art. The news reverberated through mainstream newspapers for several months, prompting articles in the *Philadelphia Inquirer* and the *Los Angeles Times*. The following June the *Atlanta Journal and Constitution* mentioned that the *Advocate* had named Radice Sissy of the Year.

On September 18, 1992, the *San Francisco Examiner* carried a front page article reporting the homosexuality of John Schlafly, the son of antigay rights activist Phyllis Schlafly. SCHLAFLY'S SON: GAY AND GOP, read the headline above the article by gay freelance writer Larry Bush, who had once served as the *Advocate*'s Washington correspondent and was the first gay journalist accredited to the White House, and Lance Williams, an *Examiner* staff writer. Although rumors about Schlafly had been reported in the New York City gay magazine *QW*, the *Examiner* article was his first public acknowledgment.

The following day the news about Schlafly ran in other newspapers, including a front-page article in the Style section of the *Washington Post* headlined SCHLAFLY'S SON, OUT OF THE CLOSET.[45] In the meantime the *Examiner* continued to focus attention on the disclosure by carrying two follow-up stories, one on the response from the gay community and the other by Washington bureau chief Chris Matthews on the reaction among Schlafly's conservative colleagues.

The *Advocate* struck again in its September 22, 1992, issue when staff reporter Chris Bull reported that Representative Jim McCrery of Louisiana, a staunch proponent of the antigay "family values" agenda of the Republican right, had had several affairs with men. McCrery denied he was gay, but unlike Signorile's outings, which were based entirely on anonymous and secondhand sources, Bull had carefully documented the congressman's dual identity, including an on-the-record interview with a man who described his sexual relationship with McCrery and a sworn affidavit from two others with first-hand knowledge of McCrery's homosexuality. Despite widespread coverage of the *Advocate* article in McCrery's district, his constituency reelected him with more than 60 percent of the vote. The Associated Press noted, "McCrery's campaign was sidetracked at one point by an article in the *Advocate*, a national gay magazine, which called him a homosexual." Similar references appeared in the *Chicago Tribune*, the *Dallas Morning News*, and the *Houston Chronicle*.[46] The article received considerable play in local Louisiana newspapers, which were compelled to pick up on a story a gay publication had broken.

A related twist came in the spring of 1992 when a *USA Today* reporter caught wind of rumors that Arthur Ashe had contracted AIDS and called the tennis star to confirm it. Ashe avoided the reporter's question, ending the conversation without answering it. The reporter assured Ashe that his newspaper would not run the story unless it could be verified by someone with direct medical information who would comment on the record. The next morning, on April 8, 1992, Ashe called a press conference to declare that he had AIDS.[47] In most cities it was front page news and led newscasts on radio and television.

Ashe called the press conference because he wanted to make the announcement himself and because he saw the opportunity to castigate the news media for attempting to invade his privacy. He told the reporters, "Here was a very personal, very private relationship I had with my doctor, my family, my friends, and this personal relationship was to be profaned by some news organization that deemed it newsworthy." Yet the reporter was only doing his job, trying to verify a rumor with the person who was the subject of it and showing restraint when Ashe refused to do so. Indeed AIDS only added to the difficulty editors faced in determining how best to handle stories about a celebrity's sexuality and/or health within the traditional bounds of journalistic ethics, confidentiality, and privacy.[48]

Perhaps no one understood the personal and journalistic issues more clearly than the *San Francisco Chronicle*'s Randy Shilts. In February 1993, six months after Ashe's announcement, Shilts acknowledged that he had been diagnosed with AIDS. Although he had tested positive for the deadly virus six years earlier—on the day he'd finished writing *And the Band Played On*—he feared that public disclosure would hamper his work. "I don't want to be a professional AIDS patient," he said. "I'm more valuable to the gay movement as a journalist."[49]

Chronicle editor William German said he had known of Shilts's illness but saw no reason to make it public until Shilts chose to do so. Nor did he see any reason to remove him from the AIDS beat. "I do not believe we need to say a reporter is black, a reporter is Jewish," German told the *Washington Post*. "If we thought of eliminating reporters who might not be objective because of their ancestry or their politics, frankly, we'd go out of our minds and it would be impossible to practice journalism."[50]

THE EFFECT OF OUTING

Throughout 1993 evidence mounted that outing was changing the rules of journalism. Following the inauguration of President Bill Clinton, the group Queer Nation—with little evidence—outed cabinet appointees Janet Reno and Donna Shalala. The press largely ignored the actions, and both appointments were confirmed. That spring a heated controversy erupted in the New York public school system over its rainbow curriculum, a project designed to foster tolerance for diverse groups in the city, including lesbians and gays. After the school board ousted Joseph Fernandez, the head of the city's school system who was a staunch defender of the inclusion of gays and lesbians in the curriculum, rumors began to circulate about the sexual orientation of Ramon C. Cortines, the head of the San Francisco school system, who was named as Fernandez's replacement. The *New York Times* and other newspapers reported speculation by gay advocacy groups that Cortines was homosexual, a subject he politely refused to discuss. Despite the persistent rumors, his appointment was approved by the school board that had opposed the inclusion of gays in the multicultural curriculum.[51]

Even the traditionally conservative sports pages were not immune to the changes sweeping journalism. In a December 1993 column *Times* sports writer Robert Lipsyte wrote, "Outside the subculture of competitive diving, where he was simply the best of all time, Greg Louganis has never received the attention his four Olympic gold medals, his discipline, his performing beauty seemed to deserve. . . . Was it because of the whispers that he was gay?" Hollywood figures were also targets. *USA Today*, *Vanity Fair*, and *Rolling Stone* carried articles in December 1993 addressing rumors that actors Richard Gere and his model wife, Cindy Crawford, were engaged in a marriage of convenience.[52]

Outing had become so commonplace that it was incorporated in standard reporting techniques. In the March 3, 1995, edition of the *Wall Street Journal*, the front page carried the headline JANN WENNER'S RIFT WITH WIFE SHAKES UP HIS PUBLISHING EMPIRE. The story, which centered around the pending divorce of *Rolling Stone* publisher Jann Wenner, casually mentioned how the forty-nine-year-old had left his wife of twenty-six years and had begun "a relationship with a young male staffer at Calvin Klein." "Ordinarily, someone's sexuality is not something we're concerned about," the *Journal*'s managing editor Paul Steiger told the *Washington Post*. "In this case it was relevant to a very interesting story, so we included it. If you're going to profile a company that could be coming unglued, and which reflects Jann's personality as well as Jane's, you don't want to be coy. You just say what it is."[53] Editors like Steiger had finally come around to the position taken by activists nearly a decade earlier.

At the same time there was growing evidence that outing no long sparked the same degree of public furor as it had two years earlier. Even its chief instigator seemed to have backed away from it. Many expected Michelangelo Signorile's 1993 book *Queer in America* to contain several bombshells, but none of its 368 pages revealed the sexual identity of anyone new. Most of the book was devoted to rehashing old stories and debates. "Maybe it's not surprising, then, that some readers felt cheated," wrote David Boaz in a review of the book for the *Washington Blade*. Boaz, an executive at the libertarian Washington think-tank Cato Institute, described the book as a "study in contradictions" in which Signorile alternately referred to outing as a tool to change assumptions among the news media and as a weapon to punish closeted homosexuals whose views conflict with his own.[54]

With the publication of his 1995 book *Outing Yourself*, the fire-breathing champion of gay visibility had become the laid-back author of a self-help book that he dedicated to his psychotherapist. Even as a columnist in the gay magazine *Out* he had ceased ripping homosexual hypocrites from their closets.

In April 1995 former *OutWeek* editor Gabriel Rotello used his column in the *Advocate* to write outing's postmortem. "Essentially the media have grudgingly accepted *OutWeek*'s once-radical argument," he wrote, pointing out the willingness among much of the mainstream media to mention an individual's homosexuality when it is relevant. "Outing, once so contentious that it threatened to tear the community apart, is now so commonplace that it's hard to remember what the fuss was about."[55]

14

THE '90S AND BEYOND

While mainstream journalists were reassessing their journalistic assumptions about how they covered gays and lesbians in the 1990s, gay and lesbian journalists had begun to look closely at their own role in how the media portrayed their community. A growing number had begun to find that SILENCE = DEATH, the motto of AIDS activists, translated into SILENCE = LYING in the newsrooms where they worked. Fear of reprisals would have silenced them in the past, but the AIDS epidemic had changed the stakes. In the 1990s the risk of being fired seemed much less important.

Leroy Aarons understood better than anyone that a shift was taking place among gay and lesbian journalists. April 1990 marked a turning point for Aarons as he stood before his colleagues at the American Society of

Newspaper Editors (ASNE) to talk about a subject he had never discussed openly. He was acutely aware that much had changed since the day in 1965 when as a young *Washington Post* reporter he had listened to police reports about the Mattachine Society's picketing of the White House. Now a vice president of news at the *Oakland Tribune*, Aarons was standing in the ballroom of a Washington hotel to announce the results of a landmark study of gay and lesbian journalists at the nation's newspapers.

The idea for the survey had come from Loren Ghiglione, editor of the *News*, a small newspaper in Southbridge, Massachusetts. Ghiglione had become the president of ASNE in 1988. Not one to shy away from controversy, Ghiglione had served on the National News Council and was on the panel that reviewed the CBS documentary "Gay Power, Gay Politics" in 1980 and found it biased against gays. Ghiglione said,

> I'm a leftover from the sixties. I knew gays had a second-class citizenship in our newsrooms. The atmosphere made about as much sense as having a bilingual reporter who could not acknowledge that he or she was bilingual. That leaves editors unable to take advantage of that strength. In addition, I saw it as a civil rights issue. It was my feeling that newspapers would be better able to report their full community if gays were freer to acknowledge themselves.[1]

At the suggestion of an openly gay staff member at the editor's association Ghiglione contacted Leroy Aarons, whom Ghiglione had met as a college intern at the *Washington Post* in the sixties, to ask him to conduct the survey of gays. Although Aarons considered himself out to much of the *Tribune* staff, including Publisher Robert Maynard, his homosexuality was not widely known among his industry peers. The invitation from Ghiglione came as a surprise.

"I didn't feel any great fire in my belly. Here I was, the top executive of a news operation, and I wondered if it got out that I was gay in a very public way, would I be subjecting my paper to trouble?" Aarons said. "I talked to Bob Maynard, and it was pretty predictable that a black publisher would give me the go-ahead. Then I had this kind of very low-level anxiety that this may thrust me out there as a gay person on a national stage, but I agreed to do it."[2]

Arriving in newsrooms in November 1989, the questionnaire sparked controversy when some editors complained that people's sexuality was none of anyone's business. One sarcastically asked whether the organization's next survey would include "prostitute journalists" and "cocaine addicts."[3]

"What disturbs me about all of this is that while the newspaper industry is scurrying to survey various groups, it has to my knowledge failed to show equal concern about a substantial number of readers, those who have a conservative or religious orientation," wrote syndicated newspaper columnist Cal Thomas, former media director for Jerry Falwell's Moral Majority.[4]

Gay journalists, meanwhile, feared they might lose their jobs if their names fell into the wrong hands. Still, responses began to trickle in. By the time the deadline arrived, Aarons had 205 responses. It was an impressive number, considering it was the first survey of its kind, but it represented only a fraction of the estimated five thousand gay men and lesbians working on daily newspapers and therefore may not have provided an accurate picture.[5]

Aarons presented the findings at the organization's annual convention the following April in Washington, telling his colleagues that the survey confirmed "a palpable undercurrent of bias" against gay journalists. A stunning 80 percent had heard unkind comments from their newsroom colleagues; half said the comments were directed at a gay employee. One described watching a Super Bowl game: "One reporter asked who should win, and the response was 'Cincinnati—Everyone in San Francisco is a faggot; they don't have any queers in Ohio.'" A lesbian journalist said she had raised a question about gays and lesbians during a management seminar, only to be told, "Those people don't count; they're perverted."[6]

The survey also found that the journalists felt that the homophobia they observed in the newsrooms was reflected in the pages of the newspapers at which they worked. "Most reporters covering a 'gay' topic who aren't gay or informed about gay issues will write a story that presents the issues as alien, 'those' people," wrote an editor at a small daily newspaper. Eighty-three percent believed their newspaper failed to devote sufficient space to gay issues. When there was coverage, three-quarters rated it "poor" or "fair." "Apart from AIDS and the occasional public rest room bust, our paper, like many others, has virtually no coverage of the gay and lesbian community," wrote a reporter in Washington State. However, on the subject of AIDS almost three-quarters felt the coverage of the disease by their newspapers was either good or excellent. "We cover AIDS to a certain extent," wrote one journalist, "but don't even run wire briefs about civil rights issues."[7]

Even when editors knew of their orientation, gay and lesbian journalists said they were almost never called on to provide expertise. "When I proposed . . . a gay-related story," said one, "the idea was approved by my city editor, who then turned around and said I couldn't [do it]. No explanation was given and the city editor told me not to ask any questions." Another said,

"The most difficult time I ever experienced as a reporter was two years ago when my lover left me after six years. Like straight people going through particularly traumatic divorce, I was almost dysfunctional at work for a long time. Unlike straight people might have in such a situation, I received no support even from those I told."[8]

Although some journalists agreed to be quoted by name, most—87 percent—were too frightened. "If I am identified, I will probably be unemployed," wrote one lesbian. Another woman responded: "I'm not 'out' at work, but I have become more open about my personal life over the last several years." Even so, 60 percent of the journalists thought their chances of advancement were good or excellent.[9]

For several days before his presentation to the editors Aarons had wrestled with whether to say he was gay or leave it unspoken, as he and others had done so often in the past. It was only in the final minutes before he spoke that he made up his mind, telling his colleagues,

> For the first time in newspaper history, we get a glimpse into the mindset of mainstream gay and lesbian journalists—our journalists, at our newspapers—who more often than not have remained invisible. But this is more than a survey. It is a manual filled with articles that, taken together, is a sort of Whole Earth Catalogue on how to—and how not to—deal with these thorny issues in the workplace and in our news pages. . . . I want you to know that doing this report has had tremendous impact on gay and lesbian journalists across the nation—and I have talked to hundreds of them. It has given them hope and new optimism. It has enhanced their respect for this organization. And I, as an editor, and a gay man, am proud of ASNE.[10]

Articles about the survey appeared in several major publications, including *Time*, the *Los Angeles Times*, *Boston Globe*, and *New York Times*.[11] The *Washington Post* ignored it altogether even though Aarons had worked there for fourteen years and had sent editor Ben Bradlee an advance copy. A few days later, when nothing had appeared, Aarons saw Bradlee and asked why. "Well," Bradlee told Aarons, "we couldn't find an angle for the damn thing."[12]

STEPPING OUT AT THE *NEW YORK TIMES*

Even before the survey gays and lesbians were emerging from newsroom closets. Starting in the summer of 1987, a small group of gay and lesbian

journalists at the *New York Times* took part in the annual gay pride parade up
the Avenue of the Americas to commemorate the Stonewall riots. Until then
Times employees had not dared to join for fear of reprisals. But photo editor
Nancy Lee, a lesbian, had recognized a new sense of openness in the newsroom when she returned from a yearlong fellowship at Harvard. By then
Max Frankel had succeeded Abe Rosenthal as executive editor. "It was a collective sigh of relief in the newsroom," she remembered. "There was a feeling that we could be good journalists without worrying about our jobs every
second of the day."[13]

Lee contacted some of her gay and lesbian colleagues and invited them to
a picnic lunch at a spot in Central Park on the parade route. When the procession moved past them, making its way from Greenwich Village to Central
Park, Lee and the others spontaneously fell in with the crowd, walking hand
in hand. Lee said,

> At that time we didn't even know each other very well. We didn't have a sign,
> a banner, or T-shirts that would identify us. But we were very proud of where
> we worked and of each other. It wasn't that anyone said, "It's alright to be gay
> now; you don't have to hide anymore." It was that a lot of things were suddenly
> all right. The discussions about the news and the interaction with the editors
> was at a much more humane level for everyone, not just for gays but for every-
> one in the newsroom.[14]

In June 1988—the following summer—Lee and photographer Sara
Krulwich invited everyone in the newsroom they knew to be lesbian or gay
to a party and encouraged them to bring along their same-sex partners or a
guest. "I think everyone truly felt as if a door had been opened," Lee recalled.

Throughout 1988 and into 1989 some members of the group would meet
informally for lunch. The conversation would inevitably turn to being gay
and working at the *Times*. In May 1990 Tom Kulaga, who worked in the
Times's advertising department, suggested that they organize a team to participate in the city's AIDS Walk, which was held by the Gay Men's Health
Crisis. The team quickly attracted both gays and straights in the newsroom.
In addition, the *Times* sent an important signal by agreeing to make a corporate contribution.

Another important turning point came in December 1990. Reporter
David Dunlap suggested that it was time for the gay staff members to consider forming a caucus, much as women and blacks had done almost two

decades earlier. Addressing his gay and lesbian colleagues at a holiday dinner, he explained,

> Were there to be such a group on 43rd Street, it might concern itself with such journalistic issues as the thoroughness and objectivity of coverage given to lesbian and gay issues; the paper's decision to eliminate the full-time reporter on the AIDS beat, even with such small but critical details as the practice of excluding companions from the list of survivors in an obituary. It might take up even more challenging issues such as discrimination in the work place or health coverage and other benefits being made available to our companions. These are matters that are probably more effectively addressed on a collective rather than individual basis with the Times editors and management.[15]

Simultaneously, but unknown to gays at the *Times*, a similar set of events was unfolding at the *Los Angeles Times*. In November 1989 reporter David Fox mentioned to a gay colleague that he had been at the paper for six years but knew few of the other gays on the staff. The two men drew up a short list of people to invite to Christmas dinner. "It was almost underground," Fox remembered. "No one would know about it except for the people who were invited."[16]

The dinner guests became the nucleus of a rapidly growing group. In February 1990 they invited everyone they could identify to a second dinner, including a gay reporter from the newspaper's South Bay office, and someone in the business section they had only heard rumors about.

Most significantly, they extended an invitation to John Brownell, a gay editor and rising star thought to be in line to succeed the newspaper's editor in chief. When Brownell arrived, "someone shook me and said, 'That's John Brownell,'" Lily Eng recalled.[17] At the dinner Leroy Aarons, who had been invited by *L.A. Times* reporter Victor Zonana to explain the survey of gays in newsrooms and Aaron's desire to establish an organization. In listening to Aarons, Zonana and some of the others realized that the *L.A. Times*'s antidiscrimination policy said nothing about sexual orientation.

Brownell suggested that they simply ask management to change it. "Too political," grunted one reporter as the idea set off a heated debate. Finally, reporters Victor Zonana and Lily Eng agreed to draft a letter requesting the change. All but two of the fourteen present agreed to sign the letter before Zonana and Eng delivered it to the two highest-ranking executives at the *L.A. Times*, Publisher David Laventhol and Editor Shelby Coffey III.

"We were treated with utmost respect. They said no one had asked for such a thing before," Zonana said. "They wanted to check with their lawyers, but they didn't think it would be a problem. We talked to them about harassment and about hearing off-color remarks and that sort of thing. They got the idea and felt that a policy might solve it. The policy came out later that same month."[18]

In early 1990 Brownell was appointed deputy managing editor, instantly becoming a symbol for gay and lesbian employees who had wondered whether their openness would hurt their careers. Brownell was diagnosed with AIDS a few months later and died at age thirty-three. "I didn't know him well, but it was like losing a brother," Eng said.

At his funeral a small group of gays and lesbians from the newsroom huddled together, holding each other's hands. Later editor Deborah Bergman described the scene in an article for the *Advocate*: "To my left were my friends—Ann and then Greg and Lily. To my right sat Harry. As John's friend Hans began to speak, I slipped my hand into Harry's and Ann grasped my other one. I was glad to be surrounded by lesbian and gay friends, and I thought about how our shared experiences unite us. Shortly after John's death, a gay male colleague sent me a message on the computer, 'I don't believe it. How do we all go on?' Sitting in St. Viriana's, I had the answer: hand in hand."[19]

Brownell's death solidified the small group. In the months that followed they expanded their ranks to include gay journalists at the *Orange County Register* and other nearby newspapers and broadcast stations. Along with the caucus at the *New York Times* and a small group of gay journalists that already existed in San Francisco, the Los Angeles group became the nucleus for Leroy Aarons's dreamed-of national organization.

OUT IN THE BLACK PRESS

At about the same time a lesbian presence was emerging at *Essence* magazine, the most widely read black women's magazine in the nation. For months Senior Editor Linda Villarosa had rebuffed her coworkers' attempts to set her up with blind dates. Unknown to them, Villarosa had no interest in dating men.

While her colleagues talked of their husbands or boyfriends, Villarosa sat alone at staff meetings and only talked about her family. As she casually brushed off their concerns with polite excuses, staff members began to consider her distant, almost unfriendly. Finally, to quell the rumor mill she told her boss about her secret in the fall of 1990. "It was so much fun that I came out to everybody," she recalled. "I told them I was a lesbian and that I wasn't interested in meeting anyone's brother-in-law."[20]

A few weeks later someone suggested during an editorial planning meeting that the magazine commission an article about lesbians. All eyes shifted to Villarosa. "What we'd really be interested in is hearing from a mom," she heard someone suggest. "You know, somebody's mother who would speak."

Villarosa agreed to ask her mother to write the article. "I really love you, and I think this is an important thing for you, and I will do it," Clara Villarosa told her daughter after thinking about it for a day.

Villarosa told the staff she had agreed to help her mother write it. But the staff had other plans; they wanted both mother *and* daughter to describe their experiences. As they explained their idea, it suddenly dawned on Villarosa that they were asking her to come out to five million readers.

"As a journalist most of my pieces were about toxic waste or about whatever and I thought I could never talk about myself. I had always hid behind a byline," Villarosa said. "But at that time *OutWeek* magazine was going strong, and there was a lot of talk about coming out, and I realized that I was hiding behind some kind of mask by not coming out in a bigger way. I was uncomfortable, but I decided to do it."[21]

The only surprise came after mother and daughter finished their articles. Suddenly, the editor of the magazine appeared at the door of Villarosa's office. "It's fabulous," she said. "But I really think you need to use a pseudonym because this could really hurt your career."

Villarosa took the suggestion like a slap in the face. Here she was describing to readers how wonderful it was to be an open lesbian while being told to use a fake name. "No," she responded. "Not only do I want to use my real name, we want you to include our pictures."[22]

Accompanied by three photos of Linda and Clara together, the article appeared in the May 1991 issue. The introduction said, "Mothers love their daughters, unshakably and unconditionally. But learning that her daughter is a lesbian can be a difficult and painful challenge for a mother—no matter how much she loves her daughter. Here Linda Villarosa, a gay woman, and her mother, Clara, together discuss their journey of emotions from fear to disappointment and anger and finally toward peace and acceptance."[23]

In the article the two women alternately described a coming out process that would sound familiar to most gays and lesbians but unfamiliar to most

Essence readers. Linda wrote about her attempts to live up to the expectations of her parents, while knowing that she was somehow different from other girls. Clara described her suspicions when her daughter showed little, if any, romantic interest in men. Then came the confrontation, followed by their eventual resolution and acceptance.

Linda Villarosa recalled that

> there was a long period between the time the magazine was finished and it hit the newsstands. The fear was paralyzing. It was too late to do anything, but the thought occurred to me that maybe I could just pull all of the magazines off the stands or something. My mother was afraid. People at my job were very afraid for me. But actually, after they talked about their fears, I stopped being so afraid. My friends were going to open my mail and take out all of the negative letters first. I thought, "No, I've made this decision, I'm going to go with it." It was the most important decision I ever made, both for myself and for my career.[24]

The article inspired more letters than any in the magazine's twenty-one-year history. Some men wrote, "Just one night with me . . ." or "You seem like a nice person, but . . ." The tone of the letters shifted as mail began to arrive from young readers. Some expressed their appreciation, and others said they were concerned that the article might cost Villarosa her job. The editors asked the two women to write a second article five months later in which they would respond to some of the letters.[25]

"It's been wonderful," Linda Villarosa later told a group of gay and lesbian journalists. "It really changed my life for the better. It helped me become a better writer and interviewer, because it's about me and how I feel about myself."[26] (In August 1994 *Essence* promoted Villarosa from senior editor to the top position of executive editor.)

MORE ROOM AT THE TOP

Linda Villarosa was not the only openly gay person to hold a ranking position in the media in the fall of 1991. By then twenty-nine-year-old British-born Andrew Sullivan had worked at the *New Republic* for nearly five years, beginning as a summer intern in 1986 after his graduation from Oxford. He had decided he wanted to work on the staff of a American magazine and approached the magazine about being an intern while he worked on his master's degree in political science at Harvard. "I wrote to a half dozen of them," he recalled. "But I really wanted to go to the *New Republic*. I thought it was the smartest and the least boring."[27]

Although Sullivan was aware of his attraction to other men, he had never acknowledged it to anyone until the fall of 1987. When he returned to Harvard for his doctoral degree in political science, he had his first serious relationship. "It was like being in a black-and-white movie and suddenly finding out it's in color," he said.

Sullivan had his first brush with homophobia in the media the following summer during another stint at the *New Republic*. To prepare an article about homoerotic imagery in American advertising he had collected examples of advertisements for Calvin Klein and Ralph Lauren products. He was studying them in the magazine's conference room when another journalist, whom Sullivan refuses to name, suddenly entered the room. Sullivan asked him for his reaction. "Well," the man responded, "they're all faggots!" Sullivan said,

> I was just staggered that someone who works at the *New Republic* would ever use that word, in that way. He would never say, "They are all niggers!" I didn't say anything, but I did make a mental note. In fact, he has been the consistently most difficult person on this whole subject. But his homophobia is very open, and now we can discuss it, which is what I prefer. He actually believes that people are hounded into being homosexuals in college these days and that all gay men prey on younger insecure heterosexuals—all of which is bullshit. If it were the Jews, it would be like "The Protocol of the Elders of Zion." But I must say I find it hard to think of him in quite the same way.[28]

Sullivan did not address his sexuality openly among the staff until magazine owner Martin Peretz invited him to a farewell lunch. Peretz asked whether he planned to return to England and enter politics. "Frankly," Sullivan responded, "a political career is now complicated because I'm gay— openly gay—and who knows how people will deal with that?" "Don't worry about it," Peretz counseled him.

Sullivan earned his Ph.D. and briefly wrote a column for *Esquire* before returning to the *New Republic* in 1990. Peretz had asked him to come back as deputy editor. Within a few months he was out to the magazine's readers. Set on a large pink triangle, the headline on the December 17, 1990, story read GAY LIFE, GAY DEATH. As the story unfolded, it seemed as much about the progress of Andrew Sullivan's coming to terms with his homosexuality as it was about the escalating tensions between gays who tested HIV positive and those who were HIV negative.

The article began in a detached third-person tone: "By protecting themselves against the virus, gay men also find themselves protected against intimacy." But as the story developed, the descriptions involved "us." "There is no light beneath us in this hole," he wrote. "The hopeful idea that a community is being forged in the face of death is untrue, not because it is beyond the capacity of gay people, but because there is nothing as isolating as one's own extinction."[29]

At about the same time the magazine installed a special telephone to record readers' comments. "I love your magazine," said one caller. "But why on earth do you keep Andrew Sullivan on your staff? It's out of character with the magazine; he doesn't fit."

Sullivan also came under stinging criticism from other gays. The December 30, 1990, issue of the gay magazine *Christopher Street* featured a cover story that proclaimed that Sullivan's article about AIDS was GAY BALONEY. Writer Bob Satuloff accused him of being out of touch on the issue.

But Sullivan took the criticism in stride and so did Peretz. In the summer of 1991 Sullivan became acting editor of the magazine. In addition, the magazine continued to focus on gay and lesbian issues, including legalization of gay marriage (which it supported), ACT UP (whose confrontational tactics it criticized), and outing (which it deplored).

The next October Peretz officially named Sullivan to the editor's post, making him the highest-ranking openly gay editor in the mainstream media.

"Thirty years ago, it would have been incredible to think that an editor at the *New Republic* would be an open homosexual—that's a staggering thought. It shouldn't be, but that's where we are," said Sullivan. "I mean, there were plenty of homosexuals in my position before now, but the difference is in being out."[30]

The naming of an openly gay conservative as editor of the seventy-seven-year-old magazine sent media writers to their keyboards gushing with enthusiasm. A FLAGSHIP HEELS TO STARBOARD, proclaimed *Time* magazine. "Which of these characteristics might not normally be used to describe the editor of the *New Republic*: a) conservative; b) Catholic; c) British; or d) gay. Try 'All of the above,'" the article suggested.[31]

NEW EDITOR IS RETHINKING NEW REPUBLIC'S DIRECTION, the *New York Times* announced. It did not mention that Sullivan was gay until the fourth paragraph. The *Washington Post* took note of Sullivan's ascent to the editorship six months later. THE NEW BOY AT NEW REPUBLIC was the headline beside a photo of Sullivan that engulfed most of the upper half of the page.[32]

But the publicity had its drawbacks. Sullivan found that he had become a lightning rod for gay activists. Because the magazine had criticized the disruptive tactics used by ACT UP, Sullivan was confronted at a gay dance club in Washington by Michael Petrelis, a gay activist who smashed his cocktail glass at Sullivan's feet to dramatize his anger.

But the most important test of his future as an editor came from the magazine's sponsors. Although advertising pages—the standard measure of magazine profitability—had been dropping when Sullivan took the helm of the *New Republic*, and circulation had hit an even steeper decline, there were signs that the pattern was quickly reversing. In March 1992 the *New York Times* reported that despite a rough year for magazine publishers generally, the *New Republic* had managed a respectable gain and expected a significant increase during the rest of the year. "The thought is always in the back of your mind that Mr. Sullivan's sexuality would discourage advertisers," magazine president Jeffrey Dearth acknowledged. "But no, thank God it hasn't, and I'm delighted."[33]

TROUBLE AT THE PRINTING PRESS

Not all gay journalists were so lucky. Juan Palomo had been a reporter at the *Houston Post* for almost all of his eleven years in journalism. In 1990 he began writing a thrice-weekly column that quickly attracted a wide audience. He earned a reputation as a columnist who was willing to tackle some of the most incendiary local and national topics.

In early July 1991 Palomo learned of the savage beating of a young man outside a gay bar; the victim later died. The attack was only the latest in a rash of gay bashings, but neither of the city's two newspapers paid much attention. As Palomo read about the arrival of the young man's mother to claim the body, he felt compelled to speak out, even though he knew that in order to write forcefully about homophobia he would have to reveal his own homosexuality.

The next day Palomo incorporated his anger into an article that condemned the crime wave: "I feel a special responsibility to speak out because I have this forum and, more importantly, because like Paul Broussard, I am gay." Palomo said there was little to decide:

I felt that I had no choice; I had to do it. I couldn't continue doing my job, in effect, trying to pretend that I was a straight man. I wrote a lot about gay issues and every time people would say, "Oh, you're so sensitive and you're so good. You write like you're one of us." I didn't like the hypocrisy. I didn't like writing like one of "them" instead of "us." It bothered me every time I had to do it, and it was time to end that charade—especially when that murder took place."[34]

When Palomo finished the column, he pressed a key on his computer terminal and sent it to his editor for approval. After several hours the editor called him into his office and asked, "Are you sure you're ready for this? Are you sure you're ready for the consequences?" Palomo assured him he was, but after the newsroom brass held several meetings, Palomo was told that his column would be stronger if he removed the references to himself. Palomo held firm. He did not want to write from behind a veil of secrecy but relented when it appeared that if he pressed the issue, the column would be killed and his basic message about gay bashing would be lost.

Readers responded to the column with an outpouring of two hundred letters and telephone calls, almost all supportive. "Most readers saw it as a straight man writing sympathetically about a gay issue," Palomo later reflected. "And in that sense, it was a lie."[35]

Several weeks later the *Houston Press*, a small alternative weekly, ran an exposé of Palomo's confrontation with his editors, CUTTING OUT THE CONSCIENCE OF A COLUMN. "The *Houston Post*'s Juan Palomo had something important to tell his readers,' the article began. "His own newspaper wouldn't let him, so we will."[36]

When he returned from a short vacation a few days after the *Houston Press* article ran, Palomo was fired by the *Post*. "He was fired because he had one too many confrontations with his superiors," not because of his homosexuality, insisted Charles Cooper, the newspaper's senior vice president and editor.[37]

As word of the ouster swirled through the city's Hispanic and gay communities, Queer Nation, a militant gay group that had split off from ACT UP, organized picket lines outside the newspaper and at the high-rise apartment building where Cooper lived. One picket sign read, "Rehire Palomo! Who cares if he's a homo?" Several reporters at the *Post* started a petition opposing his dismissal. Articles began to appear in media throughout the country. The *Washington Post* ran an article entitled GAY COLUMNIST KEPT IN THE CLOSET.[38]

In the midst of the uproar Palomo received a bitterly worded letter from former *Houston Post* editor David Burgin, who had left the paper to become the editor in chief of the *Daily Review* in Hayward, California. After reading an account of the flap in the newspaper trade magazine *Editor & Publisher*, he could remain silent no longer, Burgin said. In his letter Burgin described Palomo as a "shrill, arrogant, humorless voice" who was passing out "sanctimonious bullshit." He told the columnist that if he were still Palomo's boss, he would "throw your ass out."[39]

A week after the firing the *Houston Post* rehired Palomo but with one major change. His column would no longer appear a prized position on the front page of the local news section. He would become a columnist for the opinion-editorials section and serve as a member of the editorial board. Earlier, Palomo had turned down a similar offer, calling it a demotion. This time he accepted because "it boiled down to the fact that I'm happier being a columnist than a martyr. Martyrs are forgotten very quickly, and I didn't want that to happen."[40]

Palomo was not the only gay journalist who ran into trouble. In September 1990 the *Morning News Tribune* in Tacoma, Washington, demoted lesbian writer Sandy Nelson to the night copy desk after she spoke out in support of gay-related antidiscrimination legislation. For a number of years Nelson had taken part in a number of political campaigns for abortion rights, open housing, and civil rights. When she served as a "communications coordinator" for one organization, her responsibility had been to establish contact with other community organizations, not with the news media. But her newspaper claimed that Nelson, an award-winning education reporter, had compromised its "appearance of objectivity," even though she confined her activism to her off hours. Nelson denied any breech of ethics and slapped the *Morning News Tribune* with a lawsuit in August 1991, claiming wrongful discharge and breach of contract.[41]

A Tacoma, Washington, Superior Court judge ruled against Nelson on May 2, 1995, deciding that the *News Tribune* was within its rights to reassign the lesbian journalist because of her public support for gay rights. "She can still have her views and be politically active," commented Executive Editor David Zeeck. "She just can't do it for a newspaper that's trying to be neutral." Nelson vowed to appeal the ruling.[42]

United Press International reporter Julie Brienza faced a situation similar to Nelson's in April 1990 after she wrote a freelance article on "hate radio" for the *Washington Blade*, the gay newspaper. For the article she had interviewed Vic Eliason, a Milwaukee-based evangelical broadcaster who had helped defeat a Wisconsin gay rights law by urging his listeners to oppose it.

When he returned her telephone call, Brienza answered the phone in the Washington bureau by identifying UPI, and Eliason contacted officials at the wire service to protest. When that failed, he took his complaints to the airwaves. "If she does work for the *Washington Blade* . . . how can she report objectively on national issues?" Eliason demanded on the nationally syndicated radio show *Point of View*. "She controls the news coming out of the Supreme Court! . . . I am outraged at this type of infestation of what appears to be homosexual influence within what has been billed as [a] totally objective news service." At Eliason's urging his listeners jammed UPI's telephone line, demanding that the wire service fire Brienza because she was a lesbian who was freelancing for a gay newspaper.[43]

Although Brienza had received permission to freelance, she realized she could be disciplined for using company time and company telephones to write the story. A few days later she was fired, not because she was a lesbian but, she was told, because she had worked on the story during her work hours at UPI. In November 1990 Brienza filed a $10 million libel suit against Eliason and a $2.5 million suit against UPI that alleged unlawful employment discrimination.

Eliason settled out of court in April 1995, agreeing to pay Brienza $255,000 in damages. "I couldn't be happier," the reporter told a news conference. "We have corrected a devastating wrong—a wrong that was motivated by two equal forces: the hatred of a radical right-wing broadcaster and the cowardice of a crumbling wire service."[44]

A NEW TONE FOR THE *TIMES*

The *NewYork Times* had begun to reflect the profound changes made after Max Frankel became executive editor in 1986. Its transformation was reinforced by two other developments in the early 1990s. On February 26, 1990, Iphigene Ochs Sulzberger, the ninety-seven-year-old daughter of the *Times*'s founding publisher, died. Although she had had no direct involvement in the newspaper's content, she had discouraged coverage of gays and lesbians in the mid-sixties, helping to establish an unofficial antigay policy that prevailed for more than two decades.

Two years later, on January 16, 1992, the *Times* underwent an even more significant change when Arthur Ochs Sulzberger stepped down as publisher after nearly three decades and passed the mantle to his forty-year-old son,

Arthur Jr., who had been carefully groomed for the position since 1978. The elder Sulzberger described it as "another important step in forming the management team that will lead the *New York Times* in the years ahead."[45] His son's appointment was particularly significant for gay and lesbian journalists on the *Times* staff.

"The difference was like night and day," Jeffrey Schmalz recalled. "I don't know how much of it was Max Frankel and how much was Arthur Junior. I suspect Arthur Junior has been leading the way. He was all along more receptive to gay people and felt that the paper had been cruel. I think that as he gained in power, the paper more and more took the right stand on gay employees and gay issues."[46]

The younger Sulzberger had assumed control of the newspaper only days after Schmalz was well enough to return to work after being diagnosed with AIDS. Schmalz had tried to resume his duties as deputy national editor, but the pace had proved too grueling. As the *Times*'s AIDS reporter, he could work a reduced schedule, and he could offer readers penetrating insights into the disease and the dilemmas it presented for the people who contracted it.

"Two years ago tomorrow, I collapsed at my desk in the newsroom of the *New York Times*, writhed on the floor in a seizure and entered the world of AIDS," he wrote in his December 20, 1992, article, COVERING AIDS AND LIVING IT: A REPORTER'S TESTIMONY.

Only a few years earlier no major newspaper would have allowed a reporter to cover an issue in which he was personally involved. The conflict of interest, the thinking went, would have so biased the reporter's perspective that the truth would have been lost. But in this case at least, Schmalz's personal experience provided readers with a deeper insight and context that made the epidemic meaningful.

"The gay struggle for individual rights is running head-on into America's deep ambivalence about homosexuality," Schmalz wrote in late January 1993. "The dispute over gay men and lesbians in the military reflects a kind of continuing national referendum on homosexual rights, revealing just how tenuous support can be despite big political and social advances and polls showing that a majority of Americans oppose job discrimination against homosexuals."[47]

Edwin Diamond, then *New York* magazine's media writer, referred to Schmalz as "the *Times*'s new gay voice." "As the institutional *Times* and other news organizations come to terms with the past, a new level of journalistic honesty inevitably results," wrote Diamond. "The chestnut non-issue of whether gays should cover gays, Jews should cover Jews . . . blacks . . . blah blah blah . . . has been overtaken by events, as Jeff Schmalz suggests."[48]

Although he was not the first *Times* reporter to contract AIDS—several had died from the disease—Schmalz was the first in the upper echelon of editors and was by far the most visible. Employed by the *Times* for nearly twenty years, he had practically grown up in the newsroom. Arthur Sulzberger Jr. said,

> When you have someone of that caliber diagnosed as having AIDS, clearly that had to have had an effect. But the question is: an effect on whom? On Max [Frankel] or Joe [Lelyveld]? They knew he was gay. On me? I knew he was gay. On my father? Sure, I'm sure that helped elevate things. All of a sudden there was a face on which to attach the disease. He humanized it, I suspect, for a lot of people. His journalism then led to a different level for our readers—including all of us—and led to a higher level of understanding. But I wouldn't say his collapse did that. The journalism that followed did that.[49]

In the spring of 1993 Schmalz profiled Randy Shilts, fellow journalist and compatriot in the personal battle against AIDS. In some sections of the article, WRITING AGAINST TIME, VALIANTLY, it was easy to forget that Schmalz was writing about Shilts and not about himself: "One minute he is the old Randy Shilts, a blur of energy and issues and passion, musing over the possibility of a new book, railing against the abuse of gay and lesbian Americans in the military. The next, he isn't Randy Shilts at all. He's just another gay man with AIDS."[50]

FORMATION OF AN ORGANIZATION

Despite the challenges facing gay and lesbian journalists, growing numbers were emerging from their silence. When Aaron's newly formed National Lesbian and Gay Journalists Association held its first annual convention in July 1992 in San Francisco, it attracted nearly three hundred journalists from as far away as New England, Florida, and Alaska.

"A kind of electricity crackled through the event," boasted Aarons in the organization's newsletter. "Consider the implications of those 300 people headed home and fired up for action—ready to engage their colleagues with strategies for change that will in turn affect millions of people whose perceptions are shaped by the media."[51]

Joe Yonan was among them. The twenty-six-year-old editor in chief of the *Monadnock Ledger* had not come out to his publisher or his staff at the small weekly in rural New Hampshire until a writer for the trade magazine *Editor & Publisher* asked whether he could quote him at the conference. "Sure, go ahead," he responded. "Being here with all of these journalists has been very inspiring for someone like me, and I've been struggling with how to come out to my staff."[52]

Arthur Sulzberger Jr., who had been publisher of the *New York Times* for only six months, set the tone for the convention by predicting that the success of the nation's news media would be determined by their openness to a diverse newsroom. He could not attend the convention in person but videotaped his speech, telling the journalists,

> I'm convinced that if newspapers are to survive, they can no longer be exclusionary bastions of a single view of the world. We can no longer offer our readers a predominately white, straight, male vision of events and say that we are doing our job. . . . Only when we offer our readers a wide spectrum of viewpoints can we say we are fulfilling our role as journalists. We need to find the courage to cover the world the way it is. We must offer our readers coverage of the broad gay community, its people, and its issues.[53]

Sulzberger's address reflected the enlightened attitude of a new generation of media movers and shakers. The National Lesbian and Gay Journalists Association listed fifteen news organizations that had officially barred discrimination against lesbians and gays, including such large metro dailies as the *Baltimore Sun*, the *Philadelphia Inquirer*, *St. Paul Pioneer Press*, *San Francisco Examiner*, *San Francisco Chronicle*, and smaller newspapers, including the *York (Pennsylvania) Dispatch*, *Terre Haute (Indiana) Tribune-Star*, *Central New Jersey Home News*, and the *Sheboygan (Wisconsin) Press*.[54]

Newspapers in Brattleboro, Vermont, and Salina, Kansas, began to publish commitment announcements for same-sex couples among wedding engagements. "Our editorial policy has always been in favor of equal rights," said George Pyle, editor of the *Salina Journal*. "It would be kind of hypocritical to say that on the editorial page, and then to say on the lifestyle pages that "We're not going to include you.'"[55]

Between 1990 and 1993 nine other small- to medium-sized newspapers took similar steps, including papers in New Hampshire, Massachusetts, Washington, and California. Among the largest were the *Minneapolis Tribune*,

Seattle Times, and *San Jose Mercury-News*. In Austin, Texas, Roger Kintzel, publisher of the *American-Statesman*, responded to an outpouring of criticism from fundamentalist Christians by saying the newspaper was following its stated policy of nondiscrimination on the basis of sexual orientation.[56]

With so many changes taking place so suddenly backlash could have been predicted. Writing in the *Columbia Journalism Review*, former *Washington Monthly* editor William McGowan described an undercurrent of hostility that had resulted from attempts to diversify newsrooms. Citing the *New York Times* as a primary example, McGowan accused Arthur Sulzberger of turning diversity into "a personal crusade."[57]

GAYS AND LESBIANS REPORTING ON GAYS AND LESBIANS

Jeffrey Schmalz and Randy Shilts may have been the most widely recognized gay journalists working at major newspapers, but they were not the only ones emerging in the media. On May 8, 1992, the *Detroit News* broke new ground when it carried the first regular column by an openly lesbian reporter, Deb Price.[58]

"While newspapers across America, including our own, have increased news coverage of gay issues, no voice is regularly heard that looks at life from a gay perspective," said the newspaper's editor and publisher, Robert Giles, in an introduction that accompanied Price's first column.[59] The column was carried by other newspapers owned by the Gannett chain in other cities, including Palm Springs, Des Moines, and Rochester, New York. The columns appeared occasionally in the national Gannett newspaper *USA Today*.

Price was deluged with letters—both supportive and critical. "I have been reading the *Detroit News* from cover to cover for more than 30 years," wrote one reader. "I am canceling my subscription today." "Today it's gay issues," wrote another. "Will the next 'feature' be wife-swapping or a column for pornographers?" Giles took the letters in stride. "I think the negative backlash is the best argument for the need for this kind of column," he said. "It reflects two themes: first, the obsession with the sexual aspects of homosexuality. The second is the prejudice against people who are of a different sexual orientation."[60]

Price went on to write columns about the alienation of gay teenagers, the antigay military witch-hunts, how the Bible has been used to justify discrimination, and her twentieth college reunion at which she introduced her former classmates to her partner, Joyce. "It is the column that I always wanted to read," she said.[61]

The *Philadelphia Daily News* became the nation's second newspaper to incorporate a gay-written column. "As a good independent newspaper we should address the needs of all of our readers," said editorial page editor Richard Aregood. "Especially, now, when members of the 'Party of God' want to string gays up, we think people have a legitimate right to have other opinions in their daily newspaper."[62] The column began in October 1992 by alternating between a lesbian, Victoria Brownworth, and a gay man, Mubarak S. Dahir.

In late January 1993 *New York Newsday* added a gay voice to its pages when it hired Gabriel Rotello, the openly gay former editor in chief of *OutWeek*, the fiery magazine that had shaken the industry two years earlier by outing prominent gays. Within two months two other newspapers followed suit. The *St. Louis Post-Dispatch* began running a monthly column by Amy Adams Squire Strongheart. And David Jones, a well-known gay activist in North Carolina, began writing a column for the *Chapel Hill Herald*.

The broadcast industry also was showing signs of change. In July 1993 NBC president Robert Wright adopted a "work force diversity" policy. His memo to employees said,

> Simply put, diversity is providing an environment which removes all barriers so people can excel. . . . It's a fact that the United States' population is rapidly becoming more diverse, and that competition for television viewers, currently at an all-time high, continues to escalate. NBC's ability to compete will increasingly depend on how successful we are in attracting the majority of television viewers with programming that appeals and is relevant to the largest segment of the viewing public. By diversifying our own work force, we are able to diversify our product and speak to that broader audience.[63]

Wright's memo did not mention gays and lesbians specifically, but the memo's importance as a signal of support for them became clear a few weeks later. Medical reporter Steve Gendel was out to many of his colleagues at the network but had never made his orientation known among the top ranks. Then Gendel was invited to appear on *Real Personal* on CNBC, the cable network owned by NBC. The topic that night was a newly released scientific study that showed a genetic basis for homosexuality. After he was introduced by show host Bob Berkowitz as someone with an interest in the findings, Gendel told viewers, "I have a personal interest and a professional interest because as you know, I am a gay man—something I never thought I would say on national television." After a burst of applause from the studio audience, Berkowitz asked, "How do you feel about saying that, by the way?" "It's important," Gendel responded. "It's an important part of this story because if people are going to understand what homosexuality is they have to understand who we are and the only images people have is when we are dancing or marching. They don't see us in suits and ties as doctors, lawyers, businessmen, and their fellow neighborhood reporter."[64]

Gendel took his acknowledgment a step further in the summer of 1994 in a story on the Stonewall 25 celebration for the *Today Show*. "Few will deny the riot was a great catalyst for the American gay movement, allowing many of us who are gay, including myself, to come out of the closet and fight for acceptance," he said at the end of his report.[65]

But the subject of homosexuality arose in a much different context a few days later on New York's NBC affiliate WNBC. During an interview with actor Tom Arnold, *Live at Five* anchor Sue Simmons suddenly found herself embroiled in controversy. As she peppered Arnold with questions about his personal life, Arnold suddenly said, "Let's get into your personal life. Are you married?"

"No," Simmons responded.

"Are you a lesbian?" he asked.

"Yes," said Simmons.

"Now we've got something in common," Arnold quickly added.

"Now that I've lied about my life, lie about yours," Simmons shot back at Arnold.

"I'm blessed to be sitting here with you, a confirmed lesbian," he continued as Simmons insisted that her remark had been a joke. But the popular anchor later felt it necessary to issue a statement saying she hoped her comment would not "destroy" her career. NBC followed up with a statement that called Simmons a "valued and important member of the NBC family," adding that her personal life was her own business.

The exchange with Arnold and the subsequent statements from Simmons and the network quickly became a hot topic in New York gossip columns. "Let's face it," she told one columnist. "This could possibly be a career-ender."[66]

But the increasing presence of gay and lesbian reporters and gay coverage in the mainstream media triggered an identity crisis for the gay press. The *Advocate*, the oldest gay newspaper, was for the first time facing competition from straight newspapers and magazines as well as from several new gay and lesbian publications that were also looking for a slice of the national gay readership. Joining the *Advocate* on newsstands were such names as *Out*, *Genre*, and *NYQ*, each of which was trying to outgloss the other with slick, full-color layouts and advertising. In response, the *Advocate* went to glossy paper and jettisoned its controversial sexually explicit classified advertising.

In 1992 the United States had approximately 160 gay-targeted publications. But by that summer the heightened competition was beginning to take its toll on small weeklies that could not compete with the slick new national magazines. After nineteen years as a mainstay of gay journalism, Boston's *Gay Community News* suspended publishing on July 4. "The economics of 1973 are not workable in 1992," said longtime contributor Michael Bronski. "We managed to get by on hook or by crook, but hippy economics are no longer tenable." The nonprofit collective of gays and lesbians that ran the newspaper predicted it would have a restructuring plan finished by November and vowed to reopen the next January.[67]

Out magazine claimed in 1994 that it had doubled its circulation in just two years to more than 100,000. Time, Inc., unveiled plans to start *Tribe*, a gay and lesbian version of *Mirabella* and *Esquire*. Former *QW* editor Maer Roshan had been chosen as the magzine's editor. But after extensive research and several business plans Time suddenly decided the marketplace would not support another gay magazine and dropped the idea.

Within days rumors began to circulate that Time had been pressured into killing the magazine. A *New York Times* article quoted unnamed sources who claimed that the American Family Association (AFA) had threatened the media conglomerate with a boycott. Not only did company officials steadfastly deny the reports, but AFA head Donald Wildmon denied any knowledge of the magazine.[68] In the meantime *Gay Community News* struggled against the new slick breed of gay press. After publishing special issues (on the 1993 March on Washington, RACE, CLASS, SEX, and Stonewall), *GCN* resumed publishing in the fall of 1994 as a quarterly with aspirations of rebuilding itself financially to become a monthly, but it clearly was not the forceful voice it had been a decade earlier.

Increasingly, gays and lesbians were seeing news about themselves in the mainstream press. Coverage in 1992 was fueled by the presidential campaign, which was followed by an intense national debate over gays in the military. The television networks booked gay and lesbian military personnel for interviews on their most popular morning and evening news programs. As the political debate reached a boiling point in Washington, national magazines featured photos of gay and lesbian soldiers on their covers.

In addition, the news media were facing increasing pressure from a growing number of gay and lesbian activists in a growing number of cities. By the fall of 1993 GLAAD's membership had climbed to more than ten thousand with a fledgling network of local chapters in Atlanta, Dallas, Denver, Kansas City, Los Angeles, San Diego, San Francisco, and Washington.[69] All of them were ready to respond with cards and letters or with picket lines to the slightest media misstep.

LESBIAN AND GAY JOURNALISTS MEET

When the National Lesbian and Gay Journalists Association held its second convention in the fall of 1993, attendance had doubled to nearly 600, and membership in its dozen chapters in major cities had climbed from about 600 to more than 800.[70] The organization also had grown in stature.

Arthur Sulzberger continued his support of the organization by personally hosting a reception, as did Knight-Ridder, publisher of several major newspapers, including the *Miami Herald*, *Philadelphia Inquirer*, and *San Jose Mercury-News*. Panel participants featured such high-profile media luminaries as Tom Brokaw of NBC, Robert MacNeil of PBS's *MacNeil-Lehrer Newshour*, Dan Rather of CBS, and Judy Woodruff of CNN. "You have all said several times that it would be OK if someone were to come out—that you would be supportive of that, but I wonder how much you have articulated that within your news organizations to the people who may be closeted," gay journalist Michelangelo Signorile railed at the distinguished foursome.[71]

The combative mood tempered a bit when Brokaw told the audience he had happily worked with a number of homosexuals during his broadcast career. The audience applauded MacNeil when he mentioned that he has a gay son. Covering the event for the *Washington Post*, media critic Howard Kurtz said it represented a "sea change in the industry's mainstream." "If any doubts remain that gay journalists have become part of the media mainstream, they were dispelled here this weekend," he wrote.[72]

Many of those changes were personified by reporter Jeffrey Schmalz of the *New York Times*. After hiding his sexual orientation for almost twenty years at a newspaper with a long history of slighting the gay community, he spoke to his gay and lesbian colleagues as an openly gay journalist with AIDS. "I actually came very late to this fight and have borne an incredible guilt complex because of that," he told them. "I'm sorry, and I'm very grateful to you for having borne that fight for so long, and I thank you." Then he asked, "But are we to spend all of the time here applauding ourselves? I think not. I think the question for this room full of hundreds of gay men and women is, where are we going from here? And, I don't know the answers to that. . . . I'm not sure we have the professionalism; I'm not that sure we have the answers about where to go, and how to go, and how to move. I'm not sure. I wish us all well. But I just don't know what the future holds for all of us."[73]

Schmalz was especially unsure of his own future. For more than a year he had undergone intense medical treatment as he entered the final stages of the disease. The thirty-nine-year-old survived for only five weeks after NLGJA's convention. His death on November 6, 1993, was noted in a *Times* obituary written by his colleague and friend Richard Meislin, the reporter who had been brought home from Mexico ten years earlier after his superiors realized he was gay. It was a fitting illustration of how far the *Times* had come. "Part of the price of his ascent at The Times, Mr. Schmalz long believed, was that he hid his homosexuality from at least some of this superiors," the obituary noted. "But after his illness became known, and his sexual orientation was no longer a secret, he became an outspoken supporter of equal rights for gay people."[74]

Three weeks later the *New York Times Magazine* carried Schmalz's final story, one he had worked on since the spring. The long feature began in a traditionally dispassionate reporter's voice but evolved into a moving account of Schmalz's own anguish that the disease had all but disappeared from the public landscape. With nearly ninety Americans dying daily, he aimed the brunt of his anger at President Bill Clinton for not doing enough:

> I had hope when I interviewed Bill Clinton about AIDS and gay issues for this magazine in August 1992. He spoke so eloquently on AIDS. I really did see him as a white knight who might save me. How naive I was to think that one man could make that big a difference. At its core, the problem isn't a government; it's a virus. Still, in interviews with researchers and Administration officials, it was clear that we are talking about different planets. I need help now, not five years from now. Yet the urgency just wasn't there. Compassion and concern, yes; even sympathy. But urgency, no. I felt alone, abandoned, cheated.[75]

Three days later, in observance of World AIDS Day, President Clinton spoke to a gathering at Georgetown University and referred to the article and described Schmalz as a "remarkable man" who had interviewed him "in a very piercing way" during the campaign. Clinton accepted the rebuke in the article, saying, "I invite you to tell me what else you think I can do, and to ask yourselves what else you can do."[76]

Randy Shilts, who had been too ill to attend the NLGJA convention, survived Schmalz by only three months. His death on February 17, 1994, at age forty-two garnered headlines in newspapers across the nation. The man who had done the most to chronicle the outbreak of the AIDS epidemic ultimately had become one of its victims.

At his funeral in San Francisco hundreds of gay and lesbian mourners filed into Glide Memorial Church, while religious fundamentalists picketed outside. Some of them handed out flyers that read, "Another filthy media fag has died of AIDS." "The fag-dominated entertainment, and media worlds are making a hero of this gerbil-mongering moron," said Fred Phelps, pastor of the Westboro Baptist Church, who had traveled to San Francisco from Topeka to stage the protest. But speakers lavished praise on Shilts. "Randy Shilts is one of the truly great journalists of our time," said Michael Denneny, his editor at St. Martin's Press. "His career is a shining example of what journalism at its best can be and can accomplish."[77]

A MEASURE OF PROGRESS

On April 25, 1993, thousands of lesbians and gays filled Pennsylvania Avenue in front of the White House and the Capitol for the third National March on Washington. The level of media coverage was unprecedented.

In the two weeks before and after the march the *New York Times* alone carried 50 articles, compared with only 5 stories about the previous march in 1987. The number of articles in the *Washington Post* rose from 12 in 1987 to 51 in 1993. The same trend was reflected in the *Los Angeles Times* where only 5 articles appeared in 1987, compared with 26 in 1993. A study by New York activist Bill Dobbs the day after the march showed that 156 newspapers across the nation had reported the story. Most featured it on their front page.[78]

Army Sergeant José Zuniga contributed to the drama when he used the march to personalize the gays-in-the-military debate by acknowledging that he was gay during a fundraiser for the National Gay and Lesbian Task Force on the evening before the march. Wearing an array of military decorations, including Sixth Army "Soldier of the Year," Zuniga spoke to a crowd that included a large contingent of television camera crews and reporters who had been alerted to the pending announcement. "It's an opportune time to come out," Zuniga said. "People realize we are in the military, but these ludicrous excuses are fogging the issue. We are in. We are serving with distinction. I want to show the nation that this is discrimination, pure and simple."[79]

Commenting on Zuniga's announcement, *New York Times* op-ed columnist Anna Quindlen wrote, "Stereotypes fall in the face of humanity. You toodle along, thinking that all gay men wear leather after dark and would never, ever be permitted around a Little League field. And then one day your best friend from college, the one your kids adore, comes out to you. Or that wonderful woman who teaches third grade is spotted leaving a lesbian bar in the next town. And the ice of your closed mind begins to crack."[80]

"The media really seemed to get it this time," commented Gregory Adams, the communications director for the march. "Consistent and distinct messages of justice, fair treatment, and equality ran through nearly every article or broadcast we saw." His assessment was echoed by Ohio University professors Joseph Bernt and Marilyn Greenwald who analyzed coverage of the march in thirty newspapers. "It extended over a really long period of time, including the week after the march," said Bernt. "This [march] generated much more sophisticated stories; it got into local gay and lesbian communities."[81]

While gay activists reveled in the attention, media critics were pointing out the lapses. *Washington Post* ombudsman Joann Byrd blasted her newspaper's coverage: "What was really missing in the coverage—and what would have improved the paper's credibility on the whole subject—was a comprehensive reporting of the debate surrounding gay rights. Not to encourage conflict, not to provide 'the other side,' but to fully tell the gay rights story."[82]

The biggest controversy among the media involved their own gay and lesbian journalists. The *New York Times* and NBC had no objection to their staff members taking part, provided their jobs did not involve covering or supervising the coverage of the issues involved. The Associated Press and the *Washington Post*, however, objected to any of their reporters participating in any "partisan activities." The National Lesbian and Gay Journalists Association had planned to sponsor a contingent in the march but later reconsidered and decided not to.[83]

In June 1994 coverage of gays and lesbians revolved around Stonewall 25 in New York, the twenty-fifth anniversary of the Stonewall riots. The *New York Times*, which had paid scant attention to the riots in 1969, ran fifty-six articles on a variety of gay-related topics in the ten-day period surrounding the anniversary. Six of those stories ran on the *Times*'s front page. The *CBS Evening News* highlighted the gay rights movement with an entire segment. It referred to the 1969 Stonewall riots as an event that changed America.

That same month gays were also staging the fourth annual Gay Games, the gay and lesbian sporting event modeled after the Olympics. Few among the media approached the games as a major international sporting event, even though eleven thousand athletes participated, more than participated in the Summer Olympics in Barcelona in 1992. Although *Sports Illustrated* ignored it, *ABC Sports* carried a report on the games and a brief history of earlier Gay Games events. Two New York dailies, the *Times* and *Newsday*, gave it considerable play.[84]

Writing about the games in the *Washington Post*, staff writer Rachel Alexander not only publicized the games but attempted to explode the macho lesbian stereotype. The article quoted Susan Kennedy, one of the games organizers, as saying, "There is this picture of lesbians as these motorcycle dykes—really short hair, combat boots and a pack of cigarettes rolled up in one sleeve. The truth is that while there are some lesbians who fit that description, there are also some straights who fit that description and just as many lesbians who don't fit that description at all."[85]

Organizers had hoped the Gay Games and using the United Nations as a backdrop for the Stonewall 25 march would focus attention on gay rights worldwide. But these angles were largely overshadowed in news stories that concentrated on the historical aspect of the Stonewall commemoration and a controversy that erupted when members of ACT UP organized a separate, unofficial march from the site of the old Stonewall Inn to Central Park, hoping to focus attention on the AIDS epidemic.

The day after the march, articles appeared in newspapers across the nation. People who had never before heard of the Stonewall rebellion were now reading about its commemoration in their morning newspapers:

Miami Herald: MANHATTAN MARCH IS 'A CRY FOR JUSTICE'
Philadelphia Inquirer: GAYS RALLY IN N.Y. TO DEMAND EQUALITY
Minneapolis Star Tribune: GAYS MARK ANNIVERSARY OF NEW YORK UPRISING
St. Louis Post-Dispatch: MARCHERS CELEBRATE GAY PRIDE
Los Angeles Times: THOUSANDS JOIN MARCH IN N.Y. FOR GAY RIGHTS

USA Today, the *Washington Post*, *Baltimore Sun*, and *Boston Globe* carried pictures of the march on their front pages and directed readers to articles on their inside pages. *Newsweek* ran a two-page feature by gay journalist Charles Kaiser. The June 20 edition of *New York* magazine showcased the celebration with a cover that asked IS EVERYBODY GAY? TIME included a brief article in its June 27 issue but then listed the march as a loser in its Winners and Losers column after the organizers ran into financial trouble.

One other measure of progress was how far the media had come in allowing openly gay and lesbian journalists to cover news involving gays. As the coordinator of the gay and lesbian caucus at the *New York Times*, David Dunlap asked management of the newspaper how it would regard gay staff members who participated in Stonewall 25. Most newspapers have policies that prevent journalists from participating in a variety of political functions if that participation could be seen as a conflict of interest. In the case of gays and lesbians, covering any story involving gays was routinely considered a conflict.

Times managing editor Joseph Lelyveld took the same position the newspaper took in regard to the March on Washington a year earlier, cautioning that gay and lesbian journalists at the *Times* should not take part "if they currently cover gay-related news, or expect to in the future." Dunlap suspected the directive carried an especially strong message for him personally, because Lelyveld was slated to succeed Executive Editor Max Frankel on July 1—five days after the march. Dunlap and his colleague Richard Meislin were careful to keep their distance from the official activities, choosing to watch and wave at friends from the sidewalk behind police barricades as the march passed. (In September 1994 Lelyveld assigned Dunlap to cover gay and lesbian issues in addition to his real estate beat. In essence, Dunlap filled the void left by the death of his friend Jeffrey Schmalz.)[86]

USA Today reporter Debbie Howlett was another who would not march. As an open lesbian on the newspaper's staff, she was busy covering the march for the next day's edition, writing the story that was headlined THOUSANDS MARCH FOR GAY RIGHTS. She had already written an extensive preview article for the newspaper in which she explained the historical significance of the celebration and the progress of the gay rights movement since 1969. In her coverage of the march she singled out veteran lesbian activist Barbara Gittings, noting that Gittings was among those who had picketed the White House in 1965. "For all of us marching here in New York, there are thousands in small towns across America who feel they can't speak out. People should not be complacent and merely celebrate the victories," Gittings said.[87]

Most of the criticism leveled at the media centered on the lack of coverage given to a lesbian march late in the afternoon the day before the official

Stonewall 25 march. One explanation given by the newspapers was that the lesbian march, the largest of its kind ever held, was scheduled too late in the day to make Sunday edition deadlines. The July 5, 1994, *Village Voice* carried a separate article on the lesbian march.

The most glaring gaps in the coverage involved lesbians and international human rights violations against gays—which was a main theme of Stonewall 25; these omissions prompted criticism that the coverage overall was shallow. "It was saccharine," remarked former *New York Times* media writer Alex Jones in an interview with the *Advocate*. "The one thing that was really lacking was any serious discussion of the status of gay affairs. It did a disservice to the news aspect of the event, because there's a real national debate going on about the issue of gay rights."[88]

But even with its flaws news coverage of Stonewall 25 offered a striking measure of the heightened visibility gays and lesbians had attained throughout the media since 1969. "Here in New York, you really could not open a newspaper or turn on a TV set without seeing something about gays," Ellen Carton, executive director of GLAAD's New York chapter, told the *Washington Blade*.[89]

There were missteps and oversights by the media, but none was describing gays and lesbians as the "forces of faggotry," as the *Village Voice* had on its front page in 1969. Whereas the Stonewall riots merited only two single-column stories in the *New York Times* in 1969, the commemoration in 1994 was front-page news. Gay and lesbian activists had denounced the press in 1969. In 1994 activists were seeing coverage that had been only a dream of their predecessors. And, for the first time, some gay activists had begun to describe much of the news media as "fair and accurate."[90]

EPILOGUE

In 1996 gays and lesbians appear in the news almost routinely—nearly as routinely as they were excluded fifty years ago. The news media often go beyond the once-prevalent stereotypes to tackle many core issues facing gays and lesbians. As a result the American public sees and hears more about the wants and concerns of the gay community today than ever before.

"Lesbians and gay men today wake up to headlines alternately disputing their claim to equality under the law, supporting their right to family status, denying their desire, affirming their social identity," wrote the late, openly gay editor Andrew Kopkind in the *Nation* in May 1993. "They fall asleep to TV talk shows where generals call them perverts, liberals plead for tolerance and politicians weigh their votes. 'Gay invisibility,' the social enforcement of the sexual closet, is hardly a problem anymore."[1]

It seems almost inconceivable that a decade ago the *New York Times* refused to use the term *gay*. The *Times* now has openly gay reporters covering gay stories—and the stories appear with remarkable frequency. As recently as 1974 a front page headline in the *Los Angeles Times* used the term *fag*. But in the summer of 1995 the newspaper carried a story about the twenty-fifth annual gay pride celebration in West Hollywood under the headline A DAY TO BE PROUD.[2]

Issues the media would have overlooked or given only a passing glance as recently as five years ago now receive extraordinary attention. *Vanity Fair* devoted a special section of its February 1995 issue to an in-depth report on antigay hate crimes in Texas. The message about the pervasive antigay violence in America was carried to an even larger audience when ABC's *Primetime Live* aired a segment on the issue a few days after *Vanity Fair* appeared on newsstands.[3]

Today's media are more likely than ever to call attention to discrimination faced by gays and lesbians. After a gay man became embroiled in an anonymous hate-mail campaign in a southeastern Missouri town in July 1995 and was fired from the funeral home where he'd worked for fifteen years, the *St. Louis Post-Dispatch* responded with an editorial: "For those who believe that homosexuals don't need legal protection of their civil rights, Roger Moore's story is sadly instructive. Absent legal protection, Mr. Moore and other homosexuals have only the good will and moral courage of others to rely on. As his case vividly demonstrates, that's not enough."[4]

Some editors and reporters also have begun to incorporate gays in broader community stories instead of marginalizing them in sidebars that set them apart and emphasize their differences. The *Washington Post*, for example, spotlighted several couples on the front of its Style section for Valentines Day 1995, describing how they had met and had fallen in love. Among such political luminaries as Al and Tipper Gore and movie star sweethearts Matthew Broderick and Sarah Jessica Parker were playwright and gay activist Larry Kramer and his boyfriend, architect David Webster. As the newspaper had with the heterosexual couples, it described when the two men had met (1968), when they began dating (in the 1970s), and how long they had been a couple (since April 1993).[5]

Likewise, the *Statesman Journal* in Salem, Oregon, ran a September 1995 feature on National Singles Week and included comments from a single gay man. In a Father's Day feature the *CBS Evening News* included two gay fathers and their adopted sons.[6]

How gays are portrayed in television series also has changed significantly. During the 1995 season, for example, at least nine network series contained a recurring gay and/or lesbian character, including ABC's *NYPD Blue* and *Roseanne*; CBS's *High Society*; Fox's *Melrose Place*, *Party of Five*, and *The Crew*; and NBC's *Friends* and *The Pursuit of Happiness*. ABC took the formal step of extending its fairness policy to include gays in 1995, adding them to a list of groups that are not to be "misrepresented, ridiculed or attacked" on the network's programming.

"Prime-time television never has been a hospitable climate for gays and lesbians, but there are genuine signs of a thaw as the networks prepare to launch the 1995–96 season," noted *San Francisco Chronicle* TV writer John Carman. "It's not a huge splash in a year with a record number of new shows, yet there is a difference that marks an uptick in the history of gays and lesbians on television."[7]

Another sign of the trend sweeping the media was the willingness of an increasing number of news executives to allow gay and lesbian journalists to cover gay-related news. Before the *San Francisco Chronicle* hired Randy Shilts in 1982, the few journalists who were openly gay were thought to be too biased to cover stories involving gays. Jeffrey Schmalz emerged from the newsroom closet of the *New York Times* in 1991, and only extreme right-wing media watchdog groups ran forward to accuse him of "having an agenda" during his two decades at the newspaper.

Not only are gays writing about gays, they are breaking big stories. Syndicated *Detroit News* columnist Deb Price sparked an uproar in August 1995 when she reported that Robert Dole's presidential campaign had accepted, then returned a $1,000 contribution from a gay Republican organization, even though the campaign had actively solicited the money. The story set off a flurry of embarrassing headlines for Dole in newspapers nationwide, including the *New York Times*, *Washington Post*, *Los Angeles Times*, *Boston Globe*, New Orleans *Times-Picayune*, and *Wall Street Journal*. THE DOLE WAY: IF YOU'RE DOWN, KICK A GAY, read a *San Francisco Chronicle* headline.[8]

Two months later another gay journalist confronted Dole about the check during a press conference. Responding to a question from the *Cleveland Plain Dealer*'s Washington correspondent, Sabrina Eaton, Dole called the action a mistake and blamed it on his campaign staff. The comment set off a rash of articles suggesting he was fickle. DOLE FLIPS, FLOPS AND IRKS, the *Los Angeles Times* opined the next day. MR. DOLE FLIPS BACK, said the headline on the *Washington Post*'s editorial.[9]

These changes may seem sudden to millions of readers and television viewers across the nation. But the shift in how the media portray gays and lesbians did not happen overnight. What we see in today's media is the result of many years of protesting, cajoling, and negotiating by gay and lesbian activists who complained that much of what the media were saying about their community was neither fair nor accurate.

What may also seem sudden is that after shrugging off their demands, the news media have begun to respond. But here too the change has not been as sudden as readers and viewers of the news might think. The basis for what we see in the news media today dates back several decades to one of the most chaotic periods of social change in the nation's history: the 1960s.

The 1960s were a time of turmoil and protest that was punctuated by civil rights demonstrations, urban riots, antiwar protests, and a revolt by women who had grown weary of their second-class status. The nation's traditional power structure was under assault, including the white male-dominated news media.

In 1969 the Kerner Commission, established by President Lyndon Johnson to examine the reasons behind a rash of urban riots, blamed the news media for failing to provide the nation with an accurate picture of everyday life for inner-city black Americans: "Our evidence shows that the so-called 'white press' is at best mistrusted and at worst held in contempt by many black Americans." The commission strongly suggested that to correct the problem the news media had to employ, promote, and listen to black journalists.[10]

That same year the nation's first gay riot erupted outside the Stonewall Inn in New York City. Many of the gays and lesbians who established the gay liberation movement had been involved in the civil rights movement and the student antiwar protests, where they had learned how to attract media attention and, through the media, public recognition.

Like blacks, gays distrusted the news media, where they too were virtually invisible. Only weeks after the Stonewall uprising in 1969 angry gays picketed the *Village Voice* over that newspaper's refusal to use the term *gay*. Six weeks later they picketed *Time* because its cover story, NEWLY VISIBLE, NEWLY UNDERSTOOD, portrayed them as sick, sad, and hopeless. Within weeks gays picketed the *Los Angeles Times* and the *San Francisco Examiner* for similar reasons. As they had in response to the Kerner Commission report, the media waxed indignant, vowing never to allow anyone to tamper with their First Amendment right to cover the news.

Although blacks and women made significant gains under the Civil Rights Act of 1964, in 1973 half the nation's commercial television stations still had no blacks, women, Native Americans, or Asian Americans on their staffs. No Hispanic held the title of anchor, reporter, producer, or manager. In the case of women three-quarters of those working in commercial television held clerical or secretarial positions.[11]

Several women reporters at the *New York Times* filed a class action suit in 1974 after they found out that the newspaper was paying them an average of $3,000 a year less than their male counterparts—a gap that widened throughout the '70s. (Similar suits were filed by women against the *Washington Post*, Associated Press, *Newsday*, *Detroit News*, *Baltimore Evening Sun*, and *Reader's Digest*.) In the midst of the women's suit black reporters at the *New York Times* filed a similar grievance. Of the 586 reporters and editors at the *Times* in 1979, only 36 were nonwhite. Executive Editor Abe Rosenthal described their complaints as "social blackmail" and was outraged to learn that among some employees he was known as an "equal opportunity oppressor."[12]

Although legal avenues were open to blacks and women, gay and lesbian journalists were not afforded similar legal protections by the Civil Rights Act and had little option but to hide inside their newsroom closets. Earlier sections of this book described the experiences of Leroy Aarons at the *Washington Post* in 1965, Perry Dean Young in the Saigon bureau of United Press International in 1968, and Sharon Shaw Johnson at the *Rockford Morning Star* in 1972.

In the meantime other minority journalists began to make small but significant inroads. In 1978 the American Society of Newspaper Editors (ASNE) set the ambitious goal of hiring enough minority journalists by the year 2000 to match the ratio of minorities in the national population. But within a short time media executives complained of an insufficient number of qualified black and female applicants. Women and minorities complained of a lack of commitment by owners and editors to hire and promote them, especially into management ranks. In 1990 more than half of the estimated sixteen hundred daily newspapers in the United States still had no minority employees in their newsrooms, prompting black journalists like Ben Johnson, assistant managing editor of the *St. Petersburg Times*, to remark to white colleagues,

"Y'all ain't serious." Merv Aubespin, chairman of the minorities committee of ASNE, called the rate of progress "not only unfortunate, but embarrassing for our industry."[13]

Pressure on the news media intensified in the early nineties when the industry fell into what proved to be a protracted economic slump. The traditional suppliers of information faced stiff competition from cable television, VCRs, online computer networks, talk radio, and other sources of news and entertainment that were siphoning off a growing share of their audiences and viewers and thus putting greater pressure on the media's profits. Advertising revenue at newspapers, magazines, and television stations had fallen into one of the deepest slumps on record by 1990. "In my 31 years, this is the worst I have ever seen it," the owner of a New Jersey newspaper told the *Wall Street Journal*.[14]

The dire outlook jolted the upper echelons of the nation's news media into a new reality. Audiences had changed, and the media had failed to keep pace with peoples' tastes and expectations. In ever-increasing numbers consumers were bypassing newspapers and newscasts and turning to raw sources: cable television and talk shows. It wasn't just women and minorities who were abandoning conventional media. White men were turning in droves to talk radio, exemplified by the politically reactionary Rush Limbaugh. Under these pressures media executives and editors in New York and elsewhere began to take a hard look at what they were doing. For the first time many began to examine long-held assumptions about how they defined news and how it should be covered.

WATCHWORD OF NEWSPAPER PUBLISHERS AT CONFERENCE IS AUDIENCE DIVERSITY, the *Wall Street Journal* reported in May 1991, signaling that newspaper executives were ready to find ways to attract a broader audience. "They said they are looking to appeal to practically every identifiable demographic group—senior citizens, teenagers, baby-boomers, city dwellers, suburban families—despite newspapers' traditional role as a mass medium," the article reported.[15]

The diversification of news staffs, which had been an empty promise during the seventies and eighties, was getting serious attention from news executives throughout the industry. Newspaper consultant Nancy Woodhull commented that before 1992 editors called her to ask how they could keep the National Organization for Women from picketing their newspapers. "Now I'm getting calls from [editors] seeing women as a market, as readers," she said.[16]

As women and blacks joined news staffs in increasing numbers, they began to influence the media's definition of news. Diversity was becoming synonymous with good journalism. "Newspapers are uniquely positioned, it seems to me, to be instruments for community understanding across communities," said Robert Maynard, the late publisher of the *Oakland Tribune* who was one of the news industry's strongest advocates of diversity. "I honestly believe that it is to our benefit to build a community made up of a set of smaller communities that share a continuing and enduring respect for each other."[17]

By the time the news media began to reassess their future, gays and lesbians had become increasingly visible. They were easily ignored in the mid-1960s when they could muster only a dozen pickets for a protest at the White House. But in the mid-1970s the situation began to change as tens of thousands of gays staged political demonstrations in Washington in 1979 and again in 1987. Even if the lowest estimate was correct, the 1987 March on Washington was the largest civil rights demonstration in that city since 1963. In the 1990s the media's commitment to reflecting cultural diversity, coupled with the heightened visibility of gays and lesbians, compelled the news media to recognize that they had overlooked a variety of issues and concerns important to several segments of society, among them African-Americans, women, and gays.

The AIDS crisis was another major catalyst in changing how the news media viewed the gay community. The worsening epidemic intensified the soul searching that had already begun in some newsrooms. As they had for decades, gay and lesbian activists pushed the media to resolve a long-standing confusion about whether to cover the emerging gay community and how it should be done. The media were slow to recognize the burgeoning AIDS crisis in much the same way they were slow to recognize the problems facing inner-city blacks in the sixties. Because journalists had no personal experience with these problems, they didn't exist. In the case of AIDS, as the death toll rose and gay and lesbian activists demanded fair and accurate reporting of the epidemic, the importance of the AIDS story overcame the prudishness, prejudice, and indifference that had long guided how the media portrayed gays and lesbians.

At the same time mainstream journalists began to adjust to the idea that gays and lesbians were in their midst—so much so in fact that gay and lesbian journalists began to play an active role in determining how their community was being covered. Membership in the National Lesbian and Gay Journalists

Association (NLGJA) surged. Between 1992, when the organization held its first national convention in San Francisco, and its 1995 convention in Washington, D.C., membership rolls climbed from 545 to 1,200 in eighteen chapters, including Canada.[18]

The changes we see in today's media coverage of the gay community are the result of all these factors working simultaneously and converging in the 1990s. Whereas the news media had routinely excluded gays and lesbians for decades lest coverage of such topics offend "family-oriented" readers and viewers, by the early nineties the media were eager to attract gays. As gays became more visible, they became an appealing segment of the marketplace. By some liberal estimates attendance at the 1993 March on Washington topped one million—only a fraction of the millions of gays in America. Advertising executives and marketers began to figure out that if gays one day proved to be 10 percent of the population, as some have claimed, their annual disposable income could be as high as $500 billion.[19]

In addition, editors and producers in some newsrooms began to see gay journalists as resources who can provide understanding and insight into the gay community and can spot stories that straight reporters fail to recognize. "Being gay and covering a gay story to me are never inconsistent—never," said *Miami Herald* urban affairs editor Justin Gillis. "Having a gay reporter cover a gay issue in a sophisticated way is, as a rule, a good thing. That person brings a skill and an ability at dialogue with people being covered, sources, and knowledge of the community."[20]

As might be expected, given the history of gays, lesbians, and the news media, gays' heightened visibility in the news and in newsrooms brought backlash. Televangelist Pat Robertson, for example, regularly complained of a gay conspiracy to shape coverage of gays. In the spring of 1995 his *700 Club* carried a report that used the NLGJA as evidence that the national news media had lost touch with basic American values.[21]

Syndicated columnist Cal Thomas, the former media director for Jerry Falwell's now-defunct Moral Majority, was another vocal critic of the gay presence in the nation's newsrooms. "Never has it been more necessary for the public to analyze the information it receives from the media in order to determine whether it is truth or propaganda," Thomas wrote after the NLGJA's Washington convention in 1995. "Increasingly, when it comes to homosexuality, the press cannot be trusted."[22]

Thomas's criticism was echoed in articles by conservative columnist and media critic L. Brent Bozell III of the Media Research Center in Alexandria, Virginia: "We are supposed to believe that an association of journalists would not have an ideological agenda because its members insist they are objective? There's nothing objective about a group whose agenda is far left of Mr. Clinton's."[23]

In Texas a newspaper began receiving threatening phone calls after it ran two gay-related stories on the same day. Soon afterward a pipe bomb exploded in one of the paper's vending racks.[24]

Elizabeth Weise, a lesbian reporter in the Associated Press's San Francisco bureau, began receiving faxes from Fred Phelps, a fundamentalist Baptist minister from Topeka, Kansas, who picketed the memorial service for Randy Shilts, the *San Francisco Chronicle* reporter who died of AIDS in 1994. Phelps addressed his intimidating faxes to "Elizabeth Weise, Fag Reporter."[25]

An openly lesbian reporter at the Portland *Oregonian* became embroiled in a controversy over a proposed state-wide anti-gay ballot measure, after she spoke as a panelist at an NLGJA conference in 1994. But after supporters of the measure picketed the *Oregonian*, publisher Fred Stickel dismissed their complaints as a"tempest in a teapot."[26] In an earlier era such criticism would have sent news executives into hasty retreat. But in the 1990s some in the news media—the *Oregonian* in particular—have begun to show resolve in defending their efforts to portray a broader perspective of society, despite the criticism. In a sense the backlash from antigay critics is a measure of success.

Despite all the improvements in how the media approach stories about gays and lesbians, the news continues to reflect an undercurrent of bias. Even in the 1990s the news media fail to apply the same standards of fairness to gays and lesbians that are afforded other minorities. The news media continue to practice a double standard when writing about gays and lesbians. Although many more stories appear with far greater frequency than in the past, the visibility is obscured by numerous examples of journalists' failing to apply the same standards of fairness to news about gays that guide their coverage of other minorities.

In particular the reporters continue to write about the rights and dignities of gays as controversial topics that require "balance," giving antigay fanatics a platform from which to propound their bigotry under the guise of providing "the other side." Although it would be unthinkable for journalists to interview a Ku Klux Klan member or neo-Nazi for stories about African

Americans or Jews—or to interview a misogynist for a story on women's rights—the media think nothing of routinely including demeaning and hateful remarks from bigots and antigay zealots in stories about gay rights.[27]

In a similar manner many reporters continue to provide a platform for those who want to castigate gays and lesbians with the rhetoric of "family values" without recognizing their underlying prejudice. And columnists are equally unthinking. Antisemitic remarks by televangelist Pat Robertson and by Patrick Buchanan have sparked an outpouring of condemnation. But the editorial boards and columnists leave unchallenged derogatory characterizations of gays by Robertson and Buchanan. Buchanan has said that gays are "medically ruinous" (by spreading disease to the population at large) and terms AIDS as "nature's form of retribution" against homosexuals.[28] On his *700 Club* Robertson has compared gays to satanists.

The media's double standard was at work in 1992 when former presidential candidate Robertson attacked supporters of an equal rights amendment in Iowa, claiming the feminist agenda "encourages women to leave their husbands, kill their children, practice witchcraft, destroy capitalism and become lesbians." The Associated Press wire crackled as it sent Robertson's bizarre assessment of Iowa's equal rights amendment to newspapers and broadcast stations across the nation. But when Robertson attempts to demonize only gays, as he has on numerous occasions, those attacks go unreported. On his *700 Club* in 1993 and 1994 Robertson blamed gays for a series of natural disasters, including California earthquakes and midwestern floods. After showing a segment on gay protests at churches Robertson said,

> And now we have a country, ladies and gentleman, that permits blasphemy in our motion pictures, blasphemy in our literature, blasphemy on our television, blasphemy in our schoolrooms and classrooms, and in our colleges and universities. [It] not only accepts homosexuality but protects it. . . . It's wrong and we say it boldly, and they don't want to be told that their lifestyle is sinful. But God's word is immutable, and we will violate it at our peril. . . . We're not standing in judgment; we're telling the truth of what God Almighty is doing.[29]

The average American probably never heard of attempts by the Montana legislature in March 1995 to pass a measure requiring anyone convicted of a consensual homosexual act to register with the police as a violent offender, as murderers and rapists are required to do. The proposal, which was defeated in committee, was vastly underreported by the media. As lawmakers in Utah and South Dakota considered measures that would legalize same-sex unions, the news media carried little in-depth reporting on the importance of marriage to gays.

When Secret Service personnel donned protective rubber gloves to process a delegation of gay leaders visiting the White House in June 1995, the incident made headlines only after President Bill Clinton apologized for their actions.[30] If there was an outpouring of condemnation on the op-ed pages of the nation's newspapers, it was hard to detect. *New York Times* columnist Frank Rich, for one, recognized that the rubber gloves were only an example of the much larger problem of discrimination against gays. Imagine the outcry if a delegation of African Americans or women had been greeted in similar manner.

In some cases news about gays goes unreported because the media have simply failed to ask pertinent questions. Few examined the basis of an advertisement that ran in midwestern newspapers to condemn Gay and Lesbian History Month in public schools. The advertisement cited a study claiming that homosexuals are "a group of people who prey on the innocence of minors." The *St. Louis Post-Dispatch* dug into the story and found that the conservative group that placed it had misrepresented the study's findings.[31]

It is safe to predict that the media would condemn a referendum to deny civil rights protection to blacks or women. But when ballot initiatives were considered in Maine, Ohio, Florida, Colorado, Idaho, and Oregon to remove legal protections for gays, few in the mainstream media condemned them as legislative homophobia.

The news media also continue to fall into homophobic traps without realizing it. In the summer of 1991, for example, the media ran a rash of stories describing evidence of a genetic basis for homosexuality. Seeing it as a story about a scientific advancement, a host of newspapers—including the *New York Times* and the *Washington Post*—ran the gene story on page one, and it got prominent play on network television. It even merited a segment on ABC's *Nightline. Time* reported the story and *Newsweek*'s cover line gave it a dramatic touch: IS THIS CHILD GAY?[32]

In an early edition a *New York Times* headline referred to a "brain discrepancy" among gays. It was not clear whether the phrase was used by a scientist quoted in the story, but that terminology did not appear in other major newspapers, including the *Washington Post, Chicago Tribune,* and *Wall Street Journal. Times* editors changed the headline for later editions, dropping the reference to a discrepancy. The *Post* has continued to report on the gene research, carrying at least four stories on further developments, three of them on its front page, since August 1991.[33]

No doubt some gays would welcome evidence that homosexuality is not a chosen lifestyle—as many antigay critics have long maintained—but the tone of the articles and their prominent placement imply that the discovery may lead to a "cure." Clearly many journalists do not recognize that the "cure" for a minority that does not consider itself ill is tantamount to genocide.

It is difficult to believe that stories about the origins of any other minority would produce news stories as simplistic and superficial as the articles about the gay gene. But the news media routinely report scientific hypotheses as if they were fact. Compounding the problem for gays is a tendency among the media to continue to underreport or ignore stories that are considered too complex for a general audience. As a result the media often dwell on conflict and controversy involving gays but gloss over more complex stories that speak to what it is like to be gay.

Another example of this pattern is the news media's approach to covering the gay movement. Although audiences frequently see stories about the heads of the NAACP or NOW, the news media rarely focus on the leaders of the gay and lesbian rights organizations. When they do cover the gay political movement, journalists often fail to pose difficult—but fair—questions, motivated perhaps by their new-found desire to please gay readers. Who are the leaders of the gay and lesbian political organizations? How do these groups spend their money? How effective are they? Do they offer a compelling vision of the role of gays and lesbians in American society? Are their claims valid?

The upshot of all of this is that many journalists still have not helped the public grasp the complexities of gay life. Seldom do they focus on what it's like to be a gay teenager, a gay in the military, a gay professional, a gay victim of a hate crime, or the length of the struggle for gay rights. Gay activists must have been stunned to hear Cynthia Tucker, editorial page editor of the *Atlanta Constitution*, comment on the importance of the 1993 March on Washington. "I think one thing many citizens don't understand, including many citizens here in Georgia, is that gays can be actively discriminated against," she said in an appearance on PBS's *MacNeil-Lehrer Newshour*, for which she is a regular analyst. "Many people don't yet understand that gays can be discriminated against in housing and in the workplace, and I think that's part of the public education campaign that has to continue."[34] What Tucker did not say was that it was the news media—not gay activists—that have failed for decades to inform the public about what it's like to be gay in America.

This is not to say that gays and lesbians should be allowed to veto stories they find offensive, any more than that right should be given to any other segment of the political landscape. The First Amendment guarantees the press's freedom to report the news however it chooses. Bias, like beauty, is in the eye of the beholder, and even the earliest gay activists recognized that the remedy for the distortions they saw in the news was not censorship but enlightenment.

The critical point here is this: There is a pretense to journalism that provides journalists with a false sense of security, leading them to believe that, despite the many pressures they face each day, they cover news accurately and fairly. In reality they frequently fall short of their own standards, particularly in covering minorities. In the case of gays and lesbians the reporting falls short of the ideal in numerous ways:

- A fair press cannot claim to reflect society but exclude groups of people because they might hurt media profits.
- A fair press cannot overrely on official sources, who have their own axes to grind, and claim to offer objective news.
- A fair press cannot preclude members of minority groups from covering their own communities because editors fear they will be any more biased than another reporter.
- A fair press cannot exclude minority voices from the ranks of newsroom management and claim to support equality and justice.
- A fair press cannot let the facts speak for themselves but must put them in a context that readers, viewers, and listeners can understand.
- A fair press does not restrict itself to both sides of an issue but as many sides as necessary for people to be understood.
- A fair press cannot perpetuate derogatory stereotypes and consider itself an accurate source of news.
- A fair press cannot rationalize its motives but must examine itself to see if it is what it claims to be.
- A fair press must find ways to reflect all segments of society.

In looking at the coverage of gays and lesbians from the 1940s to today, it is striking how often the double standard has been defended by the media, most often under the guise of protecting the sensitivities of their audiences. But gays and lesbians—like anyone else—have a right to expect fair and accurate coverage from the news media, regardless of the personal beliefs and values of journalists who write the news. They have this right because this is what the news media promise—to report the news fairly and impartially.

What journalists have failed to grasp is that it is as unfair for them to render gays invisible or paint them as a menace as it is for society to deny them employment or housing. Many journalists do not realize that traditional reporting techniques—so-called straight news—can produce distortion that hurts people. Whether the news media can accurately and fairly report on the many facets of our society is a long-debated topic on which there has been no consensus. But what is increasingly clear is that the news media play a critical role in how we understand the world around us, especially aspects of the world and society that are beyond our personal experiences. We look to the news media for information and for a sense of how we should respond.

Few journalists have understood as well as noted magazine editor Frederick Lewis Allen how difficult it is for the news media to portray reality accurately and fairly. Newspapers, Allen wrote in *Atlantic Monthly* in 1922, "are the eyes through which largely we see life in our time, and the news that they print is in great measure the raw materials of our ideas. Nothing is more important than that through these eyes we shall see, not a distorted picture, but the reality."[35]

NOTES

INTRODUCTION

1. Stephen J. Flynn, "Turn-About Not Fair Play, Say Beach Police," *Miami Herald*, November 21, 1953, p. 1.

2. Gay journalist and historian Jim Kepner, writing under the pseudonym Lyn Pedersen, called attention to the hysteria surrounding the Miami witch-hunt in the January 1954 issue of *One* magazine in a cover story headlined MIAMI JUNKS THE CONSTITUTION and again in the April–May 1956 issue. His articles are the most complete accounts available.

3. Editorial, "Treat with Them for What They Are," *Miami Herald*, July 28, 1954, p. 6-A. In 1952 Miami adopted an ordinance that banned "femmics"—men who dressed as women—and prohibited drag shows. But the authorities allowed the gay bars along Powder Puff Lane to remain open. The police claimed the bars made it easier for them to keep tabs on the "perverts." This has been a traditional rationale for police in many cities.

4. Cited in "This Is Miami!" *ONE*, October 1954, pp. 16–17.

5. Chester Eldredge, "Official Urges Society to Face Pervert Problem," *Miami Herald*, August 11, 1954, p. 1.

6. Cited in Lyn Pedersen, "Miami Hurricane," *ONE*, November 1954, p. 5.

7. Stephen J. Flynn, "Beach Police Round Up 35 in Pervert Crackdown," *Miami Herald*, August 13, 1954, p. D-1.

8. Letters to the Editor, "Just Execute Them All," *Miami Herald*, July 18, 1954, p. 3-F.

9. Michael Browning, Karen Branch, and Jack Wheat, "Papers Show How Gays Were Rooted Out," *Miami Herald*, July 2, 1993, p. 1-A. By May 1964 the Johns Committee had pulled the certifications of seventy-one teachers throughout the state's public schools and caused the firing of some fourteen professors or assistant professors at state universities. Ironically, the only person who was confronted with criminal charges was a reporter at the *Orlando Sentinel* who had written articles exposing the committee's activities.

10. Jack Nelson, "1,500 Sex Deviates Roam Streets Here," *Atlanta Constitution*, October 11, 1954, p. 2. Today Nelson is chief Washington correspondent and former bureau chief for the *Los Angeles Times*.

11. Cited in John Gerassi, *The Boys of Boise: Furor, Vice, and Folly in an American City* (New York: Macmillan, 1966), p. 3.

12. Ibid., p. 14.

13. "Parkway Police Seizing Soliciting Homosexuals," *New York Times*, February 23, 1978, p. 38.

14. Dennis McQuail, *Mass Communication Theory*, 3d ed. (Thousand Oaks, Calif.: Sage, 1994).

15. Robert C. Doty, "Growth of Overt Homosexuality in City Provokes Wide Concern," *New York Times*, December 17, 1963, p. 1; Columbia Broadcasting System, "The Homosexuals," *CBS Reports*, March 7, 1967; Jack Star, "The Sad 'Gay' Life," *Look*, January 10, 1967, p. 30; Susan Banashek and Al Martinez, "Night Shoppers—Fantasy in the Market Aisles," *Los Angeles Times*, August 14, 1974, p. 1.

16. Quoted in David L. Altheide, *Creating Reality: How TV News Distorts Events* (Beverly Hills, Calif.: Sage, 1976), p. 17.

17. An example of the subjective nature of news was the December 1993 ABC News special, "The 12 Most Fascinating People of 1993." When asked how the twelve had been selected, host Barbara Walters explained, "The names came from our staff and whoever happened to be walking by during those weeks we were putting the list together" (John Carmody, "TV Column," *Washington Post*, November 19, 1993, p. D-4).

18. Herbert J. Gans, *Deciding What's News: A Study of CBS Evening News, NBC Nightly News, Newsweek, and Time* (New York: Pantheon, 1979), p. 39.

19. William L. Rivers, "The Negro and the News: A Case Study," in Wilber Schramm and Donald F. Roberts, eds., *The Process and Effects of Mass Communication* (Urbana: University of Illinois Press, 1971), pp. 151–68.

20. Lincoln Steffens, *The Autobiography of Lincoln Steffens* (New York: Harcourt, Brace, 1931), p. 223. Ironically, in the 1970s a New York beach that was named for Riis became a popular gay cruising area.

21. Nan Robertson, interview by author, May 11, 1992, Washington, D.C.

22. In his book *Deciding What's News* sociologist Herbert Gans says that 70 to 85 percent of all domestic news during the late 1960s and early 1970s concerned well-known people and those in official positions. Media consultant Tom Koch says Gans's figures are probably conservative (Richard Harwood, "Reporting on, by, and for an Elite," *Washington Post*, May 28, 1994, p. A29).

23. Gans, *Deciding What's News,* p. 101.

24. Leon V. Sigal, *Reporters and Officials: The Organization and Politics of Newsmaking* (Lexington, Mass: D. C. Heath, 1973), p. 5; Warren Breed, "Social Control in the Newsroom: A Functional Analysis," *Social Forces* 33 (May 1955): 326–35.

25. Ben H. Bagdikian, *The Media Monopoly,* 4th ed. (Boston: Beacon Press, 1992), p. 3–26.

26. David Shaw, "The Press and Sex," *Los Angeles Times,* August 19, 1991, p. A-19.

27. David Harris, *Dreams Die Hard* (New York: St. Martin's/Marek, 1982), p. 329. Harris did not divulge the names of the individuals who complained.

28. Stuart Byron, "The Closet Syndrome," in Karla Jay and Allen Young, eds., *Out of the Closets: Voices of Gay Liberation* (New York: New York University, 1982), pp. 58–65.

29. The first public protest by gays was held in New York on September 19, 1964, when the League for Sexual Freedom sponsored a picket line at the Whitehall Street Induction Center to protest the long-standing discrimination against gays by the military. The picket line at the White House in April 1965 was the first by an organization of gays and lesbians.

30. Leroy Aarons, interview by author, August 8, 1990, Rosslyn, Va.

31. "10 Oppose Gov't on Homosexuals," *Washington Afro-American,* April 20, 1965. A cameraman from a local television station watched the protest, but no coverage was ever broadcast, according to the *Insider,* newsletter of the Mattachine Society of Washington, April 1965, p. 1 (from the files of Franklin Kameny).

32. Perry Deane Young, interview by author, July 13, 1990, Washington, D.C.

33. Perry Deane Young, "South Toward Home," *Independent Weekly,* March 11–17, 1992, p. 7; Young interview.

34. Sharon Shaw Johnson, interview by author, July 24, 1992 (telephone).

I. A COMMUNITY DISCOVERS ITSELF

1. George Chauncey, *Gay New York: Gender, Urban Culture, and the Making of the Gay Male World 1890–1940* (New York: Basic, 1994), p. 310.

2. Miriam Ottenberg, "How the Navy's 'Mind Detectives' Seek Men of Sound Nerve for Warfare," *Sunday Star,* January 10, 1943, p. B-5.

3. Carl Binger, M.D., "How We Screen Out Psychological 4-F's," *Saturday Evening Post,* January 8, 1944, p. 19.

4. "Homosexuals in Uniform," *Newsweek,* June 9, 1947, p. 54.

5. Jeffrey Weeks, *Coming Out* (London: Quartet Books, 1977), p. 31; Jonathan Ned Katz, *Gay American History: Lesbians and Gay Men in the U.S.A.,* rev. ed. (New York: Meridian, 1992), pp. 23–24.

6. John D'Emilio, *Sexual Politics, Sexual Communities: The Making of a Homosexual Minority in the United States, 1940–1970* (Chicago: University of Chicago Press, 1983), p. 35.

7. "K-Day," *Time,* August 31, 1953, p. 52.

8. Cited in Martin Duberman, "1948," *New York Native,* June 29–July 12, 1981, p. 15.

9. "Something Ought to Be Done," *WMCA,* cited in Duberman, "1948," p. 15.

10. Max Lerner, "Scandal in the State Department, *New York Post,* July 13, 1950, p. 2.

11. Allan Bérubé, *Coming Out Under Fire: The History of Gay Men and Women in World War II* (New York: Free Press, 1990) p. 266.

12. "Perverts Called Government Peril," *New York Times,* April 19, 1950, p. 25; "Object Lesson: Problem of Homosexuals in the Government," *Time,* December 25, 1950, p. 10; "State Department Fires 531 Perverts, Security Risks," *Los Angeles Herald-Express,* July 2, 1953; "U.S.

Ousted 425 on Morals," *New York Times*, April 13, 1953, p. 20. For the number of firings see John D'Emilio, *Making Trouble* (New York: Routledge, 1992), p. 60.

13. Max Lerner, "Scandal in the State Dept.," *New York Post*, July 10–23, 1950. Lerner wrote a second in-depth report on homosexuality, a nine-part *New York Post* series titled, "The Tragedy of the 'Gay'" (January 18–27, 1954). As a starting point, he described the grisly poisoning of a New York couple and the arrest of their homosexual son and his lover on homicide charges. The series went on to describe homosexual life, the views of psychiatry, methods used in schools and homes "to deal with the problem," and the alleged connection between homosexuality and crime. He pointed out, "They dislike the words 'homo,' 'fairy,' 'fag,' 'Nance,' 'fruit,' 'pansy,' 'queer,' and others by which a hostile world expresses its contempt. They call themselves 'gay,' using the word as both a noun and an adjective." In the case of the homicide Lerner concluded that "the homosexuality of the boys did not lead to the crime itself, it was part of the total web of their distorted growth."

14. Lerner, "Scandal in the State Dept.," July 23, 1950, p. 2.

15. Anthony Leviero, "New Security Plan Issued; Thousands Face Re-Inquiry," *New York Times*, April 28, 1953, p. 1.

16. "Performers Get Network Edicts," *Variety*, March 29, 1950, p. 33.

17. Turner Catledge, *My Life and the Times* (New York: Harper & Row, 1971), p. 225.

18. D'Emilio, *Sexual Politics*, pp. 49–50.

19. Eric Gordon, "March 12th Dinner Honors Gay Liberation Movement," *Heritage*, newsletter of the Southern California Library for Social Studies and Research, Winter 1994, p. 1.

20. Dale Jennings, interview by author, June 10, 1994, Los Angeles.

21. Ibid.

22. Katz, *Gay American History*, p. 415.

23. Marvin Cutler, *Homosexuals Today* (Los Angeles: One, Inc., 1956), p. 29.

24. Dale Jennings, interview by author, January 30, 1993 (telephone).

25. Several books have described Slater as a member of the Mattachine Society. However, in a May 3, 1995, letter to the author he said he never had joined the organization.

26. D'Emilio, *Sexual Politics,* pp. 87–88. The name *One* was suggested by Mattachine Society member Guy Rousseau, who borrowed it from the writings of Thomas Carlyle: "A mystic bond of brotherhood makes all men one."

27. Don Slater, letter to author, May 3, 1995.

28. Paul V. Coates, "Well, Medium, and Rare," *Los Angeles Daily Mirror*, March 12, 1953, p. 8.

29. Cutler, *Homosexuals Today,* p. 48.

30. W. Dorr Legg, interview by author, February 8, 1993, Los Angeles.

31. Newsletter, San Francisco Mattachine Society, June 25, 1954.

32. Transcript, Mattachine Society file, ONE Institute, Baker Memorial Library, Los Angeles.

33. Television column, *Daily Mirror,* May 5, 1954, sec. 2, p. 7; KAP, "Confidential File," *Daily Variety*, May 4, 1954, p. 9.

34. David L. Freeman, "For Courage: One Salutes Curtis White," *ONE*, May 1954, p. 27.

35. Curtis White, Letters to the Editor, *ONE*, July 1954, p. 25. White, who still does not want to be identified, later dropped out of the Mattachine Society and became a successful executive at a leading Los Angeles public relations firm.

36. Don Slater, interview by the author, October 24, 1995 (telephone).

37. Jennings interview, 1994.

38. Ann Carll Reid, "Editorial," *ONE*, March 1957, p. 9. For details of the court cases see 241

F. 2d 772 or *ONE*, March 1957, pp. 5–20. The ruling stemmed from the 1957 decision in *Roth v. United States* (354 U.S. 476) in which the Court sustained the conviction of a pornography dealer but at the same time declared that "sex and obscenity are not synonymous." From then on only materials that appealed to an individual's "prurient interest" could be successfully prosecuted [John D'Emilio and Estelle B. Freedman, *Intimate Matters: A History of Sexual America* (New York: Harper & Row, 1988)].

During the 1950s and 1960s gay and lesbian organizations used the term *homophile* as a euphemism for *homosexual*. Activists thought using *homophile* would deemphasize the sexual aspect of homosexuality and reflect a broader emotion. In addition, they used the word as a signal that acknowledging one's homosexuality or even being gay was not a requirement for membership.

39. "Court Voids City Law on Union Aides," *Los Angeles Times*, January 14, 1958, p. 8.

40. Almost a decade earlier "Lisa Ben" had written a small newsletter in Los Angeles called *Vice Versa*. From June 1947 to February 1948 she relied on a laborious process at her office at the RKO Movie Studios where she would type one original with four carbon copies, then reload her typewriter, and repeat the process until she had ten copies. At first she relied on the postal service for delivery but learned that it was illegal to send material about lesbians through the mail, so she began to deliver them by hand. After her ninth issue she left RKO, and *Vice Versa* ended. But for several years copies of the newsletter continued to circulate among women who had never seen any other information about lesbians.

41. Barbara Gittings, interview by author, August 12, 1992 (telephone).

42. Lorrie Talbot, "A Daughter Watches T.V.," *The Ladder*, March 19, 1958, p. 10; Ann Warren Griffith, "Conversation at Midday," *New York Herald Tribune*, March 9, 1958, TV sec., p. 7. According to Talbot, the women who did appear on the program were author Helen King and psychiatrist Helen Hendin.

43. Ronald Bayer, *Homosexuality and American Psychiatry: The Politics of Diagnosis* (New York: Basic, 1981), pp. 21–27.

44. Edmund Bergler, *Homosexuality: Disease or Way of Life?* (New York: Basic, 1956), pp. 27, 7.

45. Max Lerner, "The Tortured Problem," *New York Post*, January 14, 1957, p. 28.

46. D'Emilio, *Sexual Politics*, p. 115.

2. OUT OF THE SHADOWS

1. Del Martin, "Public Press Goes Wild!" *The Ladder*, November 1958, p. 6.

2. "Society Probes Problem of Perversion," *Denver Post*, September 5, 1959, p. 3; Letters to the Editor, "The Open Forum," *Denver Post*, September 14, 1959, p. 25.

3. Ron Johnson, "Wolden in 'Smear' Campaign," *San Francisco Examiner*, October 8, 1959, p. 1; Del Martin, "History of S.F. Homophile Groups," *The Ladder*, October 1966, p. 9; Editorial, "Wolden Should Withdraw," *San Francisco Chronicle*, October 10, 1959, p. 1.

4. "'Organized Homosexuals' Issue in S.F. Election," *The Ladder*, October 1959, p. 8.

5. Del Martin, "2-Hour Broadcast on Homophile Problem," *The Ladder*, January 1959, pp. 7–14.

6. In 1973 Pacifica's WBAI in New York set off a storm of controversy when it broadcast a twelve-minute segment from a George Carlin comedy album titled "Filthy Words," which Carlin described as seven words "you couldn't say on the public airwaves." After receiving complaints from listeners, the Federal Communications Commission reprimanded the station and ordered stations to restrict the broadcast of indecent language to hours when children were not in the audience. The Pacifica Foundation challenged the reprimand in court but lost. Ultimately, the U.S.

Supreme Court also ruled against Pacifica, holding that the First Amendment does not bar the government from prohibiting the broadcast of words that may not be obscene but are "patently offensive" (*Federal Communications Commission v. Pacifica Foundation*, 438 U.S. 726 [1978]).

7. John D'Emilio, *Sexual Politics, Sexual Communities: The Making of a Homosexual Minority in the United States, 1940–1970* (Chicago: University of Chicago Press, 1983), p. 35.

8. "Big Sex Raid—Cops Arrest 103," *San Francisco Chronicle*, August 14, 1961, p. 3.

9. Ernest Lenn, "Special Cops for 'Gay' Bars," *San Francisco Examiner*, October 12, 1961, p. 3.

10. Laud Humphreys, *Out of the Closet* (Englewood Cliffs, N.J., Prentice-Hall, 1972) p. 114.

11. Beth Hughes, "San Francisco's Own Stonewall," *San Francisco Examiner*, Gay in America series, June 4, 1989, p. 3.

12. Transcript, "The Rejected" (San Francisco: Pan-Graphic Press, 1963), p. 9.

13. Ibid., p. 24.

14. Mattachine Society of New York Collection, International Gay Information Center Papers, New York Public Library.

15. "Television Breakthrough Brings Favorable Comment," *Mattachine Review*, October 1961, p. 2.

16. All three reviews are quoted in "Calling Shots," *Mattachine Review*, October 1961, p. 17.

17. "Paul Coates Interviews," *The Ladder*, July 1962, p. 15.

18. John M. Goshko, "House Group Continues Homosexuality Hearing," *Washington Post*, August 10, 1963, p. C-2.

19. Robert Doty, "Growth of Overt Homosexuality in City Provokes Wide Concern," *New York Times*, December 17, 1963, p. 1.

20. A. M. Rosenthal did not respond to letters or telephone calls requesting an interview. This account comes from Harrison Salisbury, *Without Fear or Favor* (New York: Times Books, 1980), p. 416, and Harrison Salisbury, interview by author, August 12, 1992 (telephone).

21. Curtis Dewees, interview by author, November 21, 1993 (telephone).

22. Jack O'Brien, "Jack O'Brien Says," *New York Journal-American*, July 9, 1962, p. 47.

23. Jack Gould, "Radio: Taboo Is Broken," *New York Times*, July 16, 1962, p. 48; "Minority Listening: Homosexuals on Radio Station WBAI," *Newsweek*, July 30, 1962, p. 48.

24. John LeRoy, "The New Publicity Break: Where Do We Go from Here?" *The Ladder*, December 1962, pp. 16–17.

25. Randolfe Wicker, interview by author, September 24, 1992, New York.

26. Ronald Bayer, *Homosexuality and American Psychiatry: The Politics of Diagnosis* (Princeton: Princeton University Press, 1981), pp. 49–53.

27. Doty, "Growth of Overt Homosexuality."

28. Bayer, *Homosexuality and American Psychiatry*, pp. 49–53.

29. Wicker interview.

30. Philip Gerard, "Symptom of the Times," *The Ladder*, December 1964, pp. 9–12; "City Side," *Newsweek*, December 30, 1963, p. 42.

31. Wicker appeared on the *Les Crane Show* on January 31, 1964.

32. Data obtained from *Readers' Guide to Periodical Literature*, March 1963–February 1965 and March 1965–February 1966.

33. Robert Trumbull, "Homosexuals Proud of Deviancy, Medical Academy Study Finds," *New York Times*, May 19, 1964, p. 1.

34. "Breakthrough: When Will It Come?" *Mattachine Review*, April–September 1964, p. 4.

35. Paul Welch, "Homosexuality in America," *Life*, June 26, 1964, pp. 68–80.

36. Don Slater, interview by author, January 3, 1993 (telephone).

37. "Breakthrough," p. 7; *One*, June 1964, p. 2; L.E.E., "Cross-Currents," *The Ladder*, July 1964, p. 23.

38. Jean White, "Homophile Groups Argue Civil Liberties," *Washington Post*, October 11, 1964, p. B-10.

39. Max Frankel, "President's Aide Quits on Report of Morals Chase," *New York Times*, October 15, 1964, p. 1.

40. Editorial, "Law and the Homosexual Problem," *Life*, June 11, 1965, p. 4; "Tangents," *ONE*, August 1965, p. 14.

41. "The Homosexual in America," *Time*, January 21, 1966, pp. 40–41.

42. "Cross-Currents," *The Ladder*, March 1966, p. 18.

43. Kopkind, who died in 1994, left *Time* in 1965 to become an associate editor at the *New Republic*, founded two magazines in the early 1970s, and later became a top editor at the *Nation*. Andrew Kopkind, interview by author, March 21, 1992. See also Andrew Kopkind, *The Thirty Years' Wars: Dispatches and Diversions of a Radical Journalist, 1965–1994* (New York: Verso, 1995).

44. Paul Hofmann, "Cuban Government Is Alarmed by Increase in Homosexuality," *New York Times*, April 16, 1965, p. 2.

45. "10 Oppose Gov't on Homosexuals," *Washington Afro-American*, April 20, 1965.

46. "Picketing Results," *The Ladder*, May 1966, p. 19.

3. FRONT PAGE NEWS

1. Jean M. White. "Those Others: A Report on Homosexuality," *Washington Post*, January 31–February 4, 1965.

2. "Cross-Currents," *The Ladder*, April 1965, p. 19.

3. Bob Whearley, "'Militant Minority' Poses Serious Problem for Society," *Denver Post*, February 14, 1965, p. 25.

4. Editorial, "Editorial: Homosexuals in Denver," *Denver Post*, February 25, 1965, p. 18.

5. Letter from Mattachine Society member Elver Barker to Bob Whearley, Mattachine Society of New York Collection, International Gay Information Center Papers, New York Public Library.

6. Dick Hebert, "Detectives Watch Hangouts and Curb Some of Activity," *Atlanta Constitution*, Atlanta's Lonely 'Gay' World series, January 2–8, 1966. Quote is from January 4, 1966, p. 1.

7. Joseph Kahn, "Our Penal Code," *New York Post*, December 27–31, 1965. Quote is from December 28, 1965, p. 25.

8. James A. Wechsler, "Entrapment Inc." (editorial), *New York Post*, March 7, 1966, p. 26.

9. Eric Pace, "Garelik Urges Public to Report Police Trapping of Homosexuals," *New York Times*, April 2, 1966, p. 1.

10. Editorial, "Entrapment, Inc." *New York Post*, April 5, 1966, p. 30.

11. D'Emilio, *Sexual Politics*, p. 208. New York City prohibited homosexuals of either sex from "remaining in or being employed in cabarets" and from making "a rendezvous of dance halls." In 1971 the Department of Consumer affairs relaxed its regulations during the term of Mayor John Lindsay.

12. George Chauncey, *Gay New York: Gender, Urban Culture, and the Making of the Gay Male World 1890–1940* (New York: Basic, 1994), pp. 331–54.

13. Dick Leitsch, interview by author, September 29, 1992 (telephone).

14. Lucy Komisar, "Three Homosexuals in Search of a Drink," *Village Voice*, May 5, 1966, p. 15.

15. Charles Grutzner, "S.L.A. Won't Act Against Bars Refusing Service to Deviates," *New York Times*, April 26, 1966, p. 55.

16. Bob Rose, "Dateline Chicago," *Chicago Daily News*, November 17, 1965, p. 3; "Bob Rose, Daily News columnist," *Mattachine Midwest Newsletter*, December 1965, p. 5.

17. Lois Wille, "The Homosexuals—A Growing Problem," *Chicago Daily News*, The Twilight World series, June 20–23, 1966; Lois Wille, interview by author, February 11, 1993 (telephone).

18. Lois Wille, "Homosexual Clergyman Tells of His Bizarre Double Life," *Chicago Daily News*, The Twilight World series, June 20–23, 1966, p. 3.

19. Irv Kupcinet, "Kup's Column," *Chicago Sun-Times*, September 29, 1966, p. 106. Despite Kupcinet's arch tone, he often publicized events involving Chicago gays in his newspaper column and on his TV talk show when few, if any, in the media showed any interest.

20. L.E.E., "The Invisible Woman," *The Ladder*, June 1965, p. 4.

21. Donn Teal, *The Gay Militants* (St. Martin's Press, 1995 [1971]), p. 214.

22. Psychiatrists' estimates reported in Irving Bieber, "Speaking Frankly on a Once Taboo Subject," *New York Times Magazine*, August 23, 1964, p. 75; activists' claim cited in Jean M. White, "A Moral-Medical Dilemma, *Chicago Sun-Times*, May 30, 1965, p. 23.

23. Phyllis Lyon, interview by author, September 15, 1992 (telephone).

24. Ibid.

25. Judy Klemesrud, "The Disciples of Sappho, Updated," *New York Times Magazine*, March 28, 1971, p. 28.

26. Warren D. Adkins, "The Washington-Baltimore TV Circuit," *Homosexual Citizen*, newsletter of the Washington Mattachine Society, May 1967, p. 6. Adkins was a pseudonym that Jack Nichols used.

27. Ibid.

28. Jack Nichols, letter to the Executive Board, Mattachine Society of Washington, October 14, 1963. Personal files of Jack Nichols.

29. "Off the Cuff," *The Ladder*, special report, October 1964, p. 8.

30. Frank J. Howell, "Toward a Positive View of the Functioning Homosexual," *Vector*, March 1966, p. 11.

31. "The Homosexual in America," *Time*, January 21, 1966, pp. 40–41.

32. Stanley Kauffmann, "Homosexual Drama and Its Disguises," *New York Times*, January 23, 1966, p. C-1.

33. In his 1992 book *Acting Gay: Male Homosexuality in Modern Drama* (New York: Columbia University Press) drama scholar John M. Clum describes the article as "a classic example of the mixed signals that entrapped American playwrights: a few liberals posturing about society's responsibility for the closet, as if Kauffmann himself weren't maintaining the closet, followed by gross oversimplifications that dismiss the work of dramatists in question" (p. 181).

34. Stanley Kauffmann, "On the Acceptability of the Homosexual," *New York Times*, February 6, 1966, p. II-1.

35. David Halberstam, *The Powers That Be* (New York: Alfred A. Knopf, 1979), p. 303.

36. Turner Catledge Papers, Special Collections, Mitchell Memorial Library, Mississippi State University, Mississippi State, Mississippi.

37. Ben H. Bagdikian, *The Media Monopoly* (Boston: Beacon Press, 1983), p. 42.

38. Turner Catledge, *My Life and the Times* (New York: Harper & Row, 1971), p. 190.

39. John Brannon Albright, interview by author, September 8, 1992 (telephone).

40. Catledge, *My Life*, pp. 190, 246.

41. Fred Friendly, interview by author, October 6, 1992 (telephone).

42. William Peters, interview by author, November 5, 1992 (telephone).

43. Ibid.

44. Ibid. When the documentary finally aired, *New York Times* writer George Gent noted in a preview article that the network had "unveiled its long-awaited study on homosexuals." The story said, "It was not the program originally planned more than two and a half years ago, which was said to stress the more sensational aspects of the gay life" (George Gent, "TV: C.B.S. Reports on Homosexuals," *New York Times*, March 8, 1967, p. 91).

45. Lars Larson, interview by author, December 27, 1992 (telephone).

46. Jack Nichols, interviews by author, May 14, 1992, and October 25, 1992 (telephone).

47. Transcript, "The Homosexuals," *CBS Reports*, March 7, 1967.

48. Vito Russo, *The Celluloid Closet: Homosexuality in the Movies* (New York: Harper & Row, 1987), p. 153; Richard M. Levine, "How the Gay Lobby Has Changed Television," *TV Guide*, May 30, 1981, pp. 3–6; David Rothenberg, "Media Watch," *New York Native*, June 15–28, 1981, p. 8.

49. Rothenberg, "Media Watch," p. 7.

50. Mike Wallace, interview by author, October 13, 1992 (telephone).

51. "TV Key Previews," *Washington Star*, March 7, 1967, p. A-16; Gent, "TV: C.B.S. Reports on Homosexuals"; Clay Gowran, "Repeat: TV No Spot to Unload Garbage," *Chicago Tribune*, March 8, 1967, sec. 2-A, p. 4; Dean Gysel, "A Frank Look at Homosexuality," *Chicago Daily News*, March 8, 1967, p. 67. CBS officials adamantly rebuffed attempts to view the original documentary or the production notes from either the Peters or the Morgan versions, which are believed to be housed in the network's archives. "For a very long time CBS News has maintained the view that such materials, including outtakes, are, in essence, our notes and therefore not freely accessible," said Donald DeCesare, network vice president.

52. Larson interview.

53. Wallace interview.

54. Leon V. Sigal, *Reporters and Officials: The Organization and Politics of Newsmaking* (Lexington, Mass.: D. C. Heath, 1973), p. 69.

55. David Perlman, "A Medical View of the Homosexual," *San Francisco Chronicle*, June 19, 1968, p. 1.

56. David Perlman, interview by author, September 27, 1992 (telephone).

57. David Perlman, "The Homosexuals Reply to Doctor," *San Francisco Chronicle*, June 21, 1968, p. 1.

58. James W. Cheseboro, ed., *Gayspeak: Gay Male and Lesbian Communication* (New York: Pilgrim Press, 1981), p. 351.

59. "Where the Boys Are," *Time*, June 28, 1968, p. 80.

60. Richard Schickel, "Shock of a Hidden World," *Life*, November 1, 1968, pp. 34–38; "Where the Boys Are," *Time*.

61. Ronald Forsythe [Donn Teal], "Why Can't 'We' Live Happily Ever After, Too?" *New York Times*, February 23, 1969, p. II-1.

62. Donn Teal, "How Anguished Are Homosexuals?" *New York Times*, June 1, 1969, p. 23.

63. Donn Teal, interview by author, June 25, 1994, New York.

64. In October 1961 San Francisco gay activist Guy Strait began publishing the *League for Civil Education News*, which was the first attempt to distribute information about the homophile movement among patrons of the San Francisco gay bars. The magazine attracted a large readership by featuring stories about police harassment written in an inflammatory style. In 1963 Strait changed

the name of the publication to *Citizens' News* and claimed he was distributing seven thousand copies each month, outstripping sales of *One*, *The Ladder*, and the *Mattachine Review* combined. But the publication was never a financial success, and by the early 1970s *Citizens' News* had declined into a small smut magazine and then died. Strait also started a publication called *Cruise News &World Report* but ran into legal problems when *U.S. News and World Report* claimed copyright infringement.

65. Jeff Yarborough, "We Are Born," *Advocate*, October 6, 1992, p. 8. Dick Michaels and Bill Rand were pseudonyms, according to Yarborough. Jim Kepner, archivist of the International Gay and Lesbian Archives, Los Angeles, says that Michaels may have embellished his story a bit—the person actually arrested was Rand (Kepner, Letter to the Editor, *Advocate*, November 17, 1992, p. 12).

66. Stephen J. Sanswett, "A Homosexual Paper, the Advocate, Widens Readership, Influence," *Wall Street Journal*, November 3, 1975, p. 1.

67. Alan D. Winter, "The Gay Press: A History of the Gay Community and Its Publications" (Library of Congress, 1976), p. 48.

68. Rob Cole, interview by author, October 9, 1992 (telephone).

69. Nancy Tucker, interview by author, October 14, 1992 (telephone).

4. COVERING STONEWALL

1. "Police Begin Times Sq. Cleanup After Night Workers Complain," *New York Times*, February 6, 1969, p. 78.

2. Editorial, "Crime in Times Square," February 17, 1969, p. 34.

3. Letter from Theodore Bernstein to Marty Robinson, published in the Mattachine Midwest *Newsletter*, March 1969, p. 4.

4. Ronald Bayer, *Homosexuality and American Psychiatry: The Politics of Diagnosis* (Princeton: Princeton University Press, 1981), p. 40. In its annual index the *Times* listed articles about homosexuals under the category "Sex," one category ahead of "Sex Crimes," until 1971 when it created the category "Homosexuality."

5. Herb Caen column, *San Francisco Chronicle*, December 7, 1969, p. B-1.

6. Richard Goldstein, "Stonewall Riots," *New York*, April 19, 1993, pp. 121–22. Information about police treatment of lesbians comes from oral history tapes that were part of "Becoming Visible: The Legacy of Stonewall," an exhibit at the New York Public Library, June 18–Sept 24, 1994; the speakers were not identified.

7. This edition of the *Les Crane Show* aired on WABC-TV on January 31, 1964. Toby Marotta refers to Wicker's TV appearance and its influence on Hoose in *The Politics of Homosexuality* (New York: Houghton Mifflin, 1981), p. 93; Jerry Hoose, interview by author, November 9, 1992 (telephone).

8. Harold Pickett, "I Like to Call It an Uprising," and Frank Esselourne, "Doorman Remembers," *Gay Community News*, June 23, 1979, p. 10; Lucian Truscott IV, "Gay Power Comes to Sheridan Square," *Village Voice*, July 3, 1969, p. 1.

9. Jeremiah Newton, "Stonewall 25," anniversary panel discussion, Lesbian & Gay Community Center, New York, March 15, 1994. Newton participated in the Stonewall riots.

10. Dick Leitsch, "First Gay Riot: Police Raid on N.Y. Club Sets Off First Gay Riot," *Advocate*, September 1969, p. 3.

11. Ibid.

12. Ibid.

13. There is no way to confirm that Sikes was the reporter on the story. However, Mark Hawthorne, a former reporter at the *Times*, recalls that it was Sikes. Although interviews with

other staff members who worked on the metropolitan and copy desks at the *Times* on the night of the Stonewall riots failed to confirm this, the process of elimination confirms Hawthorne's recollection. During his ten-year career at *Times*, Sikes never advanced beyond the newspaper's copy desk. As was sometimes the practice at the *Times*, Sikes was sent from the copy desk to act as a reporter on the story but was not credited with a byline. Sikes probably knew of the Stonewall Inn because he lived in a small apartment on West Tenth Street, only a half block from the bar.

14. Albin Krebs, interviews by author, August 3, 1992, and March 9, 1993 (telephone).

15. Krebs interview, 1992.

16. Martha Shelley, interview by author, October 9, 1992 (telephone). Martha Shelley is a pseudonym.

17. Dennis Eskow, "3 Cops Hurt as Bar Raid Riles Crowd," *Sunday News*, June 29, 1969, p. 30.

18. Martin Duberman, *Stonewall* (New York: Dutton, 1993), pp. 194–200.

19. "Police Again Rout 'Village' Youths," *New York Times*, June 30, 1969, p. 22.

20. Jay Levin, "The Gay Anger Behind the Riots," *New York Post*, July 8, 1969, p. 36.

21. Jerry Lisker, "Homo Nest Raided, Queen Bees Are Stinging Mad," *New York Daily News*, July 6, 1969, p. B-1.

22. Ibid.

23. Lucian Truscott IV could count on the *Village Voice* to run his essays because his conservative point of view contrasted sharply with the newspaper's plentiful supply of essays by vocal and often combative liberals. The owners of the *Voice* saw their newspaper as a journalistic laboratory that would reflect a variety of opinions, generate controversy, and sell newspapers. Truscott proved to be a competent journalist. While in the army in 1970 he wrote an article for the *Voice* in which he described how soldiers in his platoon were returning from Vietnam addicted to heroin. One collapsed from an overdose and died in Truscott's arms. The article infuriated his superiors who arranged to have him ousted. He then became a full-time staff writer until the *Voice* was sold in 1974 to a group of investors headed by Clay Felker, editor of *New York* magazine. Truscott turned his attention to writing the novel *Dress Gray* (1979) and later became a Hollywood screen writer.

24. Lucian Truscott IV, interview by author, April 8, 1993 (telephone).

25. Howard Smith, "Full Moon over the Stonewall," *Village Voice*, July 3, 1969, p. 1.

26. Leitsch, "First Gay Riot," p. 1; Toby Marotta, *The Politics of Homosexuality* (Boston: Houghton Mifflin, 1981), p. 77. Reference to dropping hairpins was a humorous code among gays that goes back to the 1940s. "He let a hairpin drop," gays would say, describing a cue someone had given that he was homosexual.

27. Jack Nichols and Lige Clarke, "Pampered Perverts," *Screw*, July 25, 1969, p. 16.

28. Ellen Frankfort, *The Voice* (New York: William Morrow, 1976).

29. Another source of news about gays was *Gay Power*, a newspaper started by the underground newspaper *East Village Other*. Because it was owned by straights, GLF accused it of exploiting gays and denounced it. Even so, the newspaper thrived, according to Donn Teal in *The Gay Militants* (New York: St. Martin's Press, 1995 [1971]), and became "a near-diary of militant activities" until editor John Hayes left in the spring of 1970 and it became a porno newspaper. *Gay* published from November 1969 through July 1973 when Nichols and Clarke resettled in Florida. The two men chronicled their experiences at the newspaper in their book *I Have More Fun with You Than Anybody* (New York: St. Martin's Press, 1972).

Although Goldstein was a close friend of Nichols and Clarke's, and enabled them to begin *Gay*, his attitude toward gays was fraught with contradictions. In December 1983 he was quoted as referring to AIDS as a "wonderful disease" that transforms those who are infected "from fruits to vegetables." (Mark Thompson, ed., *Long Road to Freedom: The Advocate History of the Gay and Lesbian Movement* [New York: St. Martin's Press, 1994], p. 247.)

30. The term *homophobia* was coined by Dr. George Weinberg in his book *Society and the Healthy Homosexual* (New York: St. Martin's Press, 1972); John Paul Hudson, letter to the author, November 10, 1993.

31. Robert Patterson, "Clubs Won't Fix Breakfast, But Will Get You a Fast Fix," *San Francisco Examiner*, October 24, 1969, p. 8.

32. Robert Patterson, "The Dreary Revels of S.F. 'Gay' Clubs," *San Francisco Examiner*, Oct. 25, 1969, p. 5.

33. Larry Littlejohn, interview by author, October 12, 1993 (telephone).

34. "S.F. Cops Arrest 12 After Melee at Examiner," *Advocate*, January 1970, p. 2.

35. Morris Kight, interview by author, October 13, 1992 (telephone).

36. Ibid.

37. "Homosexual Unit Pickets the Times," *Los Angeles Times*, November 6, 1969, p. 11; "Gays Picket L.A. Times over Paper's Ad Policy," *Advocate*, January 1970, p. 2.

38. Nancy Ross, "Homosexual Revolution," *Washington Post*, October 25, 1969, p. C-1.

39. Enid Nemy, "The Woman Homosexual: More Assertive, Less Willing to Hide," *New York Times*, November 17, 1969, p. 62.

40. Julie Smith, "How Does Girl Meet Girl?" *San Francisco Chronicle*, July 1, 1969, p. 17; "Cross-Currents," *The Ladder*, October–November 1969, p. 38.

41. Gerald Caplan, M.D., "A Psychiatrist's Casebook," *McCall's*, November 1969, p. 65.

42. Richard Foster, "The Homosexuals: A Newly Visible Minority," *Midwest Magazine* (*Chicago Sun-Times*), December 14, 1969, pp. 40–41; Richard Foster, "Three Speak Out on Harassment, Parents, Analysts and Girls," *Chicago Sun-Times*, December 14, 1969, pp. 43–45.

43. "Policing the Third Sex," *Newsweek*, October 27, 1969, pp. 76–77.

44. Christopher Cory, "The Homosexual: Newly Visible, Newly Understood," *Time*, October 31, 1969, p. 56–67.

45. Bob Kohler, interview by author, November 11, 1992 (telephone).

46. Teal, *Gay Militants* p. 97.

47. Kohler interview.

5. GAY NEWS, STRAIGHT MEDIA

1. The founders of Gay Activists Alliance were Jim Owles, Arthur Evans, Kay Tobin, Marty Robinson, Tom Doerr, Richard Flynn, Arthur Bell, Donn Teal, Leo Martello, Steve Adams, Fred Orlansky, Gary Dutton, and Fred Cabellero.

2. Hamill's comment is cited in Donn Teal, *The Gay Militants* (New York: St. Martin's Press, 1995 [1971]), p. 52; Harriet Van Horne, "Enough of All This," *New York Post*, April 9, 1969, p. 54.

3. John Hammond, "Obituary: Craig L. Rodwell," *New York Native*, July 5, 1993, p. 13.

4. Arthur Bell, *Dancing the Gay Lib Blues* (New York: Simon & Schuster, 1971), p. 28.

5. "Homosexuals Hold Protest in 'Village' After Raid Nets 176," *New York Times*, March 9, 1970, p. 29. New York police continued to target gay bars until at least October 1982 when twenty officers raided Blues at 264 West Forty-third Street, a bar located almost directly across the street from the *New York Times*. According to an account in the *New York Native* ("Midtown Cops Go Berserk in Gay Bar," October 11–24, 1982, p. 1), the crowd of "black gay men and women were being savagely beaten by a commando squad," including a man with a wilted arm who was beaten when he

couldn't put his hands up. According to this account, the manager claimed he alerted the *Times*, but "he was told no one was available."

6. Lacey Fosburgh, "Thousands of Homosexuals Hold a Protest Rally in Central Park," *New York Times*, June 29, 1970, p. 1; Teal, *The Gay Militants*, p. 309.

7. Steven V. Roberts, "Homosexuals in Revolt," *New York Times*, August 24, 1970, p. 1.

8. Joseph Epstein, "Homo/Hetero: The Struggle for Sexual Identity," *Harper's*, September 1970, p. 51.

9. Bell, *Dancing the Gay Lib Blues*, p. 133.

10. Pete Fisher, interview by author, November 12, 1992 (telephone).

11. Midge Decter's homophobia surged into print exactly ten years after publication of Joseph Epstein's article. In the September 1980 issue of *Commentary* Decter wrote a hostile account of life on Fire Island, titled BOYS ON THE BEACH. She claimed that gay liberation had ruined homosexuals and attempted to discredit the gay rights movement by saying gay life centered around arrests, beatings, and "an appalling rate of suicides." (She described the Epstein essay as "elegant and thoughtful.") In a letter to the editor in the December 1980 issue of *Commentary*, psychiatrist Ernest van den Haag called her essay "the most brilliant description I have read of a male homosexual way of life." Decter reiterated her views in another article, again published in *Commentary* (March 1993), in which she attacked the "rainbow curriculum" in the New York public schools.

12. Teal, *Gay Militants*, p. 249; Kay Tobin and Randy Wicker, *The Gay Crusaders* (New York: Paperback Library, 1972), p. 192. Wicker played no part in writing the book. His name was included on the jacket after the publisher told Kay Lahusen (Kay Tobin) that the book would not sell unless it carried a man's name. She and Wicker were members of New York's Gay Activists Alliance.

13. Bell, *Dancing the Gay Lib Blues*, p. 134.

14. Teal, *Gay Militants*, p. 251.

15. Letter from Merle Miller to Willie Morris, October 27, 1970, Arthur Bell Papers, International Gay Information Center, New York Public Library.

16. Victor Navasky, interview by author, April 20, 1992 (telephone); Merle Miller, *On Being Different* (New York: Random House, 1971), p. 47. In his 1987 book *The Celluloid Closet* gay film critic Vito Russo describes *Cruising* as "homophobic in spirit and in fact.": "It sees all its gay characters as having been 'recruited,' condemned to the sad gay life like modern vampires who must create new victims in order to survive. . . . Walker's killer intimates that the homosexual lifestyle is an inherently violent one—not that the cruising scene is violent, but that to be homosexual is to be violent" [rev. ed. (New York: Harper & Row, 1987), p. 236]. *Cruising* did not become controversial until it was made into a movie in 1980 and set off angry protests in Greenwich Village, where major portions of it were filmed.

17. Miller, *On Being Different*, p. 47; Navasky interview.

18. David Rothenberg, "Merle Miller Speaks Plainly," *Advocate*, July 13, 1977, pp. 29–31; Miller, *On Being Different*, p. 49.

19. "Three Candidates Support Rights of Homosexuals," *New York Times*, October 27, 1970, p. 36; Walter H. Waggoner, "Fight Is Pressed by Homosexuals," *New York Times*, November 5, 1970, p. 32.

20. E. M. Forster died in 1970, so *Maurice* was not published until fifty-five years after its completion. The story concerns the coming of age of two young men who meet at Cambridge. It was particularly unusual in the era in which it was written because the novel not only described homosexuality as an inherited trait (rather than as a behavior) but had a happy ending.

21. Navasky interview.

22. Merle Miller, "What It Means to Be a Homosexual," *New York Times Magazine*, January 17, 1971, p. 9.

23. Miller, *On Being Different*, p. 6.

24. The first letter is cited in Peter Hadley, "Gay Author Merle Miller Hailed by GAA," *Gay*, July 5, 1971, p. 3. The second letter is cited in Merle Miller, "A Homosexual [Continued]," *New York Times Magazine,* October 10, 1971, pp. 67–81.

25. For reaction of Miller's family and friends see Thane Hampton, "Barbara Walters Comes Out!" *Gay*, September 18, 1972, p. 4; ABC's reaction and that of gay critics is recounted in Merle Miller, "Gay Liberation Is Not Lovable," *More* 2 (3) (March 1972): 9.

26. Jane E. Brody, "Homosexuality: Parents Aren't Always to Blame," *New York Times*, February 10, 1971, p. 48.

27. Jane E. Brody, "More Homosexuals Aided to Become Heterosexual," *New York Times*, February 28, 1971, p. 1. Jane Brody responded to my August 11, 1992, letter requesting an interview about her articles on homosexuality by writing, "I am not an expert and should not be quoted on such matters."

28. Stuart Byron, "Gay News and the Times: An Indelicate Balance," *Village Voice*, April 1, 1971, p. 13.

29. Judy Klemesrud, "The Disciples of Sappho, Updated," *New York Times Magazine*, March 28, 1971, p. 28.

30. Letter from Judy Klemesrud to Jim Owles, president of Gay Activists Alliance, April 16, 1971, Gay Activists Alliance Papers, International Gay Information Center, New York Public Library.

31. Bell, *Dancing the Gay Lib Blues,* pp. 142–45.

32. GAA flyer, GAA Papers, International Gay Information Center, New York Public Library.

33. Stuart Byron, "The Closet Syndrome," in Karla Jay and Allen Young, eds., *Out of the Closets: Voices of Gay Liberation*, pp. 58–65 (New York: New York University Press, 1972).

34. Miller, "Gay Liberation Is Not Lovable," p. 9.

35. Ibid.; Joseph Lelyveld, "Militant Homosexuals to Stage March to Central Park Today," *New York Times*, June 27, 1971, p. 30.

36. Jill Johnston, "Fictions of the Self in the Making," *New York Times Book Review*, April 25, 1993, p. 1.

37. Jill Johnston, "Of This Pure But Irregular Passion," *Village Voice*, July 2, 1970, p. 29.

38. "Cross-Currents," *The Ladder*, April–May 1970 p. 32; Jill Johnston, interview by author, May 24, 1993 (telephone).

39. Johnston interview; Jill Johnston, "Lois Lane Is a Lesbian," *Village Voice*, March 4, 1971, p. 8.

40. "Cross-Currents," *The Ladder*, October–November 1970, p. 24;

41. "Cross-Currents," *The Ladder*, September–October 1970, p. 30; Marcia Cohen, *The Sisterhood: The Inside Story of the Women's Movement and the Leaders Who Made It Happen* (New York: Ballantine, 1988), p. 278.

42. Jill Johnston, "On a Clear Day You Can See Your Mother," *Village Voice*, May 6, 1971, p. 37.

43. Quoted in Cohen, *Sisterhood,* p. 289.

44. Rosalyn Drexler, "Theater for Ideas: A Night of Lib and Let Lib," *Village Voice*, May 6, 1971, p. 28.

45. Johnston interview; Jane Howard, "End of the Stag Nation," *Washington Post*, March 3, 1973, Book Review sec., p. 8.

46. Ellen Frankfort, *The Voice* (New York: William Morrow, 1976), p. 266.

47. Johnston interview.

48. Jill Johnston, letter to the author, May 3, 1995. To a large degree Johnston's decision to leave the *Voice* marked her departure from the spotlight of radical lesbianism-feminism in exchange for a far quieter life. In 1993 Johnston and Ingrid Nyeboe were married in Nyeboe's native Denmark under a 1989 partnership law that made Denmark the first nation to legalize gay and lesbian marriages.

6. BECOMING VISIBLE

1. Arthur Bell, "The Sixties," in Michael Denneny, Charles Ortleb, and Thomas Steele, eds., *The Christopher Street Reader* (New York: Perigee Books, 1984), p. 29.

2. Ibid.

3. Early in his career Arthur Irving Bell's work appeared under the name Arthur Irving.

4. Arthur Bell, "Hairdresser Shelters Agnew's Son," *Gay*, September 28, 1970, p. 1; Arthur Bell, *Dancing the Gay Lib Blues* (New York: Simon & Schuster, 1971), pp. 105–106.

5. Editorial, "Any Old Jobs for Homos," *New York Daily News*, April 5, 1972, p. 61.

6. Lacey Fosburgh, "Attack Charges Denied by Maye," *New York Times*, June 28, 1972, p. 46; "Grand Jury Clears 2nd Fire Union Aide," *New York Times*, July 8, 1972, p. 30.

7. The 1975 film *Dog Day Afternoon* was based on the true story of John Wojtowicz and Sal Naturale, who robbed a branch of Chase Manhattan Bank of $29,000. Naturale was killed in the robbery attempt, and Wojtowicz was sentenced to twenty years.

8. Arthur Bell Papers, International Gay Information Center, New York Public Library.

9. Arthur Bell, "Let *Boys in the Band* Die," *New York Times*, April 8, 1973, sec. 2, p. 15.

10. Kay Longcope, interview by author, May 4, 1993 (telephone).

11. Cited in Linda Reed, "A Paradox: The Role of Women in Journalism," *Communication: Journalism Education Today* (Winter 1975): 2.

12. Longcope interview.

13. Kay Longcope, "Minister Marries Gays over Bishop's Objection," *Boston Globe*, April 8, 1973, p. 5.

14. Longcope interview.

15. David Perlman, "The Psychiatrists & the Protesters," *San Francisco Sunday Examiner & Chronicle*, May 24, 1970, This World sec., p. 18; Ronald Bayer, *Homosexuality and American Psychiatry: The Politics of Diagnosis* (Princeton, N.J.: Princeton University Press, 1987 [1981]), p. 104.

16. Stuart Auerbach, interview by author, February 9, 1995 (telephone). Perlman, another reporter tipped by the gay organizations, wrote, "It was certainly the first scientific meeting in history in which scholars were told off with phrases like 'f– you,' or their research papers loudly called b– s–'" (Perlman, "The Psychiatrists & the Protesters").

17. Stuart Auerbach, "Gays and Dolls Battle the Shrinks," *Washington Post*, May 15, 1970, p. 1.

18. Letter from Morris Kight to the author, October 26, 1995; *Advocate* Staff Report, "Zap! Boff! Pow!" in Mark Thompson, ed., *Long Road to Freedom*, (New York: St. Martin's, 1994, pp. 38–39.

19. Bayer, *Homosexuality and American Psychiatry*, pp. 104–107.

20. Ibid.

21. Rob Shivers, "Psychiatry Convention Hears 'Gay Is Healthy,'" *Advocate*, June 7, 1972, p. 12.

22. Barbara Gittings, interview by author, November 6, 1995 (telephone).

23. Bayer, *Homosexuality and American Psychiatry*, p. 115–16.

24. Ronald Gold, interview by author, April 3, 1994, New York City; "Therapy Scored by Homosexuals," *New York Times*, October 9, 1972, p. 32.

25. Boyce Rensberger, "Psychiatrists Review Stand on Homosexuals," *New York Times*, February 9, 1973, p. 24.

26. Gold interview.

27. Charles Socarides continues to promote his theories on homosexuality. In a July 15, 1993, segment of the *MacNeil-Lehrer Newshour* (PBS) on "sexual chemistry" he commented, "In my opinion, the causation for homosexuality has been discovered. . . . We feel that the homosexual becomes homosexual due to a disturbance in the early development." On *Larry King Live* on CNN on June 9, 1994, he stated, "Homosexuality is a developmental disorder. . . . There's homosexual behavior, which is not the true condition, and obligatory homosexuality, which we feel is one of the sexual deviations." What Socarides neglected to tell the interviewers in both cases was that his gay son Richard sits on the board of the Lambda Legal Defense Fund, one of the most successful gay rights litigation organizations in the nation.

28. Associated Press, "Doctors Urged Not to Call Homosexuality Illness," *New York Times*, May 10, 1973, p. 20.

29. Brown noted in his biography *Familiar Faces, Hidden Lives: The Story of Homosexual Men in America Today* (New York: Harcourt, Brace, Jovanovich, 1976) that he was prompted to make his announcement when he learned that Pearson had written a series of articles about homosexuals working in the administration of California governor Ronald Reagan and was planning to write a similar exposé about the New York mayor's staff (p. 15). Literary critic Webster Schott cited Pearson's disclosure in a *New York Times Magazine* article, A 4-MILLION MINORITY ASKS FOR EQUAL RIGHTS (November 12, 1967, p. 44).

30. Marcia Chambers, "Ex-City Official Says He's Homosexual," *New York Times*, October 3, 1973, p. 1; Howard Brown, "Here I Am—I'm Gay," in Mark Thompson, ed., *Long Road to Freedom* (New York: St. Martin's Press, 1994), p. 88.

31. Richard D. Lyons, "Psychiatrists, in a Shift, Declare Homosexuality No Mental Illness," *New York Times*, December 16, 1973, p. 1.

32. Robert E. Gould, "What We Don't Know About Homosexuality," *New York Times Magazine*, February 24, 1974, p. 13.

33. Barbara Trecker's series in the *New York Post* is cited in "Newspaper Series Surprises Activists," *Advocate*, April 24, 1974, p. 4.

34. Arthur Bell, "Has the Gay Movement Gone Establishment?" *Village Voice*, March 28, 1974, p. 10.

35. During its annual convention in May 1994 the American Psychiatric Association presented awards to Kameny and Gittings, citing them for their contributions to psychiatry. "That represented a closure of the whole issue," Kameny later commented. See Jack Nichols's interview with Kameny, *TWN*, April 5, 1995, p. 22. *TWN* is the gay weekly in Miami.

36. "CBS Denies Manford Equal Time," *Advocate*, February 27, 1974, p. 21.

37. William Safire, "Don't Slam the Closet Door," *New York Times*, April 18, 1974, p. 41.

38. Mike Royko, "Going Bananas over Liberation," *Chicago Daily News*, March 22, 1974, p. 3.

39. Mike Royko, "There'll Be No Apology," *Chicago Daily News*, March 28, 1974, p. 3. Royko's bias was even more blatant in an incident twenty years after he compared gay rights with monkey rights. During his arrest on charges of drunken driving and resisting arrest in Chicago on December 17, 1994, Royko began shouting at police, "Fuck you, fag. Get your fucking hands off

me. Jag off, you queer." The incident became public when the *Advocate*'s West Coast correspondent, John Gallagher, received a tip to check the police records. He reported his findings in the *Advocate*, June 27, 1995, p. 21. Royko pleaded guilty and apologized for his behavior.

40. Ann Landers, *New York Daily News*, July 23, 1976, p. 48; Jane E. Brody, "Study Finds Some Homosexuals Are Happier Than Heterosexuals," *New York Times*, July 9, 1978, p. 22.

41. Robert Rawitch, "Gay Movement Fights Stigma of Prostitution," *Los Angeles Times*, October 28, 1973, p. II-1.

42. Atlanta was also the site of gay protests against the media. In July 1973 about fifteen picketers from the Lesbian Feminist Alliance demonstrated in front of the *Atlanta Journal* after the newspaper refused to cover gay pride festivities the previous month. The newspaper took the unusual step of reporting it. See "Homosexuals Stage Protest at Newspapers," *Atlanta Journal*, July 8, 1973, p. 7-C.

43. Douglas Sarff, "Tiny Protest Group Risks Arrest, Makes Nation's Third Largest Newspaper Promise Coverage," *Advocate*, November 20, 1974, p. 3.

44. Kight, interview by author, October 21, 1992 (telephone).

45. Cecil Smith, "Hal Linden: He Holds the Lid on *Barney Miller*," *Los Angeles Times*, April 26, 1975, TV sec., p. 2.

46. Susan Banashek and Al Martinez, "Night Shoppers—Fantasy in the Market Aisles," *Los Angeles Times*, August 14, 1974, p. 1.

47. Memo from Gregg Kilday to Lynn Lilliston (entertainment editor) and senior writers, April 28, 1975. (From the files of Gregg Kilday)

48. Mark Murphy, interview by author, May 20, 1993 (telephone).

49. Lenny Giteck, "Cancer Takes Life of Gay Activist, Advocate Owner David Goodstein at 53," *Advocate*, July 23, 1985, pp. 10–11.

50. Lou Romano, "The Advocate," *Washington Blade*, June 1977, p. 11.

51. Thompson, *Long Road to Freedom*, p. 113.

52. Stephen J. Sansweet, "A Homosexual Paper, The Advocate, Widens Readership, Influence," *Wall Street Journal*, November 3, 1975, p. 1.

7. TV BECOMES A BATTLEGROUND

1. Nicholas Johnson, "Television and Violence—Perspectives and Proposals," *Television Quarterly* (Winter 1969): 31.

2. George Gerbner and Larry Gross, "Living with Television: The Violence Profile," *Journal of Communication* (Spring 1976): 174–99.

3. For a description of the *Laugh-In* skit, see Mattachine Midwest Newsletter, March 1969, p. 4; for gay jokes on *Laugh-In* see Dennis Altman, *Homosexual Oppression and Liberation* (New York: Avon, 1971), p. 108.

4. Neither Arthur Bell [*Dancing the Gay Lib Blues: A Year in the Homosexual Liberation Movement* (New York: Simon & Schuster, 1971), p. 135], nor Toby Marotta [*The Politics of Homosexuality* (Boston: Houghton Mifflin, 1981), p. 186], cites what comedian Mort Sahl said on *The Dick Cavett Show*. However, Jim Kepner quoted the comedian as referring to gays as homos, faggots, and as a "negative social force," among other remarks ("Mort Sahl Stirs Gay Rage," *Advocate*, March 3, 1974, p. 37).

5. Arthur Bell, *Dancing the Gay Lib Blues*, p. 163.

6. John J. O'Connor, "TV: Homosexuality Is Subject of Two Programs," *New York Times*, November 3, 1973, p. 79.

7. T. Perew, "Gays on TV Not the Real Thing," *Advocate*, May 8, 1974, p. 37.

8. Richard Levinson and William Link, *Stay Tuned* (New York: St. Martin's Press, 1981), p. 105.

9. Diller's sexuality was the subject of heightened speculation two decades later when TV talk show host Arsenio Hall publicly suggested that the then-chairman of Fox, Inc., was gay. "I don't know if I outed him," Hall later told the *Advocate*. "I know that Barry Diller isn't the only gay guy in town. There are a lot of gay people who run the studios" (Bruce Mirken, "Woo! Woo! Woo!" *Advocate*, June 18, 1991, p. 58).

10. Levinson and Link, *Stay Tuned,* pp. 120, 135.

11. Harold Fairbanks, "ABC to Air Sensitive Story on Real-Life Gays," *Advocate*, December 20, 1972, p. 10.

12. Ronald Gold, interview by author, July 31, 1992, New York City.

13. Richard Casey, "But the Big Story Tonight Is . . . Youths Get Piece of 'Action' on Channel 6," *Philadelphia Inquirer*, August 16, 1972, p. 1.

14. Mark Segal, interview by author, March 24, 1993 (telephone).

15. In April 1991 Merv Griffin was named in a $200 million palimony suit filed by Brent Plott, a thirty-seven-year-old Florida man. Griffin termed the suit a "shameless attempt to extort money from me" and denied that his relationship with Plott was sexual. However, Plott told *NBC Nightly News*, "We lived together, shared the same bed, the same house. He told me he loved me." In November 1991 a Los Angeles Superior Court judge dismissed the case with prejudice, meaning that it could not be refiled. However, one month later Griffin was slapped with another suit by an entertainer who charged the *TV* star with sexual harassment. That suit was also dismissed. Michaelangelo Signorile, *Queer in America: Sex, the Media, and the Closets of Power* (New York: Random House, 1993) p. 263–65; John Gallagher, "Hollywood Watchers: Griffin Suit Exposes Industry's Intolerance," *Advocate*, May 21, 1991, p. 14.

16. "Tonight Show Zapped by Gay Raider," *Advocate*, March 28, 1973, p. 3.

17. "2 Gays Arrested at NBC-Burbank," *Advocate*, April 11, 1973, p. 15.

18. Richard Rusinow, "'Raider' Hits Mike Douglas Show," *Gay*, June 18, 1973, p. 1.

19. "Activists in Lather over NBC Slurs," *Advocate*, November 21, 1973, p. 3; "Gay Philadelphian Invades 'Today' Set," *Philadelphia Inquirer*, October 27, 1973, p. B-1.

20. Les Brown, "N.B.C. Acts After Complaints by Homosexual Organizations," *New York Times*, October 27, 1973, p. 63.

21. Segal interview.

22. Transcript, *CBS Evening News with Walter Cronkite*, December 11, 1973, p. 13; "'Gay Raiders' Invade Cronkite News Show," *New York Times*, December 12, 1973, p. 94.

23. Tommi Avicolli, "Two Flags: Segal and Cronkite," *Drummer*, August 27, 1974, p. 3.

24. Segal interview.

25. Transcript, *CBS Evening News with Walter Cronkite,* May 6, 1974, pp. 17–19.

26. Libbe S. HaLevy (formerly Loretta Lotman), interview by author, April 19, 1993 (telephone). After 1975 Lotman dropped out of gay activism and pursued a career as a writer. She relocated to Los Angeles and, as part of her recovery from childhood abuse issues, changed her name to Libbe S. HaLevy.

27. Ibid.

28. Ibid.

29. Kathryn C. Montgomery, *Target: Prime Time* (New York: Oxford University Press, 1989), pp. 79–100.

30. "How to Put Pressure on Network Affiliates," memo from Loretta Lotman, media direc-

tor of Gay Media Action, to local gay activists, September 1974. (From the personal files of Libbe S. HaLevy)

31. "How to Book A TV or Radio Program," memo from Loretta Lotman, media director of the National Gay Task Force, to local gay and lesbian media advocates, October 1975. (From the personal files of Libbe S. HaLevy)

32. "ABC's Sell Job in Ad Exit on 'Welby' Issue," *Variety*, October 9, 1974, p. 42; Harry F. Waters, "TV: Do Minorities Rule?" *Newsweek*, June 2, 1975, pp. 78–79; Bruce Voeller, interview by author, October 21, 1992 (telephone).

33. *Hollywood Reporter* is cited in "'Police Woman' Backs Down," *Advocate*, November 6, 1974, p. 31; Richard M. Levine, "How the Gay Lobby Has Changed Television," *TV Guide*, May 30, 1981, pp. 3–6.

34. Lesbian Feminist Liberation grew out of the Lesbian Liberation Committee of the Gay Activist Alliance in the spring of 1973 when the women formed a separate organization. Many members later tired of internal conflicts and became involved in the National Gay Task Force (which later became the National Gay and Lesbian Task Force) after it formed in 1974.

35. Joe Johnson, "Outraged Lesbians Zap NBC," *Advocate*, December 18, 1974, p. 1.

36. Douglas Sarff, "NBC Asks for Gay Stamp of Approval," *Advocate*, January 29, 1975, p. 4.

37. "Network Heads Cite Realities of 'Family' Life," *Broadcasting*, February 17, 1975, p. 35; David L. Aiken, "'No to T.V. Code Request," *Advocate*, June 4, 1975, p. 5.

38. HaLevy interview.

39. "Protests Against NBC (Again)," *Advocate*, November 19, 1975, p. 9; Ginny Vida, interview by author, December 13, 1994 (telephone).

40. John J. O'Connor, "The Preoccupation with Sex," *New York Times*, November 26, 1978, p. 33.

41. In September 1991 the major networks faced renewed resistance from advertisers. In the case of an episode of *Quantum Leap* about a gay teenager NBC apparently told the producers they would have to accept financial responsibility unless they made changes in the episode. When it finally aired the following winter, one network executive was quoted as saying the episode had lost $500,000 in revenue from advertisers who pulled out. A year earlier ABC reportedly lost $1.5 million in canceled ads after an episode of *thirtysomething* showed two men kissing in bed (Victor Dwyer, "Prime-Time Sparks," *MacLean's*, March 2, 1992, p. 53).

42. Kathryn Montgomery, "Gay Activists and the Networks," *Journal of Communication*, Summer 1981, pp. 49–57.

43. Richard M. Levine, "How the Gay Lobby Has Changed Television," *TV Guide*, May 30, 1981, pp. 3–6; Nicholas Von Hoffman, "Out from TV's Sit-Com Closet: The Presentable Gay," *Rocky Mountain News*, November 4, 1976, p. 75.

44. Lotman spoke to the third annual "counter-convention" sponsored by *More* magazine in 1974. Other panelists included Ronald Gold, communications director for the National Gay Task Force; Merle Miller, author; and Allen Young, journalist and co-editor with Karla Jay of the landmark *Out of the Closets: Voices of Gay Liberation* (New York: New York University Press, 1977). The moderator was George Whitmore, an openly gay journalist who had contributed many articles to the *Advocate*.

45. John Zeh, "Media: To Be or Not to Be Visible?" *Advocate*, June 5, 1974, p. 25. Two years later, in the spring of 1976, CBS television revised the nondiscrimination statement on its job application forms to include sexual preference. ("Briefs," *Advocate,* March 10, 1976, p. 10.) But the change was essentially meaningless because gays and lesbians had no legal protections on which to rely if the policies were ignored.

46. Zeh, "Media."

47. Burdette Bullock, interview by author, February 9, 1990, Orlando, Fla.

48. Glaser went on to work as a reporter at television stations in Miami, Norfolk, Detroit, Ft. Wayne, and New York City, and on the syndicated *Entertainment Tonight*. In December 1994, as the media-entertainment reporter for KNBC in Los Angeles, he acknowledged his homosexuality during an on-air obituary for AIDS activist Elizabeth Glaser (no relation), saying, "As a gay man who has lost many friends to AIDS——."

49. Garrett Glaser, interview by author, June 26, 1992.

50. Tom Cassidy, interview by author, July 25, 1990.

51. Hank Plante, interview by author, November 17, 1990.

8. WORKING IN NEWSPAPERS

1. For accounts of their disappearance see Edward Bliss Jr., *Now the News: The Story of Broadcast Journalism* (New York: Columbia University Press, 1991), p. 347, and Malcolm Forbes, *What Happened to Their Kids?* (New York: Simon & Schuster, 1990), p .87.

2. Perry Deane Young, interview by author, July 13, 1990, Washington, D.C.

3. Ibid.

4. John Kifner, "Sexuality Issue Put to Rest: Elaine Nobel Is Ready for Office," *New York Times*, November 14, 1974, p. 60; "Moments in Gay and Lesbian History," *San Francisco Examiner*, June 7, 1994, p. A-2.

5. Deborah Howell, "State Sen. Allan Spear Declares He's Homosexual," *Minneapolis Star*, December 9, 1974, p. 1.

6. Carl Griffin Jr., interview by author, January 30, 1993 (telephone).

7. Ibid.

8. Carl Griffin Jr., "Woman Describes Forming Group to Help Parents of Gay Children," *Minneapolis Tribune*, September 29, 1975, p. 11-B. In his essay "The Closet Syndrome" in Karla Jay and Allen Young, eds., *Out of the Closets* (New York: New York University Press, 1977), openly gay journalist Stuart Byron wrote, "I know of only one establishment daily in the country which has an openly gay reporter assigned to the gay beat—the *Minneapolis Star*." Byron was apparently referring to Griffin, although Griffin worked at the *Minneapolis Tribune*, and his coverage of gay stories was not specifically defined as a beat.

9. Griffin interview.

10. David L. Aiken, "Gay Is Now Okay in 2.6 Million Federal Jobs," the *Advocate*, July 1975, p. 3; "Homosexual Hiring Is Revised by U.S.," *New York Times*, July 4, 1975, p. 45.

11. John Leo, "Gays on the March," *Time*, September 8, 1975, pp. 32–43.

12. "I Am a Homosexual," *Time*, September 8, 1975, p. 32; David Gelman, "'Gays' and the Press," *Newsweek*, October 20, 1975, pp. 93–94.

13. Cliff Jahr, "The All-Gay Cruise: Prejudice and Pride," *New York Times*, April 6, 1975, sec. 10, p. 1. Jahr, whose specialty was celebrity profiles, had a history of approaching a taboo subject head on. He was asking about and reporting the sexuality of closted celebrities long before it was fashionable—and getting his stories into print. In his interviews with Janis Ian in 1975 and Elton John in 1976, both stars acknowledged their homosexuality for the first time. See "Janis Ian Comes Out from 'Between the Lines,'" *Village Voice*, December 15, 1975, p. 136, and "Frank Talk: The Lonely Life of a Superstar," *Rolling Stone*, November 7, 1976. Jahr died of AIDS-related causes on August 6, 1991.

14. Cliff Jahr, "Fit to Print: The *Times* They Are A-Changing," *Advocate*, June 18, 1975, p. 34; Robert Stock, interview by author, January 29, 1992 (telephone).

15. Joseph C. Goulden, *Fit To Print* (New York: Lyle Stuart, 1988), p. 397.

16. "New York Intelligencer," *New York*, April 21, 1975, p. 72.

17. After Eric Nadler described the rumored firing and rehiring of Max Frankel in *Forum* in October 1985 ("Sex & the New York Times," pp. 10–17), Frankel called him and denied it had happened.

18. Jahr, "Fit to Print."

19. Grace Lichtenstein, "Homosexuals Are Moving Toward Open Way of Life as Tolerance Rises Among the General Population," *New York Times*, July 17, 1977, p. 34.

20. Grace Lichtenstein, interview by author, March 30, 1992 (telephone).

21. A. M. Rosenthal did not respond to letters or telephone calls requesting an interview.

22. Grace Lichtenstein, "Homosexuals in New York Find New Pride," *New York Times*, October 25, 1977, p. 41.

23. Lichtenstein interview.

24. Dave Anderson, interview by author, March 27, 1992 (telephone).

25. Roger Wilkins, interview by author, January 18, 1991 (telephone).

26. Wilkins, interview by author, July 20, 1991 (telephone).

27. Peter G. Davis, interview by author, September 21, 1993 (telephone).

28. George DeStefano, "The New York Times vs. Gay America," *Advocate*, December 9, 1986, p. 43+.

29. David Rothenberg, "Homophobia at the New York Times," *New York Native*, June 1–14, 1981, p. 15.

30. Nan Robertson, interview by author, May 11, 1992 (telephone).

31. Peter Millones, interview by author, April 16, 1992 (telephone).

32. Martin Merzer, "Anita Bryant Continues Fight Against Gay Rights Ordinance," *Atlanta Constitution*, February 6, 1977, p. 7.

33. Adon Taft and Susan Burnside, "Group Raps Homosexual Ordinance," *Miami Herald*, January 17, 1977, p. B-1.

34. Bob Kunst, letter to the author, June 26, 1995.

35. Ibid.

36. Editorial, "An Unneeded Ordinance," *Miami Herald*, June 5, 1977, p.2E.

37. Tom Braden, "Remember When 'Gay' Meant Gay?" *St. Paul Pioneer Press*, March 27, 1977, p. 36.

38. Jeff Greenfield, "Why Is Gay Rights Different from All Other Rights?" *Village Voice*, February 6, 1978, p. 1.

39. Amy Larkin, "Enough! Enough! TV Is Killing Us with Gays," *Atlanta Constitution*, September 18, 1977, p. 26.

40. Cited in "Darts and Laurels," *Columbia Journalism Review*, March–April 1978, p. 23.

41. Richard M. Levine, "Our Only Allies Now Are Our Worst Enemies," *TV Guide*, June 6, 1981, p. 50; "ABC Series Attacked in Christian Mailing," *Advocate*, October 16, 1980, p. 13.

42. Richard Goldstein, interview by author, February 2, 1993, New York.

43. Ibid.

44. Roger Ricklefs, "Some Top Concerns Rule Out Job Bias Against Gay People," *Wall Street Journal*, December 8, 1978, p. 31; the Taylor memo is cited in Alexander Cockburn, "Press Clips," *Village Voice*, January 1, 1979, p. 21.

45. Fred Taylor, interview by author, September 3, 1992 (telephone).

46. Kunst letter.

47. John Jacobs, "Briggs' Wild Rumors About Gay Teachers, *San Francisco Examiner*, October 3, 1978, p. 6; the reaction of the *Los Angeles Times* is cited in Mark Thompson, ed., *Long Road to Freedom* (New York: St. Martin's Press, 1994), p. 164.

48. Lenny Giteck, interview by author, December 13, 1994 (telephone). Giteck went on to serve as the *Advocate*'s editor in chief from 1985 to 1988.

49. Lenny Giteck, "How Things Used to Be," *San Francisco Examiner*, Gays and the City series, October 30, 1978, p. 25.

50. Giteck interview.

51. "Introducing Randy Shilts," *Advocate*, June 18, 1975, p. 9.

52. Garry Wills, "The Rolling Stone Interview with Randy Shilts," *Rolling Stone*, September 30, 1993, p. 47.

53. Randy Shilts, interview by author, June 3, 1993 (telephone).

54. Jo Thomas, "75,000 March in Capital in Drive To Support Homosexual Rights," *New York Times*, October 15, 1979, p. A14; Craig Davidson, "Can We End Media Bias Against Gays?" *USA Today*, magazine sec., November 1991, p. 72.

55. Bill Kreidler, "Boston's LAGMA Tells You How To Monitor Media and Talk Back Effectively," *Advocate*, November 24, 1983, p. 38.

56. Christine Madsen, interview by author, February 23, 1992, Freeport, Maine.

57. Peter Freiberg, "Court Upholds Firing of Lesbian," *Advocate*, October 1, 1985, p. 13; Chris Bull, "Still Looking For Justice," *Gay Community News*, October 4–10, 1987, p. 3.

58. Madsen interview.

59. Jill Clark, "Lesbian Journalist Fired by Christian Science Monitor," *Gay Community News*, March 20, 1982, p. 1.

60. Madsen interview.

61. Katherine Triantafillou, interview by author, June 29, 1993 (telephone).

62. Ann Flornaday, "Monitor Charged with Discrimination," *Ms.*, May 1983, p. 29.

63. Larry Bush, "AP Turns Down Union Request for Gay Job Protections," *Advocate*, April 14, 1983, p. 9. The Associated Press reiterated its position in 1994 when it turned down another request to include gays and lesbians in its antidiscrimination policy [National Gay and Lesbian Journalists Conference, *Alternatives* (newsletter), Fall 1994, p. 3].

64. Madsen interview.

65. Ibid.

9. GAY POWER, GAY POLITICS

1. "Documentary on TV Fails the Gay ABCs," *Advocate*, November 15, 1979, p. 7.

2. John Carmody, "The TV Column," *Washington Post*, December 18, 1979, p. B-10.

3. Former San Francisco vice mayor Hadley Roff, interview by author, May 25, 1993 (telephone). Requests for an interview with Diane Feinstein (now a U.S. senator) were rejected by her staff.

4. Sally Gearhart, interview by author, September 9, 1993 (telephone).

5. Transcript, "Gay Power, Gay Politics," *CBS Reports*, CBS News, April 26, 1980, p. 1.

6. Ibid.

7. Randy Alfred, interview by author, July 25, 1992 (telephone).

8. Randy Alfred, complaint filed with the National News Council against CBS News, July 10, 1980, p. 1, International Gay and Lesbian Archives, Los Angeles. The archives and the papers of

the ONE Institute were scheduled to move to the University of Southern California, Los Angeles, in the spring of 1996.

9. Alfred interview.

10. Alfred complaint to National News Council, p. 16.

11. Ibid., p. 15.

12. Alfred complaint to the News Council, p. 20

13. Transcript, *CBS Reports,* p. 3.

14. J. Stone, "Diane Feinstein: A Brave New Mayor," *Ladies' Home Journal*, March 1979, p. 96.

15. Alfred complaint to National News Council, p. 14.

16. Alfred interview.

17. Randy Alfred, "Lesbian Bites Dog," *Advocate*, January 1982, p. 24.

18. Ibid. A glory hole is an opening carved in the partition between stalls in a men's restroom and used for anonymous sexual liaisons.

19. Alfred complaint to National News Council, p. 34.

20. Jarvis and O'Flaherty are cited in Lenny Giteck, "Gay Politics Special Stirs Protest, Probe," *Advocate*, June 12, 1980, p. 10; Michael Munzell, "The Perverts Are Coming!" *Peninsula Times Tribune*, April 25, 1980, p. C-9.

21. Robert Chandler, letter to the National News Council, September 4, 1980, pp. 1, 7. Chandler was vice president and director of public affairs broadcasts for CBS News in New York. A copy of the letter can be found in the International Gay & Lesbian Archives, Los Angeles.

22. Ibid., pp. 2, 11.

23. National News Council Report, p. 38, International Gay & Lesbian Archives, Los Angeles. (The reports of the council also were printed in the *Columbia Journalism Review*. The decision on "Gay Power, Gay Politics" appeared in the issue of January–February 1981, pp. 76–83.)

24. Ibid., p. 41.

25. Ibid., p. 43.

26. Randy Alfred, "A Victory for High Journalistic Standards," *Sentinel*, October 3, 1980. (From the files of Randy Alfred)

27. Grace Diekhaus and George Crile, memo to "Our Colleagues at CBS Reports," undated, International Gay & Lesbian Archives, Los Angeles. Authenticity verified by George Crile.

28. George Crile, interview by author, June 18, 1993 (telephone). A year after the uproar over "Gay Power, Gay Politics," CBS producer George Crile became embroiled in another controversy over a documentary he had produced. Retired Army General William Westmoreland slapped CBS with a $120 million libel suit over "The Uncounted Enemy: A Vietnam Deception." The program accused the military of conspiring to undercount enemy strength in Vietnam in order to make the war more palatable to the public. Westmoreland called the allegation unfair and unjust." However, he dropped his suit when he found that libel laws do not require accurate reporting, only that the story not intentionally damage someone's character. The court never addressed his complaints about unfairness.

29. Transcript, "Update," *CBS Reports*, October 21, 1980.

30. Alfred, "High Journalistic Standards."

31. "CBS' 'Gay Power' Resurfaces in Austin," *Advocate*, October 1, 1981, p. 15.

32. Cited in Larry Bush and Richard Goldstein, "The Anti-Gay Backlash," *Village Voice*, April 8–14, 1981, p. 1.

33. Ann Northrop, interview by author, April 7, 1992.

34. Ibid.

35. Jon Katz is a veteran journalist who had been a reporter and editor at the *Boston Globe*, the *Philadelphia Inquirer*, the *Washington Post*, the *Dallas Times-Herald*, and the (Baltimore) *News-American*. He worked at CBS News from 1982 to 1987. More recently he has been media critic for *Rolling Stone*, *New York* magazine, and *Wired* and writes the Suburban Detective series.

36. Northrop interview. Katz remembers the *CBS Morning News* segment, but he does not recall the conversation with Northrop (Jon Katz, interview by author, May 23, 1995, telephone).

37. Northrop interview.

38. Joe Lovett, interview by author, September 7, 1993 (telephone).

39. Ibid.

40. Todd Gitlin, *Inside Prime Time* (New York: Pantheon, 1983), p. 262.

41. Richard M. Levine, "Our Only Allies Now Are Our Worst Enemies," *TV Guide*, June 6, 1981, p. 50. By 1991 it had become increasingly clear that Wildmon could not support his threats against advertisers on programs that portrayed gays in a positive light. The *New York Times* reported on May 19, 1991, "None of the product boycotts announced by the American Family Association seems to have been very successful" (John J. O'Connor, "Gay Images: TV's Mixed Signals," *New York Times*, May 19, 1991, sec. 2, p. 1.

10. LESSONS FROM THE RAMROD

1. "Two Dead, More Wounded in NY Shooting Spree," *Advocate*, December 25, 1980, p. 7.

2. Josh Barbanel, "Gunman Kills One and Wounds 7 in Village," *New York Times*, November 20, 1980, p. B-1. The Ramrod murders were not the only important local story that slipped past the *Times*. In fact, the *Times* became notorious for concentrating on national and international news while virtually ignoring important stories at its doorstep. One of the clearest examples was New York City's 1975 financial crisis, which the *Times* and several other New York dailies virtually ignored until the city slipped into bankruptcy. See Martin Mayer, "Default at the New York Times," *Columbia Journalism Review*, January–February 1976, pp. 16–20.

3. Josh Barbanel, interview by author, April 8, 1992 (telephone).

4. Edward Hudson, "Rest Room Shut to Foreclose Use by Homosexuals," *New York Times*, August 1, 1980, p. B-1.

5. David Rothenberg, interview by author, June 27, 1992.

6. Jeffrey Schmalz, interview by author, June 27, 1992, San Francisco. Schmalz was not open about his homosexuality when he argued for giving the story bigger play because it was worth more prominent display.

7. Peter Millones, interview by author, December 14, 1994 (telephone).

8. Kieran Crowley, "Bloodbath in the Village," *New York Post*, November 20, 1980, p. 1.

9. Joe Nicholson, "Confessions of a Closeted Newspaperman," *New York Native*, December 29–January 8, 1981, pp. 14–17.

10. Ibid.

11. Joe Nicholson, interview by author, November 12, 1992 (telephone).

12. Ibid.

13. Nicholson, "Confessions of a Closeted Newspaperman," p. 14.

14. Joe Nicholson, "Coming Out at the New York Post," *Columbia Journalism Review*, March–April 1982, pp. 26–27. Nicholson did not actually come out in print in the *New York Post* until 1993 during the "gays in the military" controversy, when he wrote a firsthand account of his own military service. GAY IN THE NAVY, read the front page headline on January 29, 1993.

15. Nicholson interview.

16. The *Philadelphia Inquirer* and the *Philadelphia Daily News*, two newspapers owned by Knight Newspapers (now Knight-Ridder), are believed to be the earliest media outlets to adopt antidiscrimination protections for gays and lesbians. A 1974 story in the *Advocate* quoted *Inquirer* sources who said a clause to protect "sexual preference" from discrimination was added to the union contract "at the suggestion of an unnamed company employee" ("Sex Preference Bias Ends at Two Major Newspapers," *Advocate*, November 20, 1974, p. 16). Coincidentally, John S. Knight III, an heir to the Knight newspaper fortune, was a closeted homosexual. This became known after his murder by a gay male hustler at his Philadelphia apartment in the early 1970s. Knight's double life became the subject of a 1979 book by Arthur Bell, *Kings Don't Mean a Thing* (New York: William Morrow, 1978).

17. Frank Perich, interview by author, March 23, 1993 (telephone).

18. Jeff Weinstein, interview by author, September 16, 1994 (telephone).

19. Richard Goldstein, interview by author, February 2, 1993, New York.

20. Randy Shilts, interview by author, June 3, 1993 (telephone).

21. Ransdell Pierson, "Uptight on Gay News," *Columbia Journalism Review*, March–April 1982, p. 32.

22. Arthur Sulzberger Jr., interview by author, November 23, 1993, New York.

23. David Dunlap, interview by author, April 16, 1992 (telephone).

24. David Dunlap, interview by author, September 17, 1993 (telephone).

25. Ibid.

26. David W. Dunlap, "Archdiocese Seeks Accord with City," *New York Times*, June 18, 1984, p. 1; Dunlap interview, 1993.

27. Lindsy Van Gelder, interview by author, November 4, 1990, New York.

28. Marcia Cohen, *The Sisterhood: The Inside Story of the Women's Movement and the Leaders Who Made It Happen* (New York: Ballantine, 1988), p. 150; Van Gelder interview.

29. Van Gelder interview.

30. Lindsy Van Gelder, letter to the author, February 5, 1993.

31. Van Gelder interview.

11. RESPONDING TO AIDS

1. Lawrence Mass, M.D., "Disease Rumors Largely Unfounded," *New York Native*, May 18–31, 1981, p. 7.

2. Cited in David Black, *The Plague Years*, (New York: Simon & Schuster, 1985), p. 49.

3. Harry Nelson, "Outbreaks of Pneumonia Among Gay Males Studied," *Los Angeles Times*, June 5, 1981, p. 3.

4. David Perlman, "A Pneumonia That Strikes Gay Males," *San Francisco Chronicle*, June 6, 1981, p. 4.

5. "'Gay' Pneumonia? Not Really, Says Researcher," *Advocate*, July 23, 1981, p. 12.

6. U.S. Centers for Disease Control, *Morbidity and Mortality Weekly Report*, July 3, 1981.

7. Lawrence K. Altman, "Rare Cancer Seen in 41 Homosexuals," *New York Times*, July 3, 1981, p. 20.

8. A study by David Shaw, media writer at the *Los Angeles Times*, found that the *New York Times* published sixty-two stories on Legionnaires' disease during August and September 1976—eleven of them on the front page. In the first nineteen months of the AIDS crisis the *New York Times* printed only seven stories on the epidemic. It took four years for AIDS to make eleven appearances on the

New York Times's front page (David Shaw, "Anti-Gay Bias? Coverage of AIDS Story: A Slow Start," *Los Angeles Times*, December 20, 1987, p. 1).

9. The founders of New York's Gay Men's Health Crisis were Larry Kramer, Dr. Lawrence Mass, Paul Popham, Paul Rapoport, Nathan Fain, and Edmund White.

10. James Kinsella, *Covering the Plague: AIDS and the American Media* (New Brunswick, N.J.: Rutgers University Press, 1989), p. 17.

11. Lawrence Mass, M.D., "Cancer as Metaphor," and "KS: Latest Developments," *New York Native*, August 24–September 6, 1981, pp. 12–13.

12. The program was broadcast on June 14, 1982.

13. Joe Salzman, "AIDS and the Media," *USA Today Magazine*, July 1992, p. 31.

14. Jerry Bishop, interview by author, August 2, 1993 (telephone).

15. Jerry Bishop, "Mysterious Ailment Plagues Drug Users, Homosexual Males," *Wall Street Journal*, December 10, 1981, p. 41.

16. Jerry Bishop, interview by author, August 2, 1993 (telephone).

17. Jerry E. Bishop, "Epidemic: A Grave Disease First Found in Homosexual Men Is Spreading," *Discover*, September 1982, pp. 35–38.

18. Bishop interview.

19. The 1970 novel *Cruising*, by *New York Times Magazine* editor Gerald Walker, was a murder mystery set in New York's S&M underground. Some readers complained that it was homophobic and exploited gays. When director William Friedkin made it into a feature film ten years later, the production set off angry protests in Greenwich Village where major portions of it were filmed.

20. Dr. Lawrence Mass, interview by author, July 27, 1993 (telephone).

21. Lawrence D. Mass, M.D., *Homosexuality and Sexuality: Dialogues of the Sexual Revolution* (New York: Harrington Park Press, 1990), p. 124.

22. The *Voice* ran its first major article about AIDS, a long and detailed personal account by Stephen Harvey, on December 21, 1982, DEFENSELESS: LEARNING TO LIVE WITH AID. (The disease was later named AIDS.)

23. Harry Nelson, "Mysterious Fever Now an Epidemic, *Los Angeles Times*, May 31, 1982, p. 1.

24. Richard Saltus, "New Worry About Gay Disease," *San Francisco Examiner*, October 24, 1982, p. 1.

25. Shaw, "Anti-Gay Bias?" and David Shaw, "Press Watch," *Los Angeles Times*, April 8, 1990, book review sec., p. 5.

26. Lawrence Mass, M.D., "AIDS and What to Do About It," *Gay Community News*, September 25, 1982.

27. Mark Thompson, interview by author, March 11, 1994 (telephone).

28. Ransdell Pierson, "The Experts Confer on A.I.D.S. and Call for Federal Research Funds," *Advocate*, January 6, 1983, p. 19.

29. The Fain and Bush coverage is cited in Mass, *Homosexuality and Sexuality*, p. 122.

30. Story count for *Gay Community News* is based on *Alternative Press Index*, January–May 1983.

31. Lawrence Mass, letter to the author, April 30, 1995.

32. Two years later the *St. Paul Pioneer Press* carried a similar series by Jacqui Banaszyneki, AIDS IN THE HEARTLAND. The 1987 series tracked the lives of two men with AIDS who lived on a Minnesota farm until their deaths. The articles won both the Pulitzer Prize and the Society of Professional Journalists Distinguished Service Award. Okie is quoted in David Shaw, "His Death Focused Attention on Disease; Hudson Brought AIDS Coverage Out of the Closet," *Los Angeles Times*, December 21, 1987, p. 1.

33. Mass interview. Altman, medical writer for the *New York Times*, declined to be interviewed for this book.

34. David Rothenberg, interview by author, February 7, 1992, New York.

35. Craig Claiborne, interview by author, April 8, 1992, New York.

36. Robin Marantz Henig, "AIDS: A New Disease's Deadly Odyssey," *New York Times Magazine*, February 6, 1983, p. 28; Robin Marantz Henig, interview by author, December 3, 1993 (telephone).

37. Rothenberg interview.

38. Ibid. A. M. Rosenthal did not respond to letters or telephone calls requesting an interview.

39. Rothenberg interview.

40. Letter from A. M. Rosenthal to Gay Men's Health Crisis quoted in Susan Mulcahy, "Page Six," *New York Post*, June 26, 1983, p. 6.

41. Dudley Clendinen, interview by author, July 21, 1993 (telephone).

42. Clendinen publicly acknowledged his homosexuality in an op-ed article in the *New York Times* on the appeal by Bill Clinton for "the gay vote" during the 1992 presidential race. ("The Gay Vote: Music to My Ears," *New York Times*, August 1, 1992, p. A-23.

43. Clendinen interview.

44. Richard Meislin, interview by author, September 11, 1993.

45. Ibid.

46. After his retirement Rosenthal began a weekly column for the *Times* op-ed page called On My Mind. In several of his columns he chose AIDS as his topic and seemed to have reversed his earlier indifference to the epidemic. In one 1988 column he referred to the epidemic as "the story of the decade." In his October 9, 1991, column headlined, SILENCE ON AIDS IS A LIE, he criticized then-President George Bush for a lack of leadership in establishing an AIDS commission.

Frankel had covered the 1964 arrest of presidential assistant Walter Jenkins on a morals charge, writing the front-page story in a straightforward, nonjudgmental manner. In a 1992 interview for the New York gay magazine *NYQ* Frankel remarked to writer Charles Kaiser how impressed he'd been by the compassion shown by President and Mrs. Johnson. Despite the political liability Jenkins represented, Johnson wept, Frankel recalled. "What they did for the kids, and the wife, very quickly, was quite amazing," Frankel said (Charles Kaiser, "The Max Factor," *NYQ*, April 5, 1992, pp. 43–46).

47. Jane Gross, "The Devastation of AIDS: Many Dead, More Dying," *New York Times*, March 16, 1987, p. 1. The four-part series ran March 16–19, 1987.

48. David Shaw, "Anti-Gay Bias?" p. 1.

49. Michelangelo Signorile, "Out at the New York Times," *Advocate*, May 19, 1992, p. 40.

50. Arthur Ochs Sulzberger Jr., interview by author, November 23, 1993, New York.

51. Stephanie Poggi, " 'Gay' Finally Fit to Print," *Gay Community News*, June 28–July 4, 1987, p. 1.

52. Peter Freiberg, "The New York Times Finally Okays Use of Gay," *Advocate*, June 2, 1987, p. 23.

53. Gina Kolata, "Lesbian Partners Find the Means to Be Parents," *New York Times*, January 30, 1989, p. A-13.

54. Urvashi Vaid, interview by author, December 23, 1994 (telephone).

55. Debra Chasnoff, interview by author, February 14, 1995 (telephone).

56. Randy Shilts, "The Strange Deadly Diseases That Strike Gay Men," *San Francisco Chronicle*, May 13, 1982, p. 6.

57. Jeff Yarborough, "The Life and Times of Randy Shilts," *Advocate*, June 15, 1993, pp. 32–39.

58. Randy Shilts, "Gay Freedom Day Raises AIDS Worries," *San Francisco Chronicle*, May 27, 1983, p. 2.

59. Kinsella, *Covering the Plague*, p. 144.

60. Ibid., p. 266.

61. Larry Bush, interview by author, April 29, 1993, Washington, D.C.

62. Number of articles in *New York Times* is from David Shaw, "Anti-Gay Bias?" p. 1; Randy Shilts, *And the Band Played On: Politics, People, and the AIDS Epidemic* (New York: St. Martin's Press, 1987), p. xxi.

63. Paul Berg, "To Know You've Been Exposed," *Washington Post*, September 4, 1985, health supplement, p. 11; Erik Eckholm, "Fears on AIDS Termed Largely Without Cause," *New York Times*, September 13, 1985, p. B-3.

64. Arnie Kantrowitz, interview by author, December 12, 1992 (telephone).

65. Marshall K. Kirk and Erastes Pill (pseudonym), "Waging Peace," *Christopher Street*, December 1984, pp. 33–41.

66. Jewelle Gomez, interview by author, October 1, 1993 (telephone).

67. Other GLAAD founders included Barry Adkins, Allen Barnett, Arnie Kantrowitz, Gregory Kolovakos, Jim Owles, Marty Robinson, and gay film historian Vito Russo. Owles and Robinson both were former presidents of GAA.

68. John A. Fall, "The New Stonewall?" *New York Native*, November 25–December 1, 1985, p. 11.

69. Peter Freiberg, "Gays Protest NY Post Homophobia," *Advocate*, December 1, 1986, p. 16.

70. Joe Nicholson, interview by author, November 12, 1992 (telephone).

71. William F. Buckley Jr., "AIDS: And Then, What?" *National Review*, May 22, 1987, p. 56.

72. Based on figures that appeared in "AIDS and the Press, *Time*, August 22, 1994, p. 15. *Time* credited NEXIS and the World Health Organization for the information in its graphic.

73. Garry Wills, "The Rolling Stone Interview: Randy Shilts," *Rolling Stone*, September 30, 1993, p. 47. *And the Band Played On* became a best-seller and earned Shilts an $800,000 advance for his next book, about gays in the military.

74. Chris Bull, "Media Watchers Say Day of Desperation Caught Nation's Eye," *Advocate*, February 26, 1991, pp. 14–15.

75. Gerry Yandel, "Gay Group Disrupts CNN Broadcast," *Atlanta Constitution*, July 27, 1991, p. C-2.

76. Wendy Melillo, "Whatever Happened to AIDS?" *Washington Post*, September 24, 1991. 10–11.

12. THE EXPERIENCE OF AIDS

1. Bill Cox, "A Journalist with AIDS," *Honolulu Star-Bulletin*, September 1, 1986, p. A-8.

2. "Journalist Bill Cox Dies After Long AIDS Battle," *Honolulu Star-Bulletin*, May 20, 1988, p. 1.

3. Robert O'Boyle, interview by author, July 6, 1991, Seattle.

4. Ibid.

5. Julie Fanselow, "Living with AIDS," *Editor & Publisher*, January 19, 1991, p. 17; Mark Thompson, ed., *Long Road to Freedom: The Advocate History of the Gay and Lesbian Movement* (New York: St. Martin's Press, 1994), p. 243.

6. Robert O'Boyle, "Painful Side Effect: Seeing the Fear in Others' Eyes," *Seattle Times*, June 17, 1990, p. H-1.

7. Robert O'Boyle, "AZT Curses User with Nausea, But Blesses Him with Better Life," *Seattle Times*, July 1, 1990, p. K-6.

8. O'Boyle interview.

9. John Caiman, "Paul Wynne's Subject: His AIDS," *San Francisco Chronicle*, January 11, 1990, p. E-1.

10. Jane Gross, "On-the-Air Diary of a Passage Toward Death," *New York Times*, January 22, 1990, p. A-1.

11. Tom Cassidy, interview by author, July 25, 1990, New York.

12. Frank J. Prial, "TV Crew Leaves Set of AIDS Victims' Interview," *New York Times*, March 28, 1985, p. B-5.

13. Cassidy interview.

14. "Tom Cassidy; CNN Business Correspondent" (obituary), *Los Angeles Times*, May 28, 1991, p. 26.

15. Elinor Burkett, panelist, "The State of AIDS Coverage," first annual national conference of the National Lesbian and Gay Journalists Association, San Francisco, June 27, 1992 (tape recording).

16. Elinor Burkett, interview by author, June 2, 1995 (telephone).

17. Charisse L. Grant, "His Desperate Secrecy: Questions for Us All," *Miami Herald*, September 9, 1990, p. 1-C.

18. Burkett interview.

19. In February 1991 the *Herald* named Doug Clifton, forty-seven, to succeed Janet Chusmir as executive editor. An editor with the *Herald* for seventeen years, he had more recently been managing editor of the *Charlotte Observer*, which is owned by Knight-Ridder, as is the *Herald*, the chain's flagship.

20. Jean Latz Griffin, interview by author, June 18, 1993 (telephone).

21. Andy Knott, "2 Sought in Ex-Prof's Killing," *Chicago Tribune*, December 19, 1982, p. 3.

22. Paul Varnell, interview by author, June 1, 1993 (telephone).

23. Griffin interview.

24. Joseph Sobran, "Homosexuality Isn't Healthy," *Chicago Sun-Times*, January 13, 1986, p. 29.

25. Dan Layman, interview by author, August 20, 1993 (telephone).

26. Ibid.

27. In 1992 Al Wardell received a Stonewall Award from the Anderson Prize Foundation for his leadership of the Illinois Gay and Lesbian Task Force. Among the accomplishments cited by the foundation was "persuading both the *Chicago Tribune* and the *Chicago Sun-Times* to create and staff gay reporting beats."

28. Mary Dedinsky, interview by author, June 2, 1993 (telephone).

29. Tom Brune, interview by author, June 15, 1993 (telephone).

30. Ibid.; Tom Brune, "NU Women Hear AIDS Expert, Not Victim," *Chicago Sun-Times*, February 12, 1987, p. 12.

31. Griffin interview.

32. The quilt was scheduled to return to Washington on October 11, 1996; organizers expected the number of panels to reach forty-five thousand.

The Supreme Court defeat for gays drew a burst of interest from newspapers, but many characterized the ruling as an infringement on privacy rather than a matter of gay rights. Among the papers that saw an infringement on privacy was the *New York Times*, which carried two front page articles on the decision and an editorial the following day condemning it. (Linda Greenhouse and Stuart Taylor Jr., "High Court, 5–4, Says States Have the Right to Outlaw Private Homosexual

Acts," *New York Times*, July 1, 1986, p. 1; Editorial, "Crime in the Bedroom," *New York Times*, July 2, 1986, p. A-30.)

33. Urvashi Vaid, interview by author, December 23, 1994 (telephone).

34. Barbara Gittings, interview by author, August 12, 1992 (telephone).

35. Victor Zonana, "AIDS Quilt Helps Thousands Remember," *Los Angeles Times*, April 10, 1988, p. II-9.

36. Victor Zonana, interview by author, March 21, 1992, Boston.

37. Ibid.

38. Victor Zonana, "Profile in Courage, Anger: Brad Davis Battled AIDS, Hollywood," *Los Angeles Times*, September 11, 1991, p. 1.

39. In 1990 Victor Zonana moved off the AIDS beat at the *Los Angeles Times*. Because of his accomplishments he was promoted to senior business correspondent in the newspaper's New York Bureau. In 1993 he left the *Times* to become a deputy assistant secretary of health for public affairs in the Clinton administration.

40. Jacqi Tully, "Changes Invade the Newsroom," *San Francisco Examiner*, Gay in America series reprint, June 8, 1989, p. 22.

41. Frank McCulloch, interview by author, May 17, 1994 (telephone).

42. Ken Maley, interview by author, May 22, 1994 (telephone).

43. Lenny Giteck, "Gays and the City," *San Francisco Examiner,* thirteen-part series beginning October 30, 1978. p. 26.

44. Greg Brock, interview by author, November 16, 1994 (telephone).

45. McCulloch interview.

46. Quoted in H. Glenn Rosenkrantz, "Welcome to the Gay '90s," *Washington Journalism Review*, December 1992, p. 31.

47. Maley interview.

48. Randy Alfred, "How the Examiner Fares: Sensational Coverage Called Rare," *San Francisco Examiner*, Gay in America series (June 4–20, 1989) reprint, June 8, 1989, p. 22.

49. William R. Hearst III, "From the Publisher," *San Francisco Examiner*, June 4, 1989, Special Report, p. 2.

50. According to Brock, the section was designed as a showcase, and the concept never included ads. Letters to the Editor, *San Francisco Examiner*, Gay in America series reprint, p. 15.

51. Rita Reed (photographer) and Kurt Chandler (reporter), "Growing Up Gay: A Crisis in Hiding," *Minneapolis Star Tribune*, December 6, 1992 (reprint), pp. 15–145.

52. For a time the findings of the federal study had been suppressed by the Bush administration under pressure from right-wing groups and conservatives in Congress (Chris Bull, "Suicidal Tendencies," *Advocate*, April 5, 1994, pp. 35–42); Rita Reed, interview by author, June 13, 1995 (telephone).

53. Reed interview.

54. Reed and Chandler, "Growing Up Gay," p. 25.

55. Jane Hoffman, interview by author, September 21, 1994 (telephone).

56. John Lancaster, "Iowa Sailor Exonerated in Blast," *Washington Post*, October 18, 1991, p. 1.

57. Peter Johnson, "Rooney Under Fire for Remarks About Gays," *USA Today*, January 25, 1990, p. D-3.

58. Andy Rooney, "In My Opinion," *Morning Advocate* (Baton Rouge), September 22, 1989, p. 7-B.

59. Peter Johnson, "Rooney Under Fire"; Eric M. Breindel, "The Andy Rooney Affair," *Commentary*, May 1990, p. 56.

60. Andy Rooney, "Rooney's Letter to Gays," *Advocate*, February 27, 1990, p. 13.

61. Ibid. Rooney had expressed similar sentiments a decade earlier, during a publicity appearance before TV critics to tout the upcoming season on CBS. Asked by journalists about the CBS documentary "Gay Power, Gay Politics," Rooney became infuriated that the reporters—one of them a Pulitzer Prize winner—would attempt to impugn (as he saw it) the reputation of CBS News. He twice questioned the sexuality of some reporters present and accused them of representing special interests rather than journalism. "I am impressed by the arrogance of many of the questions," he was quoted as saying. "Why were so many of the questions from gays? . . . I thought it was unbecoming for anyone in an advocacy position to press it so much." At another point he told the writers, "Prejudice saves me a great deal of time in making quick judgments" (William A. Henry III, *San Francisco Examiner*, July 4, 1980, p. E-1). The *Chronicle* said the session ended after Rooney suffered some type of seizure and left the room screaming at the reporters, "Get outa here! Get outa here! Get outa here!"

62. Chris Bull, "Andy, We Hardly Knew Ye," *Advocate*, February 27, 1990, pp. 10–12.

63. "'60 Minutes' Rooney Suspended by CBS," *Chicago Tribune*, February 9, 1990, p. 3-A.

64. Craig Davidson, "Media Coverage of Rooney Affair," *GLAAD Tidings*, February 16, 1990.

65. Chris Bull, interview by author, November 2, 1990, New York.

66. Roxanne Roberts, interview by author, December 13, 1994 (telephone).

67. Breindel, "The Andy Rooney Affair," p. 56.

68. Nat Hentoff, "Tuning Out Andy Rooney," *Washington Post*, February 13, 1990, p. A-21. Hentoff cites Carmody.

69. Bull interview.

70. Jay Martel, "The Year in TV," *Rolling Stone*, December 13–27, 1990, p. 236.

71. "AIDS and the Press" (illustration) *Time*, August 22, 1994, p. 15; Kim Painter, "A Checkered History of Tragedy, Despair and Hope," *USA Today*, June 4, 1991, p. 6-D; Dr. Diane Colasanto, "Public Still Holds Faulty AIDS Beliefs," *San Francisco Chronicle*, November 29, 1989, p. A-5.

72. Jeffrey Schmalz, interview by author, February 7, 1992, New York.

13. THE CONSEQUENCES OF OUTING

1. Benjamin Webster and Jackson Diehl, "Rep. Bauman in Court," *Washington Post*, October 3, 1980, p. 1; Ron Shaffer and Benjamin Webster, "Bauman Pleads Innocent on Solicitation Charge," *Washington Post*, October 4, 1980, p. 1.

2. Joann Stevens, "The Boy-Whore World, *Washington Post*, October 7, 1980, p. 1. Bauman struggled to salvage his political career. Several conservative groups rallied to his side and tried to shift the spotlight from his personal life to his conservative record in Congress. But the voters pulled away from him, and he lost to moderate Democrat Roy Dyson.

3. Tom Sherwood and Joann Stevens, "Hill Police Arrest Congressman on Sodomy Charge," *Washington Post*, February 5, 1981, p. 1. Several months earlier Hinson startled voters in his home district by announcing at a press conference that he had been among the survivors of a 1977 fire at a Washington gay porno theater that killed eight men. He also acknowledged that he had been accused of "an obscene act" on the grounds of the Iwo Jima Memorial, a notorious gay cruising area. After his arrest in 1981 Hinson pleaded not guilty to a reduced charge but resigned from Congress.

4. John Robinson, "Frank Discusses Being Gay," *Boston Globe,* May 30, 1987, p. 1. Frank was concerned about how his disclosure would be portrayed. "I don't want a headline that says BARNEY FRANK IS GAY," he told the *Globe* reporter. He wanted the acknowledgment to be part of an all-encompassing article about his life, not the entire focus. Even so, *Globe* editors felt otherwise. The front-page article, which was headlined FRANK DISCUSSES BEING GAY, began, "U.S. Rep. Barney Frank, after years of ambivalence about disclosing the nature of his private life, has decided to acknowledge publicly that he is gay." Ted Gup, "Identifying Homosexuals," *Washington Journalism Review,* October 1988, pp. 20–22.

5. Larry Gross, *Contested Closets: the Politics and Ethics of Outing* (Minneapolis: University of Minnesota Press, 1993), p. 57; Kim I. Mills, "Gays Crying Gay," *Washington Journalism Review,* October 1990, pp. 23–25.

6. Angelo d'Arcangelo, *The Homosexual Handbook* (New York, Ophelia Press, 1968), p. 259.

7. "'Homosexual Handbook' Names Dozens of Living Showbizities as Such," *Variety*, March 5, 1969, p. 2; "'Times Nixes 'Homo,'" *Variety*, April 23, 1969, p. 77; "The Fringe," *Saturday Review*, June 14, 1969, p. 48; Donn Teal, *The Gay Militants* (St. Martin's Press, 1995 [1971]) p. 65.

8. John Francis Hunter, *The Gay Insider* (New York: Stonehill, 1972), pp. 621–622.

9. Taylor Branch, "Closets of Power," *Harper's,* October 1982, pp. 35–50.

10. Edwin Diamond, *Media Show: The Changing Face of the News, 1985–1990* (Cambridge, Mass.: MIT Press), p. 92.

11. Edwin McDowell, "Merle Miller Is Dead at 67; A Novelist and a Biographer," *New York Times,* June 11, 1986, sec. 2, p. 10. A precedent for listing gay spouses was actually set in 1979 upon the death of one of Siegal's predecessors, Assistant Managing Editor Theodore Bernstein.

One of Bernstein's duties was to set and enforce newspaper style policies on grammar and content, including the ban on listing unmarried partners in obituaries. But when Bernstein died in June 1979, a closeted gay writer at the *Times* listed in Bernstein's obituary the name of his live-in girlfriend, guessing that out of a sense of respect for the late editor no one would delete her name. "With Mr. Bernstein when he died was his longtime friend Ethel C. Spiegel," the obituary said ("T. M. Bernstein Dies; Language Authority and Ex-Times Editor," *New York Times*, June 28, 1979, p. 1).

Months later the *Times* received an obituary for a gay man listing his male partner as a survivor, and the same writer included the name in the obituary. But as he expected, his editors objected and removed the name, citing the *Times*'s policy and the fact that the two men were not married. "Neither was Ted Bernstein married to that lady," the writer retorted. Still, the precedent had been set, and the *Times* ban on listing gay partners had begun to crumble.

12. Andrew Rosenthal, "Paul Popham, 45, a Founder of AIDS Organization, Dies," *New York Times,* May 8, 1987, p. D-17.

13. Robert W. Peterson, "Gay Survivor Challenges Paper's Obituary Policy," *Advocate,* August 30, 1988, p. 22.

14. Mills, "Gays Crying Gay."

15. Gross, *Contested Closets*, p. 38.

16. The owners of *OutWeek* were New York business executives Kendall Morrison, Michael Carver, and Lawrence Basile. Steven Polakoff, a successful Miami businessman, served as the publisher.

17. Cited in Jeanie Kasindorf, "Mr. Out," *New York,* May 14, 1990, pp. 85–91.

18. William A. Henry III, "Forcing Gays Out of the Closet," *Time,* January 29, 1990, p. 67.

19. Michelangelo Signorile, interview by author, August 27, 1993 (telephone).

20. Michelangelo Signorile, *Queer in America: Sex, the Media, and the Closets of Power* (New York: Random House, 1993), p. 73.

21. Jeannie Williams, "Mag Explores Forbes' Sex Life," *USA Today*, March 12, 1990, p. 2-D.

22. Gabriel Rotello, "The Inning of Outing," *Advocate,* April 18, 1995, p. 80; Michelangelo Signorile, "The Secret Gay Life of Malcolm Forbes," *OutWeek,* March 18, 1990, cover story.

23. Michelangelo Signorile, "Gaystyles of the Rich and Famous," *VillageVoice,* April 3, 1990, pp. 23–24.

24. David Gelman, "Outing: An Unexpected Assault on Sexual Privacy," *Newsweek,* April 30, 1990, p. 66.

25. Rick Harding, "Activists' List Casts a Pall Over the Potomac," *Advocate,* July 17, 1990, p. 8–9.

26. John Gallagher, "Actor's Libel Lawsuit Leaves Media Asking How to Cover Outing," *Advocate,* August 13, 1991, p. 21.

27. Ibid.

28. "Outing," *Newsweek,* p. 66; Cheryl Lavin, "The Light in the Closet," *Chicago Tribune,* June 8, 1993, Tempo sec., p. 1.

29. Eleanor Randolph, "At Odds over Outing of Gays," *Washington Post,* July 13, 1990, p. C-1; Randy Shilts, "Naming Names," *GQ,* August 1990, pp. 160–66. After *Advocate* publisher David Goodstein died of bowel cancer in June 1985, he was succeeded by Niles Merton. In 1992 the magazine was sold to a group of five investors led by Sam Waters, a forty-one-year-old Yale-educated art historian who had no prior publishing experience. In May 1995 *Business Week* reported that circulation at the money-losing magazine had climbed by 50 percent and it was nearing financial viability.

30. Fred W. Friendly, "Gays, Privacy and a Free Press," *Washington Post,* April 8, 1990, p. B-7.

31. Stuart Byron, "Naming Names," *Advocate,* April 24, 1990, p. 37.

32. Maer Roshan, "Front-Page News," *OutWeek,* June 26, 1991, p. 39.

33. Barbara Grizzuti Harrison, "Don't Make Gays Go Public," *Mademoiselle,* August 1990, p. 126.

34. According to the February 1, 1993, issue of *Newsweek,* about thirteen thousand men and women were cashiered as homosexuals between 1982 and 1992.

35. Elaine Sciolino, "Voice of the Pentagon Delivers Press Curbs with a Deftness Honed on TV," *New York Times,* February 8, 1991, p. A-9; the "open secret" is cited in Signorile, *Queer in America*, p. 101.

36. Richard Goldstein, "The Outer Limits," *Village Voice*, July 30, 1991, p. 40.

37. Signorile interview.

38. Michelangelo Signorile, "The Outing of Assistant Secretary of Defense Pete Williams," *Advocate,* August 27, 1991.

39. Editorial, "Comment," *Advocate,* August 27, 1991, pp. 6–7.

40. William A. Henry III, "To Out or Not to Out," *Newsweek,* August 19, 1991, p. 17.

41. David Astor, "Controversial Piece on Pentagon Official," *Editor & Publisher,* August 17, 1991, p. 40.

42. Signorile, *Queer in America*, pp. 133–34.

43. Lucian Truscott IV, "Truman's Legacy to Clinton, *New York Times,* February 1, 1993, p. A-19.

44. Donna Minkowitz, "Not Even Worth an Outing," *Advocate,* June 16, 1992, p. 11.

45. Laura Blumenfeld, "Schlafly's Son, Out of the Closet," *Washington Post,* September 19, 1992, p. D-1.

46. Chris Bull, "The Outing of a Family-Values Congressman," *Advocate,* September 22, 1992, pp. 38–45; "Brother Easily Defeats Brother to Win Re-Election in Louisiana," *Chicago Tribune,* October 4, 1992, p. 9; Todd J. Gillman, "Louisiana Congressman Defeats Brother, Incumbents to Face Off," *Dallas Morning News,* October 4, 1992, p. 16-A; "Louisiana Primary Results," *Houston Chronicle,* October 4, 1992, p. 10.

47. Christine Spolar, "Privacy for Public Figures?" *Washington Journalism Review,* June 1992, pp. 20–22.

48. Debra Gersh, "Doctors, Patients and the Press," *Editor and Publisher,* January 19, 1991, p. 14; Christine Spolar, "Privacy for Public Figures," *Washington Journalism Review,* June 1992, p. 20; Alex S. Jones, "Report of Ashe's Illness Raises an Old Issue for Editors," *New York Times,* April 10, 1992, p. A-25; Debra Gersh, "Unclear Boundaries," *Editor and Publisher,* April 18, 1992, p. 7.

49. Jeff Yarbrough, "The Life and Times of Randy Shilts," *Advocate,* June 15, 1993, p. 38.

50. Howard Kurtz, "Is Being Positive a Negative on the AIDS Beat?" *Washington Post,* February 18, 1993, p. C-1.

51. Sam Dillon, "New Chancellor's First 24 Hours in New York," *New York Times,* September 2, 1993, p. B-3.

52. Robert Lipsyte, "Louganis Approaches the Edge of the Stage, and Leaps," *New York Times,* September 19, 1993, p. 11 (Louganis publicly disclosed his homosexuality in February 1995 in his best-selling autobiography *Breaking the Surface*); "Covering Sexuality and the Geres," *USA Today,* December 7, 1993, p. 2-D.

53. Patrick M. Reilly, "Jann Wenner's Rift with Wife Shakes Up His Publishing Empire," *Wall Street Journal,* March 3, 1995, p. 1; Steiger is quoted in Elisabeth Bumiller, "The Wenner Story's Out," *Washington Post,* March 6, 1995, p. D-1.

54. David Boaz, "Queer in America: Study in Contradictions," *Washington Blade*, August 5, 1994, p. 45.

55. Gabriel Rotello, "The Inning of Outing," *Advocate,* April 18, 1995, p. 80.

14. THE '90S AND BEYOND

1. Loren Ghiglione, interview by author, September 6, 1993 (telephone).

2. Leroy Aarons, interview by author, August 26, 1990, Rosslyn, Va.

3. Andrew Radoff, "ASNE Survey Creates Controversy," *Editor & Publisher*, November 18, 1989, p. 12.

4. Kathryn C. Montgomery, *Target: Prime Time* (New York: Oxford University Press, 1989), p. 168.

5. Estimate is based on the Kinsey figure (that 10 percent of any population is gay) and is used by George Garneau, "Groundbreaking Survey," *Editor & Publisher*, April 7, 1990, p. 12.

6. American Society of Newspaper Editors, Human Resources Committee, *Alternatives: Gays and Lesbians in the Newsroom*, April 1990 pamphlet.

7. Ibid.

8. Ibid.

9. The survey findings were underscored in 1993 when the National Lesbian and Gay Journalists Association conducted a study of gays in the broadcast media. A significant number of the gay men and lesbians who responded knew of antigay slurs made by their coworkers. Although many said they were generally satisfied with their working environment, they also expressed "a sense of foreboding, fear of the unknown, and feeling that things could be better." Only a few on-air reporters and anchors participated in the voluntary study. Of those who did, most were leery

of talking on the record, fearing "the potential wrath of viewers and management" (The National Lesbian and Gay Journalists Association and the Radio and Television News Directors Foundation, *Another Perspective: A Report on Gay and Lesbian Issues in Electronic Journalism*, 1995 pamphlet).

10. American Society of Newspaper Editors, official record, pp. 12–14.

11. A year later, in June 1991, researchers at the E. W. Scripps School of Journalism at Ohio University compared the responses of the gay journalists with responses from 134 senior newspaper editors. The editors gave consistently higher ratings to the reporting and coverage of gay-related issues than the gay journalists did. The authors, Joseph Bernt and Marilyn Greenwald, concluded that the discrepancy reflected a lack of knowledge of the gay community rather than any conscious bias.

12. Aarons interview.

13. Nancy Lee, interview by author, September 9, 1993 (telephone).

14. Ibid.

15. David Dunlap, memo, December 1990 (Courtesy of David Dunlap).

16. David Fox, interview by author, September 7, 1993 (telephone).

17. Lily Eng, interview by author, July 29, 1993 (telephone).

18. Victor Zonana, interview by author, March 21, 1992, Boston.

19. Deborah Bergman, "Has AIDS Finally Bonded Lesbians and Gay Men?" *Advocate*, December 18, 1990, p. 106.

20. Linda Villarosa, panel discussion, "Coming Out in the Mainstream," OutWrite, the Third National Lesbian and Gay Writers Conference, Boston, March 21, 1992 (tape recording).

21. Villarosa, OutWrite panel discussion.

22. Villarosa, OutWrite panel discussion.

23. Linda Villarosa, "Coming Out," *Essence*, May 1991, pp. 82–84.

24. Ibid.

25. Linda Villarosa, "Readers Respond to Coming Out," *Essence*, October 1991, pp. 89–90.

26. Villarosa, OutWrite panel discussion.

27. Andrew Sullivan, interview by author, June 5, 1991, Washington, D.C.

28. Ibid.

29. Andrew Sullivan, "Gay Life, Gay Death," *New Republic*, December 17, 1990, pp. 19–25.

30. Sullivan interview.

31. Michael Duffy, "A Flagship Heels to Starboard," *Time*, October 14, 1990, p. 82.

32. Deirdre Carmody, "New Editor Is Rethinking New Republic's Direction," *New York Times*, November 11, 1991, p. D-1; Charles Trueheart, "The New Boy at New Republic," *Washington Post*, May 27, 1992, p. C-1.

33. Dearth is quoted in Stuart Elliott, "'Hot Editor' Phenomenon Benefits the New Republic," *New York Times*, March 26, 1992, p. D19.

34. Juan B. Palomo, "Censored Columnist Tells His Story," *Alternatives* (newsletter of the National Lesbian and Gay Journalists Association), September 1991, p. 1; Juan Palomo, OutWrite panel discussion.

35. Palomo, "Censored Columnist Tells His Story," p. 1.

36. Quoted in Tony Case, "Columnist Closeted," *Editor & Publisher*, August 3, 1991, p. 19.

37. Ibid.

38. Howard Kurtz, "Gay Columnist Kept in the Closet," *Washington Post*, February 18, 1993, p. C-1.

39. Tony Case, "Fired, Rehired," *Editor & Publisher*, September 14, 1991, p. 14.

40. Lenny Giteck, "Journalists Struggle to Come Out in Mainstream Newspapers," *Advocate*, October 8, 1991, pp. 48–51.

41. M. L. Stein, "Lesbian Journalist Sues over Transfer," *Editor & Publisher*, August 7, 1993, p. 10.

42. "Newspaper May Limit Activism of Its Reporting Staff," *Washington Blade*, June 2, 1995, p. 18.

43. Sue Fox, "Former UPI Reporter Wins Settlement with Reverend," *Washington Blade*, April 7, 1995, p. 8.

44. Associated Press, "Lesbian Reporter Wins Settlement," *Washington Post*, April 6, 1995, p. B-12.

45. Alex S. Jones, "Arthur Ochs Sulzberger Passes Times Publisher's Post to Son," *New York Times*, January 17, 1992, p. 1.

46. Jeffrey Schmalz, interview by author, February 7, 1992, New York.

47. Jeffrey Schmalz, "Homosexuals Wake to See a Referendum: It's on Them," *New York Times*, January 31, 1993, p. IV-1.

48. Edwin Diamond, "Out of the Closet," *New York*, May 24, 1993, p. 14.

49. Arthur Ochs Sulzberger Jr., interview by author, November 23, 1993, New York.

50. Jeffrey Schmalz, "Writing Against Time, Valiantly," *New York Times*, April 22, 1993, p. C-1.

51. Leroy Aarons, "The Spirit and the Substance," *Alternatives* (NLGJA newsletter), Summer 1992, p. 1.

52. Edward Iwata, "Stepping Out," *Editor & Publisher*, August 22, 1992, p. 10.

53. Arthur Sulzberger Jr., speech to National Lesbian and Gay Journalists Association Convention, San Francisco, June 25, 1992 (transcript of tape recording).

54. List appears in *Alternatives* (NLGJA newsletter), Winter 1993, p. 3.

55. Margaret Allen, "Gay Wedding Coverage," *Editor & Publisher*, April 24, 1993, p. 30.

56. Ibid.

57. William McGowan, "The Other Side of the Rainbow," *Columbia Journalism Review*, November–December 1993, p. 53.

58. The decision came on the heels of an Ohio University survey of senior newspaper editors that found that more than three-quarters rated their coverage of gays and lesbians as fair or poor. Only 4 percent thought their coverage was excellent ("Editors Admit Gay Coverage Needs Improvement," *Editor & Publisher*, February 22, 1992, p. 17).

59. Quoted in Tony Case, "Life from a Gay Perspective," *Editor & Publisher*, July 11, 1992, p. 13.

60. Ibid.

61. Deb Price, keynote speaker, National Lesbian and Gay Journalists Association Annual Convention, New York City, September 11, 1993 (tape recording).

62. Mubarak S. Dahir, "Gay on the Way at Daily News," *Philadelphia Gay News*, October 2–8, 1992, p. 1.

63. Cited in John Carmody, "The TV Column," *Washington Post,* July 6, 1993, p. C-4.

64. Transcript, "Real Personal," CNBC Television, July 15, 1993.

65. Gabriel Rotello, "Broadcast News: Gay and Not Gay," *New York Newsday*, August 25, 1994, p. A-36.

66. Ibid.

67. Deirdre Carmody, "New Gay Press Is Emerging, Claiming Place in Mainstream," *New York Times*, March 2, 1992, p. 1; Stephanie Schorow, "One of Nation's Oldest Gay Newspapers Must Change or Die," Associate Press, July 24, 1992.

68. Wayne Hoffman, "Time Pulls the Plug on Tribe," *Washington Blade*, June 17, 1993, pp. 35–36.

69. Sheila Walsh, "GLAAD Decides the Time Is Right to Expand," *Washington Blade*, October 8, 1993, p. 25; *GLAAD Rag*, newsletter of the National Capital Area chapter of GLAAD, October 1993 and September–August 1994. The merger of the New York and Los Angeles chapters in August 1994 set the stage for GLAAD/USA to become the umbrella organization that its executive director, Craig Davidson, and its founders had envisioned eight years earlier. The pooling of resources gave gay men and lesbians the loudest and clearest voice they had ever had to combat homophobia and encourage positive images for gays at all levels of the media.

70. Tony Case, "Recruiting Gay Journalists," *Editor & Publisher*, September 11, 1993, p. 10.

71. From the tape recording of the 1993 convention of the National Lesbian and Gay Journalists Association, New York, September 10, 1993.

72. Howard Kurtz, "Gay Journalists 'Asserting Themselves' in the Media," *Washington Post*, September 12, 1993, p. A-4.

73. Jeffrey Schmalz, keynote address, NLGJA convention, New York, September 11, 1993 (tape recording).

74. Richard J. Meislin, "Jeffrey Schmalz, 39, Times Writer, on Politics and Then AIDS, Dies," *New York Times*, November 7, 1993, p. 46.

75. Jeffrey Schmalz, "Whatever Happened to AIDS?" *New York Times Magazine*, November 28, 1993, p. 56.

76. Thomas L. Friedman, "President Defends His Efforts in Combating AIDS," *New York Times*, December 2, 1993, p. 1.

77. Sidney Brinkley, "Fundamentalist Picket the Funeral of Randy Shilts," *Washington Blade*, February 25, 1994, p. 17.

78. The story count provided here is the result of searching NEXIS and LEXIS by screen for dates and the phrase "March on Washington." Dobbs's study is described in William K. Dobbs, "Front Page: How American Newspapers Covered the 1993 March on Washington for Lesbian, Gay and Bi Equal Rights and Liberation," NLGJA convention, New York, September 10–12, 1993.

79. Howard Schneider, "A Decorated Soldier Joins the Ranks of the Open," *Washington Post*, April 25, 1993, p. A-17.

80. Anna Quindlen, "The Power of One," *New York Times*, April 28, 1993, p. A-21.

81. Peter Freiberg, "The Media Really Seemed to Get It," *Washington Blade*, June 11, 1993, p. 5.

82. Joann Byrd, "They Marched, We Missed," *Washington Post*, May 2, 1993, p. C-6.

83. Elizabeth Kolbert, "Covering Gay Rights: Can Journalists Be Marchers?" *New York Times*, April 24, 1993, p. A-10; Kim Mills, "Taking It to the Streets," *American Journalism Review*, July–August 1993, p. 22.

84. An analysis by Judith Cramer, a communications lecturer at Buffalo State College, found that during a two-month period surrounding the 1994 Gay Games (May 18–July 18, 1994), the games were featured in twenty-one *New York Times* articles and twenty-nine articles in *Newsday*. Cramer presented her findings in a paper delivered to the annual meeting of the Association for Education in Journalism and Mass Communication, Washington, D.C., August 9–12, 1995.

85. Rachel Alexander, "Lesbian Athletes Find Strength in Numbers," *Washington Post*, June 25, 1994, p. D-2.

86. David Dunlap, interview by author, June 26, 1994, New York. Lelyveld had covered the second annual commemoration of the Stonewall rebellion for the *Times* in 1971 in a manner that

was remarkably balanced for that era. According to writer Merle Miller, it was the first article of its kind that did not include comments from antigay psychiatrists (see note 35 in chapter 5).

87. Debbie Howlett, "Thousands March for Gay Rights," *USA Today*, June 27, 1994, p. 3A.

88. John Gallagher, "Juiceless," *Advocate*, July 26, 1994, pp. 28–30.

89. Walsh, "GLAAD Decides the Time Is Right."

90. Ibid.

EPILOGUE

1. Andrew Kopkind, "The Gay Moment," *Nation*, May 3, 1993, p. 1. Kopkind died of bladder cancer in October 1994.

2. Stephanie Simon, "A Day to Be Proud Parade," *Los Angeles Times*, June 26, 1995, p. B-1.

3. "Vanity Fair Covers Gay Issues from A to Z," *GLAAD Rag*, newsletter of the National Capital Area Chapter of Gay and Lesbian Alliance Against Defamation, January–February 1995, p. 3.

4. Editorial, "A Buried Hate Surfaces," *St. Louis Post-Dispatch*, July 15, 1995, p. 14-B.

5. Staff report, "How They Met," *Washington Post*, February 14, 1995, p. B-1.

6. "Media Briefs," *GLAAD Rag*, November 1995, p. 5; "Gay Fathers on the Evening News," *GLAAD Rag*, August 1995, p. 5.

7. Jess Cagle, "America Sees Shades of Gay," *Entertainment Weekly*, September 8, 1995, pp. 20–44; "The ABC's of Fairness," *GLAAD Rag*, July 1994. p. 2; John Carman, "Gay Characters Get a Life on TV," *San Francisco Chronicle*, August 17, 1995, p. E-1.

8. Deb Price, "Gays' Campaign Gift to Dole Turns Out to Be a Hot Potato," *Detroit News and Free Press*, August 26, 1995, p. C-6; Debra J. Saunders, "The Dole Way: If You're Down, Kick a Gay," *San Francisco Chronicle*, August 30, 1995, p. A-21.

9. Editorial, "Dole Flips, Flops and Irks," *Los Angeles Times*, October 19, 1995, p. B-8; Editorial, "Mr. Dole Flips Back," *Washington Post*, October 19, 1995, p. A-22.

10. Cited in William J. Drummond, "About Face," *American Enterprise*, July–August 1990, pp. 23–29.

11. Edward Bliss Jr., *Now the News* (New York: Columbia University Press, 1991), p. 327.

12. Nan Robertson, *Girls in the Balcony* (New York: Random House, 1992), p. 182; Maurine H. Beasley and Sheila J. Gibbons, *Taking Their Place: A Documentary History of Women and Journalism* (Washington: American University Press, 1993), p. 26. In the *Times* case the newspaper agreed to a settlement just before the suit was set for trial in 1978. Each of the paper's 550 women employees was paid $454.54.

13. Katherine Corcoran, "Reaching for Diversity," *Washington Journalism Review*, July–August 1992, pp. 38–42.

14. Patrick M. Reilly, "Newspapers Gird for Even Tougher 1991," *Wall Street Journal*, October 17, 1990, p. B-12.

15. Patrick M. Reilly, "Watchword of Newspaper Publishers at Conference Is Audience Diversity," *Wall Street Journal*, May 10, 1991, p. B-3-B.

16. Daniel Pearl, "Newspapers Strive to Win Back Women," *Wall Street Journal*, May 4, 1992, p. B-1.

17. Robert Maynard, panel discussion, "Closing Roundtable: Gay Issues Go Mainstream—How Do You Cope?" National Lesbian and Gay Journalists Association Convention, June 27, 1992, San Francisco.

18. Steve Chaney, welcoming remarks, National Lesbian and Gay Journalists Association Convention, Washington, D.C., October 19–22, 1995. The numbers include journalists and asso-

ciate members (associate members are people working in related fields, such as public relations). Also, as one member reminded NLGJA officers, "Just because we're here doesn't necessarily mean we're out in our newsrooms."

19. Lucy Kaylin, "Can the Gay Press Survive?" *GQ*, March 1994, p. 158. Census figure is cited in John Gallagher, "Ikea's Gay Gamble," *Advocate*, May 3, 1994, pp. 24–26.

20. Keith Eddings, "Should Gays Cover Gay Issues?" *Columbia Journalism Review*, March–April 1994, pp. 47–49.

21. Cited in Louise Sloan, "Is Gay Coverage Suffering from Right-Wing Backlash?" *Alternatives*, NLGJA newsletter, Summer 1995, p. 1.

22. Cal Thomas, "Of Dubious Genetic and Press Proclivities," *Washington Times*, November 5, 1995, p. B-1.

23. L. Brent Bozell III, "Pandering to Media with Its Own Agenda," *Washington Times*, November 3, 1995, p. A-1.

24. Debra Gersh Hernandez, "Reflections of a Gay Journalist," *Editor & Publisher*, November 18, 1995, p. 19.

25. Elizabeth Weise, panelist, "Between a Rock and a Hard Place: Gay Reporters Covering Gays," 1995 convention of the National Lesbian and Gay Journalists Association, Washington, D.C., October 21, 1995.

26. David Tuller, "Right Wing Focuses on 'Gay Media Bias,'" *Alternatives*, NLGJA newsletter, Winter 1994, p. 1.

27. For an extended discussion on the media's failure to hold the religious right accountable for the damage caused by its antigay views, see Chris Bull and John Gallagher, *Perfect Enemies: The Religious Right, The Gay Movement, and The Politics of the 1990s* (New York: Crown Publishers, in press).

28. Buchanan is cited in Judy Keen and Richard Benedetto, "Buchanan Ads Try to Paint Bush as a Liberal," *USA Today*, February 28, 1992, p. A-3.

29. "Robertson Letter Attacks Feminists," *New York Times*, August 26, 1992, p. A-16; Transcript, *700 Club*, January 18, 1994, People for the American Way Data Bank Archives, Washington, D.C.

30. Frank Rich, "The Gloved Ones," *New York Times*, June 18, 1995, sec. 4, p. 15.

31. Jo Mannies, "Anti-Gay Ad Draws Criticism: Fund-Raising Maneuver or Statement of Facts?" *St. Louis Post-Dispatch*, October 18, 1995, p. 1-B.

32. David Gelman, "Is This Child Gay?" *Newsweek*, February 24, 1992, p. 46.

33. Natalie Angier, "Zone of Brain Linked to Men's Sexual Orientation/Brain Discrepancy May Be Key to Homosexuality," *New York Times*, August 30, 1991, pp. 1, D-18, and "Zone of Brain Linked to Men's Sexual Orientation/Zone of Brain May Be the Key to Homosexuality," pp. 1, D-18.

34. Transcript, "MacNeil-Lehrer Newshour," PBS, April 26, 1993.

35. Frederick Lewis Allen, "Newspapers and the Truth," *Atlantic Monthly*, January 1922, pp. 44–54.

INDEX

DATE DUE
